PART 1
A PROCESS FOR COMPOSING

CONTENTS

The DK Handbook

ANNE FRANCES WYSOCKI
University of Wisconsin, Milwaukee

DENNIS A. LYNCH
University of Wisconsin, Milwaukee

Longman

New York   San Francisco   Boston
London   Toronto   Sydney   Tokyo   Singapore   Madrid
Mexico City   Munich   Paris   Cape Town   Hong Kong   Montreal

Text design, page layout, and cover design: **Dorling Kindersley**

Pearson Longman
Publisher: Joseph Opiela
Executive Editor: Lynn M. Huddon
Senior Development Editor: Michael Greer
Senior Supplements Editor: Donna Campion
Senior Marketing Manager: Windley Morley
Director, Market Research and Development: Laura Coaty
Production Manager: Bob Ginsberg
Project Coordination: Elm Street Publishing Services
Cover Design Manager: Wendy Ann Fredericks
Cover Photos: (clockwise from top left) Thomas Northcut/Getty Images/
    Photodisc; Apple/Splash News/News.com; C. Squared Studios/Getty
    Images/Photodisc; Howard Shooter/© Dorling Kindersley; and Siede Preis/
    Getty Images/Photodisc
Photo Researcher: Dorling Kindersley; additional photo research by Linda Sykes
Senior Manufacturing Buyer: Alfred C. Dorsey
Printer and Binder: RR Donnelley & Sons Company/Crawfordsville
Cover Printer: Coral Graphic Services, Inc.

For permission to use copyrighted material, grateful acknowledgment is made to the copyright holders on pp. 624–625, which are hereby made part of this copyright page.

Library of Congress Cataloging-in-Publication Data

Wysocki, Anne Frances
  The DK handbook / Anne Wysocki.
    p. cm.
  Includes bibliographical references and index.
  ISBN-13: 978-0-205-74333-9 (alk. paper)
  ISBN-10: 0-205-74333-1 (alk. paper)
  1. English language--Rhetoric--Handbooks, manuals, etc. 2. Report writing--Handbooks, manuals, etc.
  3. English language--Grammar--Handbooks, manuals, etc. I. Title.
  PE1408.W97 2008
  808'.042--dc22

                                                                              2007044386

This book includes 2009 MLA guidelines.

1 2 3 4 5 6 7 8 9 10—DOC—12 11 10 09

Longman
is an imprint of

www.pearsonhighered.com

ISBN-13: 978-0-205-74332-2 (spiral bound)
ISBN-10:   0-205-74332-3 (spiral bound)

WHY WE WROTE THIS HANDBOOK

We wrote this handbook to be useful. We wrote the previous sentence knowing it can be read in two ways, both of which we intend: **We** want to be useful and we want *the handbook* to be useful.

We want to be useful to a community that matters to us, the community of writing learners and writing teachers. We offer this book—shaped out of the particular strengths we each bring to teaching and writing—in small return for this community's generosity in sharing knowledge and optimism.

We want *the handbook* to be useful to the many students we have watched try to find their ways through the dense and complex details that characterize any comprehensive handbook. We hope that our particular approaches—making visible the patterns of composition, keeping details visibly discrete, emphasizing the rhetorical nature of all aspects of writing—support learners in easily comprehending the details (and the pleasures) of writing...

...for, finally, we also wrote this handbook to be pleasurable in its use and application. We both know the delights of writing when we are confident and engaged with our words, when we can play with a range of possibilities and know that we can choose among them appropriately. We want those who use this book to use it with confidence and even delight so that they can then write with confidence and take delight and satisfaction in the shape and effectiveness of their words.

HOW WE WROTE THIS HANDBOOK

Because we wanted this handbook to be useful, we commissioned a usability test for it early in the development process. Participants in the user testing were first-year writing students in both community college and research university classrooms. In considering the results of this test—which included over 27 hours of videotaped student feedback and an extensive summary report—we learned what worked and what frustrated students in early drafts of our sections on evaluating sources, using commas, and MLA documentation. By watching students work with these drafts, we learned how and why they got stuck at certain points in the tasks assigned them—and we applied what we learned to help us shape and refine some of the core principles of the handbook's design.

We describe these principles to the right.

1 **Pages can be designed to support the conceptual work of learning.**
Learning to compose requires learning the communication genres, conventions, and processes around us. Once we are familiar with them we can use them inventively to meet our needs; becoming familiar with them means (as in any learning) moving from their general shapes to their specific applications.

Our handbook's *layered structure* helps learners move from the general to the specific. Each new topic begins with a two-page spread that is a *topic overview*; each overview helps students grasp quickly and visually the key steps of processes and concepts.

Students needing more information can turn to the *detail pages* following each overview. The detail pages expand on one step or concept at a time, helping learners *zoom in* on strategies or ideas.

Finally, *application pages* (again, made up of two-page spreads) present illustrated examples demonstrating how to apply processes.

The following principles follow from this first one.

2 **Consistent and uncluttered layout helps learners find what they need.**
Each topic fits on its two-page spread, making information and ideas readily graspable visually and so conceptually. The topic of every two-page spread appears dependably at its top left corner. Because finding and seeing information is made easy, students can focus on what they need to learn instead of on finding it.

3 Students search for visual and verbal patterns that match the problems they wish to solve.

Our user testing reminded us just how much students—unfamiliar with rhetorical or grammatical terminology—navigate handbooks by flipping pages, looking for what matches a current composing need. Two aspects of this handbook's design support such learning:

- **Pattern pages** provide learners with straightforward visual explanations of compositional processes or grammatical structures. If students can see a pattern, they can hold it in their minds for later application.

- The pattern pages are visually differentiated from other pages in the book so that students can find them quickly.

4 Students look for examples first.

In the user testing, students turned through the handbook looking for sample sentences or other examples that matched their needs; only after finding the examples did they read accompanying explanatory text.

Our handbook's design puts **examples front and center**. We've included as many examples—of sentences, student writing, or source evaluation—as we could and we built explanations inductively from the examples. We want students to find easily what will help them solve their writing and editing concerns—and then (as above) we want them to remember the pattern of what they learn so they can apply it later.

5 The processes of research and documentation process can be presented visually.

Many of our reviewers told us how frustrated students are by the details of documentation. We worked **to make visible the patterns of documentation**, so that students won't feel as though each citation requires starting anew. We have provided as many citation examples from different media as possible.

From our user testing, we also learned that students often don't know the kinds of sources they are using: How do they tell a personal homepage from a nonprofit website or a corporate author from an individual author? In addition, students—like many of us—can be vexed by the complexities of database searches. We designed our research coverage to provide as much visual support as possible for such needs. You will find many **visual samples of different print and online sources** and detailed step-by-step **visual explanations of how to use databases of journals**.

Our hope is that these approaches help students make informed and critical judgments about the media and information that now fill their—and our—lives.

SUPPLEMENTS

MyCompLab is a Web application that offers comprehensive and integrated resources for every writer. With MyCompLab, students can access a dynamic eBook version of *The DK Handbook*; learn from interactive tutorials and instruction; practice and develop their skills with grammar, writing, and research exercises; share their writing and collaborate with peers; and receive comments on their writing from instructors and tutors. Go to http://www.mycomplab.com to register for these premiere resources and much more.

A booklet of **Exercises to accompany The DK Handbook** provides assignments and activities that allow students to practice the writing and grammar lessons in the handbook. Instructors can assign the exercises according to their own teaching styles and their students' needs. The variety of short answer and open-ended questions also allows instructors to use the exercises as both an assessment and a diagnostic tool. A separate **Answer Key** is available to instructors for this *Exercises* booklet.

An **Instructor's Resource Manual,** developed by Anne Wysocki, Dennis Lynch, and Kristi Apostel, offers guidance to new and experienced teachers for teaching composition with *The DK Handbook* and using its media resources.

VangoNotes are audio chapter reviews and practice tests students can download to any mp3 player. Visit vangonotes.com for details.

ACKNOWLEDGMENTS

Although composing this handbook took longer than we imagined and than our editors hoped, the process has been deeply pleasurable. We have learned much and have valued the time we have gotten to spend with others—either in person or through their work.

Lynn Huddon got us started on this project, kept her humor and patience, and contributed finer features. Michael Greer's intelligence, thoughtfulness, humor, and energy are present on every page, and his evenness and encouragement are also a reason this book is now in your hands. Joe Opiela gently kept us focused and determined. Stuart Jackman kept us colorful and delighted us with each new page. Christine Holten provided valuable insight and contributed much to our sections for multilingual writers. Megan Galvin-Fak has creatively and energetically thought about how to get this book into people's hands and infectiously kept us excited. In working with our advisory board and focus groups, Laura Coaty kept us thinking about this work's real applications. Bob Ginsberg and Kim Nichols managed the production process with grace and style. And Tharon Howard carried out the smart and detailed user testing—with live students—that helped us understand how others really do use handbooks.

We thank (and will continue to thank for a long time) all the above for the extraordinary efforts they have made on behalf of this book—but nonetheless our most emphatic thanks go to our reviewers (listed below), whose generosity with their time and care for student learning has contributed to and strengthened every bit of this book.

John Bennett, Lake Land College; Paula Berggren, Baruch College; Lori M. Butler, Rogers State University; Arnold Bradford, Northern Virginia Community College; Joel R. Brouwer, Montcalm Community College; Shanti Bruce, Nova Southeastern University; Ron Christiansen, Salt Lake Community College; Joseph Colavito, Northwestern State University; Dean R. Cooledge, University of Maryland Eastern Shore; Philip Kevin Coots, Ashland Community and Technical College; MaryAnn K. Crawford, Central Michigan University; Joe Davis, North Iowa Area Community College; Darren DeFrain, Wichita State University; Erika Deiters, Moraine Valley Community College; Ronda Leathers Dively, Southern Illinois University–Carbondale; Scott Douglass, Chattanooga State Technical Community College; Kerith Dutkiewicz, Davenport University Online; Jacqueline Gray, St. Charles Community College; Ann E. Green, Saint Joseph's University; Dianne Gregory, Kaplan University; Max Guggenheimer, Lynchburg College; Monica Fortune Hatch, Southwestern Illinois College; Gail Odette Henderson, Baton Rouge Community College; Joel B. Henderson, Chattanooga State Technical Community College; Charlotte Hogg, Texas Christian University; Ned Huston, Eastern Illinois University;

WHAT IS COMPOSING?

Composing a paper, you arrange words into sentences into paragraphs, hoping that the arrangement will engage your readers. Composing a poster, you arrange words, photographs, and colors, so that viewers will want to look at the poster and will heed its purposes. Composing a podcast, you arrange voices and other sounds so that others will want to listen.

The New London Group—British and American teachers who research how we learn to communicate—argues that composing requires three steps:

1 No matter the medium—written, visual, oral, or some mix—we always compose with elements and arrangements already familiar to others. These existing elements and arrangements are called *Available Designs* by the New London Group.

2 As we compose our texts out of available designs, we are *Designing*, trying out new shapes and combinations of what is available.

3 When we finish composing, we have made the *Redesigned*, something new out of past possibilities. The redesigned, in turn, becomes new available designs for our, or others', future composing.

This process shapes what we propose in this handbook. If you are to be an effective and satisfied composer, you need to learn the designs that are available to you—the conventions, grammars, and expectations—so you can make what audiences can understand but also so that you can design for your own purposes.

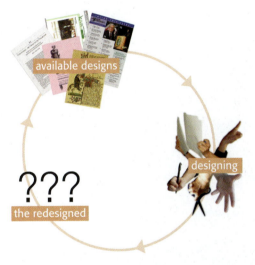

available designs

designing

???
the redesigned

WHAT IS RHETORIC?

Rhetoric is a method for understanding how communication happens.

Rhetoric developed in the western Mediterranean area over 2,000 years ago as political systems became democratic and as legal institutions came into being. People saw that audiences were moved by some speeches and writings more than by others, and that some speeches and writings not only failed but achieved the exact opposite of what their composers had hoped.

Some people—*rhetoricians*—started systematically studying what underlay effective speeches and writing.

The result of the rhetoricians' studies was rhetoric.

AUDIENCE

Rhetoric begins with the understanding that writers (and composers of any text) address audiences. Audiences are not mindless and automatically under a composer's sway; instead, audiences come to texts with beliefs, values, and ideas. Using rhetoric, composers consider the relationships they can build with audiences so that audiences will want to listen and engage with the composer around the issue at hand.

PURPOSE

The earliest rhetoricians realized that composers need to have purposes. This might seem so obvious as to be useless, but if composers cannot articulate their purposes in detail, then they cannot decide how to proceed in composing. (As when one young woman went to court to appeal a ticket for driving through a red light, it was only after her appeal was denied that she realized her purpose was not to tell the judge how the traffic light was hidden by a truck, but rather how she did not know there even was a traffic light where she should have stopped.)

CONTEXT

Where and when do composer and audience meet? Is it face to face or through an essay? Late Saturday night or early Monday? How will recent events influence an audience's attitude? Rhetoricians recognize that composers need to consider the contexts of communication because the contexts shape how audiences respond.

STRATEGIES

Once composers have a sense of audience, purpose, and context, they can begin making all the particular decisions—big and small—that shape a composition. Composers need to consider how a choice of a particular word, just as much as a choice of what comes first in a text, are likely to affect an audience's attitude toward a purpose.

RHETORICAL SITUATIONS

The combination of audience, purpose, and context make up what rhetoricians (starting in the twentieth century) call *the rhetorical situation*. This term helps us keep in mind that communication is not a simple transfer of information but is rather an interaction of real, complicated people within the real, complex events of lives and cultures.

Even classrooms are rhetorical situations, where writing an essay involves people with different cultural and educational backgrounds: students and teachers. How do you use the audiences, purposes, and contexts of classrooms—and the strategies available to you—to learn to communicate as you hope?

■ ■ ■

THIS HANDBOOK

This book is about helping you discover as much as you can about your audiences, purposes, and contexts so that you can use the available strategies of writing (and also, to a lesser extent, of visual and oral communication) to construct the connections you want to build with your audiences.

WHAT IS RHETORIC?
AUDIENCE

WHO WILL BE READING, VIEWING, OR HEARING WHAT YOU COMPOSE? WHAT ASPECTS OF YOUR AUDIENCE MATTER TO WHAT YOU HOPE TO ACHIEVE?

That a text you are composing has to be shaped for other people is the central concern of rhetoric.

Perhaps the need to think about your audience when you compose seems obvious to you, but the understanding that we write and compose texts for others takes a while to develop.

Before entering college, most writing education focuses on grammar, research, and the logical structures of writing. Before college, most people move in fairly small circles of friends and family, and so their communications are informal and relaxed: Most often, people in high school know well the people to whom they are writing and speaking. After high school, when we go to college, start working to support ourselves, and start taking more active roles in our communities, we have to learn how to communicate with people we may not know so directly.

We need, in other words, to build upon what we learned about writing in high school: We need to start thinking about the people who read, view, or hear what we compose, and how those people are likely to respond to the many choices we make while composing.

AUDIENCES ARE NEVER FULL, REAL PEOPLE

Even when you are talking with your mother or best friend, you are addressing only some part of that person. Your mother is your mother, after all, and so you speak to her as *mother*; she may also be a boss, an employee, a sister, a daughter—but, when **you** talk with her, you are addressing only that part of her that is *mother*.

Likewise, when you write work memos, they go to your boss and co-workers insofar as they have the role of **boss** and **co-worker**; you do not address the sides of them that are *parent*, *churchgoer*, or *novel reader*.

People have rich emotional and intellectual lives and different cultural backgrounds. When you compose texts for others, you focus on a particular topic and hope your audience will pay attention to your concerns. What emotions play around your topic—and how can you compose to arouse or to dampen those emotions? What possible opinions and values might your audiences hold on your topic—and how can you compose to focus their attention on some particular aspect they might not have considered before or are likely to dismiss?

Audiences, in other words, are always a bit imaginary, in that you ask them to step into the roles and beliefs that the purposes and contexts of your composing require. You call audiences into being from where they really are.

→ Because the consideration of audience is so important, a whole part of this book is focused on shaping writing for audiences. See pages 149–184.

WHAT IS RHETORIC?
PURPOSE

WHAT DO YOU WANT TO HAPPEN AS A RESULT OF YOUR COMPOSING EFFORTS?

What do you hope your audience will think, feel, believe, or do after engaging with you through your text? What do you want to learn through engaging with your audiences?

PURPOSE IS NOT THE SAME AS THESIS

A thesis is the idea—usually with reasons—you hope readers will take away from a piece of argumentative writing. But when you compose such writing, you hope readers will do something with that idea: Do you hope they will write to their national or state political representatives, buy energy-saving light bulbs, or think a little differently about religion or women's lives?

Purposes take into account the emotions and possible actions of readers as well as their thoughts.

PURPOSES ARE NEVER SIMPLE

Here are some purposes for composing:

"I hope that my paper will encourage readers to feel angry enough about teacher salaries in this district that they will join the demonstration to be held at the state capitol next month."

"Because of my poster, I'd like my audience to look more carefully at how others treat pets, knowing there is a relation between pet and child abuse."

"I want my readers to be happy that women's rights have advanced so much in the last century, and to understand why it's important to protect those rights. I want them to see the connection between what happened in the last century and the improved lives of their mothers, sisters, daughters, and themselves."

By thinking about purpose, you start thinking about what your writing and composing need to do, and you start thinking concretely about how to do it.

IMAGINING PURPOSE

As with audience, you need to imagine your purpose as closely as you can: If you picture for yourself exactly the response you hope the text you are composing brings about, you will be more likely to compose texts that appeal in concrete and engaging ways to audiences.

What emotions should your composing arouse or dampen in your audience?

Are you working to build connections with individuals by themselves or to bring people together?

Are you hoping people will take specific action, or quietly consider an issue in more depth?

→ Considerations of purpose weave throughout the rest of this book, but if you want specific help with purpose, see pages 14–15, 23, and 160–165.

WHAT IS RHETORIC?
CONTEXT

WHERE ARE YOUR READERS AT THE MOMENT THEY ENGAGE WITH THE TEXT YOU ARE COMPOSING?

WHAT IS GOING ON AROUND THEM? HOW ARE THE PLACE AND TIME LIKELY TO AFFECT HOW THEY READ?
How can you take those circumstances into account while composing so that the text fits its context and reaches its readers?

LOCAL AND IMMEDIATE CONTEXTS

When you write an essay for a class, the teacher has to respond to your essay as well as to the essays of everyone else in your class, usually at night or on the weekend, at home. How is this likely to shape how your teacher reads?

When you write a memo at work, your boss or co-workers will receive the memo amid a pile of other paperwork, in the middle of distracting days. How is this likely to shape how they read?

When you design a flyer for a campus event, it goes up on walls or telephone poles alongside hundreds of others; it has to attract the attention of people who are hurrying by, ten feet away.

When you design a website for a non-profit organization, readers will probably read it alone, at their computers.

Each of these circumstances, describing the particulars of how audiences come to texts, can help you consider composing. What do you need to do to show a tired, weary-eyed teacher that you've done what an assignment asked? How can you compose a memo so that your busy boss and co-workers will understand exactly what you want? What photographs and words—and what sizes, and how many—can help you attract the eyes of a passing poster audience? What words, colors, and photographs can help you take advantage of the intimacy of a computer screen reader?

The more you can imagine the time and place in which someone will read your text, the more you can shape the text to fit when and where the text will be read.

LARGER CONTEXTS

What are the values and concerns of your time and place? What has happened recently—in your town or country or in the world—that might affect how someone responds to a text?

For example, after September 11, 2001, no one could write an editorial about travel or world events without taking September 11 into account. It was a long time before people felt it was appropriate to tell jokes and be humorous about politics or world events.

But also imagine that your town is struggling over whether to allow Wal-Mart to build a megastore or over how to find funding to keep the hospital open or the factory from shutting down. If you were to write a letter to the editor about school funding, for example, or about the need for a new stoplight on your corner, taking into account those larger community concerns shows readers that you understand the consequences of what you argue—and so readers are more likely to listen.

Composing texts while mindful of the larger contexts in which your readers move can help you figure out what tone of voice to use, the beliefs and values that shape how readers read, and the mood your readers are likely to be in. Considering all these details helps you understand how and why readers might respond. It helps you build bridges to readers, and thus helps you shape a text that readers are more likely to read, understand, and want to engage.

WHAT IS RHETORIC?
STRATEGIES

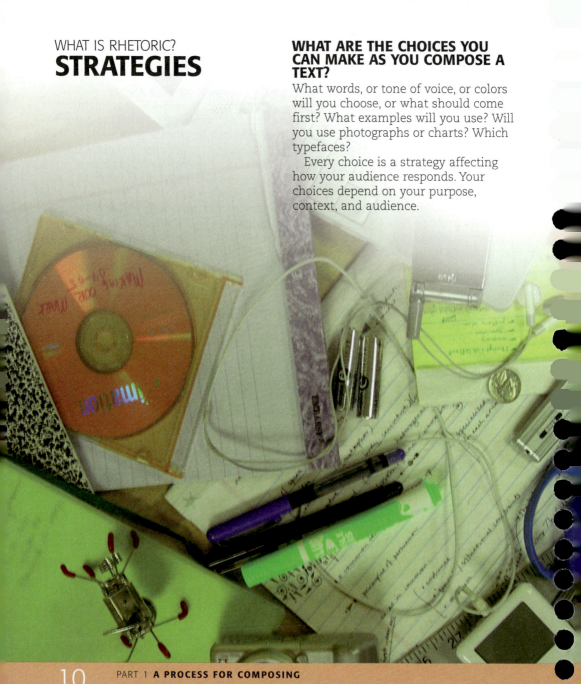

WHAT ARE THE CHOICES YOU CAN MAKE AS YOU COMPOSE A TEXT?

What words, or tone of voice, or colors will you choose, or what should come first? What examples will you use? Will you use photographs or charts? Which typefaces?

Every choice is a strategy affecting how your audience responds. Your choices depend on your purpose, context, and audience.

IN TERMS OF STRATEGIES,

becoming an effective composer of texts involves:

1 Your ability to identify the widest possible range of choices—of strategies—available to you in your rhetorical situation.

2 Your ability to shape choices to address your audience, given your purpose and context.

Regarding the first ability: When you first start considering a text you have to compose (or even when you are partly into composing it), if you list every choice you could make, you'll see how much room there is for you to experiment with possibilities; you're more likely therefore to achieve your purposes. (You'll also probably realize the impossibility of listing every possible strategy—but it's useful to try.)

Regarding the second ability: If you want your audience to write to their congressional representatives to support a bill funding more space exploration, don't begin with a discussion of where the money should come from: That starts your readers thinking about why space exploration might be bad. Start instead with a discussion of the wonders of space, and then describe the medical and industrial advances resulting from space exploration; your audience will approach your request with a positive point of view.

You can consider every possible strategy in light of how your readers are likely to respond, and how your choice will shape their attention and thus their receptiveness to your purpose.

THE STRATEGY OF ARRANGEMENT

In the example of space exploration, the strategy we discussed is arrangement. Arrangement is about what comes first in a composition, and what follows.

For some rhetorical situations, audiences expect certain arrangements. When you write a business letter, the letter starts with a date and a greeting, and then discusses the matter at hand, with (often) a final paragraph suggesting what the next actions should be. Scientific papers are usually arranged with an abstract first, then a description of experimental method, then a description of the results of the experiments, then a discussion of the results, and finally a list of other papers consulted during the research.

→ Because arrangement is such a crucial strategy in composing, a whole part of this book is devoted to it; see pages 185–236.

THE STRATEGY OF MEDIUM

Sometimes you enter a composing situation with all choices open to you, including that of the medium. If, for example, you have been asked to help a nonprofit organization improve its outreach to teenagers, would you recommend composing webpages or brochures, organizing a fair or school visits, or handing out printed T-shirts at the mall? Each of these media engages with the audience in different ways, and so can help you achieve your purpose in different—and differently effective—ways.

RHETORIC AND A PROCESS FOR COMPOSING A RESEARCH PAPER

People who study writers and writing have learned that all effective writers have processes they follow to develop writing. These processes differ in their particulars from writer to writer, but generally—when it comes to composing a research paper—the processes contain the steps shown on the next page.

(Keep in mind that, although the process looks linear, writers often move back and forth through the steps, especially between revising and getting feedback, as they produce several drafts of the work.)

With each step, you become more certain about audience, purpose, context, and—eventually—strategies, until it is time to declare a project finished.

We include the chart on the right at the beginning of each part of this book to help you stay oriented in a project. When we do this, we won't show the rhetorical concerns, because they will be spelled out in each part.

Understanding your project

Getting started audience? AUDIENCE? audience?
purpose? *purpose?* **purpose?**
CONTEXT? CONTEXT? *context?*

Asking questions AUDIENCE
PURPOSE → CONTEXT

Shaping your project for others AUDIENCE + PURPOSE + CONTEXT

Drafting a paper

Getting feedback STRATEGIES

Revising STRATEGIES

Polishing AUDIENCE + PURPOSE + CONTEXT
+ STRATEGIES

RHETORIC AND A PROCESS FOR
COMPOSING A RESEARCH PAPER

UNDERSTANDING YOUR PROJECT OR ASSIGNMENT

To understand any new project or assignment—whether you are in school, at work, or anyplace else where you need to develop communication— you need to understand the rhetorical situation of the project or assignment:

❏ **Who is your audience?**

❏ **What is the purpose?**

❏ **What is the context?**

UNDERSTANDING A CLASS ASSIGNMENT

❏ **Who is your audience?**

In a writing class, you will often hear that the audience is your classmates— but probably your teacher will give you a grade on how well you address the concerns and beliefs of your classmates, so the teacher is also a very important part of your audience. (Sometimes teachers ask you to write for other audiences besides the class; you will have to ask how you are to learn about those audiences.)

❏ **What is the purpose?**

There are three levels of purpose within a class writing assignment, all of which you probably hope to satisfy:

• There are the teacher's purposes. You might be asked to demon-strate that you know how to pro-duce polished prose; can carry out research, integrate it into a paper, and document it; and can develop and produce a persuasive argument. Look at each new assignment for explicit state-ments of what the teacher hopes you will learn; if they are not there, ask.

- You can have your own purposes related to your own learning: If there are skills on which you need to focus (such as some particular aspect of grammar, or transitions, or writing complex paragraphs), how can you work them in?
- There is your particular purpose within the paper you write and its audience, such as *I want to persuade the people in class that replacing the light bulbs in their houses with compact fluorescent bulbs is a useful thing to do* or *I would like to persuade people to write to their representatives about [xxx].*

When you are trying to understand what a teacher is hoping you will achieve, look for the following key terms in an assignment:

summarize: to describe as concisely as possible the main points of writing

define: to explain a term or concept

inform: to tell others about an issue, with supporting examples and data

analyze: to break a process or object into its conceptual parts while showing how the parts relate to make a whole

persuade: to present your opinions on a topic using evidence, so that others might come to agreement with you

❏ **What is the context?**
The classroom is the immediate context, of course—but so is your campus and its values and recent events. The values of the community around the school, current national and international events—how are these likely to shape how your audience will read?

Once you have done some thinking about these questions, you will help yourself tremendously if you reflect on the assignment in writing, asking any questions that come up, as the person who wrote the following did:

The assignment says that I am to write an argumentative research paper on a topic of my choosing, providing lots of evidence, with the class as my audience. I've written research papers before, but I don't know what "argumentative" means regarding research, so I have to ask what that means. But that sounds like the overall purpose for the teacher, to show that I know how to make research be an argument. (I'm also not sure what counts as evidence; I'll have to ask about that, too.) And I don't really know the people in class yet, but they seem to be just like everyone else I know on this campus, so I can ask my friends to help me think about this paper. The context? Well, it's this writing class—so I guess that means I also have to be careful about how I write. But we also just had that big sports scandal here, so maybe that's something to write about.

UNDERSTANDING OTHER PROJECTS

Here are questions to help you start your initial thinking about new communication projects. Later parts of this book will help you continue to develop your understanding of your rhetorical situation, as your questions and concerns become more focused with further work.

❑ **Who is your audience?**

What particular people will read, see, or hear the communication I am building? What are my relationships with those people? What values and beliefs do they hold concerning the topic of the communication? Why should this communication matter to them? What will be most important to them in this communication? Is there an immediate audience and then a secondary audience (as, for example, when someone writes a report for a boss, who will then pass the report on to the next boss)?

→ Part 4 of this book goes into detail about audiences; see pages 150–159.

❑ **What is the purpose?**

Why am I doing this? What am I hoping to achieve? What should my audience think, feel, or do when they are finished reading? What relationships am I hoping to build with my audience?

→ Part 4 of this book goes into detail about purposes; see pages 160–165.

❑ **What is the context?**

Where and when will my audience receive the communication from me? How does that context shape them to respond? Are there any recent events that might affect how they respond?

PART 2
FINDING IDEAS

CONTENTS

WHERE ARE WE IN THE PROCESS FOR COMPOSING?

Understanding your project

Getting started
Finding a topic
Narrowing the topic
Developing research questions
Finding sources
Keeping track of sources

Asking questions

Shaping your project for others

Drafting a paper

Getting feedback

Revising

Polishing

COMPOSING TO LEARN & COMPOSING TO COMMUNICATE

PART 2 OF THIS BOOK IS ABOUT COMPOSING TO LEARN

At the earliest stage of the composing process, you need to let yourself wander through the possible opinions and perspectives on a topic, finding as wide a range as you can. By letting yourself wander, you are more likely to come upon ideas that resonate for you and your audience. That is why this part of the book—Part 2—is set up to help you identify and narrow a topic and then find a wide range of sources on your topic.

Part 3, Analyzing Arguments and Evaluating Sources, will help you consider the ideas, opinions, and perspectives you discover in relation to your audience.

WHY DO YOU NEED TO KNOW ABOUT THIS DISTINCTION?

Effective and successful writers understand that sometimes they need to lose themselves in their own words in order to figure out what ideas matter to them; they also recognize that sometimes they need to look at their ideas from a little distance in order to think about how to shape words for readers.

If you can recognize when you are composing to learn versus when you are composing to communicate, or if you can recognize that sometimes you need to back off from shaping your ideas for readers in order to figure out your own ideas, your composing process will be quicker and easier and will yield stronger results.

COMPOSING TO LEARN

If you are writing, sketching, or reading to figure out what *you* think, believe, or feel, then you are composing to learn. You have no one else in mind as you work: You are simply working things out for yourself. In this stage, you think about possible audiences as little as possible.

Composing to learn can take place on scraps of paper, in journals, on white boards, on dinner napkins and tablecloths, in dreams.

COMPOSING TO LEARN SUPPORTS…

JOURNALS, DIARIES, AND MEMORIES

This is writing meant to be read only by you.

COMPOSING TO COMMUNICATE

When you alertly shape your ideas so that others can understand them, you are composing to communicate. You make clear reasons for and connections between ideas. You think about how others might respond, and you shape all aspects of a text so that others can understand what you do.

Composing to communicate requires composing to learn. Until you have a pretty good idea of what matters to you, you can't know what it is you want others to hear or see.

A RESEARCH PROCESS

Successful writers articulate for themselves exactly what they know at each step of their composing process. This helps them see what they know—and what they still need to learn. This also helps them see when they can really be confident that they have an argument to put on the page (or screen) for others.

What moves writers from step to step of the composing process is research that becomes more focused.

Almost all writers—all composers in almost any medium—start with a general idea or general interest in a topic. By doing initial and broad research into their area of interest, they learn what aspects of the topic might be of concern to their audiences.

Once writers have a narrowed topic, they can generate questions about the topic. These questions help writers learn what further research—now very focused research—they need to do.

All this time, writers are moving toward a thesis statement, which is a statement of the logical aspects of a focused argument, one that is appropriately narrowed for the audience.

Once they have a thesis statement, writers can then build a statement of purpose, which uses a thesis statement and a writer's knowledge about an audience to describe the various compositional strategies that will help the writer reach the audience.

With all that research behind them, writers are well prepared to draft an effective and strong composition.

GENERAL TOPIC

the economy
politics   technology   file sharing
the draft   war   video games   health
global warming   immigration   music
globalization   education

NARROWED TOPIC

electronic voting machines
file sharing
the success of new bands
global warming
the distribution of tree species
charter schools and public schools

QUESTIONS TO GUIDE RESEARCH

What is electronic voting? Why do people suggest we use electronic voting? What makes electronic voting machines better (or worse) than other voting methods? Who oversees electronic voting machines? Who makes electronic voting machines? Who recommends electronic voting machines? Who says we shouldn't use electronic voting machines?

THESIS STATEMENT

Government-developed and owned electronic voting machines that print receipts for voters will help voting be faster and fairer.

STATEMENT OF PURPOSE

Because I am writing to people in class, many of whom will not even yet have voted, I need to explain about different kinds of voting machines—and how each one causes troubles in tracking and counting votes. I also need to show how electronic voting machines—given how they are now developed—seem more vulnerable to tampering and fraud than other existing kinds of voting.

FINISHED WRITING

COMPOSING TO LEARN

COMPOSING TO COMMUNICATE

TIP: THE RESEARCH PROCESS IS NOT LINEAR

This graphic makes the research process look fast and streamlined. It isn't. You will probably repeat steps as you come across sources that lead your thinking in new directions or as you think more about your own position.

A RESEARCH PROCESS, CONTINUED

GENERAL TOPIC

RESEARCH

NARROWED TOPIC

RESEARCH

QUESTIONS TO GUIDE RESEARCH

RESEARCH

THESIS STATEMENT

RESEARCH

STATEMENT OF PURPOSE

RESEARCH

FINISHED WRITING

RESEARCH BROADLY, THEN DEEPLY

During the early stages of research, *general and popular sources* can help you research broadly to get a general sense of what matters to people. Online sources like Google and Wikipedia and popular magazines like *Time* and *Newsweek* can provide help with this broader, preliminary inquiry.

During the later stages of research, *academic journals and other specialized sources* can help you deepen your research and develop your thesis. In academic and other kinds of formal writing, audiences also expect you to provide multiple sources to support your main points.

→ See pages 38–59 for more on kinds of sources and the expectations audiences have about them.

A SKETCH OF ONE WRITER'S PROCESS

GENERAL TOPIC
file sharing

NARROWED TOPIC
file sharing and the careers of new bands

QUESTIONS TO GUIDE RESEARCH
Developing a set of guiding questions can help you gain a better sense of what is at stake, for whom, and why.
Who shares files? How many files are shared in a year? What is file sharing? What are different ways to file-share? What kinds of files are shared? Are there competing interpretations of what counts as file sharing? Who assigns different interpretations? Who decides whether file sharing is good or bad? What criteria do they use? Some people think file sharing is always theft; are there conditions under which it is beneficial? Who benefits from file sharing? Who doesn't? When does file sharing help a band? Do the effects of file sharing differ when different kinds of files are shared? What aspects of file sharing ought to be protected? When should file sharing be prohibited?

THESIS STATEMENT
A thesis statement is about logic: It offers reasons for your position that will be persuasive to your intended audience.
Musicians who make their music freely available online for sharing sell more of their music than those who do not, because they attract new audiences.

→ See pages 102–103 for more on thesis statements.

STATEMENT OF PURPOSE
Writers use statements of purpose to shape a thesis statement for a particular audience. A statement of purpose helps a writer think through the details (such as tone of voice, arrangement, or kinds of examples) of how to present a thesis to an intended audience.

→ Because a statement of purpose is usually several paragraphs long, we cannot give an example here; see pages 161–163 for examples.

In this part of the book, we help you work on developing a narrow topic and questions to guide your research into that topic. Part 3 helps you develop a thesis statement. Part 4 helps you develop a statement of purpose.

GETTING STARTED WITH RESEARCH

ONE PERSON'S PROCESS

Here is how Jessica Rankin, a Senior Technical Writer for a large corporation, describes her research—including how she gets started—when she has to write manuals about a new software product:

I begin by researching and reading the feature specification documents that an engineer writes for the product. These contain descriptions of the feature and what types of things the feature should be used for. After reading through these documents, I usually have a general idea of what the feature is supposed to do, the main parts that would need to be clarified for a user, and where it has been integrated into the software. From there, I go to the software and start playing with the feature to see if it correlates to the feature specification that was written for it. At this point, I have identified odd behaviors and areas that are not intuitive to the general user. These become my starting points for what I document and discuss with the engineer. I act as his first usability tester and I can see the areas that I feel need further development in terms of documentation. Plus, the dialogue that is established between the two of us allows for greater flow of information when changes come up in the feature after development has gotten further along. I know this iterative process has come to a close when the feature no longer changes and I have no further questions about the feature. The real test comes when an outside peer who isn't familiar with the feature reviews my research and documentation. The outside peer is my gauge: Have I conveyed enough information to give the most basic user a good understanding of what they're using?

SETTING UP A SCHEDULE

Unless they are projects you start out of general interest, research projects almost always have due dates—so part of getting started with a research project is figuring out how to schedule your work to be done on time. Making a schedule is also a useful way to remind yourself of just how much work goes into a research paper that is worthy of your efforts and is a learning opportunity. Start with the due date, and work backward. Here is one student's schedule (you may have less time):

Research Paper

DUE DATE	12/15
date assigned	11/1
STEPS	DATE TO COMPLETE STEP
Analyze project (p. 14)	11/2
Find & narrow a topic (pp. 26–33)	11/6
Develop questions for guiding my research (pp. 34–37) and figure out the kinds of research I need to do (pp. 38–43)	11/7
[Will I need to do any interviews, surveys, or observations? (pp. 78–79)]	
[Do I need to do archival research? (pp. 76–77)]	
Carry out my research (pp. 60–79) and start keeping running list of sources (pp. 82–83)	11/14
Develop working thesis (pp. 102–103)	11/16
Do further research required by my thesis (pp. 104–113)	11/23
Evaluate sources, deciding what to include (pp. 130–143)	11/24
Develop statement of purpose (pp. 160–165)	11/25
Develop Works Cited list (pp. 328–350)	11/30
First draft due	12/1
Receive draft back with comments	12/8
If more research is necessary...	12/10
Revise first draft	12/13
Edit first draft	12/14
Get Dad to proofread it for me	12/14
FINAL DRAFT DUE	12/15

FINDING A TOPIC

WHAT A TOPIC IS

A topic is a general area of interest. It's often just a name or a word or two, or two ideas together:

- computer game violence
- children's education
- automobiles
- racism
- women's rights
- sports and advertising
- health and aging
- microloans
- viruses

A topic is a place to start, but it is too broad for a paper; you have to narrow it by doing research that helps you shape your topic for a particular audience in a particular context.

IF AN ASSIGNMENT GIVES A GENERAL TOPIC

You may be given broad guidelines within which to choose a topic. For example, in a history class you might be asked to *Write a short biography of a person who lived through World War I* or *Find two articles that take different positions on an event we've discussed and compare the two articles.* Start by identifying an area—a topic—within the parameters of the assignment, an area in which you want to do further research. If an idea does not immediately spring to mind, use the recommendations on the opposite page to help you choose.

IF YOUR ASSIGNMENT ASKS YOU TO CHOOSE A TOPIC

In writing classes, you are often asked to write a research paper on a topic you choose. Sometimes a topic comes immediately to mind; if not, try:

- **Asking yourself some questions.** What current issues matter to you—or are affecting a friend or someone in your family? What current events or issues do you not understand?

- **Talking to others.** Ask friends and family members what matters to them these days, and why.

- **Going online.** Some library and writing center websites provide lists of current topics that are rich with possibilities for research.

Old Dominion University Libraries' Idea Generator <http://www.lib.odu.edu/libassist/idea/index.php>

University of Illinois at Urbana–Champaign Library's Topic Ideas <http://www.library.uiuc.edu/ugl/howdoi/topic.html#ideas>

Harvard University's Research Matter's Topics <http://www.researchmatters.harvard.edu/topic_list.php>

Once you have a list of possible topics, try these strategies to determine which you want to develop further:

- **Write a little bit on each possible topic.** Use these questions to help:

Audience questions: Why might my audience care about this topic? What might they already know about it?

Purpose questions: How does this topic help me address the assignment's purposes? Will this topic expand my learning? How can I shape this topic into a purpose that will interest my audience?

Context questions: Does this topic seem rich enough to help me write a paper of the length asked by the assignment? Does it seem complex enough for the assignment? What is happening locally/nationally/ internationally around this topic?

→ See pages 2–9 to review the concepts of audience, purpose, and context.

- **Do a Google search on the topic.** Does it look like there's lots of interest in the topic? What are people's different positions on the topic? Do the webpages you visit suggest other, related topics, or other directions for research?

TIP: GET STARTED EARLY

Given the time constraints of school—and of producing a solid research paper—you usually need to decide quickly on a research topic. If you start working early enough, you'll have time to explore possibilities and find a topic that engages you.

Keep in mind, too, that a research paper takes shape in many stages, and you will (if you start early) have time to modify your topic and the research question that grows out of it as you deepen your understanding of your topic. Leaving this work until the night before doesn't necessarily doom you to failure—just to fear, nerves, and the temptation to let someone else do the work for you.

NARROWING A TOPIC

A TOPIC HAS TO BE NARROWED DOWN BEFORE IT CAN HELP YOU SHAPE RESEARCH AND WRITING

Imagine you want to write about the 1960s, and you tell this to one of your slightly more obnoxious friends, who responds, "Groovy! Are you going to tell us about the Vietnam War and the draft and hippies and the free speech movement and the civil rights movement and the Black Panthers and Women's Rights and the deaths of Jimi Hendrix and Janis Joplin and then there's Woodstock and the Young Republicans…? And do you want to talk about the 1960s in Africa, Asia, and Europe?"

You probably already had some idea of where within that long list you wanted to focus, but **until you can make your focus clear and specific to others, simply being able to name your topic sets you up to be unfocused**—and if you are unfocused, your writing will also be unfocused and you will find it hard to plan and organize your paper.

STARTING TO NARROW A TOPIC THROUGH INITIAL, BROAD RESEARCH

One way to find possibilities for narrowing a topic is to start researching the topic using general and popular research sources, as in this example where a Google search on the topic, talking with friends about the topic, and reading the paper and watching television give this writer a sense of how to focus the topic:

TOPIC:
microloans

GOOGLE SEARCH:
Microloans are small loans (usually under $100) made to people without credit, usually in developing countries; they support self-employment and are often made to women because then the whole family benefits; one example is the Grameen bank in Bangladesh, whose founder won the Nobel Peace Prize in 2005.

READING THE PAPER:
The *New York Times* has an editorial by Nicholas Kristof on how anyone in the U.S. can loan even a little bit of money to individuals in other countries, through websites like kiva.org.

TALKING TO OTHERS:
A friend's mother has made loans to women in other countries (through online organizations) so that the women can buy sewing machines and start businesses; all the loans she's made have been repaid.

TELEVISION SHOW:
Small Treasures: Microcredit and the Future of Poverty on PBS says that many microloans are to small businesses that make products out of what others have thrown away, like a woman who makes shopping bags out of discarded cement bags.

After such initial research, this writer could narrow the possibilities to these:

• Microloans and the role of women in developing countries
• Small business options for people living in poverty
• Ways of using your money to help others
• Alternative approaches to traditional economic development

NARROWING A TOPIC

HOW DO YOU KNOW WHEN YOU HAVE A NARROWED TOPIC?

A NARROWED TOPIC IS LINKED TO AN ISSUE OR CONTROVERSY THAT WILL BE OF INTEREST TO YOUR AUDIENCE

Using what you know about your audience, use your initial, broad research (as described on the previous page) to find possible areas that might be useful, surprising, or provocative to your audience.

For example, if you are writing about the 1960s for a class research paper, you probably already have some sense of how others in class think about what happened in the 1960s. If everyone else thinks of the 1960s in terms of free love and music, then imagine how you will catch their attention if you can narrow your topic to *The liberatory social movements in the United States in the 1960s and the conservative political responses of the 1980s and 1990s.*

> **TIP: KEEP YOUR MIND OPEN**
> While doing initial informal research, cast a wide net and keep as open a mind as possible. The wider you look for information on a topic, the more likely you are to be surprised by what you find—and being surprised can help you be more interested and engaged and thus write more strongly.
>
> Also, don't look only for sources that support your initial thoughts on a topic. Seek a range of positions so that you have the widest sense of how people are thinking. (In Part 3 of this book we help you evaluate the sources you find through your research so that you can decide what is most useful for your project.)

NARROWED TOPICS

Notice how narrowed topics usually relate a general topic to specific places, times, actions, or groups of people. A narrowed topic can focus on one aspect of a general topic (as in the examples below about the Internet or religion), and relate that aspect to a place, time, action, or group.

GENERAL TOPIC	NARROWED TOPIC
women in the workforce →	the number of women in politics in the United States the last fifty years
advertising →	advertising and democratic participation in the United States
water as a resource →	water management in the Middle East
the Internet →	how corporations shape Internet social networking sites
poetry →	poetry written by people rooted in two cultures
racial profiling →	racial profiling and law-enforcement policies
global warming →	global warming education in elementary schools
sports →	college sports training and men's body images
religion →	the tax-exempt status of churches and their role in political races
technology →	the development of the compass, gunpowder, and papermaking in China
the civil rights movement →	organizational strategies of the civil rights movement

TIP: USE GOOGLE TO TEST YOUR TOPIC

There are two ways Google can tell you if your topic is narrow enough:

- If the first websites that Google suggests come from academic sources or respected organizations, your topic is narrow enough to be worth further research. (Pages 140–143 can help you determine if the sources are academic.)
- If Google responds with hundreds of millions of possible links, your topic is not yet focused enough.

OTHER STRATEGIES FOR NARROWING A TOPIC

BRAINSTORMING

Brainstorming is letting your brain run loose to jump from one idea to the next. Coming up with ideas that will engage an audience can sometimes happen when you think hard and with focus; other times you need simply to let your brain's associative abilities do what they will.

You can brainstorm alone or with others; with others, you have the advantage of playing off each other's ideas. In either case, work in the same way:

• Set aside five or ten minutes.

• For that five or ten minutes, say your topic out loud, and then say out loud—but also write down—every single thought that comes to mind in response.

• Do not stop to judge. If an idea seems too absurd to record, record it nonetheless: It might lead to something you can use. (And let yourself laugh: The energy of laughter is part of what makes brainstorming work.)

• If you hit a dead end, go back to an earlier term and see what other associations you have with it. (Try thinking of synonyms or opposites to spur your thinking—or come up with as absurd an association as you can.)

• At the end, read your ideas out loud to see if anything else comes up. If one or two ideas seem useful or potentially fruitful now, hold on to them. Otherwise, put the list aside and look at it the next day.

FREEWRITING

Freewriting is a little like extended brainstorming. Give yourself five minutes, and just write on your topic. As with brainstorming, just record whatever ideas come up: Let one idea lead into the next without stopping.

Freewriting becomes easier the more you do it; it's a good way to help your mind run more easily, and it's a practice of many successful writers.

At the end of your time limit, read over what you have written to see if any ideas stand out for development. If not, put the writing aside and go back to it later.

CLUSTERING

Like brainstorming and freewriting, clustering is a strategy for making your ideas visible to yourself—but instead of writing, you draw. Clustering helps you see relations among ideas, which can help you see potential arrangements you can use later when you start writing your paper.

To cluster, write your topic in the center of a page. Around the topic, write down as many related ideas as you can. Turn to each of those related ideas, and see what other ideas relate to them. If one idea suggests a chain of related ideas, follow it.

Below is the cluster Shelly made in thinking about body image, which led her to think about how the media shape our sense of our bodies and how our body image affects our health; by doing this clustering, and thinking about how pro-ani sites work, she came up with this narrowed topic: *body images in the media produced for you by others, and body images in the media that you produce about yourself.*

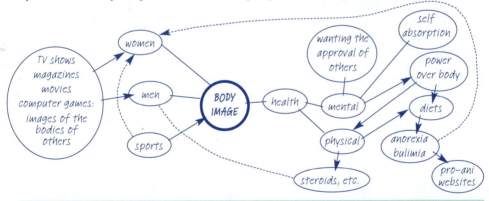

TIP: USE IDEA MAPPING TOOLS

There are free online applications that can help you cluster ideas (in information design and management, clustering is called ***mapping***): try FreeMind <http://freemind.sourceforge.net/wiki/index.php/Main_Page> or CMapTools <http://cmap.ihmc.us/>.

QUESTIONS TO GUIDE RESEARCH

Once you have a narrowed topic, you can go online or to the library to start doing more focused research. But if you take time to carry out one more step—generating questions to help guide your research—you will have a better sense of what you need to find to write a solid paper, and where to look for that information.

On the next page, we show you one way to generate questions on your topic. Doing this can help you see

- areas of research you might not have considered otherwise.
- possible ways for shaping your purpose.
- questions your audience might have that you need to address.
- the specific research directions you need to take.

You may not need to address all the questions you develop, but you won't know for sure until you start using them to dig into sources with focus.

THE ORIGINS OF THESE QUESTIONS

Courtroom observations helped rhetoricians see that most questions fit into a set of categories. Rhetoricians called the categories *stases*, the plural of *stasis*, the Greek word for *place*. Stasis questions—like the ones to the right—help communicators determine what is at stake in any argument and the complexity of what is at stake.

KINDS OF QUESTIONS TO GUIDE RESEARCH

These categories can help you not only invent questions to ask but also determine which questions are likely to lead to rich research, as we show on the next pages.

QUESTIONS OF FACT
- What happened?
- Who was involved?
- Where did it happen?
- When did it happen?

QUESTIONS OF DEFINITION
- What is the thing or issue under discussion? What is it made of?
- What is the expected way (in the particular context) of using the thing, word, title, or expression?

QUESTIONS OF INTERPRETATION
- How do we understand and make sense of what happened?
- How are we to incorporate facts and definitions into a story that makes sense to us?

QUESTIONS OF CONSEQUENCE
- What caused what happened? What changes—to which persons, processes, or objects—led to the issue at hand?
- What are the effects of what happened? What changes might result from what happened?

QUESTIONS OF VALUE
- Is what is at stake good, useful, worthy of praise, or worthy of blame?
- What audiences will value the matter at hand? What do people say about the issue?
- Which of our (or our audience's) values are called upon as we make judgments about what happened?

QUESTIONS OF POLICY
- Given the circumstances, what should we do?
- Given the circumstances, what rules should we make or enforce?
- Given the circumstances, what laws should we write?

USING RESEARCH QUESTIONS TO DEVELOP A TOPIC

USING THE QUESTIONS

Use the research questions to generate as many other questions on your narrowed topic as you can, as the examples to the right suggest.

Doing this work will help you gain a sense of questions your audience might have, questions your research and composing will need to answer.

Generating questions will also help you see what research you need to do to gain authority on your topic.

Finally, generating questions will help you see whether your initial opinion on your topic is sufficiently informed. You will learn whether your opinions really are the ones you want to hold.

■ ■ ■

When you use the research questions to help you generate more questions, just let the questions come: Don't judge them, but let one question lead to another. The more questions you can generate, the more you will have a sense of what further research you need to do.

→ See pages 42–43 for using the questions to help you determine the kinds of research to do.

TIP: TRY TO ANSWER ALL THE QUESTIONS YOU GENERATE

Even though (as you will see in coming pages) you will eventually further narrow your research to focus on one or two questions, using your research to find answers to all the questions you generate will help you.

1 Learn the broad information you will need to give your readers at the beginning of your writing so that they understand why the topic matters.

2 Develop the most thorough and complete answers in your writing.

USING THE RESEARCH QUESTIONS, EXAMPLE 1

Kwan chose the topic of stem-cell research for an argumentative research paper, and has narrowed his topic to the possibilities of stem-cell treatments for paralysis. Using the research questions, he brainstorms the following questions:

QUESTIONS OF FACT
What are researchers able to do now with stem cells to help paralysis? How far away do viable stem-cell treatments seem?

QUESTIONS OF DEFINITION
What are stem cells? What is stem-cell research? What is paralysis?

QUESTIONS OF INTERPRETATION
Do stem-cell treatments cure paralysis? Should paralysis always be treated?

QUESTIONS OF CONSEQUENCE
What happens to people who have stem-cell treatments for paralysis? How do stem-cell therapies work in treating paralysis?

QUESTIONS OF VALUE
Who thinks stem-cell research is worthwhile, and who doesn't? Why? What values are called upon as people make judgments about stem-cell research? What values *aren't* called upon? Are the bad results of stem-cell research offset by the good results?

QUESTIONS OF POLICY
What are the different policies we could have toward stem-cell research and paralysis? What are the policies of other countries on stem-cell research?

USING THE RESEARCH QUESTIONS, EXAMPLE 2

Eva has chosen the topic of road building, and has narrowed her topic to the effects of road building on rural communities. Using the research questions, she brainstorms the following questions:

QUESTIONS OF FACT
Who decides where and when roads are built? How expensive is a new road? What affects the cost of a new road? Who pays for roads in rural areas?

QUESTIONS OF DEFINITION
What counts as a new road? What, really, is a road?

QUESTIONS OF INTERPRETATION
What do new roads bring to a rural community? What do existing roads bring to a rural community?

QUESTIONS OF CONSEQUENCE
What happens when a new road is built in a rural community—or not? Who or what is affected when a new road is built, and how?

QUESTIONS OF VALUE
Are the consequences of new roads good—or bad—for a community? For whom or what are new roads good or bad (including nonhumans)? What values are at stake in making judgments about whether roads are good or bad? What values underlie the different laws that exist about road building?

QUESTIONS OF POLICY
What laws already exist about the development of roads? How have laws and policies changed over the years?

KINDS OF SOURCES, KINDS OF RESEARCH

You have a narrowed topic and a series of questions that can help you learn more about your topic, in a focused and organized manner.

Now you need to determine where to look to find answers to your questions. In these pages we cover

- **KINDS OF SOURCES** for research
- **KINDS OF RESEARCH**
- **USING YOUR GUIDING RESEARCH QUESTIONS** to determine what kinds of sources and kinds of research to carry out
- **WHERE TO FIND THE SOURCES** for the research that will help you answer your questions

UNDERSTANDING DIFFERENT KINDS OF SOURCES

Sources are the texts—written, filmed, videotaped, recorded, photographed—from which you learn about your topic. Sometimes sources provide evidence and examples to use in your writing or other composing.

PRIMARY AND SECONDARY SOURCES

To determine whether a source is primary or secondary, ask yourself if you are reading someone's original words or reading **about** the person. In a paper about Ida B. Wells, for example, speeches and books by Wells are primary sources; commentary about Wells by other writers is a secondary source.

Examples of primary sources:
- Novels, poems, autobiographies, speeches, letters, diaries, blogs, e-mails.
- Eyewitness accounts of events, including written, filmed, and photographed accounts.
- Field research (surveys, observations, and interviews) that **you** conduct.

Examples of secondary sources:
- Biographies.
- Encyclopedias.
- News articles about events.
- Reviews of novels, poems, autobiographies, speeches, letters, diaries, e-mails, blogs.

Knowing the distinction between primary and secondary sources helps you seek out both kinds, and cover all the bases in your research.

SCHOLARLY AND POPULAR SOURCES

This distinction depends on the authority and reliability of the information in the sources.

In scholarly sources:
- Authors have academic credentials: they have studied the topic in depth and know how to weigh and present different sides of the topic.
- The sources used by the writer are listed so readers can check that the sources have been used fairly.
- Topics are examined at length.
- Their purpose is to spread knowledge: These sources are usually found in libraries; they contain little or no advertising.

In popular sources:
- Authors are journalists or reporters, usually without academic study in the topic.
- The sources are not listed.
- Topics are addressed briefly.
- Their purpose is to be quickly informative or entertaining: You find these sources at newsstands and stores, and they contain advertising.

Starting research with a range of popular sources can help you quickly get an overview of available perspectives on a topic. But the expectation for an authoritative research paper is that most of its sources are academic.

KINDS OF RESEARCH

Most research projects require you to do different kinds of research, seeking sources in different places and seeking different kinds of sources. Here are general categories of the kinds of research you can carry out, in recommended order:

ONLINE RESEARCH

Not everything is online—nor does Google link to all that is online.

Unspecialized search engines—like Google and Yahoo!—are useful for the following, usually early in research:

- Developing a sense of popular opinion on topics.
- Finding popular sources on topics, in both popular magazines and in blogs.
- *Finding person-on-the-street* quotations.
- Finding links or references to academic sources.

Specialized search engines provide access to material to which popular search engines often don't have access.

→ See pages 72–73 for descriptions of some specialized search engines.

TIP: USE VISUAL AND AUDIO SOURCES

With any of the research sites we mention here you can do *visual research* and *aural research*. Almost all the kinds of research we mention access not only print sources but also photographs, videos, historic printed matter such as brochures and posters, and speeches. If any visual or aural sources can support your research, search for them online and ask librarians about them.

LIBRARY RESEARCH

There are two ways to use most libraries these days: in person and online.

We encourage you to get to know, in person, a reference librarian at your library: Being able to have a conversation with a librarian about a topic can help you open up new approaches you might not have thought of on your own. A reference librarian can help you with both in-library and online uses of the library's resources.

In-library resources include the obvious books, journals, and reference materials. But some libraries also house historical or art archives, as well as map and government repositories. If you do not know how to find these—or even what materials are available—see if your library gives tours or workshops; knowing what is in your library can help you find creative possibilities for research.

Online library resources can include catalogs of the library's holdings and databases of newspapers and journals from across disciplines. (Later we discuss how to use such databases.)

Finally, libraries usually give you access to interlibrary loans: If your library does not have a book or journal you need, they can order it for you from another library.

RESEARCH IN ARCHIVES AND SPECIAL LIBRARY COLLECTIONS

Physical archives include local history associations or museums that have collections of old manuscripts, furniture, clothing, or other items. Such archives are usually private or provide limited access in order to protect their collections; they have different access policies that you can learn by contacting the archive. To find archives that might be close to you, do an online search using *archive* or *museum* as a keyword along with the kind of information you are trying to find, look in the phone book under *museum*, or ask a librarian.

Virtual archives are online collections of digitized materials such as letters, posters, photographs, or speeches.

Many libraries also have special collections of paintings and prints, films and video, and sound recordings—often not digitized. If you are writing on a topic that has a historical dimension, or are just curious, such special collections can be fascinating.

→ For more information on finding and using both physical and virtual archives and special collections, see pages 76–77.

FIELD RESEARCH

Interviews, observations, and surveys are all forms of research. To carry them out, you have to go out *into the field*—which could be a suburban strip mall, urban nonprofit organization, classroom, or rural farm.

→ For more on carrying out interviews, observations, and surveys, see pages 78–79.

KINDS OF SOURCES,
KINDS OF RESEARCH
DETERMINING WHERE TO RESEARCH

Using the research categories to develop questions around your topic can help you with two aspects of research:

1 **Developing search terms to use for online and database searches.**

2 **Knowing the kinds of sources and research that will be useful.**

DEVELOPING SEARCH TERMS FOR ONLINE AND DATABASE SEARCHES

From your questions, pick out words and phrases directly related to your topic, and use them in search engines.

Here are terms coming from all the questions Kwan generated:

stem cell, stem-cell research, viable stem-cell treatments, stem-cell treatments, stem-cell controversy, stem-cell controversies, stem-cell results, paralysis, stem-cell therapies, consequences of stem-cell research, results of stem-cell research, stem-cell policy, stem-cell research in Europe, stem-cell research in Asia.

→ Page 73 shows how to combine several terms to do a very focused search.

WHAT SOURCES AND RESEARCH WILL HELP?

From all your questions, choose those most tied to your purpose, context, and audience. Almost all research writing starts by grounding its readers in definitions and facts on the topic; then the writing often focuses on interpretation of the issue to show a problem (which could be a consequence of an event) or to argue for certain policies. Once you have a set of focused questions, use the chart at right to choose kinds of sources and research.

Once you have a limited set of questions, use this chart to find the kinds of sources and research that will help you find answers to your questions.

	primary source	secondary source	academic source	popular source	online research	library research	archival research	field research
QUESTIONS OF FACT								
encyclopedias, atlases, and other reference works		✓	✓	✓	✓	✓		
statistics	✓			✓	✓	✓		
government or organizational documents	✓				✓	✓	✓	
firsthand accounts (interviews, autobiographies)	✓			✓	✓	✓	✓	
photographs of events	✓			✓	✓	✓	✓	
trial transcripts	✓				✓	✓	✓	
surveys and polls	✓			✓	✓	✓		
QUESTIONS OF DEFINITION								
dictionaries (for general audiences as well as specialized)		✓	✓	✓	✓	✓		
academic journal articles			✓		✓	✓		
QUESTIONS OF INTERPRETATION								
editorials and opinion pieces		✓		✓	✓	✓		
partisan news sources				✓	✓	✓		
people's stories	✓			✓	✓	✓	✓	✓
artwork (movies, novels, short stories, documentary photography)	✓				✓	✓	✓	
position statements	✓				✓	✓	✓	
biographies	✓	✓		✓	✓	✓	✓	
academic journal articles			✓					
QUESTIONS OF CONSEQUENCE								
statistics	✓	✓		✓	✓	✓		
historical accounts	✓			✓	✓	✓	✓	
photographs of the aftermaths of events	✓				✓	✓	✓	
academic journal articles			✓		✓	✓		
the items listed under INTERPRETATION								
QUESTIONS OF VALUE								
organizational mission statements	✓				✓	✓		✓
voting results	✓			✓	✓	✓	✓	
surveys and polls	✓			✓	✓	✓		
position statements	✓				✓	✓	✓	
academic journal articles			✓		✓			
the items listed under INTERPRETATION								
QUESTIONS OF POLICY								
government decisions	✓				✓	✓	✓	
organizational policy statements and decisions	✓				✓	✓	✓	✓
business records	✓				✓		✓	✓
trial decisions	✓				✓	✓	✓	
academic journal articles			✓		✓			

KINDS OF SOURCES, KINDS OF RESEARCH
CHOOSING SOURCES THAT HELP YOUR RESEARCH AND SUPPORT YOUR ARGUMENTS

Compositions that audiences take seriously offer as much support as possible from a range of supporting sources. The kinds of sources appropriate for your argument depend on the argument you are making, the audience to whom you are making the argument, and your context.

TIPS: CHOOSING WISELY

- MOST IMPORTANT: Teachers want you to compare and make judgments about a range of positions on your topic. Such thinking helps you contribute to community and civic decision making. When you do any research, seek out the widest range of others' positions.

- Sometimes teachers will give you guidelines for how many sources to use. If you have not been given guidelines and you want to indicate that you have looked carefully at a range of ideas in a 7- to 10-page research paper, a minimum of 10 sources is reasonable.

- Not just any 10 or more sources will do. Generally, use only one or two popular sources—perhaps to present the voices and opinions of others to show how and why an issue is a problem. The rest of your sources should be academic, from journal articles and books.

- Avoid using only one kind of source. Having all your citations come from one reference work (whether that work is in print or online, such as Wikipedia) indicates you have not done your research.

CHARACTERISTICS THAT DISTINGUISH SOURCES

On the next pages, we describe different often-used sources so you can judge their appropriateness for your purposes. We use the following criteria:

- **Audience**

  If a source is aimed at a general audience, the information it offers will generally be broad but shallow.

  Sources for academic or other specialized audiences will usually be more developed and better supported.

- **Writers**

  When writers are paid by the company or organization for which they write, they might offer opinions and information that is in line only with the goals of the company or organization.

- **Appearance**

  A professional appearance is a reflection of an overall ethic of care and attention to detail.

- **Format**

  If information is presented alongside advertisements, it can mean that the advertiser has some say in what information is presented.

- **Language**

  Sources using informal language are for general audiences; although they are easier to read, such sources are considered less authoritative than sources that use the language and vocabulary of specialized disciplines.

- **Review**

  If a source's information is reviewed by people who are unpaid and have no connection with the publisher, readers will grant it more authority.

- **Bibliography**

  Your readers will consider as most authoritative those sources that provide information that allows them to check the sources—such as a Works Cited list or other kind of bibliography.

- **When to use**

  We make general suggestions for using sources in ways readers will trust—but keep in mind that you always need to consider your readers, your purposes, and your context in making choices about what kinds of sources to use and how to use them. If you have any questions about using a source, ask several people from your intended audience how they would respond to your use of the source.

OTHER KINDS OF SOURCES

Almost any composition can be a source: You can cite song lyrics to show how hip-hop artists interpret current events differently than mainstream media; you can use a computer game screenshot to discuss representations of women; you can interview a neighbor about the history of local development.

We cannot possibly list all the sources you might use because what you use is limited only by what will engage your audience, given your purpose. The characteristics we consider on these pages can help you decide whether and how to use sources we have not listed.

CHOOSING SOURCES—**BOOKS**

Nonfiction Books

Such books may have more than one author but be written with a single voice throughout.

WRITERS: Publishing companies solicit writers or accept proposals from writers and choose which ones to publish.

REVIEW: Publishers approve the writing and can arrange for fact-checking.

BIBLIOGRAPHY: References are usually mentioned.

WHEN TO USE: Because publishers usually publish books only after carefully determining writers' qualifications, books tend to have authority for readers.

Reference Books

These books provide factual information such as definitions or statistics.

WRITERS: Authorities on a topic usually write entries in reference books.

REVIEW: Publishers approve the writing and check facts.

BIBLIOGRAPHY: References may be given.

WHEN TO USE: To provide definitions of words unknown to an audience or to support factual claims. Conventionally, use reference books sparingly in academic writing.

Edited Collections

An edited collection is a series of essays written by multiple authors with shared concerns, bound into one book.

WRITERS: Publishing companies solicit writers or accept proposals from writers and choose which to publish.

REVIEW: Publishers approve the writing and can arrange for fact-checking.

BIBLIOGRAPHY: References are usually mentioned.

WHEN TO USE: Because publishers usually publish books only after carefully determining writers' qualifications, collections tend to have authority for readers.

Corporate Author

Companies publish annual reports on their finances and accomplishments; they might publish books or pamphlets relevant to their products or services.

WRITERS: Written by an employee of the company or by a writer (a free-lancer) hired for the purpose at hand

REVIEW: A company might set up a review.

BIBLIOGRAPHY: References might be mentioned.

WHEN TO USE: The company's reputation on the topic about which you are writing will shape how readers respond to your use of such sources.

Government Author

The U.S. government publishes a wide range of books, pamphlets, guides, and reports on health, agriculture, economics, statistics, education, and other issues.

WRITERS: Writers can be government employees or people hired because of their expertise.

REVIEW: The writing can be reviewed by other writers in the same or other government agency.

BIBLIOGRAPHY: References may or may not be given.

WHEN TO USE: When your readers will accept the authority of the government on a topic.

KINDS OF SOURCES, KINDS OF RESEARCH
CHOOSING SOURCES—
PERIODICALS

Periodicals are so named because they are published periodically: daily, weekly, monthly, quarterly.

Daily Newspapers

AUDIENCE: General public

WRITERS: Newspaper employees (*staff writers*) or freelance journalists who are paid; writers who work for news services; a writer's credentials often are not given.

FORMAT: Articles might be accompanied by illustrations or photographs, and newspapers contain advertising.

LANGUAGE: Nontechnical, informal

REVIEW: Articles are assigned to writers and reviewed by editors working for the newspapers.

BIBLIOGRAPHY: References might be mentioned in the text, but there are usually few ways given for readers to check a writer's sources.

WHEN TO USE: When you are writing to a general audience, examples and supporting evidence drawn from newspapers can be appropriate; introductions for more specialized audiences can be enlivened with examples from newspapers.

Popular Journals

AUDIENCE: General public

WRITERS: Employees of the journal (*staff writers*) or freelance journalists who are paid; a writer's credentials often are not given.

FORMAT: Articles are usually accompanied by color illustrations or photographs, and the journals contain advertising.

LANGUAGE: Nontechnical, informal

Popular Journals
continued

REVIEW: Articles are selected and reviewed by editors working for the journal.

BIBLIOGRAPHY: References might be mentioned in the text, but there are usually few ways given for readers to check a writer's sources.

WHEN TO USE: When you are writing to a general audience, examples and supporting evidence drawn from popular journals can be appropriate; introductions for more specialized audiences can be enlivened with examples from popular journals.

Academic Journals

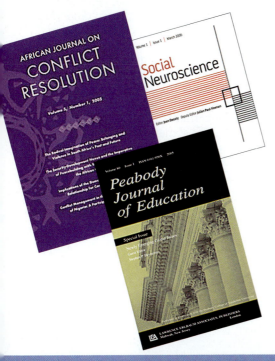

AUDIENCE: Researchers, scholars, specialists

WRITERS: Experts or specialists in a field or discipline, whose credentials are often provided and who are usually not paid for writing.

FORMAT: If articles contain illustrations, charts, tables, or maps, it is usually because they directly support the articles' arguments.

LANGUAGE: Uses the specialized language of a field or discipline

REVIEW: Reviewers who are recognized experts in the field review the articles, for no pay.

BIBLIOGRAPHY: Articles end with a list of works cited (and/or contain footnotes) to document the research performed by the writer so that readers can check the sources.

WHEN TO USE: When you want to show readers that your arguments are as well informed as possible, draw on the research in academic journals.

KINDS OF SOURCES, KINDS OF RESEARCH
CHOOSING SOURCES—
WEBPAGES

Just as there are many kinds of books, there many kinds of webpages.

Because there are so many kinds of webpages, and because webpages can be published by anyone with design abilities and access to hardware and a server, it is often hard to judge webpages' potential to support your research. On these next pages, we provide strategies for recognizing kinds of webpages as well as considering what kind of webpage might be appropriate to support the arguments you are making.

As always, keep in mind that—as with any source—the appropriateness of a webpage for supporting your argument depends on the argument you are making, the audience to whom you are making the argument, and your context. The most important question you can ask yourself in considering whether to use a source is **"Will the audience to whom I am writing see the makers of this website as authoritative on the issues with which I am concerned?"** (Keep in mind, though, that sometimes you will use sources to show how the opinions and ideas of some writers are not well argued or well supported.)

→ For ideas on judging the relevance and credibility of websites, see pages 130–143.

Personal Websites and Blogs

These present the very personal opinions of individuals who may or may not have credentials to write on a particular topic.

AUDIENCE: General public or people interested in the particular topic addressed by the website or blog

WRITERS: Such websites can be produced by anyone with at least minimal technical understanding and access to a computer and the appropriate software.

APPEARANCE: Such websites can look amateurish or completely professional; they may or may not have ads. Look at the URL to see if the website is sponsored by a company or organization.

LANGUAGE: Nontechnical, informal

REVIEW: No one reviews this information except the writer.

BIBLIOGRAPHY: Writings can be accompanied by listings of sources or links to supporting webpages.

WHEN TO USE: If the writer is an authority on the topic you are researching and your audience is likely to have heard of the person, you can use the writings to support claims you make—but you will probably also want to offer other support. If the writer is unknown to you, it is probably a good idea to use the person's opinions only as illustration of opinions people might hold on your topic.

Group Blogs

Several people who care about similar issues can agree to work on a blog together; each contributes individual entries.

suggest a link | defeat censorware | rss | archives
podcast feed | mark | cory | david | xeni | john

Search Boin

boingboing
A DIRECTORY OF WONDERFUL THINGS

A 72 Hour Conversation
mix
April 30 - May 2, 2007 | Las Vegas

SUPER DELUXE

FROM THE MAN WHO BROUGHT YOU WASHINGTON

WEDNESDAY, MARCH 28, 2007

Stasi chief was an Orwell fan, bent reality to get room 1

Erich Mielke, the head of the East German secret police, was a g Orwell's novel 1984, and desperately wanted his office to be in location of the torture chamber in the novel). His office was or floor. So he renamed the first floor the mezzanine.

"I'd long been fascinated by George Orwell's work, but I r reading 1984 until I finished the manuscript for Stasiland devoured it, and I couldn't believe Orwell's prescience. v into Mielke's office, I saw it had the number 101, which number of the torture chamber. 1984 was banned in th course, Mielke and Honecker had access to banned m told me that Mielke wanted this number so much tha office was on the 2nd floor, he had the entire first fl Mezzanine so that he could call his room 101."

--Anna Funder, author of Stasiland

Link
posted by Cory Doctorow at 05:23:11 PM permalink | blogs' comm

White House subpoena evaders put nation

OUT OF THE
CROOKED TIMBER
OF HUMANITY, NO STRAIGHT THING WAS EVER MADE.

« Gnomewatch | Main | Bookstores again »

The White Tyger
Posted by Henry

I blogged a while back about Paul Park's "A Princess of Roum which was the first in a series of four fantasy novels. I recentl finished the third in the series, The White Tyger (Powells, A which is just as wonderful. The novels are profoundly chara in a way that few genre novels are; they deliberately and sp refuse to conform to a conventional quest narrative. None characters know exactly what they're supposed to do; all to a greater or lesser extent, making it up as they go alor main protagonists (and some of the minor ones) are in s another *doubled*; their selves are split in two so that th difficulty in explaining their motivations to themselve less a conventional fantasy story in which the story is characters, determining who they are and what they working through of the ways that individuals make fantasies, spinning out *ex post* narratives to explain themselves and others. The main protagonists don

This is most fully drawn out in the character of th Ceaucescu, who sees herself as the heroine of an

are we?
ris Bertram ∞
chael Bérubé ∞
arry Brighouse ∞
Daniel Davies ∞
Henry Farrell ∞
Maria Farrell ∞
Eszter Hargittai ∞
Kieran Healy ∞
John Holbo ∞
Scott McLemee ∞
Jon Mandle ∞
Montagu Norman ∞
John Quiggin ∞
Ingrid Robeyns ∞
Belle Waring ∞
Brian Weatherson ∞

Guest Bloggers ∞
Click on the ∞ symbol next to a name for a list of all of that author"s posts.

AUDIENCE: Because group blogs are usually on a shared set of interests, the audience is people interested in those issues.

WRITERS: Because these writers want to be read, they are usually careful to choose each other on the quality of their knowledge and writing.

APPEARANCE: Group blogs tend to be carefully presented so that their appearance encourages others to take the blog seriously. Advertising on the blog can indicate that the blog is taken seriously enough that others want to advertise there, or it can mean the writers are trying to make money. Academic group blogs rarely have advertising.

LANGUAGE: The writing indicates the audience the blog wants to attract: Is it academic, or conversational, or…?

REVIEW: Because writers for these blogs want to be read and care about the reputation of the blog, they often discuss with each other the quality of the writing.

BIBLIOGRAPHY: Writings can be accompanied by listings of sources or links to supporting webpages.

WHEN TO USE: If the writers are well respected in their fields or disciplines, citing their opinions can support your writing—but keep in mind that when you are writing an academic paper, citing a blog will not have as much authority as citing an article published in a journal.

Corporate Websites and Blogs

These present information about and opinions provided by companies. The companies can be large or very, very small.

AUDIENCE: General public, consumers, people interested in the particular topic addressed by the website or blog

WRITERS: Employees of the company or freelancers

APPEARANCE: Such websites can look amateurish or completely professional, depending on the ethos the company wishes to present and the resources they wish to put toward development. Well-established companies will have their name in their URL. The company name and contact information should be somewhere on the main page.

LANGUAGE: The language will reflect the company's purposes: It might be friendly and informal, to appeal to potential clients or customers; it might be formal, to show the company's solidity and authority.

REVIEW: Corporate webpages might be reviewed by lawyers to protect the company from lawsuits; otherwise, the content is provided and approved only by the company itself.

BIBLIOGRAPHY: Writings can be accompanied by listings of sources or links to supporting webpages.

WHEN TO USE: Because such websites are usually promotional, the information you find on them will rarely be useful for supporting arguments, unless you are writing about the company itself or using the company's website as an example of how companies operate.

Nonprofit Websites

*According to the Internal Revenue Service, an organization is nonprofit if its income does not go to stockholders, directors, or anyone else connected with the organization; instead, its income supports only the work the organization does. A nonprofit's URL usually ends in **.org**.*

AUDIENCE: Anyone interested in the work done by the organization, perhaps to donate or to learn more about the organization.

WRITERS: The website might be composed by an employee of the organization or by someone hired to represent the organization.

APPEARANCE: Organizations try to present themselves as competent and dependable in order to gain support from those who see the site.

LANGUAGE: Generally, nontechnical, informal language for general audiences

REVIEW: The organization approves what is on the website.

BIBLIOGRAPHY: Writings can be accompanied by listings of sources or links to supporting webpages.

WHEN TO USE: Generally, the facts and statistics you find on the websites of nonprofit organizations are reliable—although remember that organizations want to present information that supports their purposes. It is always useful to find additional supporting information. (You can always use an organization's description of itself in your writing when you want readers to know about an organization.)

Government Websites

*U.S. government website URLs usually end in **.gov**. State websites end with the two-letter abbreviation for the state followed by **.gov**.*

AUDIENCE: General public as well as specialists looking for information the government compiles

WRITERS: The website might be composed by a government employee or by someone hired as a freelancer.

APPEARANCE: The look of government websites will tell you whether the site has been designed for general-audience or specialist use.

LANGUAGE: The language of government websites can range from friendly and informal to highly technical, depending on the intended audience.

REVIEW: Governmental websites are supposed to adhere to accessibility, writing, and navigational policies established within agencies as well as across some agencies.

BIBLIOGRAPHY: Writings can be accompanied by listings of sources or links to supporting webpages.

WHEN TO USE: Use government websites when you want to give statistics or the wording of policies. Because claims made about science or social research can be shaped for political ends, use such claims in your writing only if you can back them up with support from disinterested parties whom your readers will trust.

Online Periodicals

Distinguish among online periodicals just as you would among print periodicals, as on pages 48–49.

AUDIENCE: Depending on the periodical, the audience can be general or highly specialized, academic or popular.

WRITERS: If the periodical is an online version of a print periodical, then the writers for both versions are usually the same people. Online-only journals can have paid writers or volunteer writers.

APPEARANCE: Such websites can look amateurish or completely professional, depending on the organization behind them and their purpose.

LANGUAGE: The language will depend on the audience and purpose.

REVIEW: Online versions of print periodicals tend to have the same review policies as the print version. Academic periodicals will generally have some sort of review policy for articles; look on the website to find out. For other periodicals, the website might include such policies.

BIBLIOGRAPHY: Academic periodicals will provide sources and ways to find those sources; other periodicals may or may not provide sources.

WHEN TO USE: Use each kind of periodical as you would use its print counterpart, as described on pages 48–49.

Databases of Journals

Through your school library, you probably have access to these databases, which are like search engines into collections of periodicals: You enter terms for topics of interest to you, and the database returns to you listings of articles in which those terms appear. Databases are usually specialized. Each database provides access to a particular subject, such as medicine, law, literature and the arts, newspapers, or engineering.

AUTHORITY: Unless you are writing about databases, you are not going to be citing databases; you will instead be using them to find periodical articles that help you think about your writing or that support your points.

Because of this, the authority of databases is not an issue to consider in your use of them.

WHEN TO USE: Any time you want to find a generally credible range of articles to help you think about your topic or to support your claims, use online databases of journals.

→ See pages 64–71 for more information on using databases.

Image published with permission of ProQuest LLC. Further reproduction is prohibited without permission.

Online Reference Works

These can be online versions of print reference works or reference works created only to be online.

AUTHORITY: The information and thus authority of these sites is the same as that of print reference sources.

WHEN TO USE: Generally, make only limited use of reference works: They are best used for giving a quick fact or an authoritative definition of a term. Readers of academic research papers expect you to use a range of sources, but they especially expect you to use specialized sources primarily.

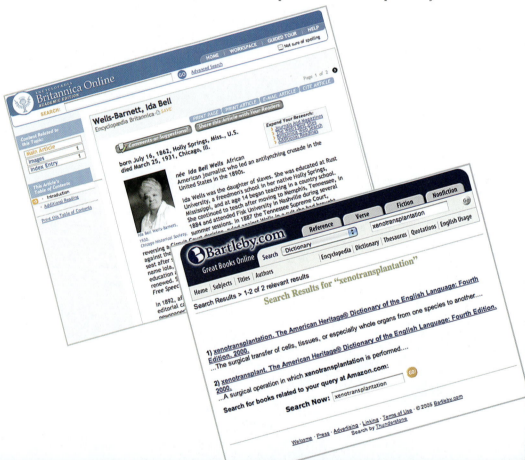

Online Reference Works—Wikipedia

Wikipedia is a particular kind of online reference, developed by volunteers who write on topics of interest to them and who edit each other's entries. Teachers consider Wikipedia use to be controversial because the entries can be shaped by nonspecialists; because there are no easy ways to check the authority and accuracy of any particular entry; and because the ease of using Wikipedia sometimes encourages writers not to seek further support for their arguments.

WHEN TO USE: Wikipedia is useful in the early stages of research, when you are looking for quick and preliminary information to help you learn how others think about a topic—just as you can use Google or any general encyclopedia. In addition, your audience (including your teacher) will probably not object if you use Wikipedia as the source for the definition of a term in your writing.

When you are ready to research a topic in depth, Wikipedia can help you go deeper because many entries include good listings of further resources—but citing Wikipedia in a Works Cited listing shows readers that you have probably done only quick and dirty research.

FINDING SOURCES

SEARCHING

You've determined that a scholarly journal article, oral history, or some census statistics ought to help you learn enough to turn your narrowed topic into a statement of purpose. Finding the sources you need means that you have to understand the way sources are cataloged, no matter the kind of source.

Prior to the Internet, libraries had card catalogs for their materials. For every book, journal, map, or governmental record kept in a library there was a small card that listed the object's title, author, date, and place of publication; a few keywords about the object's topic; and a general subject area into which the object's contents fit.

Now, instead of those cards, library objects have associated online records in databases, which carry the information that used to be on the cards. The library computer system provides a webpage into which you type search terms; the database compares your search terms to all the terms listed in the database records and then shows you any matches.

Online search engines that give you access to sources outside of libraries *look* at webpages of all kinds and develop their own database records for those pages, based on what words are on the page or in its code. When you use a search engine, it compares your search terms to its database and shows you the matches.

Both processes are similar, and both require that you know how to generate search terms that will help you find useful sources.

TIPS: SEARCHING ONLINE

BE SPECIFIC

Having a narrowed topic will help you find sources that specifically address your questions.

It is useless to enter one word into a search engine. Try two words and then three: *cars fuel* or *cars ethanol*—and then *cars alternate fuels*.

In library catalogs and databases, you can enter the key terms from your narrowed topic; you can also enter any synonyms for those terms.

In search engines like Google, you can enter the key terms from your narrowed topic—but you can also enter a question such as "Does ethanol provide better mileage than a hybrid car?" and receive the most focused information possible from the websites to which Google has access. Use the research questions you generated for such searches.

→ See page 73 to help you with this.

TRY ALTERNATE TERMS

If you cannot readily think up synonyms for the key terms of your narrowed topic, use a thesaurus, or ask someone else what other terms come to mind for your topic. The more terms you can use, the more likely you are to find helpful sources.

ASK FOR HELP

Teachers, librarians, and people in your class who seem to be good at searching are usually happy to help.

CHECK THE SEARCH ENGINE'S HELP TIPS

All search engines—the library's online catalog, a library database, or a general search engine—have a link to help or usage tips. Read this information so that you can take advantage of the particular features of a search engine.

USE A FAMILIAR SEARCH ENGINE TO FIND SOURCES YOU CAN THEN CHECK IN A MORE SPECIALIZED SEARCH ENGINE

Library joural databases can have confusing interfaces; many people, including faculty, use Google to find a source and then check to see if it's in their library. For example, you might find through Google an academic article exactly on your topic. You can then enter into your library's journal database the journal name, author, and date to have access to a full-text version of the journal. (Similarly, some researchers use Amazon.com to find books because they can usually read some of the book and check reviews. If the book looks useful, they will then see if their library has it. This is useful only for recently published books.)

PERSIST

The more creative you are with your terms and the longer you search during this stage, the more information you will find that pushes you to weigh differing opinions. This sort of thinking leads to writing others want to read.

LIBRARY RESEARCH

USING LIBRARY INDEXES

If you think information you need will be in a print source that was published before the rise of networked computers (or, roughly, before the early 1990s), then you are likely to be successful with the print indexes in your library for journal articles, newspapers, and books in several subject areas. A reference librarian can help you find the appropriate index.

TIP: GET TO KNOW A REFERENCE LIBRARIAN

Reference librarians know a tremendous amount about different kinds of sources and how to find them, in print and online. Whenever you have research questions, ask your librarian.

You can help your librarian help you if you have specific questions. "I need some statistics about how many manufacturing jobs have been lost in the U.S. in the past 10 years. What are the best places you can suggest for finding that information?" will help the librarian find you useful and specific information. "I want to learn something about job loss in the U.S." is less likely to do so.

USING LIBRARY CATALOGS

Most library catalogs have similar features to the one below. The features may show up in different places on-screen or in checkboxes instead of pop-up menus—but they will work in the same way. To prepare to use such a catalog, be sure you have a focused set of search terms, as we describe on page 61.

Pop-up menus

These pop-up menus allow you to choose how you want to search for a source. You can search using just a word or phrase or just the subject, or you can combine searches, looking for a periodical title and a word or phrase together.

Search selection

If your campus is part of a system of schools or has multiple libraries, this option allows you to search within just one of the available libraries.

Choose a language

If you are searching for a source in a specific language, this option allows you to choose from a range of available languages.

Choose your source

With this option you can choose to search specifically for a book, magazine, map, poster, or for any other type of source the library has.

Select the location of your search

This library has different archives and collections; the *location* option allows you to search within one specific location or across all of them.

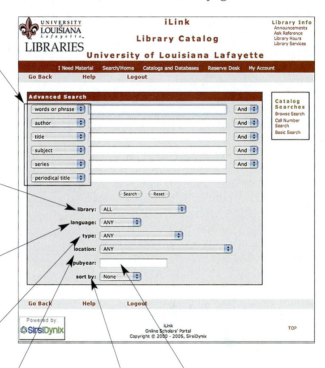

Sort the search results

This option allows you to see the search results sorted by year, author name, or title.

Select the time period of your search

If you are searching for sources from a specific year or range of years, enter that information here.

USING LIBRARY JOURNAL DATABASES

Most scholarly journals and popular periodicals are now online—and most are not accessible through Google. Different companies provide online access to these publications through subscription services; your college library subscribes to some of these services. Different subscription services give access to databases in different disciplinary areas. For example, some services provide access only to engineering or only to humanities databases.

These databases often provide only basic bibliographic information for a source—the article title, author's name(s), date and place of publication, and journal or periodical name—and an abstract giving a brief description of the source. Once you find this information, you have to find out if your library has a subscription to the journal or periodical so that you can see the full article.

More frequently, however, these databases are providing full-text versions of journal articles and periodicals that you can read online.

STEPS IN USING DATABASES

1 Find the database search page on your library website.

2 Choose a database to search.

3 Use the database's search features to find references to relevant articles.

4 Choose the references that seem the most relevant.

5 Once you decide on the most relevant references, get hold of the articles.

1 FINDING THE DATABASE SEARCH PAGE ON YOUR LIBRARY WEBSITE

On the main page of your school library's webpage will be some sort of link to the databases. There may be an option labeled **Resources for research**, **Indexes and Databases**, or **E-Resources**.

Clicking such a link will take you to a screen where you can choose the database to search, as on page 66.

WHAT IS A DATABASE?

When you have lots of data—journal articles, patient records, sports statistics, census numbers—you need to organize it so that you can find what you need. On computers, databases do this. The data are stored in particular arrangements (for example, journal articles will be stored in records that indicate the title, author, keywords, and so on); the database software can then use your search terms to find records that match. The database is the collection of data; a database management system is the software that organizes the data and shapes your search. In day-to-day conversation, however, people use **database** to mean both the collection of the data and the software used to access it.

2 CHOOSING A DATABASE TO SEARCH, PART 1

First, it helps to know about some of the more popular databases that (for the most part) give you access to general information. Here are such databases, with short descriptions, to help you decide which might be useful to your research purposes:

ABI/INFORM
(information from 1971 to the present)
This database covers U.S. and international business and management topics, with information on 60,000 companies.

AH SEARCH
(information from 1984 to the present)
This is an index to more than 1,150 arts and humanities journals and over 7,000 science and social sciences journals.

ALTERNATIVE PRESS INDEX ARCHIVES
(information from 1969 to 1990)
This is the archives for the AH Search database, and includes book, film, and television reviews, obituaries, and bibliographic information as well as articles.

CSA ILLUMINA
This is a database of other databases, giving you access to more than 100 full-text and bibliographic databases in the arts and humanities, natural sciences, social sciences, and technology.

EXPANDED ACADEMIC ASAP
(information from 1980 to the present)
This database covers subject areas in the humanities, technology, social sciences, and sciences, with full-text articles available. The database includes scholarly journals, news magazines, and newspapers.

FIRSTSEARCH
This database searches a wide variety of other databases, giving you access to educational, literary, medical, and religious topics; Latin American journals; government publications; conference proceedings; and the *World Almanac*.

JSTOR
JSTOR gives access to academic journals (dating back to 1665 in one case) in the areas of arts and sciences; health, biology, and general science; and business. (Your library may not subscribe to all the areas JSTOR covers.)

LEXISNEXIS ACADEMIC
This database provides full-text access to news, business, legal, and reference information.

PSYCFIRST
(information from 2002 to the present)
This database gives you access to citations and abstracts about worldwide research in psychology and related fields.

TIP: WHEN TO USE THESE DATABASES IN YOUR RESEARCH

The scholarly sources to which these databases can give you access are focused, detailed, and scholarly. These sources carry considerable authority for readers, but they also require effort on your part to find and to read. These sources will therefore be most useful to you when you have a solid, narrowed topic or statement of purpose to shape your searching.

→ See Part 3 on statements of purpose.

CHOOSING A DATABASE TO SEARCH, PART 2

Because there are hundreds of databases, your first step in working with the databases to which your library subscribes will probably involve a webpage that looks like the one below, which helps you choose among available databases. (The screen below comes from Michigan Technological University's Van Pelt Library website.)

Your college library's page for searching databases may not have all the features of the page shown below, but it will be similar.

Such a screen gives you many options for finding databases useful to you, as the callouts below indicate.

If you know the name of the database you want

Type its name in the *Search for Databases* box, or use the alphabetic search option to access it.

If you are new to using databases, or are searching in a new subject area, start here

These pop-up menus (which might be checkboxes on other webpages) give you access to lists of databases chosen because of their relevance to specific subject areas. Look at the list of subjects, and choose the one (or two) in which your topic best fits. (On the next pages, we show you what to do next.)

If you have some familiarity with popular databases

These are links to some of the most used databases. (Some of these are described on page 65.)

Search for Databases

[   ] ☑ Title ☑ Description (Go!)

Databases A-Z

New   All | A B C D E F G H I J K L M N O P Q R S T U V W X Y Z

Database Quick Links

- ABI/Inform
- CSA Illumina
- Compendex
- ENGnetBASE
- FirstSearch
- IEEE *Xplore*
- JSTOR
- LexisNexis
- Thomson Gale
- Web of Science
- WorldCat

Search by Subject Headings | Browse All Subject Headings

1st Subject [Agriculture, Forestry & Environmental Science ▼]

AND

2nd Subject [* (use only first subject) ▼] (Go!)

(To narrow your search select a 2nd subject heading)

Search by Providers | Browse All Providers

[American Chemical Society (ACS) ▼] (Go!)

CHOOSING A DATABASE TO SEARCH, PART 3

If you are researching a geographic topic, for example, you may find that the **Database Quick Links** databases listed in the dialogue box to the left don't get you what you need; in such a case, choose **Geography** from the **Search by Subject Heading** option on the screen shown to the left.

Below is the result of such a choice. This is a list of the databases to which this library subscribes that will most likely help you find geographic information.

How do you choose which databases to search?

Read the descriptions of the databases' scope

Look for descriptions that seem most focused in your area of interest. Below, the descriptions of scope suggest that GEOBASE, ScienceDirect, and Web of Science might be the best places to start.

Which databases give you full-text access?

Full text means that you will see the article online and not just its bibliographic information. If articles do not have full-text access, use the bibliographic information to see if your library has the journal you need; you might need to order it through interlibrary loan.

	Full Text Available Show All	Access Restrictions
Academic OneFile Coverage: 1995 - Present	F	M
Scope: premier source for peer-reviewed, full-text articles from the world's leading journals and reference sources. With extensive coverage of the physical sciences, technology, medicine, social sciences, the arts, theology, literature and other subjects.		
Article1st Coverage: 1990 - Present		M
Scope: contains bibliographic citations for items listed on the table of contents pages of over 12,600 journals in all subject areas.		
GEOBASE Coverage: 1980 - Present		M
Scope: contains citations with abstracts covering worldwide literature in geography, geology, and ecology.		
Google Scholar Coverage: 1900 - Present	F	M
Scope: web search engine designed specifically to locate scholarly literature, including peer-reviewed papers, theses, books, preprints, abstracts and technical reports across broad areas of research. **Access Note:** click **here** for additional information about Google Scholar. Also if you are coming from off campus you will be asked for your ISO Login and Password. This will grant you full text access to those full text resources that the JRVP library has secured.		
ScienceDirect Coverage: 2003 - Present	F	M
Scope: extensive and unique full-text collection covers authoritative titles from the core scientific literature. ScienceDirect is designed as a basic electronic version of Elsevier Science print allowing you to access full-text articles published since 2003.		
Social Sciences Abstracts Coverage: 1983 - Present		M
Scope: covers periodicals in anthropology, economics, geography, law and criminology, political science, social work, sociology, and international relations.		
Web of Science Coverage: 1973 - Present		M
Scope: offers Web of Science access to ISI Citation Indexes (Science Citation Index Expanded, Social Sciences Citation Index and Arts and Humanities Citation Index), which contains multidisciplinary, high quality research information from the world's leading science, social science and art and humanities journals. **We now have unlimited access to WoS.**		

TIP: THE EARLY STAGES OF RESEARCH

Keep in mind that you need to search more than one database when you are in the early stages of research looking for broad background information.

3 USING A DATABASE

Once you have chosen a database to search, you will see on your screen the search tools particular to that database; every database company presents this information somewhat differently.

WHAT DATABASE SEARCH SCREENS USUALLY HAVE IN COMMON
Here is the initial search screen for the LexisNexis database.

Start by entering your search terms

With most database searches, you will probably start by entering your search terms into the text entry box and then clicking *Search*.

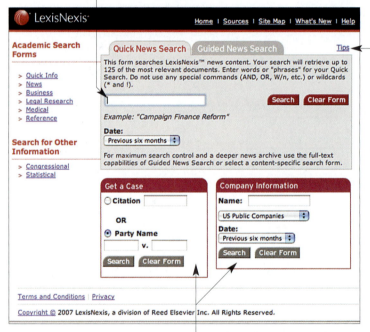

Using the database tips

As you become more comfortable with database searches, you can become more fluent by checking out how the database creators recommend you use their search features.

Explore the features of the database

Database search screens can be somewhat visually daunting, in part because they offer researchers so many possible ways to research. As you become more at ease with these sorts of searches, you will make your work and research richer if you take time to explore the features of the databases that most tie to your interests.

Searching databases that give you access to other databases

Sometimes, when you choose a database following the advice we've given in step 2, you will come to a screen like the one below; this screen shows that you have chosen a database that gives you access to still other databases. These other databases tend to be focused and specialized.

To use a screen like this, look over the databases that are listed just as you would in step 2. Choose those databases that look most relevant to your topic. When you click **Continue to Search**, you will come to a screen similar to the one shown at left, where you can enter your search terms.

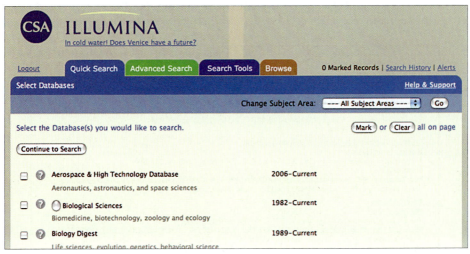

Image published with permission of ProQuest LLC. Further reproduction is prohibited without permission.

TIP: FINE-TUNING DATABASE SEARCHES

Just about every database search screen will give you a choice between a **Quick Search** and an **Advanced Search**. In **Quick Search**, you simply enter your search terms. In **Advanced Search**, you will have some set of options: You might be able to specify that the database search for articles only from within the last five years or from twenty years ago; you might be able to specify very specific subject areas for the search, or that you want only full-text searches or searches in a specific language.

Such fine-tuning can help reduce your search time if you know you need such specific information.

4 CHOOSING THE REFERENCES THAT SEEM MOST RELEVANT

After you have entered your search terms into a database search screen and clicked **Search**, you will see a screen like the one below (each database will look slightly different). This is the list of articles in the database that match your search terms.

Understanding the search results

This search was made by someone looking into recent cultural notions of beauty and the ways they affect how women think about themselves. This information shows that this researcher used the search terms *beauty* and *culture*, and was looking for articles published between 1995 and 2007. (Note that there were 4,017 matches—an indication that this search could be narrowed even more.)

Show 25 ⬍ results per page. (Display)   Results 1-25 of 4017 for « (beauty) AND (culture) AND (year:[1995 TO 2007])^0 » (0.06 seconds)

Sort by Relevance ⬍ (Sort)   Save All Citations on This Page | View Saved Citations
You have saved **0** citations

1. **The India Bonita Contest of 1921 and the Ethnicization of Mexican National Culture**
   Rick A. López
   The Hispanic American Historical Review > Vol. 82, No. 2 (May, 2002), pp. 291-328
   Link to Article I Save Citation

2. **Whatever Happened to Beauty? A Response to Danto**
   Kathleen Marie Higgins
   The Journal of Aesthetics and Art Criticism > Vol. 54, No. 3 (Summer, 1996), pp. 281-284
   Stable URL:
   http://links.jstor.org/sici?sici=0021-8529%28199622%2954%3A3%3C281%3AWHTBAR%3E2.0.CO%3B2-2
   Article Information I Page of First Match I Print I Download I Save Citation

3. **Beauty Matters**
   Peg Zeglin Brand
   The Journal of Aesthetics and Art Criticism > Vol. 57, No. 1 (Winter, 1999), pp. 1-10
   Stable URL: http://links.jstor.org/sici?sici=0021-8529%28199924%2957%3A1%3C1%3ABM%3E2.0.CO%3B2-N
   Article Information I Page of First Match I Print I Download I Save Citation

4. **The Pervasiveness and Persistence of the Feminine Beauty Ideal in Children's Fairy Tales**
   Lori Baker-Sperry; Liz Grauerholz
   Gender and Society > Vol. 17, No. 5 (Oct., 2003), pp. 711-726
   Stable URL:
   http://links.jstor.org/sici?sici=0891-2432%28200310%2917%3A5%3C711%3ATPAPOT%3E2.0.CO%3B2-4
   Article Information I Page of First Match I Print I Download I Save Citation

5. **Aesthetic Resistance to Commercial Influences: The Impact of the Eurocentric Beauty Standard on Black College Women**
   Dia Sekayi
   The Journal of Negro Education > Vol. 72, No. 4, Commercialism in the Lives of Children and Youth of Color: Education and Other Socialization Contexts (Autumn, 2003), pp. 467-477
   Stable URL: http://links.jstor.org/sici?sici=0022-2984%28200323%2972%3A4%3C467%3AARTCIT%3E2.0.CO%3B2-9
   Article Information I Page of First Match I Print I Download I Save Citation

Three promising articles

Given this researcher's purposes, these three articles look promising. He won't know for sure until he looks at the full articles, but the titles of these three suggest that they will address his concerns. (Number 2 looks as though it was written specifically in response to another article, and so won't be useful.) Note that these are not the first articles in the list; note also that there are 4,012 more articles to consider. How would you narrow this search?

5 GETTING THE ARTICLE, ONCE YOU FIND A RELEVANT REFERENCE

- The database listing to the left is from a full-text database; clicking any of the links will take you to the listed article, which you can then read.
- Sometimes, however, you will get a listing like the one below, which has no link to access a full-text version.

A listing with no link to a full text version

In such cases, look for links like these, which allow you to see if your library carries the journal from which this article comes and, in case your library doesn't, to see other libraries that have the journal. (If your library does not carry the journal, you will need to use your library's interlibrary loan service; ask a librarian for help with this if you've never used this before.)

Availability:	**Check the catalogs in your library.** • Libraries worldwide that own item: 347 • 🏛 Search the catalog at J Robert Van Pelt
Author(s):	Charles, S **Reprint Address:** Charles, S; Univ Sherbrooke, Sherbrooke, PQ J1K 2R1, Canada **Research Address:** Univ Sherbrooke, Sherbrooke, PQ J1K 2R1, Canada
Title:	**The meaning of beauty. From its origins to modern culture**
Source:	*DIALOGUE-CANADIAN PHILOSOPHICAL REVIEW* 40, no. 2 (SPR 2001): 416-419 **Additional Info:** CANADIAN PHILOSOPHICAL ASSOC: MORISSET HALL #375, UNIV OTTAWA, OTTAWA, ONTARIO K1N 6N5, CANADA
Standard No:	**ISSN:** 0012-2173
Language:	French
Reviewed Item:	**Author:** Ferry, L **Publication:** 1998 **Language:** French
References:	**Number:** 1
	SUBJECT(S)
Journal Subject:	PHILOSOPHY -- H UA
Cited Reference:	FURRY, L, 1998, SENS BEAU ORIGINES C
Article Type:	Book Review
Accession No:	000169393900022
Database:	AHSearch

TIPS: **WORKING WITH DATABASES**

- As with all research, database work takes time. You will need to try more than one database, performing variations on your basic search in each. Have patience, and look for the sources that expand your thinking on your topic.
- When you use an article from a database in your writing, you cite it differently from articles you find in a journal on the library shelf.

➡ See pages 346–347.

ONLINE RESEARCH

SEARCH ENGINES AND SEARCH DIRECTORIES

Search engines work because they access large databases of websites, which have been collected by automated programs called **spiders** or **robots**. The websites are indexed: The words and phrases they contain are compiled into lists that are structured for easy computer searching.

When you enter your search terms, the search engine compares your terms to its indexes, and returns to you a list of websites containing your terms.

Search directories are similar to search engines because each compiles databases of websites—but a directory lists or searches through only the sites that have been inspected for their relevance.

Because each search engine or directory has been designed to search the Web differently, and to index its terms differently, different search tools can return differing results for the same search terms—so you are more likely to find helpful information by using more than one search tool.

RESOURCES FOR KEEPING TRACK OF YOUR ONLINE RESEARCH
—and for taking advantage of other people's searches

If you do lots of online searches and have not yet learned about furl *<http://www.furl.com>* or del.icio.us *<http://del.icio.us>*, check them out. Each site works a little differently, but each gives you ways to save and organize links that matter to you.

In addition, each site gives you ways to search other people's collections of website links on topics related to yours; by looking at how others have labeled—or **tagged**—their finds, you can also learn new terms to use for further searching.

You are probably familiar with Google and Yahoo!, which are generalized search tools, but also check these tools, designed to aid academic searches:

INFOMINE: SCHOLARLY INTERNET RESOURCE COLLECTIONS
<http://infomine.ucr.edu/>
Infomine is constructed by college and university librarians to be a library of resources specifically for college and university students and faculty. Infomine links you to databases, electronic books and journals, and other useful resources.

ACADEMIC INDEX
<http://www.academicindex.net/>
A librarian developed this search tool, which searches through databases of information on topics of academic interest and quality, compiled or recommended by librarians, teachers, and researchers.

LIBRARIANS' INTERNET INDEX
<http://www.lii.org/>
This is a publicly funded directory, which also sends out a free weekly newsletter of websites; the online directory and newsletter websites are chosen and organized by librarians.

TIPS: USING ONLINE SEARCH TOOLS

- *Use more than one search engine.* Because each search engine is designed to search the Web differently than others, different search engines give different results for the same search terms—so you are more likely to find helpful information by searching in different engines.

- Most search engines have both *a simple search*—where you enter a few search terms—and *an advanced search*, where you can specify date ranges, the kind of file you want (html, pdf, or doc), or that the search results be only webpages containing noncopyrighted information. When you have a narrowed topic or know you need information from 1995, for example, using these features saves time. Explore these features in your favorite search engine so that—when you have a very focused search to carry out—you know what is possible.

- Many search engines will allow you to carry out what is called a *boolean search*. George Boole, a nineteenth-century mathematician, developed ways for thinking logically about how terms interact. His system has been taken up in computer searches, in which you can use the words AND, OR, NOT, and XOR (always in capital letters) to help narrow your search.

  If you are researching the Buddhist concept of Nirvana, you could enter these terms so as not to be deluged with returns about music: *Nirvana AND Buddhism NOT Cobain*

  To search once with synonyms instead of doing two searches: *women AND workplace OR office*

  Be sure to check the advanced search features of the search engine you are using for its particular approach to boolean searches.

ONLINE REFERENCES

There is a wide range of online reference materials on all subjects. Your library will probably have an online listing of all kinds of reference materials, longer than what we can include here. Here are links to some widely used sources:

BARTLEBY.COM
<http://www.bartleby.com/>
Bartleby.com gives you searchable access to dictionaries, quotations, thesauruses, usage and style references, and literature and poetry.

THE INTERNET MOVIE DATABASE
<http://us.imdb.com/>
If you are discussing a movie, this database provides you with information about the actors, directors, and writers and gives you links to reviews.

ONELOOK
<http://www.onelook.com/>
This website gives you access to over 900 dictionaries.

PERRY-CASTAÑEDA MAP COLLECTION
<http://www.lib.utexas.edu/maps/map_sites/map_sites.html>
The library of the University of Texas at Austin has produced this long list of links to all kinds of maps.

STATISTICAL RESOURCES ON THE WEB
<http://www.lib.umich.edu/govdocs/stats.html>
The library of the University of Michigan maintains this very valuable website of links to sites that track statistics about the environment, housing, the cost of living, and education, among many other topics.

WIKIPEDIA
<http://en.wikipedia.org/wiki/Main_Page>
Wikipedia is an online encyclopedia written and edited by users who wish to contribute their knowledge. This is a controversial website for teachers precisely because anyone can edit and contribute. Wikipedia is a good place to start research, when you are composing to learn: It can be a quite accurate source that gives you deeper openings into a topic. You should always check with your teacher to learn his or her position on this source. In general, however, know that using Wikipedia as a source in an academic paper will not give your paper the authority you probably want it to have—and using Wikipedia as your only source is a sure way to show readers that you have not done appropriate research.

ONLINE NEWSPAPERS

ONLINENEWSPAPERS.COM
<http://www.onlinenewspapers.com/>
This website, out of Australia, gives you access to hundreds of newspapers around the world (many in English).

ONLINE ARCHIVES
→ See pages 76–77.

GOVERNMENT SOURCES

Every government agency has a website, so if you are looking for educational or agricultural information, for example, check the websites of the Department of Education or the Department of Agriculture. Keep in mind that some of the information is shaped by the political ends of the current administration.

THE U.S. CENSUS BUREAU
<http://www.census.gov/>
The Census Bureau compiles a wide range of statistics on the U.S. population and economic systems.

MEDLINE PLUS
<http://www.nlm.nih.gov/medlineplus/>
The U.S. National Library of Medicine and the National Institutes of Health provide this nonspecialist information on health and medical issues. The site also provides a medical dictionary and encyclopedia.

THOMAS
<http://thomas.loc.gov/>
This website helps you search for U.S. government legislative information such as what is happening in Congress and its bills and resolutions.

THE WORLD FACTBOOK
<https://www.cia.gov/library/publications/ the-world-factbook/index.html>
The U.S. Central Intelligence Agency regularly updates this website of information about every country in the world. You can learn about a country's population, geography, government, and so on.

PHOTOGRAPHIC AND OTHER VISUAL RESOURCES

Many museums have collections of photographs; many U.S. government agencies also have collections of photographs. For example, check the NASA Image Exchange *<http://nix.nasa.gov/>* or the National Oceanic and Atmospheric Administration's Photo Library *<http://www.photolib.noaa.gov/>*.

NYPL DIGITAL
<http://www.nypl.org/digital/>
The New York Public Library offers this resource of "520,000 images... including illuminated manuscripts, historical maps, vintage posters, rare prints, photographs, illustrated books, and printed ephemera."

PRINTS AND PHOTOGRAPHS ONLINE
<http://www.loc.gov/rr/print/catalog.html>
This website is part of the U.S. Library of Congress. Many of the visual materials available here—posters, photographs, maps, magazines—are copyright free, but you need to check.

WIKIPEDIA: PUBLIC DOMAIN IMAGE RESOURCES
<http://en.wikipedia.org/wiki/ Wikipedia:Public_domain_image_resources>
This webpage contains a long, categorized list of online photographs and other visual text.

→ To cite photographs and other visual texts in your writing, see pages 398–402.

FINDING SOURCES
ARCHIVAL AND SPECIAL LIBRARY COLLECTION SOURCES

SPECIAL LIBRARY COLLECTIONS

Duke University has special collections related to women's history and culture, to African and African American Documentation, and to the history of sales, advertising, and marketing. Haverford College has special collections of materials related to the Quakers. The University of Idaho and the University of Utah have special collections on the history of their states.

Check your library's website to see what special collections it holds.

PHYSICAL ARCHIVES

Archives store documents of historic interest such as letters, diaries, newspapers, sermons, and postcards. Archives can store the documents of a town or county, a church or synagogue, or a person or family; they can be about labor history or African American music.

Many small museums, historical organizations, and libraries have archives of local materials. Some archives collect materials related to the life of a political or literary figure who was from or lived in the area.

To find archives in your area, look in the phone book under *Historical Organizations* and *Museums*.

To learn about archives at your university, check the library website, which will list the library's collections.

Archival research can be captivating: Holding a pioneer woman's diary from the 1860s will give you an exciting sense of differences in lives then and now—and using the diary's words in your writing will give your writing life and authority.

VIRTUAL ARCHIVES

Many physical archives have digitized their materials and made them available online. (If you use a virtual archive, keep in mind that digitization is time-consuming and costly; an archive may have only a small portion of its collection online, so you may still want to try to visit the physical archive if possible.) Each archive will have its own system for searching its collection. Individual archives might also tell you how they would like to be cited if you use their materials in your work.

Some rich virtual archives are

THE INTERNET ARCHIVE

<http://www.archive.org/index.php>
This is an archive of video, music, sound, and texts.

THE LIBRARY OF CONGRESS'S AMERICAN MEMORY PROJECT

<http://memory.loc.gov/ammem/index.html>
This collection gives you access to "written and spoken words, sound recordings, still and moving images, prints, maps, and sheet music that document the American experience."

THE NATIONAL ARCHIVES OF THE UNITED STATES

<http://www.archives.gov/research/arc/education/>
The Archives have a tremendous collection of materials (primarily government related) about this country. You have to go to the archive to look at most materials, but some are available digitally. If you are carrying out research in genealogical, social, political, or economic areas, check out the archives that have been put in searchable databases: *<http://aad.archives.gov/aad/>*

TIP: FINDING ARCHIVES OUTSIDE YOUR AREA
Go online if historical materials will answer your research questions and there are no useful local archives.

Using your search terms, do at least three searches:
your topic + **archive**
your topic + **special collection**
your topic + **museum**
Try out variations on your topic, too, because you cannot know how websites describe themselves and are cataloged by a search engine.

For example, if you were researching organizational strategies used in the Civil Rights movement, you could do a Google search with the terms **civil rights movement** and **archive**. Among other useful links, this search turns up a link to the "Voices of Freedom" website at Virginia Commonwealth University, where you can listen to a recording of Dr. Joyce E. Glaise speaking about the church's role in organizing.

Keep in mind that such searches may not turn up materials you can access digitally, but may suggest books you can order through your library's interlibrary loan service.

THE UNIVERSITY MUSEUMS AND COLLECTIONS

<http://publicus.culture.hu-berlin.de/umac/>
This is an international database giving access to 150 museums.

→ To cite materials from an archive, see page 375.

FINDING SOURCES
FIELD RESEARCH SOURCES

Field research can be performed in more depth than we can describe here. Your teacher or a librarian can help you find further information.

→ See page 110 on evaluating field research.

TIP: GETTING PERMISSION FOR FIELD RESEARCH

Almost all colleges and universities have an Institutional Review Board (IRB), a committee that ensures the proper treatment of those who participate in research studies. Such boards were started to oversee medical and other kinds of technological research, but their responsibility has spread to cover research in the humanities and social sciences.

Every campus's Institutional Review Board will have different policies for field research carried out in writing classes. If you will use the results of your field research only in a classroom paper, it is possible you do not need IRB permission—but the only way to know is to ask your teacher. (If a teacher requires you to do field research, the teacher might have gotten approval for the whole class, or will help you through the process.)

If you think you might do field research on your own, ask your teacher what permissions you need.

INTERVIEWS

You can interview experts on the topic you are researching, people who have lived through an event central to your research, or those who have opinions about your topic.

Here is a sample e-mail for requesting an interview:

Dear Professor/Ms./Mr./Dr. [Name],
For my writing class, I am doing research into [your topic] and would like to interview you, informally, on this topic.

If you are willing, I would need only 30 minutes of your time. I would like to use a tape recorder during the interview.

If an interview is amenable to you, here are several times in the next two weeks when I could come to your office: [list times here].

Sincerely, [your name]

PREPARE FOR AN INTERVIEW
- What would you like to learn from this person? Write down questions that can draw that information out of the person. (You can use the guiding questions for research you developed.)

AT THE INTERVIEW
- Start by thanking the person.
- Explain your research.
- Ask your questions, and don't hesitate to ask other questions that come to you as you listen.
- End with a "Thank you!" Ask if you can contact her or him for clarifications.

AFTERWARD
- Send a thank you e-mail or note.
- Call or e-mail for clarifications.

OBSERVATIONS

If you are researching the effects of video games on social relations among men, you could observe a group of friends playing a game together and then observe a group playing softball, to see if there are differences in how the friends interact. If you are writing about cell phone use among teenagers and adults, you could go the mall and count the percentage of teenagers and the percentage of adults using cell phones.

PREPARE FOR AN OBSERVATION

- Consider where you can observe without others being very aware of you so that they don't change their behavior because of your presence.
- Determine what kinds of actions or behaviors you want to observe and record.
- Determine how you will record what you see. (If you are doing multiple observations, set the same time limit for each one.)

WHILE OBSERVING

- Start your records with the time and date of your observation.

AFTERWARD

- If you have not learned what you thought you would, have you learned something else? Do you need to change your overall purpose, or do you need to do another observation, one set up slightly differently?
- Think about how you will justify your observations to your readers; you will need to include this in your writing.

SURVEYS

Small, focused surveys (the kind you are probably prepared to carry out, instead of state or national surveys) help you learn others' opinions about events or policies.

Small surveys can take two forms (which you can mix):

YES-OR-NO QUESTION SURVEYS

For example: *Do you think there should be a traffic light at the intersection of Bridge and Montezuma Streets?*

- Solicit quick decision making with no room for gray areas.
- Allow for tabulation to make arguments; for example, *Ninety percent of the respondents favor a traffic light.*
- Tend to get more responses because they are quick and easy to take.

OPEN-ENDED QUESTION SURVEYS

For example: *What additional school programs do you think would better prepare elementary school students to use developing technologies?*

- Solicit more thoughtful responses.
- Require interpretation. Sometimes answers group together and sometimes you get a range of very different responses. You will need to present the answers you get with explanations of what you learned.

Before you give your survey, test your questions on a few people to be sure respondents understand the questions and can answer them easily.

Also, consider how many people you need to survey so that your readers will accept that your results are well supported.

WHAT IF YOU CAN'T FIND ANYTHING ON YOUR NARROWED TOPIC?

If you are not finding information on your narrowed topic, there are several possible reasons:

- You have a creative and original topic.
- Your topic might not yet be narrow enough.
- You haven't yet found the right search terms or combination of search terms.
- You haven't yet found the right places to search.
- You have not yet learned how to use search tools comfortably.
- You are not putting in enough time.

IF YOU HAVE A CREATIVE AND ORIGINAL TOPIC

You have a decision to make: find a new topic, or continue searching?

Making effective arguments around creative and original topics is challenging, and can teach you much. You still need to find supporting evidence for the points you want to make, so you have to get creative with finding sources that inform you about the positions of others; you also have to be creative and careful with weaving those sources together into supporting evidence for the position you ultimately take. The following suggestions for generating search terms can still help you.

IT'S POSSIBLE YOUR TOPIC IS NOT YET NARROW ENOUGH

If Google or another search engine returns millions of responses on your topic—none of which seems to address what matters to you—go back to pages 28–33 to work on further narrowing your topic.

IF YOU HAVEN'T YET FOUND THE RIGHT SEARCH TERMS

- Be open to what you find: Remember that, at this stage of producing a research paper, you are trying to gather as much information as you can on a topic. You might need to shift the focus of your topic as you learn what information is available.

- Develop lists of synonyms for your terms. For example, if you are searching the topic of childhood obesity and its relationship to food advertising using cartoon characters, you are going to want to search with different combinations of the following:

    childhood, youth, young
    obesity, overweight, weight
    food, junk, diet, cereal, candy
    advertising, commercials
    cartoons, animation

    To find other words for searching, look for terms people use in the articles and websites you do find; ask others—teachers, librarians, and anyone you know who is good with words or reads a lot—what terms come to mind when you describe your topic.

- Keep track of other terms that come up as you search. In any article or webpage that seems at all close to your concerns, note what terms the authors use to describe your topic, and use those for further searches.

- Try a different search tool. Because each search tool works differently, different search tools will give you different results.

KNOWING IF YOU HAVE FOUND THE RIGHT PLACES TO SEARCH

If you have tried only one search engine or database, you need to try others. If you have tried multiple databases without luck, talk to your teacher or a librarian: They can help you determine other databases that might be fruitful.

But perhaps you are searching online when you need to be interviewing others or looking in an archive. Again, talking to a teacher or librarian about your narrowed topic—and about what you are hoping to learn—can help you find out where to look.

IT'S POSSIBLE YOU ARE NOT USING SEARCH TOOLS COMFORTABLY ENOUGH

If every time you do your research you get frustrated or confused, it is definitely time to make an appointment with your teacher, a librarian, or someone from your campus's Writing (or Learning) Center. Be specific about the help you need: First, describe your narrowed topic and what you are hoping to learn, and then describe the research you have carried out so far. Finally, ask for someone to sit by you while you search, to guide you and give advice.

IT'S POSSIBLE YOU ARE NOT GIVING YOUR RESEARCH ENOUGH TIME

If you expect research to take fifteen minutes or even an hour one night, you are wrong. Effective research requires patience, spread out over hours and days: It takes time to find the information that will help you be smart.

KEEPING TRACK OF SOURCES: Starting a running source list

As you find sources that are useful to you or that contain phrases or sentences that will attract your readers' attention, keep track of both the sources and the quotations. You can do this on paper or online.

Keep all this information in order to produce writing that meets current academic expectations. In the academic world, writers acknowledge the sources from which they draw their ideas and they make it easy for readers to check their sources. There are standard forms for showing this information in a research paper.

→ For information on the forms for documenting sources, see Part 8, pages 307–462.

When you find a source you might use, enter it in a running list, recording the information you need for that kind of source:

→ For a book or part of a book, see pages 328–331 and pages 332–335 for the information you will need.

→ For a newspaper, magazine, or journal article, see pages 336–341.

→ For an article you find in a database, see pages 346–347.

→ For a webpage or website, see pages 342–345.

→ For other kinds of texts, see pages 348–349.

If you think you might quote words from any source, record the words and the pages on which they appear.

→ See pages 316–321 for how to do this with a print source.

→ See pages 342–345 for how to do this with an online source.

HELPING YOURSELF AVOID PLAGIARISM

Because respecting the work of others and therefore acknowledging when you use their work is so important in academic writing, find strategies to keep track of when you copy the words of others. Whenever you copy words off a website into your notes or into a paper, color-code or otherwise mark those words.

→ See pages 144–145 and 308–311 to learn more about plagiarism.

EXAMPLE OF A RUNNING SOURCE LIST

March 22, 2008

"Africa Debt Cancellation -- FAQ." January 2007. American Friends Service Committee. <http://www.afsc.org/africa-debt/learn-about-debt/debt-faq.htm>

"Debt: The Illegitimate Legacy of Continent's Dictators." January 25, 2007. Africa News. LexisNexis. Van Pelt Lib., Houghton, MI <http://library.lib.mtu.edu:2082/universe/document?_m=62bc476dbc43903fc53cef9fb438 32d5&wchp=dGLbVzW-zSkVA&_md5= a9cda7d0ad24dda40259c9c16d4ddad1>

Meredith, Martin. The Fate of Africa: A History of Fifty Years of Independence. New York: PublicAffairs, 2006.

TIP: KEEP A PAPER TRAIL

If you have the slightest feeling that you might use a source—to paraphrase or quote—keep track of it. It is awful to finish a paper only to realize you have a quotation whose source you don't remember: Either you have to remove the source from your writing or you have to find it.

TIP: CITE VISUAL SOURCES

If you use visual material made by others—such as charts, graphs, posters, photographs, and so on— you need to document the source.

→ See pages 348–349 for information on citing visual materials.

TIP: ORGANIZE YOUR LINKS

If you don't already know about them, take a look at websites like <www.furl.com> and <del.icio.us> for tracking your online sources. These websites can also help you see the research other people have carried out on your topic.

STARTING A PAPER

The night before she received an assignment to write a research paper, Riley was talking with a friend's mother and learned that, through an online organization, the mother makes small loans to women in other countries to help the women start or develop small businesses. The mother explained that this process of making small loans is called *microcredit* or *microloans* and is often set up to help women who might not otherwise have access to loans.

General topic

When she received her assignment, Riley decided to learn more about microcredit, and started her research.

Some of her initial research work is shown on page 29.

This initial research taught her that microcredit or microloans can also be called *microfinance*, and so she searched with this term as well as the two others. She learned how these small loans were started in Bangladesh in the 1980s and have since spread all over the world— and that such small loans are overwhelmingly made to women.

Narrowing the topic

Riley is curious about why microcredit focuses on women, so she decides to research *women and microcredit in developing countries*.

Questions for research

Based on what she had learned from her initial research, Riley brainstormed questions to guide her further research; the bold questions are those that, at this stage of her research, matter most to her:

QUESTIONS OF FACT
- How and where did microcredit get started?
- How large is a typical loan?
- How do the people who borrow the money pay it back?

QUESTIONS OF CONSEQUENCE
- Why is microcredit necessary?
- Who benefits from microcredit?
- What are negative results of microcredit?
- **How do microloans change women's lives?**

QUESTIONS OF VALUE
- Why are so many people praising microcredit now?
- Why are so many governments encouraging microcredit organizations in their countries?

QUESTIONS OF DEFINITION
- What is microcredit?
- How is it different from other kinds of loans?

QUESTIONS OF INTERPRETATION
- Why did microcredit get started?
- **Why are loans made mostly to women?**

QUESTIONS OF POLICY
- Who decides who will receive microcredit loans?
- What laws or other policies have been enacted to support microcredit?
- What kinds of organizations support microcredit?
- What organizations oppose it?

Choosing sources

From her initial work, Riley realized that her first Google searches were helping her answer questions of fact and definition but not other types of questions.

Because the questions that matter most to her are questions of interpretation and consequence, she used the chart on page 43 to help her determine where to look.

1 She knew that stories of women who had received microloans would help her, but because she couldn't interview women in developing countries, she used Google to find websites of microcredit organizations, hoping they would have women's stories. She also looked for the organizations' mission statements, to see if they discussed why they focused on women.

2 Her library's online resources helped her search databases on current economic topics, as well as women's issues and newspaper editorials. (The ProQuest database suggested additional search terms, such as *women AND poverty AND microcredit OR microfinance*.)

3 The databases also helped her find organizational and governmental reports with statistics that might show how women's lives were changed because of small loans.

→ Riley didn't find any one source that answered all her questions, but she found many that helped her develop a thesis for her own argument—as you can see in Part 3, on pages 146–147.

HINTS & TIPS FOR FINDING IDEAS

HOW DO YOU KNOW IF YOU HAVE FOUND ENOUGH SOURCES?

In the earliest stages of research, you won't know, exactly, if you have all the sources that will help you develop an argument that will satisfy readers.

But you are researching broadly enough—finding enough sources—if you can answer most of the research questions you've generated.

HOW DO YOU KNOW IF YOU ARE KEEPING AN OPEN MIND?

You might think that you should have definitive answers to all your research questions. But—*especially for questions of consequence, interpretation, value, and policy*—if your research makes you hesitate over deciding between two or three possible responses, then you are keeping an open mind. If you can offer good reasons for several differing possibilities, then you are researching as you should.

Academic writing is rarely about offering final solutions to anything; there are few situations in life where the evidence obviously supports one final conclusion. Instead, you need to acknowledge the differing possibilities and offer the best evidence and arguments you can for the position you believe to be best.

HOW CAN YOU KEEP A TOPIC FRESH AND INTERESTING?

If you get bored with your topic, you won't enjoy the writing, your writing will reflect your emotion, and your readers will pick up on it.

Because there are different ways to get bored with a topic, there are different approaches for becoming unbored:

- Perhaps you've chosen a topic that isn't controversial or challenging enough to keep you engaged. Talk with a teacher or someone who knows about the topic to determine if you can make the topic more challenging or if you need a new topic.

- Sometimes topics become boring when you've done a lot of research and feel that you know all there is to know. If this happens, remember that not everyone knows what you do: If you talk to someone else and lay out why the topic should matter, you might see how writing about your topic can help others learn important information.

PART 3
ANALYZING ARGUMENTS & EVALUATING SOURCES

CONTENTS

WHERE ARE WE IN THE PROCESS FOR COMPOSING?

Understanding your project

Getting started

Asking questions   Critical thinking and questioning
                         Evaluating sources
                         Developing a thesis statement

Shaping your project for others

Drafting a paper

Getting feedback

Revising

Polishing

WHAT IS ANALYSIS?

Analysis is about breaking something into its pieces to learn how the pieces fit together into a whole.

To learn about and prevent diseases, doctors analyze bodies, looking at organs and bodily functions: They analyze the skeletal and muscular systems, the organs of digestion and sight, and the cellular processes of those different systems and organs. Once doctors understand how these different parts fit together, they can start questioning how a change in one part affects other parts, how (for example) a disease of the liver affects stomach functioning.

Similarly, social scientists analyze crises that are the result of human action (such as wars and economic depressions) and crises that result from a mixture of human and natural causes (deaths from heat waves or hurricanes). They try first to understand the political, social, economic, and techological structures of towns, cities, countries, and regions so that they can ask how actions and events affect those different structures. They hope in this way to learn what went wrong and how a similar crisis might be avoided in the future.

Similarly, communication specialists analyze the texts we give each other. Some specialize in analyzing political speeches, some in television advertising, some in film, some in literature, some in digital communication. These specialists bring different analytic tools to their work. In this book, we use the analytic tools of rhetoric.

In the upcoming pages, we follow the scheme for analysis shown below, to help you move from analyzing to understand to analyzing to ask questions of a text.

ANALYSIS
By breaking a text down into its parts, we can:

understand
If we can describe the parts of a text and how they fit together into a whole, then we can say we understand the text, and what its composer's purpose might have been in producing it.

ask questions
Once we understand a text, we can question it:

Does the text achieve the composer's purpose?
- Do the strategies used in the text fit with its purpose?
- Is the intended audience likely to be persuaded by the strategies used?

What do I think about that purpose and the strategies used to achieve it?
- Can I support the purpose?
- Are the strategies used valid?
- Do I accept those strategies, or think they are ethical?
- Do I think the text's composer respects the text's audience?

UNDERSTANDING AND ANALYZING TEXTS

In this book, we use the analytic tools of rhetoric to understand what the parts of a communication are and how those parts fit together to make a whole—and how the parts work to make a communicator's purposes clear to the intended audience in a particular context.

BEGINNING RHETORICAL ANALYSIS

Almost any rhetorical analysis begins with these two steps:

1 Determining the choices composers make in developing a text.

2 Considering how those choices help composers achieve their purposes with their particular audience in the context at hand.

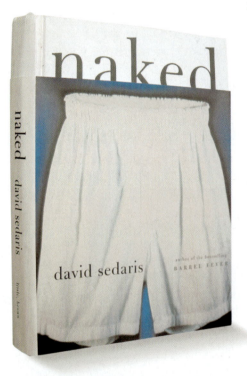

BEGINNING A RHETORICAL ANALYSIS OF A BOOK COVER

This example for starting a rhetorical analysis looks at the book cover to the left.

1 Determining the choices composers make in developing a text.

To do this, we list as many choices as we see, in any order:

- the book's title
- the book's size
- the typefaces used, and their size
- the placement of the elements, such as the title relative to the photograph
- any information about the book in addition to its title
- the book cover is different from what we usually see: The paper cover doesn't cover the whole, just part of it—so there must be something hidden under it
- the use of a photograph
- the colors used
- the overall feeling: humorous

2 Considering how those choices help composers achieve their purposes with their particular audience in the context at hand.

It's tempting to say that the cover's purpose (like any book cover) is to sell the book—and that is certainly part of the purpose. But if a cover helps persuade someone to buy the book, the cover must interest the buyer. If the buyer knows the author's writing, maybe the cover design doesn't matter; if, however, someone doesn't know the author, then the cover's purpose has to be about giving someone a strong, particular sense of what is inside **this** book. What do the strategies above suggest about *naked*?

The title and photograph are important choices because they are emphasized. The photograph is of boxer shorts, which for some reason in American culture are objects of some silliness. Their presence tells us

this book is about fairly recent topics and not about people living long ago.

Naked is a word we apply to humans, not animals, and though it can imply serious things, the word can also imply awkwardness, like losing your clothes while swimming— or being caught in public in your underwear. Because the title is printed without a capital letter— which implies informality—and is combined with the photograph, we get the sense that this book is not about heavy topics. The cover also has only the one photograph, telling us that what is in the book is probably not complicated: This is, probably, not a book of detailed history. It is about people, possibly their awkward behaviors.

THERE ARE CATEGORIES FOR ANALYZING THE STRATEGIES USED IN COMPOSING…

as we discuss on the next pages. Also, analyzing a composition is easier when we compare it to another composition, as we do with this book cover on the next pages.

UNDERSTANDING AND
ANALYZING TEXTS
DEVELOPING A SENSE OF THE AUTHOR

WE MAKE ASSUMPTIONS ABOUT THE COMPOSERS OF TEXTS

Whenever you use a text, you develop a sense of the person who made it.

Listening to the radio, you probably develop—without thinking—a sense of any speaker's gender and age, and probably also a sense that the person is serious, funny, or well-informed. You could be wrong in all your assumptions—but that doesn't stop you from making such assumptions.

We make the same assumptions when we read and even when we look at photographs, posters, or video games: We develop, consciously or not, a sense of who made the text and whether the person is trustworthy, authoritative, knowledgeable, intelligent, and so on.

WE NEVER KNOW A REAL PERSON THROUGH THE ASSUMPTIONS WE MAKE

Text producers choose how they want to appear in their texts: Writers choose tone of voice, the evidence they use, and how they describe others. Because the evidence is limited—and sometimes carefully crafted—the sense we develop of composers is always limited and partial; we never get to know a **real** person through a text.

Composers can use any strategy available to them to shape how audiences understand who the composers are. In traditional rhetorical terminology, the sense that audiences develop about composers is called

ETHOS.

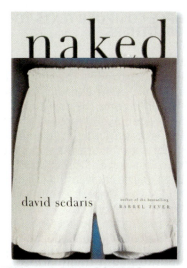

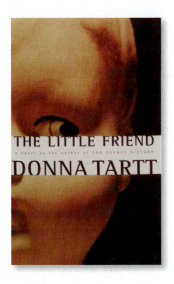

ETHOS IN BOOK COVERS

The context of book cover design says something about ethos. Rarely do writers design their own book covers; instead, a book's publisher chooses a designer. The designer works alone, or with an art director or photographer, but the work has to be approved by the publisher and (usually) by the author.

The ethos we associate with a cover is therefore not necessarily the ethos of the books—but the two should be close if the cover is to achieve its purpose of suggesting what the book is about. Notice that ethos can, therefore, be the result not of one person's decisions but of several people's.

The cover for *naked* looks professional, composed by someone who knows about using words, typefaces, and photographs together. Its humor suggests not only that the book will be funny but also that the person who made the cover has a sense of humor.

The cover for *The Little Friend* was composed by the same designer, and it too looks professional and has similar elements: one photograph, the title of the book, the author's name, and information about another of the author's books. Even though the strategies are similar, however, the second cover is a bit creepy: The extreme close-up on the face of a doll looking sideways suggests someone trying to see what's going on behind her, an undoll-like emotion.

Both covers show us someone who is able to suggest that objects have more life than we usually expect.

All these facets of this ethos—the professionalism, the humor, the attention to objects—suggest that these books are connected with makers who are clever and able to get readers to look below surfaces.

UNDERSTANDING AND ANALYZING TEXTS
UNDERSTANDING APPEALS TO EMOTIONS

PEOPLE COMPOSE TEXTS TO MOVE OTHERS

Every text is composed for a purpose—and for that purpose to be achieved, the audience has to shift. The shifting can be as simple as the audience's attention being shifted from one object to another—but most often it is larger: a shift from passivity to engagement, from not knowing or caring about a topic to knowing and caring, from feeling hopeless to wanting to act.

In all of this, there is a shifting in the audience's emotion.

What emotions does a composer consider the audience to hold on a topic before they read, see, or hear a text—and what emotions does the composer hope the audience will hold afterward?

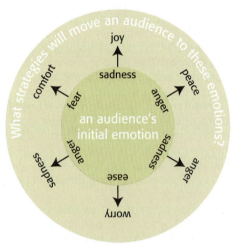

In rhetoric, a composer's use of strategies to shift an audience's emotions is called

PATHOS.

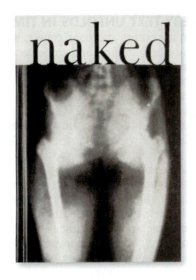

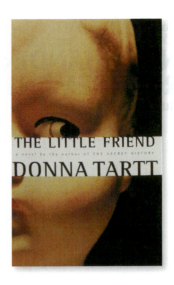

PATHOS IN BOOK COVERS

Earlier, we talked about how *naked*'s cover is about engaging with an audience's sense of humor: The title of the book and the photograph of boxer shorts are simple and funny. Perhaps we can say, then, that the cover's main pathos appeal is that of humor.

But there is another strategy we mentioned that we have not discussed: the part of the cover that comes off.

The boxer shorts are printed on a paper jacket that covers only part of the book. The jacket overlaps *naked*; the paper does not—as we expect with most book covers—cover the whole book; we are led to wonder what is under the cover, under the boxers.

In addition to its humor, the cover therefore also offers some interaction and provocation. It asks the audience to expect something under the cover … and under the cover is an x-ray, a body

more naked than we might have expected. Our emotions are called into play as we realize that we were (perhaps) hoping to see something else but instead are given a very exposed naked body. We are teased by this cover—perhaps made to laugh, perhaps made to question why we were expecting to see something else.

The second book's title, *The Little Friend*, suggests childhood—but the photograph plays emotionally with the associations we probably have with childhood. A close-up photograph of a face engages us with the face's emotion. A close-up of a face turning its eyes toward shadows behind it suggests worry, concern, fear of something about to happen. When the face is a doll's, we have entered the realm of fairy tales and fantasy. The emotions encouraged by this cover are in your face, and unsettling.

UNDERSTANDING AND
ANALYZING TEXTS
A SAMPLE ANALYSIS ESSAY

As we wrote earlier, the first step of doing analysis is to analyze for understanding. Can you describe what you think the purpose of the text is, and for whom it was intended? Can you find evidence from the text— quotations, your observations about how ethos, pathos, and logos are used— that supports your understanding? If you can do that, then you understand a text.

Your understanding may differ from others' analysis of the same text, but as long as you can use as evidence the strategies you've noted, then you have built your own understanding. Listen to how others analyze, and notice how they use the evidence of the text.

On the opposite page is a written rhetorical analysis of one of the book covers we examined on the previous pages, as an example of how you can write such an analysis for understanding.

■ ■ ■

You'll notice that the writing uses some of the descriptions from the preceding pages; this is one way to develop an analysis: Write down your observations, and then use them to build a more formal analysis (such as one required by a class assignment).

The introduction

The introduction of the essay tells readers something of what the essay is arguing— but only enough to give readers direction and (the writer hopes) curiosity.

The subject of the essay

The writer of this short essay is careful to explain to readers what the explicit subject of the essay is.

The strategy of the essay

Here the writer lists pertinent strategies used by the composer of the text being analyzed.

The conclusion

In the conclusion to the essay, the writer argues for the main strategy used by the composer of the text being analyzed, and (in the last sentences) shows how that strategy connects to the purpose of the text.

I would have thought a book cover made of a single photograph and a few words would give a reader only a bare, literal sense of the book, telling a reader, for example, that "this book is about boxer shorts." The book cover I analyze—designed by Chip Kidd for the book *naked* by David Sedaris —contains such limited elements, and yet it engages potential readers in puzzling out odd emotional relationships and so gets them engaged with the book even before they turn to page 1.

The cover of *naked* is composed, at first glance, of a simple photograph of bright white boxer shorts on a shaded blue background. The word "naked"—all in lower-case letters in a straightforward serifed typeface—is at the top, on a white background, partially covered by the photograph. The author's name is in the same typeface on top of the boxer shorts, along with a few words about another book he's published. This combination of elements is informal, straightforward, and balanced, with everything symmetric and centered. Based on such a description, this cover suggests a book that could be mundane and perhaps even boring. But boxer shorts are rarely on book covers, especially so large in proportion to everything else, and to put them together with "naked" presented so informally encourages a reader to wonder where the person is who wore the shorts: Is that person running around naked somewhere?

But there is more to the cover. Kidd has readers wondering about who was wearing those shorts, but his design also suggests an answer might be available. The boxer shorts are printed on a paper jacket that covers about three-quarters of the book. The jacket partially overlaps "naked"; the overlapping, combined with how the paper does not—unlike most book covers—cover the whole book, leads readers to wonder what is under the cover, under the boxers.

In addition to its humor, the cover therefore also offers some interaction and provocation. It asks the audience to expect something under the cover...but what is under the cover is probably unexpected.

Under the cover is an x-ray of a lower torso, a body more naked than we might have expected. Readers are teased by this cover—perhaps made to laugh and perhaps made to question why they were expecting to see something else.

Most book covers show people or objects that give readers a literal sense of what is in the book: A book cover with a dog on a leash is about dog training; a book with a palm tree is about the South Pacific. Kidd has instead used the rhetorical strategy of pathos as his primary strategy: While the arrangement of elements (including the order of seeing the boxer shorts before seeing the bony torso) encourages readers to see the informal relationship between the elements, it is the humor and surprising interaction and discovery that give readers a sense of this book. A reader who looked at this cover and in response thought that this book was a funny but edgy intimate look at a man's life would not be far off. It is possible readers would buy this book—the general purpose of the cover—because they have gotten involved emotionally with that man's life only by picking up the book to look closer.

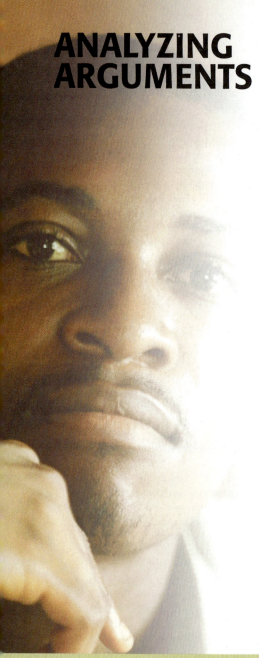

ANALYZING ARGUMENTS

Once you understand a text, you can make judgments about it.

- Do you agree with the arguments the text is making?
- Is there enough evidence to persuade you to agree? Does the evidence offered truly support the arguments being made?
- What are consequences of the arguments being made?

Experienced researchers and scholars do not respond only to isolated chunks of a text but instead try to be fair to the whole text, to how its various strategies build to a whole.

On the next pages we show steps for taking apart arguments to see whether enough evidence is offered (and thus also discuss kinds of evidence and how to judge different kinds). We suggest questions you can ask of texts to support your analysis of them.

JUDGING EVIDENCE, JUDGING SOURCES

In the next few pages on analysis, we help you judge the evidence offered in a text: Such judgments help you decide whether you accept the evidence and thus the arguments built on the evidence. Later in Part 3, we offer strategies for judging the relevance and credibility of sources you are considering using in your writing.

Judging the evidence of a text for yourself will help you decide later if your readers will see the text as a credible source that supports the arguments you are building.

Here is an editorial from the *San Francisco Chronicle*, from March 2007:

Food ad blitz

IT CAN'T be healthy for a 9-year-old— or any child—to be bombarded with an average of 21 food ads on television each day.

That's especially the case when most of the products being peddled don't come close to meeting the ordinary definition of the word "food."

According to the most exhaustive study yet done on advertising to children by the Kaiser Family Foundation in Menlo Park, one-third of all "food" ads are for candy and snacks. Just under a third are for cereals (almost all of them loaded with sweeteners). Ten percent are for fast foods.

Of the 8,854 ads reviewed, none was for fruits or vegetables.

All those commercials add up. So-called "tweens"—kids between the ages of 8 and 12—see some 7,600 food ads each year. On average, teenagers see slightly fewer—6,000 a year, or 17 a day, while 2-to-7-year-olds see 4,400, or 12 ads a day.

To view these ads as an inevitable, and even normal, part of childhood in America is not acceptable. As an authoritative report last year by the Institute of Medicine concluded, food ads have a direct impact on children's health. "Television advertising influences the food preferences, purchase requests and diets, at least of children under 12, and is associated with the increased rates of obesity among children and youth," the report found.

What's more, food ads swamp public-service advertising that promote fitness and nutrition. Children between ages 2 and 12 see a pitiful 164 such messages each year, or one every two or three days. Teenagers see one such PSA, on average, once a week.

Marketers of food products can, and must, do better. Last year, 10 of the top 10 food companies formed the "Children's Food and Beverage Advertising Initiative," and promised to devote at least half of their ads to healthier food messages that encourage fitness and nutrition.

This must be a serious effort on the part of the food industry—and must embrace more than just the major food companies. Given the high stakes—the health of future generations of Americans—it would not be premature for Congress to begin to exercise more oversight over the glut of food advertising intruding into the lives of children.

On the next pages, we offer strategies for questioning the arguments offered in this editorial. The strategies will help you:

- **Make judgments about sources you are considering using in support of your own composing.** If you question a source and find its arguments to be poorly made, you do not want to base your arguments on that source.

- **Make judgments about the validity and strengths of your own composing.** You can use the strategies we offer to be sure your arguments are well supported and are therefore more likely to be taken seriously by others.

ANALYZING ARGUMENTS
THESIS STATEMENTS

Many writers develop thesis statements to help them prepare to write—as we will be helping you do later in this part of the book.

→ See pages 146–147.

People who study how arguments work have studied the logic of thesis statements. They have learned that thesis statements with certain logical structures help writers make decisions about how to turn a thesis statement into a full paper; when thesis statements are thought about in terms of specific audiences, they can help writers make decisions about how to arrange the parts of a paper and what sorts of evidence to include.

The ideas here about thesis statements come from the work of mid-twentieth-century philosopher Stephen Toulmin. Through his studies into the structure of argument, Toulmin developed an understanding of an argument's **claims**, **reasons**, **warrants**, and **evidence**.

When you compose an argumentative paper, you can use a thesis statement (and its claim, reasons, warrants, and evidence) to help shape the paper—but when you read an argument written by someone else, you can decompose the writing: You can analyze the writing to pull out a thesis statement, along with its claims, reasons, warrants, and evidence, as we will do in a few pages.

The next page shows one way of conceiving a thesis statement for the editorial on page 101. The work of pulling out one possible thesis helps you see just what underlies the argument—and so helps you decide if enough (or the right) evidence is being offered.

WHY CAN'T A PAPER BE A THESIS STATEMENT?

Sometimes student writers ask why, instead of having to write a whole paper, they can't just present a thesis statement—or a thesis statement and its warrants and evidence. Isn't that persuasive enough?

If human beings were completely and only logical beings, this might work.

But human beings are swayed by different kinds of logic as well as by emotional appeals and the character of others. Thesis statements, warrants, and evidence are only one part of logos, and they do very little to appeal to the fullness of other humans. That is why they are only part of writing.

DO YOU THINK THE EDITORIAL ON PAGE 101 OFFERS GOOD EVIDENCE TO SUPPORT ITS CLAIM THAT CONGRESS SHOULD REGULATE TELEVISION ADS FOR CHILDREN?

Congress should have oversight of food advertising on TV because food advertising is affecting the future health of young people.

A THESIS STATEMENT is composed of…

Congress should have oversight of food advertising on TV.

Food advertising is affecting the future health of young people.

a CLAIM, which is a statement about a condition, policy, or event that a writer believes should come to pass. Notice how the claim is made up of two parts: *Congress should have oversight…* and *food advertising*.

a REASON, which states one reason the claim should come to pass. Notice how the reason is made up of two parts: *Food advertising* and *affecting the future health…*.

Congress should have oversight of what affects the future health of young people.

A WARRANT is an idea or value that a writer believes the audience is likely to accept; the whole argument hangs on this. Notice how the claim and reason each repeat a similar phrase; the warrant links the claim and the reason logically— by linking the parts that aren't repeated.

A study by the Kaiser Family Foundation in Menlo Park reviewed 8,854 ads; none was for fruits or vegetables and the majority were for foods heavy in sugars. Another report, by the Institute of Medicine, says that food ads affect children's eating habits and thus their health, and are "associated with the increased rates of obesity among children and youth." Children see almost no ads that encourage healthy eating practices.

EVIDENCE justifies the reason.

ANALYZING ARGUMENTS
WHAT COUNTS AS EVIDENCE

Evidence is what you offer audiences to persuade them that your position on a topic is worth considering.

There are many kinds of evidence composers can use to support their warrants; on these pages we consider:

1 EXPERT TESTIMONY
2 PERSONAL EXPERIENCE
3 ANALOGIES
4 FACTS (AND STATISTICS)
5 FIELD RESEARCH
6 SHARED VALUES
7 EXAMPLES

EXPERT TESTIMONY

An expert has special and thorough knowledge on a particular topic because of education, profession, study, or experience. Experts can be individuals or groups. Because of their knowledge, we believe we can rely on experts' judgments in the areas in which they know more than the average person.

Text composers can use the words of experts—their testimony—as authoritative backing on the topics about which the expert is knowledgeable.

In the editorial on page 101, for example, the Kaiser Family Foundation and the Institute of Medicine are both cited as experts; excerpts from reports they have published are offered as evidence in support of the editorial's arguments.

EVALUATING EXPERT TESTIMONY

If you are wondering whether to accept expert testimony:

- Do an online search on the person or organization. Does the person have credentials—education and experience—for offering the evidence? Does the organization specialize in the topic? Does the person or organization have an affiliation indicating potential bias?

- Ask others what they know about the person or organization.

When you compose your own texts:

- Ask people from your audience if they know and trust the experts you are citing.

- If your audience might not know an expert you are citing, include descriptions of the expert, saying why the expert has authority for you.

PERSONAL EXPERIENCE

Personal experience is what we know through living. Each of us has experiences with families, schools, jobs, and romance; we've paid taxes, driven cars, eaten, shopped, and seen changes in our communities. Every experience—and especially repeated experiences—shapes our sense of how the world works.

Personal experience is limited evidence precisely because it is personal. Without considerable research, you cannot know how many other people share your experiences; you cannot know if they draw the same knowledge from their experiences as you do.

Because personal experience is limited, it ought to play only a small part in formal writing. It can serve as a single example in support of a point. An introductory anecdote about your experiences working in a fast-food restaurant can draw readers emotionally into an argument about the moral satisfactions of low-paying jobs, but you would need much more evidence to show that others found the same moral satisfaction.

The same holds true for using others' experiences as evidence. A friend who has been to Burundi on a missionary trip might have interesting observations about how donations are spent in that country, but those observations have no place in your writing unless your friend is also an expert on the economics of donations or the observations are backed up by other evidence.

Personal experience can become facts or statistics when it is joined with and examined alongside the experiences of others through field research.

EVALUATING PERSONAL EXPERIENCE

When you see others using personal experience—whether their own or of others—as examples in their writing, ask these questions:

- Is the experience used as logical evidence in support of the composer's ability to discuss this topic (ethos), or as an emotional appeal (pathos)?

- If the experience is used as logical evidence, does the writer acknowledge that the experience is necessarily limited? Is other evidence also given as support?

- If the experience is used to show that the composer has relevant experience for taking on the topic at hand, is the experience sufficient? Does the experience indicate that the composer has any bias on the topic?

- If the experience is used as an emotional appeal, does the emotion draw the audience away from what is at issue or does it help show why the issue might be worth the audience's attention?

When you compose your own texts, keep in mind the following:

- Be wary of generalizing from your own experiences. Always try to find out if your audience has shared the same experiences—and drawn similar conclusions.

- When you use the experiences, observations, anecdotes, or opinions of others, use them only to illustrate examples and to offer other evidence of the kinds we describe on these pages.

ANALOGIES

Analogies are quasi-logical structures: When you use an analogy, you compare—usually at length—two objects, events, or processes so that the more familiar can explain the less familiar. For example, a long description of how the brain is like a computer would be an analogy in which the composer relies upon the audience's knowledge of computers to explain how the brain works.

Similarly, to call the Internet the *Information Superhighway* is to use an analogy in which one is to understand the abstract Internet networked system as being like a highway. Most people in the United States have experienced highways, and so can think of the Internet as a series of roads and inter-changes with information traveling between locations in little packets just like cars.

But analogies work more than descriptively. They carry a whole set of assumptions from the more famil-iar object being named to the less familiar. For example, the *Information Superhighway* analogy implies that the Internet should be a public resource as highways are, and regulated, supported, and repaired with public funds just as highways are.

Analogies can be used in focused ways, or can shape the argument of a whole book: The writer Malcolm Gladwell, for example, one of whose short essays we examine later, has used a whole book to consider how *ideas can be contagious in exactly the same way that a virus is.*

The following analogy is a blog entry; the writer describes a day in which he and others from his company discussed leadership and teamwork:

I mentioned something I recently read on migratory birds in flight. This study found that a flock of birds in a V-formation can fly at least 70% farther than a bird on its own. Birds at the back of the V work much less because they can take advantage of the draft created by the birds at front. When a bird at the front tires, it drops out of the lead and goes to the back to rest. The V-formation also improves visual contact and communication.

I like to tell this story to show how natural teamwork should be. This story also highlights the importance of individual excellence and leadership. Every bird in the V-formation at some point assumes the leadership role at the front. Similarly, each member of my leadership team has a key responsibility to drive the priorities and vision for their area in the company, while at the same time being able to understand how that fits into the overall vision of our company.

The comments appearing after the blog entry develop the shortcomings of the analogy: If you carry out the analogy, as one person commented, it would be appropriate for the company's *top managers to drop out of the lead positions and for some others to either die or recover;* another points out that the V-formation *is a pattern learned over the millions of years of evolution* and so not easy for humans to learn or apply.

Visual analogies also exist. The example above comes from early in World War II, when—with so many men in battle—industries encouraged women to work in factories producing weaponry and machinery needed for the war effort. The poster above uses analogies between the work to which women were already accustomed—sewing and cooking—and industrial production. The visual analogies between the two kinds of work are offered as evidence that, if women can do the familiar work, they can also do the unfamiliar work.

EVALUATING ANALOGIES

In reading and developing analogies, consider:

• Analogies are an odd sort of evidence because they prove nothing. They do not guarantee that situations will play out as an analogy suggests.

Instead, composers use analogies to shape an audience's attitudes. A compelling analogy can persuade audiences to consider an object or process in a positive light, which is a large part of any successful argument. A compelling analogy is therefore both a pathos appeal and a form of logos.

• When it is compelling, an analogy can so focus your perceptions that you cannot think outside the analogy. When you see an analogy being used as evidence in an argument, or want to use one yourself, try carrying out the implications of the analogy, as those commenting on the bird–human leadership example did.

You can also explore how an analogy shapes thinking by coming up with alternative analogies. For example, consider how the **Internet as a Superhighway** analogy asks us to think of the Internet as roads and exchanges—and implies that the Internet should be built and supported with public funds. To consider an alternative analogy, ask what implications accompany thinking of the Internet as a marketplace or huge library.

FIELD RESEARCH

If researchers are fair and open-minded in their research, honestly looking for what others think, then their interviews, observations, and surveys will create facts. When researchers compile information, they can demonstrate what a group of people think or believe in a particular place and time. They can, for example, provide statistics about how many people desire a particular policy or show, through interviewing older people in an area, what Sunday activities were popular a few decades ago.

You can use the following questions both to evaluate field research carried out by others and to help you shape field research you might perform.

EVALUATING INTERVIEWS

- Did the interviewer ask open-ended questions, allowing the person or people being interviewed to provide their opinions and beliefs?
- Did the interviewer present the interview fairly, showing where the words of the person interviewed were cut or edited?
- What sort of relationship does the interviewer appear to have had with the person being interviewed? Does the interviewer seem hostile, or overly friendly?

EVALUATING OBSERVATIONS

- Does the researcher describe the goals and methods of the observation?
- Does the researcher appear to have approached the observation seeking particular results—or been open to whatever happened?
- Does the researcher appear to have observed well, or with too much focus?
- Are the researcher's results only positive, in support of the researcher's goals, or does the researcher note any observations that went against expectations?

EVALUATING SURVEYS

- Did the survey ask open-ended questions, allowing the person or people being interviewed to provide their opinions and beliefs?
- Was the number of people surveyed sufficient for providing support for any assertions a researcher is making based on the research? (To learn how many people need to be surveyed depending on what a researcher is trying to find out, see the article "How Many People are Enough?" <http://survey.pearsonncs.com/planning/people.htm>.)
- Did the researcher seek information from an appropriately wide group of people, or only from those likely to give responses the researcher wanted?

SHARED VALUES

The editorial on page 101 relies on the warrant that *Congress should have oversight of what affects the future health of young people* (as shown on page 103). This statement presumes that its readers will be concerned about anything affecting young people's future health. Whoever wrote the editorial does not have to argue for this value or offer further evidence to support this; it can simply be assumed.

Composing an argument that does not rely on readers' values is impossible.

One could argue whether such values are evidence, but many arguments depend on such assumptions. Simple arguments such as *Don't do that—you'll get hurt!* can work only if the person at whom they are directed believes that getting hurt is a bad thing. The person who makes the statement doesn't have to explain the assumption.

Longer and more complex arguments about going to war or about health care, for example, will appeal to shared values about patriotism, nationalism, the right of people to a doctor's care, or the right not to suffer.

Because the composers of texts rely on such shared values to encourage readers to accept their arguments, these values work to support arguments just as other kinds of evidence do.

EVALUATING SHARED VALUES

When you are questioning shared values or making use of them in your own work, keep in mind:

- Using shared values to support arguments depends on what the audience believes—so you must pull assumed shared values from arguments and ask if audiences truly do believe the assumptions. Under what conditions will an audience accept those assumptions?

- People can hold contradictory values or accept some values only under certain conditions, as when some people are against violence except in response to aggression. When you are considering the shared values underlying an argument, ask if the assumptions hold in all cases or only in some.

- When you are composing your own texts, be aware of the values you are assuming your readers share with you. If you do not make those values explicit to yourself, you will not be able to use them alertly in your writing—and so you may be surprised when your audience responds negatively.

ANALYZING ARGUMENTS
FURTHER QUESTIONS TO GUIDE CRITICAL READING

In the previous pages, we have been focusing on paying critical attention to logical elements of texts. Here, we offer you questions to help you consider an even broader range of choices composers make in their texts.

Once you have done preliminary analysis to be sure you understand a text, ask these questions to help you decide if you want to be persuaded by a text:

QUESTIONS ABOUT AUDIENCE
- Whom is the composer including in the audience? Who is excluded from the audience—and why?
- To what is the composer drawing the audience's attention? What might the composer be able to overlook by focusing the audience's attention in this way?
- What does the composer assume the audience knows or believes?

QUESTIONS ABOUT PURPOSE
- Why does this purpose matter at this time and in this place?
- Are there secondary purposes as well as a main purpose?
- Is the purpose clearly stated or easy to determine? If not, why might the composer have decided not to make the purpose obvious?

QUESTIONS ABOUT CONTEXT
- Where does the audience encounter the text? How might this shape their responses?
- When is an audience likely to encounter the text? How might this shape their responses?
- What events at the time of the text's production are likely to shape an audience's expectations about the topic?

> **TIP: USING STYLE TO SUPPORT ANALYSIS**
> When you are analyzing writing, use Part 7 of this book, on style, to help you identify a writer's choices. Part 7 will help you name the strategies a writer uses for emphasizing parts of an essay and thus will help you figure out what is emphasized (logos) as well as how to describe the writer's ethos and pathos strategies. Such identifications help you see a writer's purposes more easily.

QUESTIONS ABOUT ETHOS

- Does the composer have the appropriate background or experience for pursuing this purpose?

- Does the composer seem open to multiple perspectives on the task at hand? Is the composer treating those perspectives fairly?

- What cultural backgrounds and expectations shape the composer's positions?

- Is the composer using a tone of voice appropriate to the purpose?

- What role does the composer take toward the audience? Is the composer acting as a teacher, a lecturer, a parent, a peer, a friend? Is this role appropriate for the purpose?

- Is the composer respectful of the audience, treating them as intelligent, thoughtful people?

QUESTIONS ABOUT PATHOS

- What emotion is the intended audience likely to have about the issue before they encounter the text? How does the text acknowledge that emotion, and try to shift it?

- Do the emotional appeals seem reasonable to you—or overblown?

- Are the emotional appeals appropriate to the issue?

QUESTIONS ABOUT LOGOS

- What claims, reasons, and warrants are explicit or implied in the text? (➔ See pages 102–103.)

- What kinds of evidence does the composer use? (➔ See pages 104–113.) Is that evidence relevant, credible, and sufficient? (➔ See pages 104–113.) Do you know of or can you find evidence that points to different conclusions?

- Are the sources cited so that the audience can check them? If so, are the sources relevant and credible? (➔ See pages 130–143.)

- Why might a composer start with particular examples or evidence? To what will these draw the audience's attention? (And from what will these examples distract attention?)

- How does the composition end? How will the end affect how the audience looks back on the rest of the composition?

> **TIP: GIVING EVIDENCE**
>
> If you are using these questions to do the preliminary analysis for writing a paper, include with your responses any evidence in the text that supports your responses. For example, when taking notes about ethos, you might write: *It feels as though the author is yelling at readers: All the sentences are short, emphatic, addressed to "you!" written as though readers know nothing about the topic....*

Evidence: Examples

How do we know anyone is *incorrigible* or a *decent kid*? Gladwell seems to believe that these are obvious characteristics of people, but who gets to make these decisions, and based on what evidence?

Evidence: Research

How might readers respond to this move from the made-up stories of Jimmy and Bobby to the *Tennessee study*? Is there enough evidence given in this essay for us to check on the Tennessee study ourselves, to see if we agree with how it was conducted or with Gladwell's characterization of it?

Pathos: How readers are addressed

Gladwell now refers to himself and the audience together as *we*. By assuming we are all in agreement with what he writes, what might he be trying to achieve?

Evidence: Examples

Because of the temporal context surrounding the publication of this essay, Gladwell assumes that his readers know that he is referring in this parenthetical remark to events in Iraq and at Guantanamo; he is also assuming that his readers share his interpretation of the events. Why would he insert such a serious example in parentheses here, when all his preceding examples have involved students?

Evidence: Analogy

Gladwell takes someone else's analogy and turns it around. This analogy involves an event that many take extremely seriously and would not want to see used in a lighthearted way. Do you think Gladwell's overall purpose so far justifies his use of this analogy? What sort of reader, holding what sort of beliefs, would be likely to accept this analogy and find it appropriate? (And why might Gladwell use such a serious analogy here?)

certainly ruin his career. Cambridge wasn't sure that the benefits of enforcing the law, in this case, were greater than the benefits of allowing the offender an unimpeded future.

Schools, historically, have been home to this kind of discretionary justice. You let the principal or the teacher decide what to do about cheating because you know that every case of cheating is different—and, more to the point, that every cheater is different. Jimmy is incorrigible, and needs the shock of expulsion. But Bobby just needs a talking to, because he's a decent kid, and Mary and Jane cheated because the teacher foolishly stepped out of the classroom in the middle of the test and the temptation was just too much. A Tennessee study found that after zero-tolerance programs were adopted by the state's public schools, the frequency of targeted offences soared: the firm and unambiguous punishments weren't deterring bad behavior at all. Is that really a surprise? If you're a teenager, the announcement that an act will be sternly punished doesn't always sink in, and it isn't always obvious when you're doing the thing you aren't supposed to be doing. Why? Because you're a teenager.

Somewhere along the way—perhaps in response to Columbine—we forgot the value of discretion in disciplining the young. "Ultimately, they have to make the right decisions," the Oklahoma football coach, Bob Stoops, said of his players, after jettisoning his quarterback. "When they do not, the consequences are serious." Open and shut: he sounded as if he were talking about a senior executive of Enron, rather than a college sophomore whose primary obligation to Oklahoma was to throw a football in the direction of young men in helmets. You might think that the University of Oklahoma was so touchy about its quarterback being "overpaid" it ought to have kept closer track of his work habits with an on-campus job. But making a fetish of personal accountability conveniently removes the need for institutional accountability. (We court-marshall the grunts who abuse prisoners, not the commanding officers who let the abuse happen.) To acknowledge that the causes of our actions are complex and muddy seems permissive, and permissiveness is the hallmark of an ideology now firmly in disgrace. That conservative patron saint Whittaker Chambers once defined liberalism as Christ without the Crucifixion. But

The end

Why might Gladwell have waited until the end of his essay to mention the name of the student whose actions he described back at the very beginning of the essay? (In case you didn't know, Robert Oppenheimer was one of the people responsible for the atom bomb.)

Context and ethos

What does this essay's being published in the *New Yorker* tell you about Malcolm Gladwell and how others think of his writing? If you know nothing about this magazine, what might that tell you about how Gladwell was viewing his audience while he was writing?

punishment without the possibility of redemption is even worse: it is the Crucifixion without Christ.

As for the student whose career Cambridge saved? He left at the end of the academic year and went to study at the University of Göttingen, where he made important contributions to quantum theory. Later, after a brilliant academic career, he was entrusted with leading one of the most critical and morally charged projects in the history of science. His name was Robert Oppenheimer.

New Yorker, September 4, 2006, pp. 37–38.

Below is one possible way of analyzing Gladwell's claim, reason, warrant, and evidence in the above essay. By separating these elements, you can have a better sense of whether you agree with these elements, whether you think they really do fit together logically, and whether you think the evidence works.

CLAIM: We should apply discretion rather than *zero-tolerance* policies when responding to the bad behavior of youth.

REASON: *Zero-tolerance* policies potentially prevent good people from developing to their full productive potential.

WARRANT: Discretion in response to the bad behavior of youth will help good people develop to their full productive potential.

EVIDENCE: *Facts:* The people who apply zero tolerance apply the policy outside their rightful realm, as the University of Oklahoma case shows. *Shared values:* Zero tolerance does not take into account the differences in people, as the Bobby and Jimmy examples show. Zero tolerance does not take into account the moral development of youth. Zero tolerance removes the need for institutional responsibility. *Appealing to readers' experiences:* Readers are likely to agree, based on their own experiences, that Robert Oppenheimer would perhaps not have gone on to do his important work if *zero tolerance* had been in use in 1925.

ANALYZING ARGUMENTS

A SAMPLE RHETORICAL ANALYSIS

On the opposite page, we show a written rhetorical analysis—a critical analysis—of Malcolm Gladwell's article "No Mercy," which we examined on the previous pages. You should be able to see how this essay grows out of the work of responding to the questions asked of the essay in the previous pages—as well as how this essay cuts to the heart of Gladwell's argument by questioning his warrant.

This rhetorical analysis is one example of how you can write such an analysis.

The beginning: Ethos

This writer gives a quick summary of the Gladwell article, to show that she has done the work of understanding the article. This builds her ethos postively, so her questioning of the article will thus be more persuasive to her readers.

The beginning

Now this writer helps her readers have a sense of what is to come by summarizing—quickly—her main concern about the Gladwell article; she will give evidence for this concern in the paragraphs to follow.

Analyzing ethos

The writer analyzes Gladwell's ethos: He is "confident…but not bullying" and wants to inspire others to think critically.

Logos: Evidence

Here the writer uses direct quotations from the Gladwell article to show that she has read carefully and is responding to specific Gladwell arguments.

→ See pages 316–321 for help with including direct quotations in your writing.

Ethos and pathos: The writer asks questions

After showing her readers the specific parts of Gladwell's writing that concern her, this writer can then raise the questions that motivate her concern.

How would her ethos be different if she had instead phrased these questions as statements? How does asking these questions engage readers (a pathos strategy)?

No Justice, No Mercy?
Responding to Malcolm Gladwell

In his essay "No Mercy," published in the September 4, 2006, issue of the *New Yorker*, Malcolm Gladwell argues implicitly that current "zero-tolerance" policies hurt people more than we realize. For example, Gladwell tells about the brilliant physicist Robert Oppenheimer, who under today's policies probably would have been expelled from college and denied his important career because of dangerous actions he took as a graduate student. With this example Gladwell suggests that current students who are expelled for lesser offenses are losing future careers in which they might contribute to society. While there is much in Gladwell's argument with which I agree, his examples raise for me the question of who is to judge others, and how.

I appreciate the tone of Gladwell's writing. He is a confident writer, but not bullying. There is nothing in his writing to suggest that he thinks anyone who disagrees is somehow stupid or unthoughtful. Instead, Gladwell's writing seems more of a provocation, asking us to think on these matters because they have consequences. I appreciate being drawn into this issue by the range of examples and ideas Gladwell brings into his writing—but those examples lead me to my concerns.

As a possibility for how we might treat the poorly considered actions of the young, Gladwell uses the notion of "discretion," which he describes as being based in an awareness that "every cheater is different" (119). Therefore, Gladwell argues, we need to approach each case with an awareness of who has done the action, and why, in order to decide consequences: "Jimmy is incorrigible, and needs the shock of expulsion," Gladwell writes, but "Bobby just needs a talking to, because he's a decent kid" (119). But how does anyone know these things? What would someone have to do to get to know Jimmy or Bobby well enough to make these decisions with any certainty? And what sort of person would we want to make such decisions that have so much effect on the lives of others? To live together using the discretion that Gladwell asks us to have, we would need to find people who have the time and sensitivity to look carefully into the lives of others, and who have considerable training in understanding the patterns of someone's life so as to make valid decisions.

Ethos: Adding authority by using other sources

After some online searching, this writer found a published report that helps demonstrate that her worry is concrete and real. This source ought to have authority with readers because it is published by a government source—and also because the writer describes the detailed research on which the report is based.

Ethos: Adding authority by quoting the words of others

This writer could have summarized the findings of the report she is citing, but by quoting from it she is able to let the report speak for itself, which tends to be more persuasive to readers.

Concluding

After having given her own evidence in the preceding paragraphs, the writer now summarizes her position so that her readers can leave her writing with a clear idea of her argument. (➔ See pages 292–293 on writing conclusions.)

Notice, too, how she shapes her words here: She neither dismisses Gladwell nor insists that she knows it all. How does this shape her ethos? What sort of emotional room does this leave for readers to respond?

Citing sources

➔ See Part 8 (pages 307–462) for help with citing sources.

THIS WRITER'S USE OF LOGOS…

To the right is one possible analysis of this writer's use of a claim, a reason, a warrant, and evidence. If you think that this writer has written a persuasive short essay, consider the following:

1 In what order are the claim, reason, and evidence presented in the writing? Why might they be presented in that order?

2 Notice that many other strategies weave into the writing, in support of both the logic of the claim, reason, and evidence, but also to persuade readers to have a sympathetic lean toward the writer's position: Logos matters tremendously, but it cannot stand alone.

Meanwhile, however, many examples exist of discretion that is biased. For one, the United States Department of Justice's Office of Juvenile Justice and Delinquency Prevention published a report in 1995 in which the Office analyzed the available literature on the treatment of minority youth in the juvenile justice system; after analyzing 250 published articles, with 47 being particularly relevant, the report argues that "processing decisions in many State and local juvenile justice systems are not racially neutral" (7).

Whether or not the juvenile justice system is the same now as it was in 1995, what the report shows is that racial bias can enter the system—even from people who are supposed to be professionals in deciding whether a young person committed an offense and how it should be treated. Other kinds of bias—based on class or gender, for example—also seem possible. If we do want discretion as the basis for responding to youth behavior, as Gladwell argues, how do we keep it fair?

I may sound as though I disagree with Gladwell. I do not. I think zero-tolerance policies in high schools harm the futures of people who are still too young to make certain decisions. But until an argument addresses how discretion can be applied knowledgeably and justly, without bias, I will sit uneasily with my beliefs.

Works Cited

Gladwell, Malcolm. "No Mercy." *New Yorker* 4 Sept. 2006: 37-38. Print.
United States. Dept. of Justice. Office of Juvenile Justice and Delinquency Prevention. *Minorities and the Juvenile Justice System: Research Summary.* Washington: GPO, 1995. Print.

CLAIM: Discretion is not enough for making decisions about the lives of young people.

REASON: Discretion can be biased.

WARRANT: Young people deserve fair and equal treatment.

EVIDENCE: This writer appeals to the reader's own *experiences* by asking questions about how we make decisions. The writer also uses the *expert testimony* of the U.S. Department of Justice's Office of Juvenile Justice and Delinquency Prevention, and facts supported by that testimony.

A SAMPLE ANALYSIS OF A VISUAL TEXT

The poster to the right was produced by the Mayor's Office of the City of New York as part of a campaign against domestic violence.

Pathos

This text is simple, composed of one photograph of a woman and a few lines of text. If we were looking at the original poster, the woman would seem almost life-size; as viewers, we are situated as though we were standing close to her, right behind her, as though we could touch her. What emotional relationship might this physical closeness encourage viewers to have with the woman and so the poster?

Pathos

The woman's body is bruised, and she is wearing a hospital gown. How might a viewer's attitude toward the woman and so toward the poster be different if she were wearing a low-cut dress instead?

Logos: Evidence

The poster gives one fact. What evidence is offered in its support? Whose authority is offered in support? Do we know if the fact refers just to high school students in New York City or to those in the entire United States? (Does that matter?) Why might the makers of this poster have chosen to present this fact written on this woman's bruised back instead of on a poster containing only words?

Audience

Who would be interested in this fact about high school students? Notice that the poster's composers have chosen to call attention to "high school students" and not "high school girls." Why might they have made this word choice?

Context

If the audience includes people in high school, then it is likely that the people running the campaign decided to make a poster because schools have many places where posters are easily seen. In addition, the particular visibility of posters says something about why the poster uses pathos as its major strategy: A poster has to catch the eye—quickly—of someone walking by.

Logos: Argument

This poster is encouraging viewers to make phone calls to stop abuse. Does it offer reasons to encourage this action? If so, what are they?

Logos: Arrangement

Why might the words be at the bottom of the poster rather than at the top?

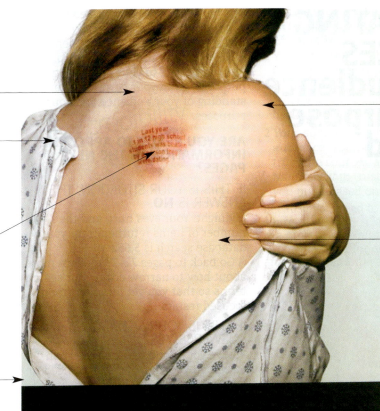

Pathos

Why do you think we are shown the woman from the back? What emotional connections does this ask the audience to make with the poster?

Pathos

Why do you think the woman is white? What does this suggest about how the poster's makers conceived of their audience?

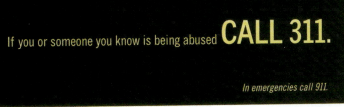

If you or someone you know is being abused **CALL 311.**

In emergencies call 911.

Michael R. Bloomberg, Mayor   Yolanda B. Jimenez, Commissioner, Mayor's Office to Combat Domestic Violence

Logos: Evidence?

Does the support of the mayor of New York City for this poster serve as expert evidence?

EVALUATING SOURCES
FOR RELEVANCE

✔ ONE
relevance

☐ TWO
credibility

IF A SOURCE MEETS MOST OF THE CRITERIA TO THE RIGHT, HOLD ON TO IT.

When you are evaluating the relevance of a source, you are evaluating how likely most readers will believe that what is presented in the source is appropriate to your arguments.

Finding sources that meet all the criteria doesn't guarantee that they'll end up in your Works Cited list at the end of your paper—but sources that meet all the criteria are much more likely to help you write a solid, strong, and persuasive argument.

ask this:
IS THE KIND OF SOURCE
RELEVANT TO YOUR AUDIENCE?

☐ **Given your research question/ purposes, what kinds of sources are likely to be most appealing and persuasive to your particular audience?**

When you are writing an academic research paper, your audience is academic readers, who tend to respect books published by academic presses, academic journal articles, and specialized encyclopedias.

Academic audiences also respect the use of primary sources. (→ See page 39 on primary sources.)

Depending on your purposes, however, you might need to supplement such sources. For example, if you are writing about the role of women in space exploration, you might want to begin your essay with one woman's personal story about how she got into the U.S. space program; in such a case, you could look in popular periodicals or blogs for such stories—and those sources would be appropriate for your purposes.

then this:
IS A PARTICULAR SOURCE
RELEVANT TO
YOUR ARGUMENT?

❏ **Is the source on topic?**
This might seem too obvious a question to ask, but it isn't. You can save yourself a lot of time if, with each possible source, you ask yourself whether the source really does provide information that is focused on your topic.

❏ **Does the source have a publication date appropriate to your research?**
If you are writing about the current state of a rapidly changing topic—such as AIDS research—you need sources dated close to the moment you are writing; if you are writing about a past event or about past situations that have led to a current event, then you need sources from those time periods as well as from people in the present.

❏ **Does the source bring in perspectives other than those of the sources you've already collected?**
You do not want to collect sources that all take the same position, for two reasons. First, if all you can find are sources that take the same perspective on your topic, then your topic is probably not controversial or interesting enough to be the subject of a paper. Second, your audience is not likely to be persuaded by writing that does not consider multiple perspectives on a topic.

❏ **Does the source provide something interesting?**
Your audience wants to be intellectually engaged with your writing. As you consider a new source, ask yourself if it contains ideas or information that is interesting—funny, provocative, puzzling—and that supports your points. Quoting or citing such ideas or information in your writing helps you write a more engaging paper.

❏ **Does the source bring in data or other information different from the sources you have already collected?**
This criterion is similar to the one preceding, but it asks you to consider how much data or other information is useful for you to collect in order to construct a persuasive position in your writing.

❏ **Does the source suggest other possible directions your research could take?**
We do want you to stay on track in your research as much as you want to stay on track, given that you have a deadline—but we also want you to stay open to the possibilities of reshaping or retouching your research question and purpose as you discover potentially new and exciting approaches.

EVALUATING SOURCES
FOR CREDIBILITY: PRINT

ONE relevance

TWO credibility

IF A SOURCE MEETS MOST OF THE CRITERIA TO THE RIGHT, HOLD ON TO IT.

When you evaluate the credibility of a source, you are evaluating whether most of your readers will accept the facts and arguments you present.

Finding sources that meet all the criteria doesn't guarantee that they'll end up in your Works Cited list at the end of your paper—but sources that meet all the criteria are much more likely to help you write a well-supported and persuasive argument.

A NOTE

Some people are nostalgic for pre-Internet days because the institutions of print publication seem to make evaluating a source's credibility easy. The costs and complexities of print publication and distribution are behind that perception.

The printing of books, magazines, and newspapers is expensive. Those who provide the money want return on their investments, so they want readers to trust what is published. Print publishing therefore developed systems of editors and fact-checkers: Often when you buy a print text its credibility has been checked in different ways. (Libraries contribute to this system, too, because librarians often buy only books recommended to them by trusted sources.)

But, as you know, not all print texts are credible (think supermarket tabloids). Some publishers have political motivations, for example. You cannot therefore count on something you find in print to be absolutely reliable—and you also have to consider what criteria your audience will use for judging credibility.

TIP: HAVE ANY QUESTIONS?
If you have any questions as you apply these criteria to a source, a librarian is a good person to ask.

DETERMINING THE CREDIBILITY OF A PRINT SOURCE

❑ **Who published the source?**
Look at page 44, on Kinds of Sources, to read about the motivations behind different kinds of publishers. A publisher's motivations can help you decide the level of credibility the source will have for your audience.

❑ **Does the author have sufficient qualifications for writing on the topic?**
Most print publications will tell you something about the author so that you can judge; you can also search online to learn about the author.
If you cannot find an author or sponsoring agency, is that because no one wants to take responsibility?

❑ **What evidence is presented?**
Is the evidence of a kind that fits the claims? What kind of evidence would be stronger?

❑ **Does the evidence seem accurate?**

❑ **Do the author's claims seem adequately supported by the offered evidence?**

❑ **Does the source try to cover all the relevant facts and opinions?**
If you are at the beginning of your research, this might be hard to answer, but as you dig deeper into your topic, you'll have a sense of the range of perspectives one can take on your topic, and you'll be able to judge how widely a source engages with the issues at stake.

❑ **What is the genre of the source?**
Is the source an advertisement (or does it contain advertisements)? Advertisers sometimes try to influence what is published near their advertisements to keep their appeal strong.
But it also matters if the source is an opinion piece, a thought-experiment or essay, or a piece of scholarship: Writers and readers have different expectations for different genres regarding how much (unsupported) opinion is appropriate.

❑ **Does the source make its position, perspective, and biases clear?**
When writers do not make their own biases clear, they often do not want readers to think about how those biases affect the writers' arguments.

❑ **Does the source make a point of seeking out different perspectives?**
If so, this is an indication that a writer is trying to understand a topic fully and not just giving a narrow view.

❑ **Does the writing seek to sound reasonable and thoughtful?**
Inflammatory language in a piece of writing is a sign that the writer is trying to move you solely through your emotional responses without engaging your thoughtfulness.

EVALUATING SOURCES FOR CREDIBILITY: PRINT
SAMPLE SOURCES

ONE
relevance

TWO
credibility

To the right are examples of how to judge the credibility of a print source based on your research question and audience.

Pedro's research question is

"What social actions ought the U.S. government be able to take in the face of pandemics?"

He is writing for his classmates and teacher.

Aaliyah's research question is

"On the Internet, how do ideas spread like viruses?"

She is doing research for a marketing company whose directors are considering new online approaches.

Gorman, Christine. "How Scared Should We Be?" *Time* 17 Oct. 2005: 30-34. Print.

Fishman, Jay A. "SARS. Xenotransplantation and Bioterrorism: Preventing the Next Epidemic." *American Journal of Transplantation* 3.8 (2003): 909-12. Print.

This source is **NOT CREDIBLE** for this audience and purpose. *Time* is well known but is not a science or policy journal; the author is not a scientist or lawmaker. Though the author quotes credible agencies, she does not give citations for us to check. The article's evidence is patchy because the questions are complex but the space for answering them is small. The language is almost inflammatory, to catch attention, not thoughts. Although this article is relevant to Pedro's question, Pedro and his readers should be skeptical about this article's depth. Pedro could perhaps use anecdotes from this article, but ought not make this a main source.

This source is **CREDIBLE** for this audience and purpose. Pedro's readers will respect the standards of the academic journal: The journal gives the author's scientific credentials (not just those of his sources), the decision to publish the article was made by other scientists (which ensures accuracy of evidence), and there are clear relations between the evidence and claims as well as strong challenges from other perspectives. The writing is exact, key words are defined, and inflammatory language is carefully avoided.

This source could be **CREDIBLE** for this audience and purpose, depending on how Aaliyah uses it. For all the reasons listed above, Aaliyah and her audience ought to be skeptical of this article. Given Aaliyah's purposes, however, the article covers enough different perspectives to be useful for developing the analogy between epidemics and Internet viruses—as long as Aaliyah notes her skepticism about the source.

This source is **CREDIBLE** for this audience and purpose. For all the reasons mentioned above, this source will carry weight with Aaliyah's audience, even if Aaliyah uses this source only to provide examples supporting her descriptions of viruses and how they spread.

EVALUATING SOURCES
FOR CREDIBILITY: ONLINE

✔ ONE **relevance**

✔ TWO **credibility**

DETERMINING THE CREDIBILITY OF AN ONLINE SOURCE

Use the criteria for evaluating print sources, with the following additions:

☐ **Who published the source?**

The domain name in the URL can indicate something about a publisher's credibility. (Example domain names are microsoft.com, whitehouse.gov, or lacorps.org.) Look at the last letters in the domain name:

.gov   A website created by an office of the U.S. federal government

.com   A website created for a company that is seeking to publicize itself or sell products

.org   A nonprofit organization—but anyone can register for the .org domain

.edu   Colleges and universities

.mil   U.S. military websites

.me.us A website for one of the fifty U.S. states: The first two letters are the abbreviation of the state name

.de   A website created in a country other than the U.S.—but websites created outside this country can also use .com, .net, and .org

.net   The most generic ending; Internet Service Providers (ISPs) as well as individuals can have websites whose URLs end in .net

What sorts of websites will your audience think are most appropriate and credible, given your purpose?

❑ **Does the author have qualifications for writing on the topic?**

With some websites you won't be able to answer this because you won't be able to determine who the author is, either because no name is given or a pseudonym is used.

If you cannot find the name of an author or sponsoring agency, perhaps no one wants to take responsibility or someone is worried about the consequences of publishing the information. If you are writing on a controversial topic, you could use information from such a site to describe the controversy and support the fact that there is a controversy—but you couldn't use the site to offer factual support for anything else.

❑ **What evidence is offered?**

In the most credible print sources, authors list the sources of their evidence; the same holds true for websites. If you cannot find the source of the evidence used, the site is not as credible as a site that does list sources.

❑ **Does the source make its position, perspective, and biases clear?**

Approach websites just as you approach print pages with this question, except that with websites you can also check where links on the site take you. A website may give the appearance of holding a middle line on a position, but if the websites to which it links support only one position, then question the credibility of the original site.

❑ **What is the genre of the source?**

Some online genres, such as newspapers and magazines, mimic print genres; approach them with the same questions as you would their print equivalents.

But webpages can easily be made to look like any genre. For example, some websites look like the informational material you pick up in a doctor's office. Just as when you receive such material in a doctor's office, however, you need to look carefully: Is the website actually advertising a company's treatments or products?

Also keep in mind that blogs are a tricky genre to use as sources. There are many well-respected blogs published by experts; if you want to cite such a blog, you will need to give evidence why that particular blog is respected by other experts. On the other hand, if you are citing words from a blog solely to show a range of opinions on a topic, the blog's credibility will not be an issue.

ALSO:

❑ **How well designed is the website or webpage?**

A site that looks professionally designed, is straightforward to navigate, and loads quickly suggests that its creators put time and resources into all the other aspects of the site; these characteristics could also indicate that the site was published by an organization rather than an individual. Do any of these factors matter for your purpose and audience?

RESEARCHING ETHICALLY

When others recognize that something legally belongs to you and that you can use it as you see fit, that thing is considered your property.

When we hear **property** we probably think of land or buildings, which, legally, are considered to be **real property**; **personal property**, on the other hand, consists of objects you can move with you. Both real and personal property are things that can be touched.

Intellectual property refers to things you cannot touch: ideas. When someone invents, writes, draws, composes, or performs something, that person's intellectual property isn't in the particular object—the thing invented or the book written—but in the ideas that make the invention or book possible.

There are two kinds of intellectual property: **industrial property**, which is inventions and trademarks like company logos, and **creative property**, which is literary and artistic works. **Creative property** is covered by copyright laws.

Copyright law developed over several hundred years, in a push-pull process between individual authors, singers, and other creators of culture and those who publish and distribute what the creators make. Copyright gives legal protection to creators so that they have control over how what they make gets used by others.

Plagiarism occurs when someone uses another's creative property without the other's consent or knowledge. This can involve using a part of another's work or passing off the whole as one's own. Plagiarism is unethical and can be illegal.

SHARED CULTURE, ACADEMIC RESEARCH, AND FAIR USE

If we had to pay the inventor every time we used certain inventions—such as speech or writing—we would probably have no culture. The same goes for some ideas: If we had to pay someone every time we told a fairy tale, sang an old lullaby, or repeated the story of George Washington chopping down the cherry tree, we would have no shared experiences to bind us as a culture. In recognition of this, it is the law that after a set number of years, creators' copyright control over their productions passes into what is called the **Public Domain**. When a creative production is in the public domain, others can use it freely, as when the Disney Company makes a movie about Pocahantas or the Little Mermaid.

But academic research—in all the disciplines of the sciences, social sciences, and the humanities—cannot wait the length of time it takes for ideas to pass into the public domain. Academic research depends on being able to use and build on the ideas of others *now*, as does artistic develop-ment. In recognition of such conditions, there is a doctrine in U.S. copyright law called *fair use*.

TIP: IS IT FAIR USE?

Fair use protects most academic uses of intellectual property—but as soon as you use that property for personal gain or commercial uses, the use is no longer protected.

FAIR USE

Fair use is a doctrine in copyright law that allows certain uses of other's copyrighted material without needing permission. Fair use does not specify exactly how much of another's work one may use; instead, four factors are considered, in legal cases, to help determine if a use is fair:

1 **The purpose and character of the use.** Is the use commercial or for nonprofit and educational purposes—such as criticism, parody, or art? Fair use is meant to support public, not personal, enrichment. If the use transforms the copied work, making something new of it, that is also more likely to be considered fair use.

2 **The nature of the copyrighted work.** Generally, uses of published non-fiction works are considered to benefit the public—and not harm the rights of a copyright holder—more so than uses of unpublished or fiction works.

3 **The amount and substantiality of the portion used in relation to the copyrighted work as a whole.** The less one copies, the more likely the copying is to be considered fair use.

4 **The effect of the use upon the potential market for or value of the copyrighted work.** If the use will not cause the copyright holder to lose income, it is more likely to be considered fair use.

The doctrine of fair use underpins academic uses of the words of others—as in research writing.

DEVELOPING A THESIS STATEMENT— AND PUTTING IT TO WORK

Riley has done initial online and library research into how microcredit changes women's lives in developing countries, as the notes on page 29 describe.

Analyzing the sources

Because Riley asked the research questions she did (page 85), she read her sources looking for why women are the focus of microcredit and how microcredit changes women's lives.

Although most sources spoke glowingly about microcredit, a few pointed out problems—and so Riley looked for more sources to support or refute those claims.

She then found more sources that questioned some of the benefits of microcredit. Through her analysis, she recognized that they tended to come from feminist perspectives—and so she is aware that various audiences will respond to those sources differently.

Because of this continued research, however, Riley believes that pointing out such problems is justified.

First thesis statement

A thesis statement has this basic form, as described on pages 102–103:

CLAIM + REASON

Based on her research, Riley writes:

> Microcredit is not always good for women because it keeps them in poverty and makes them vulnerable to familial violence.

Evaluating the first thesis statement

Effective and engaging papers are most likely to develop from thesis statements that

1 Have a concrete and focused claim.

2 Have a debatable claim.

3 Give a reason (or reasons) that can be supported.

Here's an analysis of Riley's first try:

1 The claim that *microcredit is not always good for women* is vague and broad. What do **good** or **not always** mean here? Is Riley talking about all women everywhere?

2 Because so many sources wrote only positively about microcredit, Riley's claim is certainly debatable.

3 If Riley has found several relevant and credible sources providing evidence for these reasons, then her reasons can work for her—although they still seem a little vague.

Second thesis statement

After evaluating her first try, Riley writes:

Microcredit should be offered to women in developing countries only accompanied by discussion support groups and classes in economics, because otherwise the women won't know how to change the community conditions that encourage poverty.

Evaluating the second thesis statement

1 In her paper, Riley will have to explain more clearly what she means by *discussion support groups and classes in economics*, but this claim is concrete because it makes specific recommendations; it also focuses on a few recommendations rather than many.

2 For the same reasons as before, Riley's claim is debatable.

3 Riley's reasons are now more concrete: They help her understand that she will need to write about conditions that encourage poverty in communities and give evidence that microcredit programs that don't do what she recommends do not result in community change.

The right sources? Enough sources?

By evaluating her thesis statement, Riley can see that she needs to be sure she has enough relevant and credible sources to supply the information described in points 1 and 3 above.

HINTS & TIPS FOR EVALUATING SOURCES

IF YOU ARE UNSURE ABOUT THE RELEVANCE OR CREDIBILITY OF A SOURCE...

Ask someone who might be more familiar with the source, such as your teacher, a librarian, or someone who has researched your topic before.

Knowledge about relevance and credibility of sources increases over time. Those who write repeatedly on similar research topics learn who respected writers and researchers are, and learn (in addition to what we've listed here) lots of subtle signs for what makes a source relevant and credible.

REMEMBER THAT FINDING A SUFFICIENT NUMBER OF SOURCES IS ONLY PART OF WRITING A PERSUASIVE PAPER

Have you ever started to read a letter to the editor or a blog that you had to put aside because the tone of voice was rude or obnoxious? The letter or blog might have had perfectly fine evidence in support of its arguments, but other choices the writer made in constructing the whole argument might have undone the worthiness of the research.

The same can happen to you in writing a research paper. Look on pages 160–179 for help with making choices about the other aspects of a research paper.

HOW DO YOU KNOW YOU HAVE COLLECTED ENOUGH SOURCES?

❑ Do your sources approach your question from a range of directions? Readers see it as a sign of careful and thoughtful research when writers consider a range of positions on a topic; you should not consider your research done until you have collected—and can reference—a range of positions.

❑ Do you have the right range of kinds of sources? With academic research papers, audiences usually expect sources that are academic. If your writing is for a nonacademic audience, using many kinds of sources can demonstrate that you have done broad and careful research.

❑ Do you have enough sources to support every step of the argument you are making?

❑ Do you have enough sources to help you develop solid and well-supported responses to your research questions?

❑ Before you can finally decide if you have enough sources, however, you need to know if you have the sources that will fully answer your audience's questions on this topic. Look to Part 4—where you turn your thesis statement into a statement of purpose—to help you decide if you really do have all the sources you need for your particular audience.

PART 4
CONNECTING WITH AUDIENCES

CONTENTS

WHERE ARE WE IN THE PROCESS FOR COMPOSING?

Understanding your project

Getting started

Asking questions

Shaping your project for others	Thinking in depth about audience Developing a statement of purpose
Drafting a paper	Writing a rough draft
Getting feedback	Receiving feedback to drafts Developing a revision plan

Revising

Polishing

UNDER-STANDING YOUR AUDIENCE

THE CONCERN

You know what you are writing about. For example, in Parts 2 and 3 we followed Riley's development of ideas for writing about how microcredit loans change women's lives in developing countries. As you saw, Riley put together a thesis statement: *Microcredit should be offered to women in developing countries only accompanied by discussion support groups and classes in economics,* she wrote, *because otherwise the women won't know how to change the community conditions that encourage poverty.* **But who needs to know this? For whom does this argument matter, and why?**

Through her research, Riley has accumulated some supporting evidence for her thesis, but what of that evidence will be most persuasive? Into what order should she put her evidence? What tone of voice should she use in her writing?

Riley can answer these questions only if she has some sense of who will read her writing and why.

Riley can say, *I am writing to people who know about microcredit and think it's always good*—but that level of understanding of audience is vague; it does not help her make the choices posed by the questions above.

How can Riley develop a more discerning and useful sense of her readers so that she can make specific choices about her writing?

WAYS TO ADDRESS THE CONCERN

Experienced writers will tell you that understanding their audiences is the most important step in composing writing that achieves its purposes.

Concrete and persuasive writing grows out of thinking about what your readers believe and why. For example, if Riley is writing to people who think microcredit is good, she needs to ask, *Why do they think microcredit is good? What do they think is good about it? Why haven't they heard about some of the questionable sides of microcredit? Just what do they know about it, at all?*

There is also another important question Riley has to ask, a question that any writer has to ask when addressing an audience that might not know about the topic: *Why should my readers care?*

Those questions suggest further research as well as decisions a writer like Riley has to make about readers. Riley has to research her readers—and their beliefs and opinions—because if she is going to be persuasive about microcredit, she will have to address what matters to her readers about the lives of women in developing countries.

Riley needs to develop a thicker characterization of her audience, so she needs to think about her audience as concretely as possible. If she can think of them as real, living, breathing people with emotions and attitudes toward events, then she can write to them almost as though she would talk with them, taking into consideration their opinions, thoughts, and feelings.

Whether you are writing a business memo, composing a flyer about your band, or producing a research website on the Gilded Age in the United States, taking some steps to help you think about your audiences more concretely will help you produce more effective writing.

Following, we suggest strategies for thinking about your audience in depth. Here are the steps we follow:

general observations about shared characteristics

more specific observations about what audiences know, think, and feel about a topic

narrowing further by thinking about real, specific readers

narrowing further by choosing which audiences you will address (while keeping in mind the complexities of audiences)

developing a statement of purpose

UNDERSTANDING YOUR AUDIENCE

CHARACTERISTICS YOUR AUDIENCE MIGHT SHARE

You can begin thinking about your audience by considering their general characteristics and how those characteristics can affect the attitudes they might have toward your topic.

YOU MIGHT THINK YOU ALREADY KNOW YOUR AUDIENCE…

You are writing a paper for your classmates (which, as you know, also means you are writing for your teacher). Or perhaps you are writing a memo to your boss proposing new procedures.

In each case, you think you know these people. After all, you live and work with them; you spend considerable time in varying degrees of contact.

But do you know their concerns and opinions on your topic? Do you know *why* they hold those concerns and opinions?

If your writing is to catch and hold these readers' attention, you need to give time to what they think about your topic, and why they think those things.

OR MAYBE YOU DON'T KNOW YOUR AUDIENCE

You are writing a letter to the editor of your city's newspaper. You are putting together a grant application for a non-profit organization. You are composing webpages for a new business.

In such cases, you probably don't know your audiences. Newspaper audiences are broad; people from diverse positions make grant decisions; businesses try to reach wide audiences. How do you shape your writing in these cases?

Even when you are writing to audiences with whom you are not in regular contact, you can still make judgments, based on the information you do have, about why the audiences will read what you offer and how their concerns and opinions will shape their reading.

READERS' GENERAL CHARACTERISTICS

No matter how much or how little you know about your readers, use what you do know to help you compose.

Step through the following general characteristics, asking how they might impinge on readers' responses to your thesis:

❑ age   ❑ gender
❑ ethnicity   ❑ language
❑ level of education   ❑ able-bodiness
❑ sexual orientation   ❑ class
❑ upbringing   ❑ place of living
❑ place of work
❑ other characteristics that might matter

If you know your audience well, you can focus on the characteristics they have in common, such as age or place of living. If your audience is a general audience, or if you do not know your audience, step through these characteristics to consider which matter most.

TIP: USING CARE WITH AUDIENCE CHARACTERISTICS

To define someone just by age, ethnicity, level of education, gender, or class—or even to define based on all the characteristics above—is to miss the complex mix of experiences and culture that shapes each of us. The characteristics above are just a beginning to help you think about how readers *might* respond. You can never know for sure how a person's particular life will affect his or her responses.

FOR EXAMPLE...

For Riley, both the age and gender of her readers might matter. More women are likely to identify with the plights of other women than are men; people who do not have children might not sympathize with women trying to eke out a small living for their families or get an education for their children.

In addition, people who have not traveled much or who have grown up in middle-class neighborhoods might not have experienced the social and economic conditions underlying poverty, which is what Riley wants to discuss.

If Riley is writing to a class of peers— and to her teacher—what do these observations tell her about their concerns? On which of their experiences can Riley draw to increase their interest in what she's writing?

FOR EXAMPLE...

You are writing a letter to the editor of your local paper about a proposed wind power plant that a power company wants to install on land that was once a farm. You live nearby, and are concerned about the potential noise of the plant and an increase in traffic. Are people who do not live as close to the farm going to think your concerns are simply selfish? Are people looking to bring jobs to the area going to think your concerns are only about the niceties of life instead of the essentials, like jobs?

UNDERSTANDING YOUR AUDIENCE
WHAT DO PEOPLE KNOW, THINK, AND FEEL ABOUT THE ISSUE?

The attitudes people have toward an issue can shape how committed they are to their positions.

READERS AS PEOPLE WITH OPINIONS AND ATTITUDES

Move your focus from general characteristics to what people feel about a topic or issue. Talk to potential readers, asking about

❏ what they know of the topic.

❏ their emotional responses to the topic.

❏ how they have learned what they know of the topic.

❏ personal connections they might have to the topic.

❏ values/beliefs/commitments related to the topic.

❏ questions they might have about the topic.

❏ their self-identity as it connects them to the topic. How do they see themselves connected to the topic because of their specific relations to others? That is, does it matter that a reader is a mother, a daughter, unemployed, a Republican or a leftist, rich or not, a boss or a worker, a student or a teacher, ambitious or laid back, or...?

❏ recent events—locally, nationally, or internationally—that might shape their responses to the topic.

If you cannot talk directly with readers, ask yourself the same questions, imagining how people with different backgrounds would respond.

FOR EXAMPLE...

If you were writing to argue that it might be time to build more nuclear power plants in the United States, you might learn that many people are opposed. You might learn that most people learned about the science of nuclear power in high school textbooks; they also learned about nuclear power from reading newspapers and magazines about cancer rates following Chernobyl and how people can no longer live in that community because of radiation. And, silly as it may seem, all the science fiction movies people have seen about mutations do underlie general perception, further adding to the general emotional climate of fear and uncertainty around nuclear power.

In addition, people who have children are perhaps more resistant to nuclear power because they do not want their children to be in danger. On the other hand, businesspeople (or children of businesspeople) might be more concerned about the future costs of power because of how those costs affect their ability to keep their businesses running.

These observations can help writers understand that, for most readers these days, making decisions about nuclear power is not simply a matter of coolly weighing numeric, scientific evidence; it is also about fear of mutations, cancer, and the destruction of communities. This tells writers that they probably should not compose a list of facts but will have to address people's emotional concerns about radiation and its potential long-term effects.

FOR EXAMPLE...

In quick discussions, Riley learns that most of her classmates know nothing about microcredit and the lives of women in developing countries, or they know a little bit from having seen a television show. She learns that many don't think microcredit is something they need to worry about because it happens in other countries and involves people whose lives are very different.

From her research, Riley knows that microcredit organizations are at work in the United States, too, so she thinks that she might be able to make her research interesting because it does apply here—and because she can perhaps shape her writing to help her readers think about the economic conditions of their own lives.

In addition, when Riley talks to men in her class about microcredit, she learns that they at first think it is a women's issue that does not concern them. She also learns, however, that almost all the men care deeply for their mothers and respect the work their mothers do to take care of their families—so Riley realizes that she might be able to help her male readers connect to her writing by encouraging them to keep in mind that the women who receive microcredit loans are often mothers, which she has learned from her research.

UNDERSTANDING YOUR AUDIENCE
MAKING AUDIENCES REAL AND SPECIFIC

Writing a note to friends is different from writing a paper for a group of people you have never met or know only peripherally. When you know the people to whom you are writing, you can imagine their facial expressions and their responses, and you can shape your writing to address them specifically. When you write for people you don't know well, it can feel as though your words float in air.

This is a problem all writers face, and it can cause writers to produce writing that is too abstract and that does not engage its readers.

Companies that design tools or software have the same problem: They need to design objects that real people can use. Companies test their products with real people at all stages of development, but because they can't always have real users around, they also **create** three or four imaginary people who typify the audience they are trying to reach. They name and flesh out these imaginary people as much as they can—and then they design for those **people**.

As a writer, you can do the same thing: **Imagine three to four readers who range across the characteristics that most capture who might be in your real audience.**

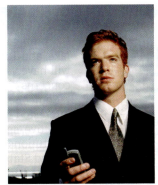

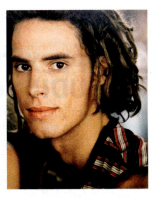

Fawn is 29 and owns a small company that builds electro-optic mechanisms for the military. She watches carefully over the bookkeeping for her company, and is very concerned about how the personal and business taxes she pays are used. She also helps support her sister, who is disabled and has two daughters.

Jake is 25 and lives in a large city where he works for a real estate development company. He was raised in a big family. His family worshipped in a denomination that holds as part of its doctrine that women should be obedient to their husbands in all things. Jake continues to attend church and finds much strength from his faith.

Tony is 18, lives in a big city, works at a nonprofit organization part time while he goes to school, and shares a large, old rowhouse with five friends, some of whom grew up outside the United States. He wants to travel after he graduates and perhaps work overseas.

Having thought about a range of readers by doing the work on the preceding pages, Riley can distill her readers into the three imaginary people above. The descriptions above are short because of our space here; Riley can make them longer, and can include specific comments made by people with whom she's spoken. By doing this work, Riley can imagine herself writing to real people, and can keep concretely in mind why her readers might be more or less resistant to microcredit.

Importantly, by thinking of these people, Riley can see that, beyond the features of age, gender, or place of birth, people's different life experiences shape their concerns in many different ways.

If you do this work, you can identify a range of concerns and attitudes that people hold that might help you decide how to shape your writing—as we explore on the next pages.

STARTING TO WRITE FOR AN AUDIENCE

MOVING FROM A THESIS STATEMENT TO A STATEMENT OF PURPOSE

A thesis statement, as we described in Part 3 of this book, is a short statement summarizing the logic of your argument.

→ See pages 102–103.

Because humans respect logic but are also, well, human, writers also must consider more than just the potential logic of their words. You need to consider how your writing will be emotionally persuasive to a particular audience and how your readers will construct a sense of you—your authority, believability, and general character—based on your words. (→ See pages 92–95 for more on pathos and ethos.) A statement of purpose helps you do this.

A statement of purpose weaves together the logical purpose of a thesis statement with what a writer learns about audience from doing the thinking and research we have described on the preceding pages.

A statement of purpose is not itself a formal piece of writing. Instead, it is thinking-on-paper, a way to help you consider what you really want your readers to think, feel, or do as they read your writing and when they are done reading it.

FOR EXAMPLE...

Here is a thesis statement for a research paper:

> We can build new nuclear power plants in the United States to help take care of our energy needs and reduce reliance on foreign oil because nuclear power plants have become safer and more reliable.

One possible statement of purpose from that thesis statement is this:

> My audience is a general audience, of different ages and backgrounds. They've heard or read about Chernobyl, Three Mile Island, and the government's tests in Utah in the 1950s. They've seen science fiction movies. So they're likely to start reading with some real fears—that nuclear energy, not carefully handled, can result in horrible children's cancers, as in Chernobyl—as well as some fears grounded in speculation, from movies.
>
> Because of those fears, I doubt I can change their minds completely—but I'm hoping to persuade them *just to look again at nuclear power*. I believe recent developments might put them more at ease.
>
> My readers also share concerns that might encourage them to be more open. They are concerned about how current energy sources—oil and coal—affect the environment. They are concerned about the costs of power production and use. So if I can show how nuclear power might just be cleaner and less expensive, they are likely to look at it again.
>
> Should I start by addressing their fears, or should I start by talking about a form of energy that's cleaner and less expensive?

HOW A STATEMENT OF PURPOSE HELPS A WRITER

By writing this statement of purpose, the person writing this paper gets help in making several important decisions:

- **Ethos.** Because this writer is trying to encourage people to be open to something that was feared in the past, he needs to have a careful tone of voice in his writing and admit that he doesn't have all the answers. If he came across as a know-it-all, how do you think his readers would likely respond?

- **Pathos.** This writer will learn that, because he is trying to shift people's thinking about something that has frightened them, he needs to acknowledge the fear and not pretend that it doesn't exist. If he made fun of the fear, or made it sound as though only stupid people are afraid, chances are he'd lose his audience.

- **Examples and evidence that will be useful, given the audience.** This writer will learn that he needs to give many—and very credible—sources to persuade his readers that nuclear power might be cleaner and less expensive than oil or coal.

STARTING TO WRITE FOR AN AUDIENCE

CHOICES A WRITER CAN MAKE BASED ON A STATEMENT OF PURPOSE

Choices about how and what to write aren't magic: You can use your statement of purpose to help you choose.

ETHOS

In Part 3, we discussed how ethos is the sense of a writer that readers get from a text, and how readers develop this sense from a writer's tone of voice, word choices, and so on.

Because Riley is writing to people who don't know about microcredit, and may not know why they should care about it, she may want to write with enthusiasm and curiosity, in order to carry readers along. When she writes in her statement of purpose about perhaps ordering her paper to re-create for her readers her experience of getting excited about microcredit before learning of its problems, this also suggests that she can construct an ethos of someone who is curious and who is learning right alongside the readers—which could be a friendly and inviting ethos.

WHAT LEVEL AND AMOUNT OF PATHOS TO USE

As we discussed in Part 3, pathos is a term for discussing how the aspects of a composition encourage audiences to have emotional responses to the composition.

Riley wants her readers to be informed, which sounds like a fairly emotionless position. But she also wants them to care, which means she wants to inspire warmth, concern, and, perhaps, enthusiasm. This tells her about the tone of voice she can use and that she should describe the people in her examples with compassion.

THE KINDS OF EXAMPLES AND EVIDENCE THAT WILL BE USEFUL FOR A PARTICULAR AUDIENCE

If your purpose is to show readers that you agree with them, use examples your audience will know, that are familiar, or that echo what they already know. If, on the other hand, you are trying to move your audience's focus, then you need carefully to choose examples that will start with what an audience knows but that will then move from the familiar into the new.

In Riley's case, however, she knows her readers don't know much about microcredit. Because she wants them to care about the people who receive microcredit, she should probably give examples about the women who receive microcredit, in order to bring them a little more to life for her readers.

WHICH SOURCES TO USE

In Part 3, we discussed how to tell if sources are relevant and credible. A statement of purpose can help you fine-tune your earlier choices.

Given that part of what Riley has to do is persuade her readers that there are problems with microcredit even though what they have heard before is positive, she is going to have to be careful to show that very credible sources have questioned microcredit—and that more than one source has questioned it. In fact, she will probably want to show that quite a few credible people have questioned microcredit, if she doesn't want readers to think the criticism comes from only one or two cranks.

WHETHER YOU HAVE DONE ENOUGH RESEARCH

A statement of purpose helps you see how much evidence your audience might need to be moved by your thesis.

By putting together her statement of purpose, Riley can see that she needs to define microcredit and perhaps give some history of it so that readers understand where it came from and what it is supposed to achieve. Thus she needs to have done enough research to answer those needs.

As above, her statement of purpose also helps her see that she is going to have to give compelling evidence that microcredit can have problems. She is therefore going to have to find a large number of sources—very reputable sources from different places—to demonstrate that a number of people find problems with microcredit.

(It can be frustrating to do all the research that leads to a thesis statement and then, after doing the work to put together a statement of purpose, to realize that you need to do more research. But it is much more frustrating to write a paper that no one cares to read and that is ineffective precisely because you stopped researching before you considered your audience. Composing is not a linear process, even if the form of a book can make it look linear; successful writers revisit earlier steps of the process continually, as they find places where they need more information or support, or where they need to rethink whom they are addressing with their writing, and so on.)

STARTING TO WRITE FOR AN AUDIENCE
A ROUGH DRAFT

WHAT IS A ROUGH DRAFT?

A rough draft is a testing ground. Written with the expectation that it can be strengthened through feedback from others and revision, it is an attempt to shape a coherent argument.

Successful writers write rough drafts, often many rough drafts. Such writers do not expect that any piece of writing will be finished in one sitting.

Instead, they allow themselves time to produce writing they know will be rough but that is necessary to help them figure out their final thoughts. Even though these writers have a pretty good idea of what they want to write before they sit down (by having developed a thesis statement and then a statement of purpose), they know that as they write, their ideas might shift or that they'll write something that doesn't quite do what they want it to.

TIP: FINDING WORDS WITH WHICH TO START

If you have prepared your thesis statement and statement of purpose, you should have a good idea of what your paper needs to include...but if you are stuck about how to start your writing, look at the suggestions for different kinds of introductions in Part 7.

➔ See pages 294–295.

Pick any of the kinds of introductions that catches your fancy; the point now is to get started writing; you can always change an introduction later if the work of the draft or feedback suggests a more appropriate introduction.

ARE YOU READY TO WRITE A FULL ROUGH DRAFT?

You are not ready to write a full rough draft until you

- have a thesis statement and have gathered good evidence in support of the reasons for your thesis's claim.

- have a statement of purpose that helps you understand how to shape your thesis for your particular readers.

PREPARING TO WRITE A DRAFT

- Review any notes you have taken from your sources.

- Keep your sources (or copies of your sources) nearby so that you can check that you are summarizing, paraphrasing, or quoting properly.

- Set up your writing area so that you will have few distractions.

- Arrange your time so that you have at least an hour, but preferably two or three hours, to write at any one sitting.

- Do not expect to complete a five- to seven-page draft in one sitting. Plan for at least two or three different times that you will write.

ARRANGING THE PARTS OF A DRAFT

See pages 202–203 in Part 5, Organizing and Shaping Texts, for suggestions on how to use your thesis statement to arrange the parts of your draft.

WHILE WRITING

- Don't stop the flow of your ideas by fixating on grammar or spelling; instead, focus on writing your argument. Because this is a draft, you will have time later to revise and edit.

  → If English is not your home language, however, see the advice on page 241 for working on drafts.

- If you get stuck in your writing, you have at least three options:

  One, get up and walk away; come back to the writing later, after you've had a chance to rest, go for a walk, chat with some friends, or otherwise refresh your mind.

  Two, start rereading your writing from the beginning to see if this sparks your thinking.

  Three, review your thesis statement and statement of purpose to see if you have covered all that you know you need to cover; if you've missed anything, start writing about it.

- If you summarize, paraphrase, or quote (→ see pages 314–315) any source, be sure to include the expected in-text citation in the format you are using. Also be sure to put any such sources into a running bibliography list at the end of your draft.

  → For **MLA style**, see pages 360–405.
  → For **APA style**, see pages 426–451.
  → For **CSE style**, see pages 453–457.
  → For **CMS style**, see pages 458–462.

STARTING TO WRITE FOR AN AUDIENCE
A ROUGH DRAFT

Riley has produced a very rough draft for an assignment that asks for a five- to seven-page paper. She is using this draft just to get her ideas onto paper, to see how they look, and to get a sense of how her ideas will work for her readers.

We've indicated some of her initial choices, as well as places she is not yet sure of her choices—and we've indicated where in this book she can look for further assistance.

As you read Riley's draft, look for how she starts to develop her argument. It's not as clear as it could be in this draft, but it is starting to take shape. Also look for how she's addressing the concerns of her readers, as she came to understand them through developing a statement of purpose.

→ Riley's polished revision of this draft is on pages 406–418.

Title

After reading the draft, return here: Do you think Riley's title accurately prepares a reader for what is to come?

Opening quotation

Will this quotation encourage readers to care for the women who receive microloans, as Riley hopes?

Introduction

Does this introductory paragraph help readers understand clearly and easily what is to follow?

→ Pages 294–295 give suggestions for introductions that meet academic expectations.

Transitions

Do you think readers will understand why Riley moves from her introductory paragraph to this sentence?

→ See pages 296–297 for information on how to write transitions that help readers follow your arguments.

A long quotation

Riley has correctly followed the standard punctuation format for quotations that take more than five lines.

→ See pages 318–319 to learn how to punctuate long quotations.

But this quotation will seem too long to practiced readers of academic texts. Riley should paraphrase and summarize at least some of this passage.

→ See pages 322–325 for information on paraphrasing and summarizing.

ROUGH DRAFT

Money Makes the World Go Round

Says Nyamba Konate, a USAID microloan beneficiary, "I can now ensure that my children go to school, and I can better support my husband by buying food and stocking it to get us through the difficult rainy season." ("Microloans and Literacy")

A Google search with "microloan" gets over 2,000,000 hits, many to organizations that offer very small loans to people who otherwise would not qualify for traditional bank loans. The websites tell stories of the changes microloans can make in the lives of poor women all over the world. But anyone who thinks microloans are always good has obviously not read enough.

Grameen Bank was the first to give microcredit.

The inspiration for Grameen Bank came to Dr. Yunus during a trip to the village of Jobra in Bangladesh during the devastating famine of 1974. He met a woman who was struggling to make ends meet as a weaver of bamboo stools. She needed to borrow to buy materials, but because she was poor and had no assets, conventional banks shunned her, and she had to turn instead to local moneylenders whose extortionate rates of interest consumed nearly all her profits.

Dr. Yunus, then a professor of rural economics at Chittagong University, gave the woman and several of her neighbors loans totalling $27 from his own pocket. To his surprise, the borrowers paid him back in full and on time. So he started traveling from village to village, offering more tiny loans and cutting out the middlemen. Dr. Yunus was determined to prove that lending to the poor was not an "impossible proposition," as he put it.

When he later formalized the loan-making arrangement as the Grameen Bank in 1983, the bank adopted its signature innovation: making borrowers take out loans in groups of five, with each borrower guaranteeing the others' debts. Thus, in place of the hold banks have on wealthier borrowers who do not pay their debts—

1

Explaining terms

Do you think Riley can count on her readers knowing what FINCA is? If you are ever in doubt whether readers will understand a term you are using, explain it.

More long quotations

Academic readers will often accept one or two quotations of this length, but you can see that Riley's paper is full of them: It looks as though her writing simply strings together the words of others. Riley needs to shorten her quotations, or to paraphrase and summarize them, to show readers that she has really thought through and made her own sense of these ideas.

→ See pages 322–325 for information on paraphrasing and summarizing.

Building ethos by using the authority of others

Riley is quoting someone named Susy Cheston here; the quotation suggests that Susy Cheston knows quite a bit about women and microloans—but why should readers trust her? If Riley explains who Susy Cheston is by including Cheston's title or explaining why Cheston has authority to speak on this topic, Riley's readers are more likely to accept the authority of this quotation and so to accept that Riley has authority, too.

→ Page 320 includes information about how to give a title to or explain the authority of someone you are quoting.

Helping readers check sources

To check a source, readers usually need the name of the person(s) responsible for the words (so that they can find the source in the bibliography list at the end of the paper) and a page number. Because the name of the person who wrote these words preceded this quotation, Riley needs only to give a page number here.

→ See pages 351–359 for how to show the sources of your quotations and evidence.

– Growth in local economies through local increases in women's spending; and

– An expanded view in the larger society of social and economic norms that relate to women.

FINCA says that it lends primarily to women because

Seventy percent of the world's poor are women, largely because of their limited access to education or to productive resources like land and credit. Another worldwide trend is an increase in woman-headed households, in which a mother provides the sole support for her children. Most victims of severe poverty are children. According to UNICEF, at least half of the 12 million children aged five or younger who die each year, die from malnutrition associated with severe poverty. The most direct way to improve childrens' survival and welfare is to strengthen their own mothers' ability to take care of them. ("Frequently Asked Questions")

Microloans are supposed to help women be confident taking care of their own money and taking part in their communities. They are expected to use any money they earn from their loans for their families. Because the families are supposed to improve, their communities are supposed to improve, too.

Research supports this, some. Susy Cheston says that:

According to research by microfinance impact assessment specialist Suzy Salib-Bauer on Sinapi Aba Trust, an Opportunity International microfinance institution (MFI) in Ghana, 42 percent of mature clients (those in the program two years or more) had an improvement in their poverty level—either moving from "very poor" to "poor" or from "poor" to "non-poor" status, as measured by a standard household asset and income index. ASHI, an MFI in the Philippines that exclusively targets poor women, found that 77 percent of incoming clients were classified as "very poor"; after two years in the program, only 13 percent of mature clients were still "very poor." (23)

Another writer describes a program that

had an important positive impact on a large number of women members. Over one third of the sample had been able to begin market

3

Logos: helping readers with summaries and transitions

Riley helps readers by ending this paragraph with a summary of the main point of her paragraph.

→ Pages 296–297 have suggestions for helping readers stay oriented in your writing.

Conclusions: a place for pathos

Riley has mostly used this last paragraph to summarize and restate her main argument, using some pathos. Academic readers expect this in essays. But what they don't expect in a conclusion is new information, such as Riley's comment about MacIsaac's report. (Riley has also not included MacIsaac in the Works Cited list.)

→ Pages 292–293 contain ideas for shaping conclusions to academic writing.

Making a works cited list

For a rough draft, it is alright to start a Works Cited listing on the same page as the rest of the paper. For a final draft, however, the Works Cited listing should start on its own page in MLA format.

→ See pages 360–405 for help in constructing a Works Cited list in the MLA format.

Enough sources?

There are many places in Riley's paper where she has made assertions without offering any evidence—so she should probably have more sources than she shows here. (There are two more sources listed on the next page.)

work with a loan, and the loans had enabled women to keep marginal businesses afloat in family crises without recourse to moneylenders. Access to loans was also estimated to have led to increased earnings for a quarter of all the sampled women, often through enabling them to switch jobs and trades to more lucrative ones. Some had diversified their activities, adding a second line of work or a secondary job. For other women the loan kept them out of further debilitating debt through diversion of the loan in times of major stress events such as illness, flood, death or desertion of husband and enabling them to carry out their ritual responsibilities necessary to maintaining social status. (Mayoux 39)

So no one is wrong to think that microloans can have positive effects in the lives of women.

Microloans have helped some women. But anyone who believes microloans will cure the world is way off. MacIsaac has written a report that shows how microloan programs ought to work. If we really honestly do want to end poverty, we must help women be in big business. We must help them make their own decisions. We must give them what will help them deal with the family and community stuff that stands in the way of them getting ahead.

Works Cited

Cheston, Susy. "Women and Microfinance: Opening Markets and Minds." *Economic Perspectives: An Electronic Journal of the U.S. Department of State* 9.1 (2004): n. pag. Web. 21 Mar. 2009.

"Frequently Asked Questions." *FINCA*. FINCA International, n. d. Web. 22 Mar. 2009.

Giridharadas, Anand, and Keith Bradsher. "Microloan Pioneer and His Bank Win Nobel Peace Prize." *New York Times*. New York Times, 13 Oct. 2006. Web. 20 Mar. 2009.

4

Enough different kinds of sources?

Some readers will note that these sources are all websites, and will not approve—even though the websites are of different kinds: a journal article published by the U.S. Department of State, a website for a respected nonprofit organization, an article from the *New York Times*, and a United Nations report. You need to judge whether your audience will accept only webpages as sources. If an assignment does not have a clear policy about using only webpages, ask.

RECEIVING FEEDBACK TO DRAFTS

To the right is feedback Riley received from her teacher.

These comments helpfully summarize the reader's understanding of Riley's argument; now Riley can understand whether readers are hearing what she hopes they will hear.

Receiving such feedback can sometimes be hard if you've put a lot of effort into writing: You might not want to hear that you have more work to do. But it's important to know how to receive feedback, because it is what helps you strengthen your writing so that it communicates what you want.

Often it is a good idea to read feedback as soon as you get it but then to put it aside for a day or two. Read it again with a little distance, and you'll be in a better position to understand it.

Feedback is what most helps you move your words from writing-to-learn to writing-to-communicate, as we discussed on pages 18–19.

When you receive feedback, keep in mind that:

- The feedback of others is what you need to become a stronger writer. Only by hearing how others respond do you learn how words communicate what they do.

- If readers do not understand your argument, or believe it to be something other than you intended, don't blame the readers. If readers miss or misinterpret your argument, ask them why they take the understanding they do from your words. If you ask readers to go through your writing sentence by sentence, explaining out loud what they understand, you will learn the particular effects your words have—and so you will learn how to revise your words so that they do what you hope.

→ See Riley's revised paper on pages 406–418.

Mayoux, Linda. "From Vicious to Virtuous Circles? Gender and
    Micro-Enterprise Development." *United Nations Research Institute
    for Social Development*. United Nations Research Institute for Social
    Development, 1 May 1995. Web. 22 Mar. 2009.
"Microloans and Literacy Are Contributing to Food Security in Poor Upper
    Guinea." *USAID*. US Agency for International Development, 2005. Web.
    23 Mar. 2009.

5

Riley—

This is a fine start: I can see you are building an
argument that, even though many people believe
microloans always have positive results and that they
can make big changes in the world, microloans won't
solve poverty and don't necessarily help women.(It's
important that you acknowledge that there are good
results for microloans and don't just make them sound
all bad.)

I sometimes get a little lost in that argument, though.

Most importantly, I wonder about the order of your
paragraphs. After your introduction, you give a little
history of microloans, then describe how they are bad,
and then describe how they are good. Why do you talk
about the bad before the good?

Also, I often have trouble understanding why you move
from paragraph to paragraph; I think you could work on
providing transitions for readers.

I look forward to seeing your revisions of this. You
should take confidence from this draft so that, as you
revise, you focus on the matters I've suggested above
but also that you don't worry about telling readers
exactly what you are doing with this argument.

Please come talk if you have any questions.

Thanks! Professor Maathai

DEVELOPING A REVISION PLAN

→ See Riley's revised paper on pages
  406–418.

After you receive feedback to a draft, make time to develop a revision plan for yourself. A revision plan is informal, just for you.

To the right, Riley's plan lays out how she understands the feedback she received and how she plans to respond.

Help for revising is offered in the next parts of this book:

→ For help with arranging the parts of writing, see Part 5, pages 187–236.

→ For help working with sources, see Part 8, pages 307–462.

→ For help with engaging readers more with your writing, see Part 7, pages 265–306.

→ For help with introductions, see pages 294–295.

→ For help with tone of voice, see pages 538–539.

→ For help with transitions, see pages 296–297.

REVISING, NOT EDITING

Notice that in her revision plan Riley doesn't mention anything about spelling or grammar: That's because revising is about focusing on your argument and how well readers understand those arguments.

When you revise, you need to be open to making large changes in your writing. You may have to throw out paragraphs, rearrange them, or add new ones as your writing helps you determine just what it is you want readers to take from your words.

Given Professor Maathai's feedback, I don't think I really got across the main point of my thesis statement, that microloan programs have their best chances of working when the women who receive the loans get classes in economics and business and have lots of time to talk with other women about their experiences and dealing with problems. I'm not sure I'm going to have enough space to make that argument, though. Maybe I need to revise my thesis, to argue just that people shouldn't expect microloans to solve poverty and liberate women because of all the problems with them; I could just suggest, at the end, about the classes and all that.

Given other feedback from people in class, I also need to

- Experiment with different arrangements of the parts of my paper, to see which most help people understand that microloans don't do what most people seem to think they will.
- Have more sources to support my claims about microloans.
- Figure out, still, how to get readers to care more: I still don't think I've got enough examples or am presenting stuff in ways that suck people in.
- Work out, like above, how to make my introduction more compelling.
- Experiment with my tone of voice, so that it's not so choppy and short.
- Work on the transitions between my paragraphs.

WRITING FOR DIFFERENT KINDS OF AUDIENCES

WRITING FOR ACADEMIC AUDIENCES

Over time, academic audiences have come to expect the most polished academic writing—as it appears in journals—to have the following nine features:

1 ACADEMIC WRITING IS ABOUT BUILDING KNOWLEDGE.

Academic audiences expect that you approach writing seriously because through writing you add to our understandings of the world and each other. This means that you have to take existing arguments seriously, research and gather evidence methodically and honestly, and make only the arguments that you can support with the evidence you have found.

2 ACADEMIC WRITING IS SERIOUS AND FORMAL.

Academic writers strive for a thoughtful tone of voice, and rarely tell jokes or use emotional language or colloquialisms (such as *no-brainer* or *oh, snap!*). In some disciplines, writers will use *I* and will use their own experiences as evidence or examples; reading examples of writing in a discipline will help you learn the particulars of the discipline. (For help with writing assignments in classes in disciplines that are new to you, ask your teacher.)

→ See pages 538–539 for more on creating a serious tone.

3 ACADEMIC WRITING GETS TO AND STAYS ON THE POINT.

An introduction moves quickly to stating what the paper is about. The writer ought to be able to explain how each and every sentence helps move a reader to the conclusion. There shouldn't be digressions or stories.

→ See pages 294–295 on writing introductions to academic papers.

→ See pages 280–281 on being explicit in your writing.

4 ACADEMIC WRITING IS EXPLICIT.

Academic writers say directly what their writing is about. In fiction and creative nonfiction, writers often use figurative language to pull readers in and suggest an overall point without ever stating the point; academic writing doesn't do this.

→ See pages 273–274 for more on the characteristics of explicit writing.

5 ACADEMIC WRITING ALWAYS HAS AN ELEMENT OF DOUBT.

Academic writers accept that there are very few thoughts and ideas that apply to everyone, everywhere, at all times. Instead, academic writers always consider a range of reasons and opinions.

To this end, academic writers often use phrases like *These facts suggest…* or *Given the available evidence, it would seem that….*

6 ACADEMIC WRITING IS NOT CONVERSATIONAL.

Academic writing usually uses longer words and sentences, more vocabulary, and more complex grammar than spoken language. Some of the more complex grammatical forms that academic writing uses are

→ dependent clauses, described on pages 483–485.

→ complex, compound, and complex-compound sentences, described on pages 480–489.

7 ACADEMIC WRITING TRIES TO BE OBJECTIVE AND UNBIASED.

The point of view of academic writing is rarely personal, rarely focused on the writer. Instead, the emphasis is on the argument being made and on ideas that benefit as many people as possible.

8 ACADEMIC WRITERS ARE RESPONSIBLE FOR THEIR ARGUMENTS AND TO OTHER WRITERS.

Academic writers can't just say anything; instead, they must take responsiblity for any claims they make by giving supporting evidence and by helping readers check that evidence. In addition, they are responsible for showing when the evidence they offer comes from the work or words of others.

→ Part 8 of this book is all about using the words and work of others; see pages 307–462.

9 ACADEMIC WRITING LOOKS SERIOUS.

→ See the section on Typography in Part 7, Style in Visual Texts, to see models for formatting your pages.

WRITING FOR WORKPLACE AUDIENCES

When you write for workplace audiences, keep the following five considerations in mind:

1 THE PLACES IN WHICH WE WORK DEVELOP THEIR OWN CULTURES.

Communities develop shared habits and expectations, and workplaces are no exception. Learning to write well professionally means learning the habits and expectations of a workplace: Is the workplace formal or informal, particularly focused on getting things done quickly or on group discussions aimed at consensus?

2 WRITING IN WORKPLACES NEEDS TO FIT THE CULTURE OF THE WORKPLACE.

All our earlier advice about audiences applies to workplace writing, but writing in workplaces is tied to how people in the organization solve problems, attend meetings, organize projects, manage tasks, evaluate documents and performance, use computer technologies, give presentations, run training sessions, and so on.

Connected to these activities is a range of specialized forms of communication with which you need to become familiar; each has general characteristics that you can recognize across various places of work and that also become adapted to specific workplaces. For example, workplace audiences all know the general form of a memo, but they also know the specific ways memos are written—and read—in their particular workplace.

3 BECAUSE WORKPLACES ARE ABOUT GETTING WORK DONE, PEOPLE AT WORK EXPECT WRITING TO BE EFFICIENT AND TO THE POINT.

This doesn't mean the writing is mechanical—it still needs to address its human audiences—but it needs to be very focused.

→ See pages 273–274 for suggestions on how to shape writing that is focused, quick, and to the point.

4 OFTEN IN WORKPLACES YOU WILL BE WRITING FOR TWO (OR MORE) AUDIENCES.

Earlier in this part we talked about complex audiences and about how sometimes you have a foreground and a background audience. In workplaces, where you may be writing a brochure or an instruction set to be read by potential consumers, it can be useful to keep these two audiences in mind. The foreground readers are the customers or clients; the background audience is those in the business or organization who will be looking at what you produce and making comments or suggestions along the way.

5 LARGER WORKPLACES CAN HAVE STYLE GUIDES YOU NEED TO FOLLOW WHEN YOU ARE WRITING FOR CLIENTS OR CUSTOMERS.

Companies have such style guides to be sure all the documents they produce are consistent and represent the company professionally. Style guides can include guidelines for using the company's logo, specific phrases to use in writing (for example, a hardware company could specify that writers tell customers to *click a button* rather than to *click on a button*), and formats for different kinds of documents. If you are not given a style guide, be sure to ask if one exists.

HINTS & TIPS FOR CONNECTING WITH READERS

ASK FOR FOCUSED FEEDBACK TO YOUR WRITING

Because getting feedback from readers is the main way to strengthen your writing, getting useful feedback is crucial. But giving good feedback is a learned skill, and many readers won't automatically know how to give you useful feedback.

When you are ready for feedback, tell readers what you need: For example, ask them to focus on your argument and to try to tell you what your thesis statement is. Or ask them to read the argument to see if you offer enough evidence, or if your transitions help them understand why you move from one paragraph to the next.

Choose only one or two areas for them to focus on in their reading.

BE SURE YOU UNDERSTAND FEEDBACK

If you hear something you don't understand from a reader, ask for clarification. If you don't understand feedback, it can't help you.

GET FEEDBACK FROM YOURSELF

Put your writing aside for at least several hours to get some distance from it, and then reread it. Reread it once to see if your thesis seems sufficiently developed, read it again to check your transitions, and so on.

You need to learn to be your own audience, because the paper you turn in is yours. You have the final responsibility for it.

PART 5
ORGANIZING AND SHAPING TEXTS

CONTENTS

WHERE ARE WE IN THE PROCESS FOR COMPOSING?

Understanding your project

Getting started

Asking questions

Shaping your project for others
Choosing a genre
Choosing an overall organization
Arranging paragraphs

Drafting a paper

Getting feedback

Revising

Polishing

WHAT IS ORGANIZATION?

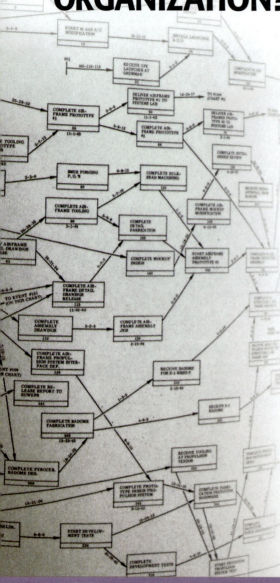

Producing a text is like building a building: You make choices to shape your audience's experience similarly to how people experience buildings.

Think of a time you visited a new acquaintance for the first time. You went to the person's apartment or house, and from the street you got a sense of the building's age. Seeing the overall style of the building—Victorian, modern, suburban ranch, or fifties apartment block—you sensed what you would see inside. Once inside, you got a sense of the overall organization of the rooms—of the layout and floorplan—which indicated how you could move through the rooms. Then there were the individual rooms with their furnishings, which told you about how comfortable it was to live in this place and what people did there. There was also the color of the walls, and what was on the walls, and what was on the shelves or tables….

As you moved from the outside to the inside, you moved from seeing large structures to seeing smaller ones, from big shapes to small objects.

Moving through a text is the same: You first see the whole, which sets up expectations about the smaller parts. As you read, listen, or look, you see the *floorplan*—the overall structure; and then you notice the parts of the *floorplan*—the paragraphs or major divisions. Finally, you notice the details, such as tone of voice, sentence length, word choice, and so on.

In this part of the book, we focus on the major elements, the overall structure and paragraphs.

BUILDING

WHOLE TEXT

POSTER

FLOORPLAN

CONCEPTUAL FRAMEWORK

CONCEPTUAL FRAMEWORK

ROOMS

PARAGRAPHS

MAJOR ELEMENTS

FURNISHINGS

SENTENCES & WORDS

DETAILED ELEMENTS

ORGANIZATION IS ABOUT HOW YOU WORK AT EACH OF THESE LEVELS

At each level, you have many choices about how to place the relevant elements in relation to each other in order to achieve your purpose, for your audience, given your context.

In this part, we focus on the major details, the framework and paragraphs.

→ In Part 7, we focus on the details.

ORGANIZATION AND MEDIUM

When you compose, your **medium** is the physical material you use to shape your composition.

Your medium can be sound waves if you are composing a podcast, or it can be paper or the electrons that light up on a digital screen if you are composing an essay. In each case, the particular material of the medium offers possibilities and limitations for what you can do, and shapes how audiences in our time and places generally think about each medium.

The chart to the right describes some of these possibilities as they relate to how audiences *generally* think about these media. You can use this chart to help you choose a medium for a project, keeping in mind that you will have to consider the particulars of the type of text you are producing.

For example, consider whether you can use color, photographs, or illustrations, or through what sort of device your audience will encounter the text you are making, and so on.

■ ■ ■

Medium might not seem like part of organization, but if you think of organization as how composers shape a text so that an audience moves through it in particular ways (as we described on pages 186–187), then an audience's first response to a new text is to encounter the material of the text in their hands, before their eyes, or in their ears.

AUDIENCE EXPECTATIONS & ASSOCIATIONS

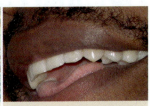

	PAPER	DIGITAL SCREENS	SOUND
Types of texts	books, posters, pamphlets, brochures, graphic novels, newspapers, manuals	Personal blogs, corporate websites, video and music sharing sites, e-mail, instant messaging	Conversations, interviews, speeches, podcasts, telephone conversations, music recordings
Scale	Most paper communications are designed for handheld use, by one person; some are designed for walls—to attract individuals out of a group.	Digital screens are usually designed for one viewer at a time, to be seen on a desk-size or handheld monitor.	Sound can be produced for many people to hear at once (as with speeches), a few people, or one person at a time.
Formality	Because of their relative permanence, print texts can seem formal and distant—although the addition of photographs, color, and illustrations can change this.	Because they can be easily changed, online texts generally have less formality than print texts. E-mail and instant messaging are very informal, like quick conversations.	When sound is the voices of others, it can seem informal because it can seem so close and direct.
Organization	Because readers can hold print texts in their hands, they can see the whole object at once and get a sense of its size and overall organization. The binding of print texts encourages linear organizations, with obvious beginnings and endings supported by section, page, and chapter numbering.	Readers rarely know if they have seen a whole digital text because the parts are visible only when they are on-screen: There is no physical whole. In addition, the parts of a print text can be designed to be accessible in many different orders; writers have to supply visual organization hints. Screen sizes also encourage shorter paragraphs than in print.	In print and online texts, audiences can look back to check what they don't remember. Because speaking does not allow this, speakers explicitly announce the organization of presentations and use repetition to help their listeners remember the main points.

ORGANIZATION, AUDIENCE, AND GENRE

SECTION ... DRIVER LICENSE/IDENTIFICATION CARD CUSTOMER

1. Has your license, ID card or operating privilege ever been revoked, suspended, cancelled, disqualified or denied? YES NO
   If yes, give date and place

2. Have you been convicted of operating while intoxicated OUTSIDE of Wisconsin?
   If yes, give date and place

3. Do you hold a valid driver's license/identification card FROM ANOTHER STATE/COUNTRY?
   If yes, list

...ars of licensed driving experience in the U.S. and ...nada?

N D - DRIVER LICENSE CUSTOMERS UNDER AGE 18 ONLY

e Certification: I certify that in the past 6 months, I have not ...ed for a moving violation that has or may result in a conviction ...d that falsifying this statement will result in the cancellation of ...ary license. Applicant Signature - Required

...ication: I certify under s.343.14(5) Wis. Stats., that this ...rolled in approved behind-the-wheel training which begins ... days from date signed.

...st Results (line out if not used)
...e Test
☐ Fail
...ficial/Instructor Signature ☐ Pass

Highway Sign Test
☐ Fail
Date Signed

Sponsor Certification ... and verify that ... requirements under ... application, has ... of which were at hig...
Minor Name - Print

Sponsor Name - Print

Sponsor Wisconsin DL...

Sponsor Signature (Mu...
X
State of Wisconsin Count...

Notary Public or DOT Auth...
X
Do NOT Use Notary Seal

...ERCIAL DRIVER LICENSE CUSTOMERS ONLY

...omplete form MV3735.
...s endorsement, complete form MV3740.

...ou had a loss of conscious- ...sed by a neurological ...ure disorder? YES NO
☐ ☐

...taken insulin to control a ☐ ☐

...aken oral medication to ☐ ☐

...f hearing) ☐ ☐

...cense in the last 10 ...ther than Wisconsin? ☐ ☐

6. In the past 5 years, have you ... offense against public mora... state? If yes, give date and p...

7. Is the vehicle you will be operat...brakes?

8. Do you meet all the driver qualifi...
   49 CFR 391 to operate a comme...
   your valid Federal Medical Certi...
   not, see publication BDS216.

9. Is the vehicle in which you will take ...
   driver license skill test representa...
   you will operate or intend to...

Imagine you are a clerk in a driver's license office, and there is no application form. Instead, each time someone needs a license, you say, *Please put the necessary information on a piece of paper.* How many different sizes and shapes of paper would you receive, with how many different arrangements of information? How messy would it be to try to work with all those different pieces of paper?

Think then of how the driver's license application form saves time and energy for both applicants and clerks.

Genres are categories of text that work like the application form: We say that something is a genre when it has a form that is repeated. Think of poetry, movies, journal articles, research papers, or posters. When your sister tells you she is going to write a poem, you don't picture a billboard; you probably picture a short piece of writing that has uneven lines and creative punctuation.

Genres save us time and effort because they help both composers and audiences know what to do and what to expect.

When you encounter a new rhetorical situation, you need to ask what genres your audience might expect, and how tightly you need to stay within the confines of the genre if you are to achieve your purposes.

As the chart to the right suggests, some genres have tighter and more detailed audience expectations than others, but exploring the wiggle room of genres allows you to create new ways for your text to unfold for its audiences.

WHAT IS THE WIGGLE ROOM IN VARIOUS GENRES?

SCIENTIFIC JOURNAL ARTICLES	CLASSROOM RESEARCH PAPERS	MOVIES	VIDEO GAMES
Conceptual framework			
For publication in most scientific disciplines, there is a ready-made framework of required sections.	Many conceptual frameworks for research papers fit classroom contexts.	Hollywood movies tend to have a "traditional" narrative structure, but independent films are often expected to have experimental forms.	Currently, video games tend to fall into the frameworks of action, simulation, role-playing, sports, and strategy/puzzle games.
NO WIGGLE ROOM	SOME WIGGLE ROOM	SOME WIGGLE ROOM	SOME WIGGLE ROOM
Major parts			
Paragraphs are expected to be direct and to the point, but can have many different structures. Charts, tables, and graphs are common.	Readers expect classroom research papers to have paragraphs. Charts, tables, and graphs are acceptable, if appropriate.	Scenes can have different lengths—but usually there *are* scenes. The screen can be divided into parts.	Depending on the framework, a particular video game can have a number of levels, a series of puzzles, one single world, a range of characters, a countdown, and so on.
SOME WIGGLE ROOM	SOME WIGGLE ROOM	SOME WIGGLE ROOM	SOME WIGGLE ROOM
Smaller parts			
The tone of voice is objective and passive.	As long as they are harmonious with the overall purpose, style experimentations are possible.	Hollywood movies tend to seek "realistic"-looking settings, lighting, and sound, but makers of films with different purposes can experiment.	Depending on the framework and major parts, a game can look 2- or 3-dimensional, be cartoonish or realistic, employ a range of sounds, or require a range of interactions.
NO WIGGLE ROOM	LOTS OF WIGGLE ROOM	SOME WIGGLE ROOM	LOTS OF WIGGLE ROOM

→ The organizations of smaller parts of texts—such as word choice, sentence structures, color, and so on—are addressed in Part 7, on styling your writing.

ORGANIZATION, AUDIENCE, AND GENRE
ONLINE GENRES

Although all genres are always in some flux because purposes, contexts, and audiences shift, online genres are unstable these days as the technologies for online communication change and new communication possibilities appear. You do need to pay attention to the genre expectations of people who use online communications frequently, but how you shape online communications depends less on genre than on the precise particulars of your purpose, audience, and context.

For example, friends and family expect your e-mails to be chatty and descriptive. To friends and family you can send e-mails that seem to have no purpose other than to say *Hello!* and stay in touch. In school and workplaces, however, expectations are different, and more formal arrangements at every level are expected. Only when you get to know a professor or fellow employee well can you write with any informality.

Blogs can be highly personal journals or sites for connecting formally with others interested in particular topics.

On the following pages, the guidelines we offer for online texts are for more formal situations.

E-MAIL

In formal contexts, e-mails will appear professional to their recipients if you:

- **Have a neutral-sounding e-mail address.** squirrlygrrrl@hotmail.com is fine for friends—but for formal communications, consider getting an e-mail account that uses your initials and last name. If your company or school gives you an e-mail address, use that for communicating with professors, staff, employers, and colleagues.

- **Write a subject that is descriptive but short and in a professional tone.** "Wanna meet?" is descriptive and short—but sounds like it's party time. For formal situations, "Budget meeting Tuesday 3pm?" is more appropriate.

- **Start with a salutation.** Until you have a relaxed relationship with others, the expected way for showing respect is to start a message with a formal salutation such as "Dear Professor:" or "Dear Dr. Murthy:" or "Dear Mo Folk:" (if you do not know someone's gender or title, write out the person's first and last names). Notice also that the expected punctuation following the salutation is a colon. When others end messages to you with their first names, then you can write to them using their first names. Otherwise, in any follow-up messages, address others the way they signed their e-mails.

- **State your purpose following the salutation.** Put two returns after the salutation, and then state your purpose.

- **Write the e-mail in short paragraphs separated by two returns.** Readers can rarely see whole messages at once, and e-mail software is rarely designed to support easy reading. Others can read more easily if they can see your paragraphs—so arrange your paragraphs to be short and easy to discern visually.

- **Avoid smiley faces.** They are appropriate only in informal e-mail.

- **Sign your message.** Even though your name is in the header, it is still considered polite to type your full name at the message end—until you know the person to whom you are writing well.

- **Keep in mind how easy it is for others to forward your messages.** If you do not want to risk the world knowing something, do not put it in an e-mail.

ORGANIZATION, AUDIENCE, AND GENRE
POPULAR GENRES

Popular genres does not mean genres everyone likes; instead, popular genres are those that can be produced **by** almost anyone or that are produced *for* broad general audiences—or both.

We give examples of three quite different popular genres here. As you look at the three, consider how the writers try to achieve their purposes by meeting audience expectations: How do they organize the parts of their texts to engage readers and make happen what they desire?

TIP: GOING ONLINE

Each of the genres we present here can be produced in print or online. Here are some differences for composers to consider when using one or the other medium:

- Paragraphs and sentences are usually shorter online than in print. Generally, readers gain a stronger sense of a text's organization when they can see the text's divisions; because screen sizes are usually smaller than paper, you can help readers see a text's organization online by using smaller paragraphs.

- For the same reasons, separating paragraphs online by two returns rather than with an indent helps readers read more easily.

- Because it requires more time and effort, a letter printed on paper and sent through the mail—rather than an e-mail—will almost always show that the writer is more serious. Such letters often therefore seem more authoritative and worthy of respect.

> **To the Editor:**
>
> In the last five and a half weeks, five schools in the United States and Canada have suffered the invasion of gunmen: Aug. 24, Essex, Vt.; Sept. 13, Montreal; Sept. 27, Bailey, Colo; Sept. 29, Cazenovia, Wis. And now, Oct. 2, Nickel Mines, Pa.
>
> In four of these five incidents, the gunman targeted girls and women.
>
> At what point do a country and its news media note this lethally combustible cocktail of gender and guns?
>
> Men and boys with guns are stalking and hunting women and girls in schools repeatedly. Until we see "the gun problem" as equally a problem of violence against women, nothing will change, and I fear that the mourning and shock will continue.
>
> Daniel Moshenberg
> Washington, Oct. 3, 2006
> *The writer is director of the Women's Studies Program at George Washington University.*

LETTERS TO THE EDITOR

After any event—horrible events like the shootings referenced in the letter above but also happier events like fund-raising picnics for local fire departments—people want to be able to share their opinions with others. They want to join in the considerations about how we should think about what happened and how we should respond.

Letters to the editor are one existing genre of writing that allows this to happen. People who send letters to the editor reach the readers of the periodical to which the letters were sent, and so extend the reach of their ideas. These letters may seem small, but if they spark responses in readers, then their ideas start to ripple out and affect others.

Whether letters to the editor are published in print or online, audiences have similar expectations about them.

Letters to the editor are

- Short and to the point.
- Focused on one topic.
- About an issue of interest to the periodical's readers. In magazines, letters to the editor are always in response to earlier published articles; in local newspapers, they can be about current or local events.
- Begun with a statement of the issue before going on to the writer's position.
- Documents in which ethos is crucial. Unlike the example letter above, rarely in a letter to the editor are a writer's credentials given. Writers have to demonstrate why they should be heard, through giving their own credentials but also through choosing a fitting tone of voice, staying focused, and using examples and evidence.

ORGANIZATION, AUDIENCE, AND GENRE

ACADEMIC GENRES IN THE DISCIPLINES

Because academic work in the United States is about careful thought and analysis for creating new knowledge, certain features are valued in almost all academic writing in this country:

• Full definition of terms.

• Logical development of ideas.

• Careful and full acknowledgment of any use of the ideas of others.

Over time, different academic disciplines have developed their own conventions for how papers within the discipline are to be arranged. These various arrangements are meant to support the particular kind of analytic work performed in the discipline.

If you are asked to write papers in classes in the humanities, sciences, or social sciences, the information to the right and on the next four pages gives you a general idea of the arrangements to use. If an assignment does not specify the arrangements to use, ask your teacher what the expectations are.

WRITING IN THE HUMANITIES

Writing in the humanities can be creative, theoretic, or analytic. We focus on analytic writing, for you will be asked to produce such writing in literature, film, rhetoric, modern languages, art, philosophy, history, and gender studies classes.

When you write analytically, you focus on a text like a short story or film or on a topic as we described in Part 2. Whether you analyze a text or a topic, you analyze to understand *how* and *why* values and decisions come to be and their effects.

ANALYZING TEXTS

When you analyze a text, you can focus on one text, describing its parts and arguing how the parts create an overall effect. You might show how a poem's line lengths and soft vowel sounds evoke a reader's reflections.

You can also analyze a text by comparing it with other texts or by explaining how it (and perhaps other similar texts) embodies cultural values, events, and structures. You might compare contemporary graphic novels and short stories, to show how both use quick, pictorial description and argue that this echoes the timing of fast food or video edits.

ANALYZING TOPICS

When you analyze a topic, you do the work we described in Parts 2, 3, and 4 of this book. You look to texts—books, journals, films, interviews—to help you learn about the topic and, using what you have learned from those other texts as evidence, you develop an argument focused on some aspect of the values, ideas, or effects of the topic.

ORGANIZING ANALYTIC PAPERS

1 **A title.** Examples: "Counterfeit Motion: The Animated Films of Eadweard Muybridge" or "'To Protect and Serve': African American Female Literacies"

2 **An introduction.** In humanities papers, an introduction can begin with a relevant quotation or example to pique interest, but the introduction's purpose is to draw readers' attention to the question or problem being discussed and to make clear why the question or problem should matter to them.

3 **Body.** This contains the writer's analysis of the text or topic. Evidence drawn from texts supports the analysis: In the analysis of a text, the evidence is drawn from the text itself, through quotation; in the analysis of topics, evidence comes from a range of texts.

   → See pages 104–113 on the kinds of evidence used in humanities writing.

4 **A conclusion.** The conclusion summarizes the paper's argument while offering no new information.

5 **Works Cited list.** At the end of the paper, list any works by other writers that are cited in the paper. (→ See pages 351–420 to learn MLA style, most often used in the humanities.)

In addition, if the writer's purpose and the context of the writing make it appropriate, writing in the humanities can be expressive: Writers can use **I**, draw on their own personal experiences or those of others, and use narratives as evidence. Check with your teacher if you are considering doing any of this in a class assignment.

WRITING IN THE SCIENCES

Research reports by scientists and engineers usually follow a specific arrangement of parts and a specific style of writing. The arrangement directs readers' attention to how an experiment was performed; readers can then judge the results and perhaps replicate the experiment.

The arrangement that scientists and engineers have developed to support communications about experiments asks that any report have, in order:

1 **A title,** which describes the experiment. One example: *The Physiological Effects of Pallidal Deep Brain Stimulation in Dystonia.*

2 **An abstract,** which is a short and concise overview of the paper; abstracts allow readers to see quickly if a paper is relevant to their work.

3 **An introduction.** This states why the research was done, what was being tested, and the predicted results—the hypothesis. There might also be a review of earlier relevant research here.

4 **Methods.** Researchers describe the procedures they undertook to perform their experiments, including the materials and equipment used.

5 **Results.** Researchers describe what they learned from the experiment.

6 **Discussion.** Here, the researchers discuss their understanding of the results. Did the results support the hypothesis? Why—or why not?

7 **A conclusion.** In this section, the researchers describe possible implications of their experiment as well as possible further research.

8 **References list.** Any works by other researchers that are cited in the report—or any reports written at an earlier time by the authors—are listed at the end of the paper. (→ See pages 453–457 to learn CSE style, which is most often used in the sciences.)

In a scientific report, all the above sections are separated and are labeled by the names listed above.

In addition, scientific writing usually has the following features:

- Because experiments are supposed to be repeatable anywhere by anyone, the experiment is emphasized, not the experimenter—and so scientific writers rarely use the first person *I* or *we* in writing; instead, they often use passive voice.

  → See pages 298–299.

- Because scientific and engineering evidence is often quantifiable, writers use charts, graphs, and tables as evidence. Photographs of objects used in experiments are also used as evidence.

- Because science and engineering research is most often carried out in labs where many people work, or across labs, research reports often have multiple authors.

TIP: CLASS ASSIGNMENTS

If you are asked to write a report in a science or social sciences class, your teacher will probably expect you to include at least several of the parts described on these pages. If the organization or features are not described in the assignment, ask.

WRITING IN THE SOCIAL SCIENCES

As the term *social sciences* suggests, the disciplines that come under this name apply scientific methods to studying people as social groups and as individuals within social groups. The social sciences include anthropology, economics, education, geography, linguistics, political science, psychology, sociology, and speech communication. (At some schools, history and gender studies might be listed as social sciences, if those areas use primarily scientific approaches to support their research.)

In writing papers for the social sciences, the arrangements that have developed over time follow the overall pattern of science writing as on the opposite page, but within the steps are some differences:

1 **A title,** which describes the study being reported in the paper. One example: *What Determines Cartel Success?*

2 **An abstract** of 100–200 words that summarize the purpose of the study, its methods, and its results.

3 **An introduction.** This defines the problem that was studied, reviews previous writing on the problem, notes the gaps in the previous writing that the current study will address, and gives an overview of the methods used. Writers also tell readers why the research being described matters.

4 **Methods.** Evidence used in the social sciences is usually observational, because social scientists are making and testing claims about human behavior. The sorts of methods for gathering this evidence are surveys and questionnaires, observations, interviews, and fieldwork. (→ See pages 78–79.) In the methods section of the paper, the writer describes which of these methods was used, and the details of how the method was carried out (how many people were interviewed or surveyed, for example, and what questions were asked).

5 **Results,** a description of what can be learned from the research.

6 **Discussion.** The researchers argue how the results of the study do (or do not) help with the problem described in the introduction.

7 **A conclusion,** which summarizes the problem, the research carried out, and what was learned.

8 **References list.** Any works by other researchers that are cited in the writing are listed at the end of the paper.

→ See pages 421–452 to learn APA style, which is most often used in the social sciences.

If the social sciences paper is longer than about five pages, the above sections are labeled by the names listed.

Because the social sciences seek as much objectivity as possible, further features of social science writing echo what we have described for science writing:

• Use of passive voice.

• Use of charts, graphs, tables, and photographs as evidence.

• Multiple authors.

RESUMÉS

Resumés summarize the experiences and education that make you appropriate for a new job. Because a resumé (and cover letter; → see pages 210–211) is often how a potential employer first encounters an employee, it deserves time and attention. And because employers often receive hundreds of resumés, they look at them quickly. Therefore, a resumé needs to be:

- short, to the point, and easy to read.
- focused on the position for which it is being sent.
- accurate.

COMPOSING A RESUMÉ

- For entry-level positions, a resumé should be one page so that employers can scan it quickly.

- Use white or cream paper. Use good-quality paper, but don't use papers such as parchment or vellum unless they are appropriate for the position (graphic designer, for example).

- Use black ink.

- Use a typeface such as Times or Helvetica. (Times takes up less space and so fits more information on a page.)

- Use 11- or 12-point type.

- Use headings, bullets, and indents so that readers can see the parts quickly.

  → See pages 300–301 on formatting.

- Look at your first draft; for each line in the body of the resumé, ask yourself, *Does this help an employer see my suitability for this position?* If the answer is no, remove or replace the information.

- If possible, get feedback from someone who works in or supervises the sort of position for which you are applying: Do they find your resumé readable, appropriately formatted, and strong?

- Always have someone else proofread it for you. Because employers receive so many resumés, they are looking for reasons to exclude; don't give them such a simple one as a typo.

- Do not lie or pad your experiences.

THE FORMAT OF A RESUMÉ

Name

Center your name at the top. Do not use nicknames. Bold your name, and put it in a slightly larger size (14 or 16 points).

Contact information

Be sure your address will be current for several months; if you are still in school or planning to move, put a permanent address. Most companies will contact you by phone or e-mail, so include both. Be sure whoever answers your phone knows to answer professionally; have a professional answering machine or voice mail message. Your e-mail address should be your name or initials; hotdude7@hotmail.com does not suggest a reliable, focused employee. If it is appropriate to the position, include a Web or blog address—as long as they are professional in both presentation and content.

Objective

Fit this on one line only; if you are responding to an ad, use the job title as part of the objective.

Education

Don't include high school unless there is something about your high school education that is relevant to the position for which you are applying.

Employment

Put your most recent employment first. Put your title first, then the place of employment, then the duration of time you held the position.

List your main accomplishments and responsibilities underneath the job title. Use action verbs in the past tense for past positions; use present tense for ongoing positions. If you have an accomplishment an employer will value, include it (such as *Website visits increased by 125%* under *Employment*).

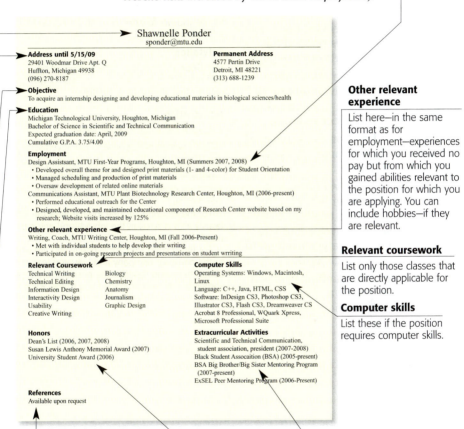

Shawnelle Ponder
sponder@mtu.edu

Address until 5/15/09
29401 Woodmar Drive Apt. Q
Huffton, Michigan 49938
(096) 270-8187

Permanent Address
4577 Pertin Drive
Detroit, MI 48221
(313) 688-1239

Objective
To acquire an internship designing and developing educational materials in biological sciences/health

Education
Michigan Technological University, Houghton, Michigan
Bachelor of Science in Scientific and Technical Communication
Expected graduation date: April, 2009
Cumulative G.P.A. 3.75/4.00

Employment
Design Assistsant, MTU First-Year Programs, Houghton, MI (Summers 2007, 2008)
• Developed overall theme for and designed print materials (1- and 4-color) for Student Orientation
• Managed scheduling and production of print materials
• Oversaw development of related online materials
Communications Assistant, MTU Plant Biotechnology Research Center, Houghton, MI (2006-present)
• Performed educational outreach for the Center
• Designed, developed, and maintained educational component of Research Center website based on my research; Website visits increased by 125%

Other relevant experience
Writing, Coach, MTU Writing Center, Houghton, MI (Fall 2006-Present)
• Met with individual students to help develop their writing
• Participated in on-going research projects and presentations on student wrriting

Relevant Coursework

		Computer Skills
Technical Writing	Biology	Operating Systems: Windows, Macintosh, Linux
Technical Editing	Chemistry	Language: C++, Java, HTML, CSS
Information Design	Anatomy	Software: InDesign CS3, Photoshop CS3,
Interactivity Design	Journalism	Illustrator CS3, Flash CS3, Dreamweaver CS
Usability	Graphic Design	Acrobat 8 Professional, WQuark Xpress,
Creative Writing		Microsoft Professional Suite

Honors
Dean's List (2006, 2007, 2008)
Susan Lewis Anthony Memorial Award (2007)
University Student Award (2006)

Extracurricular Activities
Scientific and Technical Communication,
  student association, president (2007-2008)
Black Student Assocation (BSA) (2005-present)
BSA Big Brother/Big Sister Mentoring Program
  (2007-present)
ExSEL Peer Mentoring Program (2006-Present)

References
Available upon request

Other relevant experience

List here—in the same format as for employment—experiences for which you received no pay but from which you gained abilities relevant to the position for which you are applying. You can include hobbies—if they are relevant.

Relevant coursework

List only those classes that are directly applicable for the position.

Computer skills

List these if the position requires computer skills.

References

It is fine to say these are *Available upon request*—but do check with your references that they don't mind being contacted.

Honors

List any awards, in the order in which you received them.

Extracurricular activities

If you belong to any clubs or societies relevant to the position, list them.

SHAPING PARAGRAPHS FOR AUDIENCE AND PURPOSE

In the preceding pages we've discussed the larger-scale organizational structures of different kinds of texts, and how and why to use them.

Now we discuss the next level of written organization, paragraphs.

PARAGRAPHS

Writing is not simply about conveying ideas to someone else. It also involves conveying the structure and relations of the ideas that have led writers to hold the beliefs, opinions, and values they do.

Paragraphs break reading—conceptually and visually—into units a reader can easily see. Because readers can see them, paragraphs help readers remember and so think about the structure and relations of the ideas in a text.

Readers' expectations about paragraphs have developed over several centuries. What we present on the next pages are current expectations about paragraphs in formal writing.

QUALITIES THAT READERS EXPECT IN PARAGRAPHS

- **Unity.** In the twenty-first century, readers expect a paragraph to contain sentences focused around only one idea or point.
- **Coherence.** Readers expect the sentences of a paragraph to grow out of each other.
- **Development.** Readers expect paragraphs not to repeat the same idea over and over, but instead to add to their understanding of the idea being discussed, as it relates to the writing of which the paragraph is a part.

In the next pages we go over these qualities in order.

PURPOSES OF PARAGRAPHS

There are three main categories of paragraphs:

- paragraphs that introduce readers to a piece of writing.
- paragraphs that make up the body of the writing, where the main arguments of the writing are developed.
- concluding paragraphs.

In the next pages, we focus on the paragraphs that make up the body of any piece of writing. Such paragraphs can function to

- describe.
- define.
- narrate.
- give examples.
- compare.
- classify.
- use analogies.
- divide.

Paragraphs can also mix these functions.

In the coming pages, we give examples of and discuss some of these paragraph functions. Once you understand how paragraphs perform functions like these, you can shape paragraphs to function as you need for your own purposes.

→ Pages 292–295 address introductory and concluding paragraphs.

LINKING WORDS THAT BUILD COHERENCE IN PARAGRAPHS

If you use words from the following list in a paragraph's sentences, you will help your readers understand why the sentences belong together. When you use the words below, you can repeat them to build parallel structures (→ see pages 286–287) that also show how the sentences belong together. If you do use such repetition, read your paragraph aloud to be sure you have not built a boring, singsong rhythm (unless a boring, singsong rhythm supports your purpose).

To show that information in one sentence adds to information in a preceding sentence: *additionally, also, and, besides, equally important, furthermore, in addition, moreover, too*

To emphasize the information in a sentence: *indeed, in fact, of course*

To help readers understand that you are building a sequence of events or a description of a process: *again, also, and, and then, besides, finally, first… second…third, furthermore, last, moreover, next, still, too*

To build sentences to describe events that take place over time: *after a few days, after a while, afterward, as long as, as soon as, at last, at that time, at the same time, before, during, earlier, eventually, finally, immediately, in the future, in the meantime, in the past, lately, later, meanwhile, next, now, simultaneously, since, soon, then, thereafter, today, until, when*

To help readers compare information in one sentence with that in another: *also, in the same manner, in the same way, likewise, once more, similarly*

To help readers see any important differences between your sentences: *although, but, despite, even though,* *however, in contrast, in spite of, instead, nevertheless, nonetheless, on the contrary, on the one hand…on the other hand…, otherwise, regardless, still, though, yet*

To indicate to readers that a sentence contains an example: *for example, for instance, indeed, in fact, of course, specifically, such as, to illustrate*

To help readers see cause and effect: *accordingly, as a result, because, consequently, for this purpose, hence, so, then, therefore, thus, to this end*

To make clear to readers the spatial relations among objects you are describing: *above, adjacent to, behind, below, beyond, closer to, elsewhere, far, farther on, here, in the background, near, nearby, opposite to, there, to the left, to the right*

To concede that your arguments are open to question: *although it is true that, granted that, I admit that, it may appear that, naturally, of course*

To show that sentences are summarizing or concluding: *as a result, as I have argued, as mentioned earlier, consequently, in any event, in conclusion, in other words, in short, on the whole, therefore, thus, to summarize*

USING THE LINKING WORDS AND PHRASES, AND PARALLELISM, TO BUILD COHERENCE

The paragraph below shows how each sentence connects to the next through repetition of words and phrases, as we noted on page 214. (We've highlighted *war* to help you see one repetition, and shown one pronoun use.)

But we also show how coherence is additionally built through linking words and parallelism.

You can see that only a few linking words are used; too many linking words can fragment a paragraph, so, generally, writers use only a few but combine them with the other strategies we listed on page 214 to link sentences.

parallelism

This sentence has three clauses, each of which has the same structure; the clauses are linked with semicolons. This structure shows that the three ideas have equal weight.

"in fact"

In fact precedes an explanation here and emphasizes the explanation. In this way, *in fact* indicates that the words following it amplify the words that precede it.

It is a remarkable fact about the United States that it fought a civil war without undergoing a change in its form of government. The Constitution was not abandoned during the American Civil War; elections were not suspended; there was no coup d'état. The war was fought to preserve the system of government that had been established at the nation's founding—to prove, in fact, that the system was worth preserving, that the idea of democracy had not failed. This is the meaning of the Gettysburg Address and of the great fighting cry of the north: "Union." And the system was preserved; the union did survive. But in almost every other respect, the United States became a different country. The war alone did not make America modern, but the war marks the birth of a modern America.

"this"

This refers to "that the system was worth preserving, that the idea of democracy had not failed." The pronoun carries forward those concepts into the next sentence, linking them.

"and"

And indicates to readers that the sentence it begins adds information to the sentence before it.

"but"

But signals to readers that there will be a change from what the preceding sentences were arguing.

PARAGRAPHS THAT DEFINE

If you are unsure whether your readers will understand a particular term or concept, give a definition. When you use a term or concept special to a particular discipline or field, chances are you will not be able to proceed in your argument without defining it. And if the term or concept is central to your argument, then defining it allows you and your readers to be in agreement about its meaning.

Because writers and readers have to develop a shared understanding of terms and concepts if discussion and argument are to be possible, the definition usually comes early in a text or early in a section that uses the term or concept.

Sometimes a one-sentence definition is all you will need—but if a term or concept is in any way complex or central to your purpose, then use a whole paragraph to build a detailed definition.

■ ■ ■

The paragraph to the right comes from a book arguing that food in the United States is now a petroleum product because of how crops and livestock are raised. This paragraph comes from a chapter in which the author describes Joel Salatin's farm in Virginia. The author uses this farm as an example of how crops and livestock can be raised without petroleum.

Notice how the first sentence gives a general definition of **grass farmer** (which itself includes a quick definition of **keystone species**). The following sentences add further detail and description—and use the words of an expert to support the definition being offered.

meat and milk) than anyone had ever thought possible.

Grass farmers grow animals—for meat, eggs, milk, and wool—but regard them as part of a food chain in which grass is the keystone species, the nexus between the solar energy that powers every food chain and the animals we eat. "To be even more accurate," Joel has said, "we should call ourselves sun farmers. The grass is just the way we capture the solar energy." One of the principles of modern grass farming is that to the greatest extent possible farmers should rely on the contemporary energy of the sun, as captured every day by photosynthesis, instead of the fossilized sun energy contained in petroleum.

For Allan Nation, who grew up on a cattle ranch in Mississippi, doing so is as much a matter of sound economics as environ-

TIP: WHEN USING DICTIONARY DEFINITIONS

Except when they are comparing definitions given by dictionaries, or want to comment on the shortcomings of a dictionary definition, few published writers quote from dictionaries when they need to define terms. Instead, they quote experts, people who know what a term means in practice. This gives the writer's words more authority.

PARAGRAPHS THAT NARRATE

Paragraphs that narrate tell stories. Stories personalize issues. When we hear the fortunes—or misfortunes—of others, we imagine ourselves in those situations. We know what feelings must be involved and might feel them ourselves. Stories can build emotional connections—positive or negative—between readers and topics.

Because stories are always about the experiences of one person or a few people, rarely can they stand alone as evidence: Readers will question attempts to generalize from limited experience to a broad claim. But stories can be useful in introductory or concluding paragraphs (to a whole essay or to a section) to engage readers emotionally with a topic or to make the topic memorable.

To write a narrative paragraph, tell what happened, in order. Include details—where the event took place, who was involved—but keep the narrative focused on your purpose. What is the main idea or feeling you want readers to remember?

(Note that stories based on real experiences are more effective than made-up stories; because they are not real, readers will not accept made-up stories as evidence.)

Death Nap

THE DANGERS OF TILTING BACK THE FRONT SEAT—DON'T DO IT!

By Emily Bazelon

Posted Friday, Sept. 7 2007, at 4.24 PM ET

A couple of weeks ago, I was sleeping in the front passenger seat of our car when it slammed into the vehicle in front of us. We were on the highway coming home from a family trip. The other three people in our car weren't hurt. But I'd reclined my seat, and my seat belt, which was riding high, left a long welt around my rib cage and along my stomach. As it turned out, I had internal bleeding from a lacerated spleen and three cracked ribs. I spent the next two days in intensive care.

I've recovered nicely, thank you. But the more I thought about my accident, the more I wondered whether I'd inadvertently done myself in by tilting my car seat back—as I do on just about every long drive. We worry a lot about car seats and

■ ■ ■

The paragraph to the left introduces an article on the dangers of sitting in a tilted-back front seat of a car. The author's own story makes the topic real—and scary. In the paragraphs that follow, the writer describes what she learned about tilted front seats through research and offers much more evidence than her own experience to argue that the dangers of riding in a reclined front car seat ought to be more well known.

PARAGRAPHS THAT DIVIDE

Paragraphs that define can easily become or lead into paragraphs that divide: A definition establishes a criterion that names what something is (or is not). Once you have done that, you can use the criterion to categorize and divide.

Academic writing often hinges on such categorization or division because such categorization or division is analysis. Analysis allows us to name and so to sort through the components of a process or event. We do that to learn what happened or to learn what stands in our way of accomplishing what we desire.

Paragraphs that divide are often followed by paragraphs that compare and contrast—because it is possible to compare and contrast two objects, processes, or events only when we can see that the objects, processes, or events are different.

(The opposite kind of paragraph—a paragraph that unites—is also central to academic work. Just as it is important to show that what had seemed the same is really different, it helps us when we can see that what had seemed different is really the same.)

■ ■ ■

Danah Boyd, working on her PhD at Berkeley and a Fellow at the Berkman Center for Internet and Society at the Harvard Law School, researches how young people use social networking software like MySpace and Facebook. In a recent blog article she uses sociologist Nalini Kotamraju's definition of "class" to consider differences between MySpace and Facebook. Kotamraju argues that in the United States class isn't about money but rather about social connection: who you know is going to shape your life and what you can do more than how much much money you make. Based on that distinction, Boyd argues that the difference between who uses Facebook and who uses MySpace is one of class: Facebook is where the "goodie two shoes, jocks, athletes, or other 'good' kids" go, while MySpace

> is still home for Latino/Hispanic teens, immigrant teens, burnouts, alternative kids, art fags, punks, emos, goths, gangstas, queer kids, and other kids who didn't play into the dominant high school popularity paradigm.

Boyd argues that marketers and the military have figured out this distinction and are making decisions on it; Boyd hopes that teachers and social workers will figure this out, too, in order to talk with young people about how cultural structures and decisions shape individual lives.

In this example, the writer summarizes part of the argument of another writer's work. The summary shows how the original writer—Danah Boyd—starts with a definition of **class**. She then uses that definition to show a division in an area that many had thought was the same throughout: social networking websites that allow users to make personal profiles.

By using the definition to make a division in an area that had seemed the same throughout, Boyd can point to problems we might not otherwise have seen.

PARAGRAPHS THAT BLEND ORGANIZATIONS

Depending on your arguments, paragraphs can get complex: Writers need them to perform multiple functions.

(Keep in mind, though, that even when paragraphs blend several kinds of organizations together, the paragraph will still have one main function in the overall argument of which it is a part: It needs to move the argument forward one step.)

■ ■ ■

This example is part of a newspaper editorial, published on Labor Day, in which writer Mike Rose argues that we should "honor the brains as well as the brawn of American labor."

In this paragraph, Rose lists examples of the mental work that different kinds of blue-collar work require.

But this paragraph is not only examples. The examples ground Rose's argument that we need to unite rather than divide: We need to see that blue-collar and white-collar work have much in common.

Rose thus combines examples and analysis—unifying disparate elements—in this one paragraph.

beauty salons and restaurants, auto factories and welding shops. And I've been struck by the intellectual demands of what I saw.

Consider what a good waitress or waiter has to do in a busy restaurant. Remember orders and monitor them, attend to an ever-changing environment, juggle the flow of the work, make decisions on the fly. Or the carpenter: To build a cabinet, a staircase, or a pitched roof requires complex mathematical calculations, a high level of precision. The hairstylist's practice is a mix of scissors technique, knowledge of biology, aesthetic judgment, and communication skills. The mechanic, electrician, and plumber are trouble-shooters and problem-solvers. Even the routinized factory floor calls for working smart. Yet we persist in dividing labor into the work of the hand and the work of the mind.

Distinction between blue collar and white collar do exist. White-collar work, for example, often requires a large investment of time and

TIP: MANY KINDS OF PARAGRAPHS

We have described some of the most used kinds of paragraphs. But there are also paragraphs that classify, that explain processes, that show cause and effect, and that function in other ways depending on a writer's particular purposes. As you read others' writing, try to classify their paragraphs, and to determine why they used a particular kind of paragraph when they did; such observations will not only help you expand your tool kit of kinds of paragraphs but will also help you strengthen your own argumentative choices.

BUILDING VISUAL ORGANIZATIONS

Print texts have a clear beginning, a clear order to follow, and a clear end. Films and videos have linear organization similar to print, but one-page visual texts (posters, flyers, each page in a newsletter or brochure) do not. To build visual organizations with one-page texts, construct visual relationships among the elements.

MAKE SOME ELEMENTS STAND OUT

Arranging a visual text's organization requires making obvious which elements are most important and should be seen first, and which second and third. Elements are made to stand out—and be what is first seen—through contrast, placement, and leaving some space unemphasized.

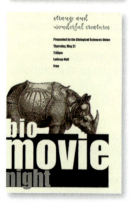

Which movie flyer to the left would catch your eye on a campus wall? What do your eyes see in each flyer?

With the top flyer, you probably see a mass of text; no part stands out. With the second, your eyes are probably caught first by the rhinoceros and the big words at the bottom; then you notice the text at the upper right. The second flyer immediately tells you what it is about and perhaps piques your interest enough that you move close to read the details—which the flyer composer knew you would read if you were pulled in by the rhino.

Contrast

The second flyer works because the bottom words are so big compared to the words at the top right. Create contrast by giving elements **very** different sizes, colors, or styles.

Placement

Western reading patterns accustom our eyes to moving left to right and top to bottom, as well as to page centers. If you organize page elements so that the biggest element is at the top left or overlaps the center, you double its visual emphasis and so make it even more eye attracting.

Unemphasized Space (or "White Space")

White space is the design term for space on a page that only appears unused. But white space (which can be any color; **white space** comes from white paper) makes visual organization possible. Areas of a visual composition cannot be emphasized if every bit of space is full. Leaving some spaces empty allows the parts that are full to stand out.

GROUP ELEMENTS OR MAKE THEM SIMILAR

When you group visual elements or make them similar (and sometimes you do both at once), you create a page that feels unified and coherent to viewers—for all the same reasons that we gave for unified and coherent paragraphs on page 214.

Also, elements that are grouped or similar can create a background against which other elements can stand out.

Group Elements

When several elements on a page serve the same function—giving the time, date, and location information about an event, for example, or serving as the eye-catching elements—group them close to each other. A viewer's eyes see and so understand that they belong together.

You can see this in the rhinoceros movie flyer, where the rhinoceros and the big words are overlapped to make one element. The words at the top right of the flyer are also grouped: A viewer can quickly see that information about the movie is in one place.

▪ ▪ ▪

Grouping can happen at the level of headings in a text, too. Compare the two text boxes to the right. The top box looks as though it contains seven different bits of text, because there is the same amount of space above and below the bold text.

The second box has more space above the bold text and none underneath; this groups the bold text with the words underneath. The grouping makes very obvious to a viewer that the bold text serves as heads for the words underneath.

Notice, too, how the second box looks as though it contains only four elements.

The components of color are hue, saturation, and brightness:

HUE

Hue describes what many of us just think of as color: When you name the hue of a color, you describe it as red or blue or yellow or green…

SATURATION

Saturation describes how much hue is present in a color. Vivid pink is highly saturated, while pastel pink is not.

BRIGHTNESS

Brightness describes how light or dark a color is.

The components of color are hue, saturation, and brightness:

HUE
Hue describes what many of us just think of as color: When you name the hue of a color, you describe it as red or blue or yellow or green…

SATURATION
Saturation describes how much hue is present in a color. Vivid pink is highly saturated, while pastel pink is not.

BRIGHTNESS
Brightness describes how light or dark a color is.

ORGANIZATION FOR ORAL PRESENTATIONS

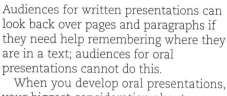

Audiences for written presentations can look back over pages and paragraphs if they need help remembering where they are in a text; audiences for oral presentations cannot do this.

When you develop oral presentations, your biggest consideration about organization should be helping your audience hear the parts of the presentation.

THE PARTS OF AN ORAL PRESENTATION

Like written papers, oral presentations have the basic structure of introduction, body, and conclusion. But as you prepare, use strategies that make the organization audible to your audience.

- **Introduction.** Explicitly and clearly tell your listeners what your presentation is about and describe the parts that make up its structure.

  As you plan your introduction, be sure to state your purpose near the beginning. If you start with an anecdote, quotation, or another attention-getting strategy, state your goal next and then describe the main points or parts that structure your presentation. You want your audience to hear your purpose and organization several times so that they will remember them.

  Vary the sentence patterns you use to describe your purpose and organization (→ see pages 470–471 about sentence patterns), but use the same or similar noun phrases to describe your purpose and organization so that audiences remember them well (→ see pages 466–467 on noun phrases).

- **Body.** As you work out the body of your presentation, choose an easy-to-remember structure and plan to keep your audience aware of each movement you make from one point to the next.

  Easy-to-remember structures have few parts: In a five- to ten-minute presentation, audiences will be able to remember three to five steps in an argument. Easy-to-remember structures are

  - *Chronological.* Audiences can easily follow presentations that present events in the order in which they occurred.

  - *Logical.* Use your thesis statement (→ as we describe on pages 202–203) to organize the body into three parts: one for the warrant, one for the reason, and one for the claim.

  - *Problem-Solution.* Describe the problem and then argue for the solution you favor.

  - *Comparative.* If you are recommending one approach to a problem over another, first present the approach you least favor and then the one you want audiences to remember.

Keeping your audience aware of your movement from one point to the next involves phrases like the following:

- My third point is...
- Now that I have described the problem, let me tell you what I think the best solution is.
- I've described what microcredit is, so let me tell you why economists think it is so important.
- Finally... or In conclusion...

  → All the phrases listed on pages 216–217 can help you help your audience hear your presentation's movements.

- **Conclusion.** Remind your audience of your argument and main points. If you can find one that fits well with your purposes, use an anecdote, story, or quotation to end memorably, so that your listeners hold on to your talk.

OTHER ORGANIZATIONAL FEATURES

- As our advice above and to the left suggests, repeating your purpose and main points in your introduction, as you move from paragraph to paragraph, and in your conclusion helps audiences follow your arguments. Use similar words as you repeat.

- Pare it down. These days, when we rarely receive instruction in how to listen, audiences benefit from straightforward, focused presentations.

TIP: AN ORGANIZATIONAL FUNCTION FOR VISUAL AIDS

If you use visual aids such as slides, overheads, or handouts during your presentation, include an opening screen or page that sketches or outlines the overall organization of the presentation.

As you move through the parts of your presentation, use screens that name the parts as you move into them.

FIGURING OUT WHAT TO DO WITH A PARAGRAPH THAT IS TOO LONG

Riley's draft (➜ see pages 168–177) has a paragraph that is too long; it starts with this:

> But one writer says that most studies of microcredit programs "find very small increases in income for quite large numbers of borrowers; in only a very small number of cases are there significant income increases" (Mayoux 39). It most often benefits women….

To break this long paragraph into paragraphs that are of expected length, Riley needs to decide how the revised paragraphs ought to function in the overall organization of her paper. Because she has given her paper an organization that follows the basic form of her thesis (➜ see pages 202–203 to see how she has done this), she has some guidelines to help her decide: She knows that she needs to start her paper by talking about her warrant—how most people believe that microcredit can end poverty—and she will conclude with her reason, that microcredit should be offered only with discussion support groups and economics classes. In the part of her paper from which the long paragraph comes, **Riley has to argue—and argue forcefully—that when microcredit is offered to women without discussion support groups and economics classes, it does not end poverty.**

Her first draft shows that she has plenty of evidence to make this case—but how should she break up her long paragraph to give it an organization that will be easier for readers to read?

THE THESIS SUGGESTS AN OUTLINE FOR THE PAPER'S BODY

One way to see what the body of a paper must address is to separate out the terms used in the thesis. Riley's thesis has four main terms:

- microcredit
- women
- discussion support groups and economics classes
- poverty

Implied in Riley's thesis are these relations among the terms:

microcredit + women = poverty

microcredit + women + discussion support groups and economics classes = end of poverty

Riley needs to devote paragraphs to each of these topics and to explaining the relationships between the topics implied by the equation.

A rough outline for the body of Riley's paper could thus be:

1 What is microcredit?
2 Why is microcredit focused on women?
3 Why does microcredit, alone, fail to bring women out of poverty?
4 What do discussion support groups and economics classes bring to the mix that can end poverty?

THE OUTLINE SUGGESTS HOW TO BREAK UP THE LONG PARAGRAPH

Riley's overly long paragraph comes in the third section: *Why does microcredit, alone, fail to bring women out of poverty?*

As she revises her paper and works on the second section—why microcredit is focused on women—Riley's research shows her that people expect microcredit to help women in two ways. First, a microcredit loan is supposed to help women gain confidence and bargaining power. Second, a microcredit loan is supposed to help women make more money and spend it in their communities, and thus help their communities move out of poverty.

The long paragraph causing Riley trouble will follow the section on why microcredit is focused on women. Riley now knows that she will use a paragraph that divides (→ see page 224) to lay out why microcredit is focused on women. In the section on why microcredit alone fails to bring women out of poverty, Riley can then build on that division to make two paragraphs out of the long one:

- One paragraph will show how microcredit alone doesn't help women gain confidence or bargaining power.
- One paragraph will show how microcredit alone has not resulted in women making money or spending it in their communities.

→ Riley's final draft, using the outline and paragraphs described here, is on pages 406–418.

HINTS & TIPS FOR ORGANIZING TEXTS

BE WARY OF SETTLING ON AN ORGANIZATION TOO QUICKLY

If you want to produce writing that is smart, complex, and creative, you have to let your writing direct you. Although you have a thesis statement and a statement of purpose, and although they can help you give a rough shape to your writing before you sit down to write, it is in writing that you really test out and find the ideas you want.

All experienced writers will tell you of times that, in working out an argument in writing, they came to different or more focused conclusions than they had originally planned. Because they listened to their words, and followed the logic of their initial ideas or of new evidence, their writing had to take on new organizations.

So don't try to force an organization on your ideas; listen to your ideas and the directions they take you. You can always reorganize a paper once you have found a new or shifted argument.

CHECKING ORGANIZATION THROUGH AN AFTER-THE-FACT OUTLINE

Once you are confident in your arguments and know that your conclusion is exactly what you want (→ see pages 292–293), check back over all your other paragraphs: Does each logically follow what precedes it and lead to what comes next?

Experienced writers often make outlines for their papers **after** they have a first (or later) draft:

• Summarize each paragraph in one sentence. (If you cannot summarize a paragraph in a sentence, then you probably need to break the paragraph into two or more new paragraphs.)

• List the paragraph summaries in order.

• Does this outline step you logically from the introduction to the conclusion? If not, you may need to add, take out, or clarify paragraphs to have different summaries.

HOW OTHERS CAN HELP YOU CHECK ORGANIZATION

When you have a draft, cut it apart so that each paragraph is on its own piece of paper. Shuffle the pieces of paper and give them to someone else; ask the other person to tape the paragraphs back into a whole, leaving out any paragraphs that don't make sense or marking any places where it is impossible to tell what should come next.

Sometimes the other person will hand you back something with a clearer order, and sometimes you will learn where you need to make clarifications, additions, or subtractions.

PART 6
WRITING FOR DIVERSE AUDIENCES

CONTENTS

WHERE ARE WE IN THE PROCESS FOR COMPOSING?

Understanding your project

Getting started

Asking questions

Shaping your project for others

Drafting a paper
Varieties of English
Writing for global audiences
Inclusive language uses

Getting feedback

Revising

Polishing

VARIETIES OF ENGLISH

 I been thru a lot of struggles to get where I'm at today.

I've struggled to accomplish what I have.

 My brother was into skydiving and he got me hooked on this stuff.

My brother, who is a skydiving fan, introduced me to the sport.

Some would react negatively to the top statement in each set above, saying, "That's not good English." By **good English**, they mean what is often called **Standard English**, represented by the second statement in each set above. Standard English—and its grammatical rules and patterns—is what is taught in schools and used in many formal situations.

Standard English is a historical accident: It resulted from the language practices of those who were economically and politically advantaged at the time people were thinking that grammar and English usage should be standardized.

LANGUAGE STANDARDIZATION AND LANGUAGE VARIETY

That we assign *good* or *bad* to different statements reflects two opposite tendencies in language use:

1
LANGUAGE STANDARDIZATION

Languages tend to become standardized in formal practice. In any language, one set of grammatical practices and speaking patterns will be favored more than others, as we noted on the page to the left.

Some argue that such standardization supports wider communication among speakers of different varieties of a language. Standard forms of language are thus often used in the media (think of how network television news reporters speak or of the writing in big-city newspapers) and in schooling, which is often meant to provide people from different backgrounds with a common culture and an ability to speak across their differences.

2
LANGUAGE VARIETY

Because of a language's use in different contexts for different purposes, different varieties of a language develop. In their daily use, people who fix cars will tend to use different sets of words than people who treat diseases. Different occupations can become so specialized—as law has, for example—that they have their own language patterns.

Similarly, different communities of people will shape local vocabularies and grammars. For example, the Gullah people, who live on islands off the southern states of North Carolina south to Florida, hold on to African words and speech patterns; these words and patterns have been brought into and have changed English in the area.

Depending on the influence that different groups have, and how much they interact with others, their words and language patterns can be accepted into the standard variety of a language, as the words of computer programming—*interface*, *platform*, and **input**—have become part of our day-to-day talk.

VARIETIES OF ENGLISH
ACADEMIC ENGLISH

" ...by the time I came to the United States as a...student in foreign and second language education..., I was not competent in writing in my second language. Although I had no trouble expressing myself in English, I was not familiar with the standards of academic writing. I remember the first assignment I had in an education course....I spent hours and hours composing the essay, and yet, with great disappointment, the paper turned out to be a Chinese composition in English, although the instructor did not comment on this. "

In the words above, Chinese student Jun Liu describes his struggles to learn to write papers in academic English. What he describes is common for all writers entering a new writing context, whether or not their first language is English.

Every time you are asked to write a document you haven't written before, there is a learning curve. You have to learn the textual conventions, style preferences, and reader expectations unique to the new context. These new exigencies may seem challenging and uncomfortable at first, but you carry some basic tools with you from all your previous reading and writing instruction that can be adapted for the new context.

Following are some principles of academic writing and some strategies to help you tackle new academic writing contexts.

THE ORGANIZATION OF ACADEMIC WRITING IN ENGLISH

Readers of academic writing in English expect written texts to be organized around the following principles:

THESIS

❏ The main argument is usually explicitly stated in the introduction and is probably also repeated in the conclusion. Writers rarely leave readers to infer the argument.

❏ Subsequent ideas and information are related to the thesis; nothing is put into the text that doesn't support or further the thesis.

EVIDENCE IN SUPPORT OF THE ARGUMENT

❏ Evidence is given to support the main argument. Different disciplines will value different types of support and will use it in specific ways; but, in general, academic writers tend to avoid using only stories or examples to support a thesis.

→ See pages 104–113 for the types of evidence used in academic and technical writing.

→ See pages 200–205 to see the kinds of evidence valued in different disciplines.

❏ The body of the writing is composed almost exclusively of evidence.

❏ Statistics, examples, and facts are used to support any generalizations needed for the argument.

ARRANGEMENT OF IDEAS

❏ Writers state the main argument in the beginning of the paper and then provide evidence for it; they do not lead the reader to the main argument.

❏ Logic is used to build arguments.

→ Pages 202–203 explain some aspects of logic used in academic writing.

❏ Each paragraph usually picks up on and develops a point from the preceding paragraph, moving readers forward with little unnecessary repetition.

❏ Writers consolidate or group issues that are related to make their writing less repetitive. They also signal the progression of their ideas using headings, transition sentences, and connecting words.

→ Pages 300–301 discuss headings.

→ Pages 296–297 discuss transition sentences and connecting words.

CONNECTING TO THE AUDIENCE

❏ Arguments are timely and provide readers with either new information or a new perspective on a topic.

❏ Writers anticipate what their readers need to know so that the readers can enter into and follow the argument. (There is one exception: When writing for courses, student writers are often expected to display what they have learned, and thus are expected to provide more background information than their readers might need.)

ENGLISH AS A GLOBAL LANGUAGE

> *I became boring.*
> **I became bored.**

> *I will climb machine to the junction. I cannot trek.*
> **I will ride my motorcycle to the junction. I can't walk the short distance.**

The two examples above show English used in different countries. In the first set of sentences, Singaporean English contrasts with what some consider to be Standard English; the second set starts with Nigerian English.

As transportation and communication technologies bring once-distant communities in touch through commerce and culture, language standardization and language variation shape English.

Standardization steps in because businesses now operate worldwide and because media are on a twenty-four-hour, worldwide news cycle. Some believe the use of one language can ease this communication. English has taken on that role, in most cases being the language of business, science, and to some extent, the Internet.

English has taken on this role not because it is a superior language but simply because of accidents of history: English happened to be in the right place at the right time. And, possibly, English will be displaced by another language at some time in the future when it is no longer politically or economically advantageous.

Language variation is also at work. Because English has been adopted in so many countries, many varieties of English have emerged, such as Singaporean English, Nigerian English, Indian English, Caribbean English, Malaysian English, and so on. Language experts refer to these varieties as **world Englishes**. Each group of new English users changes the grammar and vocabulary of what we think of as **Standard English** to reflect their culture and needs—just as, starting in the sixteenth century, people in the British colonies (including what is now the United States) changed English as it was spoken and written in England.

WRITING FOR A GLOBAL AUDIENCE

Globalization in markets, science, and media has meant that texts produced for business or technical purposes—reports, advertisements, business plans—are translated between languages. Sometimes, as the following example shows, the translation process creates problems:

> *Original meaning:* Sexual harassment is your concern.

> *Translation into another language:* Make sexual harassment your business.

Whatever the final result, the globalization of communication is influencing the language of writing. When writers of business or technical reports produce a document, they must take into account the translation process their texts will undergo.

TO ENSURE ACCURACY AND EASE OF TRANSLATION

- Use clear (not simple) sentence structures.

  For example, this sentence is difficult to translate:

The rapid level of increase in entry of women into the workforce has changed people's shopping patterns from daily shopping to weekly or monthly.

Easier to translate is this sentence:

Because more women have entered the workforce, people no longer shop daily, but weekly or monthly.

- Use straightforward vocabulary. Avoid idioms and vague word choice that might create confusion.

  The *italicized words* in the following text will be difficult to translate because they are idiomatic or make cultural references that are not shared outside the United States:

Recently I *poked fun* at those *New Age marvels* we call the multi-taskers. If you missed it, the salient point was this: Laboratory experiments prove that multi-tasking is, contrary to *all hype*, hugely inefficient.

- Anticipate vocabulary that might have multiple meanings and cause translation difficulties

  For example, **concern** in the sexual harassment example on the left causes difficulty because it has two potential meanings: **business concern** and **problem**.

USING INCLUSIVE LANGUAGE

" My name is Jane Takagi-Little. Little was my dad, a Little from Quam, Minnesota. Takagi is my mother's name. She's Japanese. Hyphenation may be a modern response to patriarchal naming practices in some cases, but not in mine. My hyphen is a thrust of pure superstition. At my christening, Ma was stricken by a profound Oriental dread at the thought of her child bearing an insignificant surname like Little through life, so at the very last minute she insisted on attaching hers. Takagi is a big name, literally, comprising the Chinese character for "tall" and the character for "tree." Ma thought the stature and eminence of her lofty ancestors would help equalize Dad's Little. They were always fighting about stuff like this.

"It doesn't *mean* anything," Dad would say. "It's just a *name!*," which would cause Ma to recoil in horror. "How can you say '*justa name*'? Name is very *first* thing. Name is face to all the world." "

This passage from Ruth L. Ozeki's novel *My Year of Meats* describes how the main character comes to be named and, in so doing, describes how we use words to shape our relations with those who may have grown up in cultures different from ours. Jane's mother is alert to the social weight of words, of how the words we use to describe ourselves—and others—shape how we are seen and treated by others. She insists that her daughter carry a name that gives her importance and so respect in the eyes of others.

This matter of how we are named comes up elsewhere in Ozeki's novel, as in the following exchange:

> Then, at the pancake breakfast where we had been filming, a red-faced veteran from WWII drew a bead on me and my crew, standing in line by the warming trays, our plates stacked high with flapjacks and American bacon.
>
> "Where are you from, anyway?" he asked, squinting his bitter blue eyes at me.
>
> "New York," I answered.
>
> He shook his head and glared and wiggled a crooked finger inches from my face. "No, I mean where were you *born*?"
>
> "Quam, Minnesota," I said.
>
> "No, no...*What* are you?" He whined with frustration.
>
> And in a voice that was low, but shivering with demented pride, I told him, "I...am...a...*fucking*... AMERICAN!"

Neither the questioning man nor Jane comes across well in Ozeki's writing, both insistent, neither willing to back off. It is precisely because our identities—the words we use to describe who we are—carry so much weight that this scene in the novel matters.

But Jane's position is the one with which Ozeki asks us to sympathize, in the end, because Jane, in spite of her expletives, is defending herself. The man wants to judge her based only on how she looks.

Instead, Jane insists on naming herself, on choosing to be seen through a word that belies the assumptions the man wants to make.

Who does not want the right to be known by a name that speaks truthfully to and respectfully of one's background and experiences?

■ ■ ■

It is important, then, that we grant each other the right to choose the names by which we are called and understood by others.

When others write or talk about us using names we believe do not reflect our backgrounds or experiences accurately or respectfully—or when they write or talk about us in ways we believe to be disrespectful—they show us either that they have made mistakes about us or that they do not see us as worthy of the same respect that they expect for themselves.

When we write about others, it would seem only right that we grant the same respect to them. If your readers feel excluded because of your word choices, because of how you refer to them, then they will either stop reading or they will read your words with a hostile, sad, or distanced attitude, thus undermining your purpose in writing.

Writing that connects with readers connects because readers feel respected by the writing. When you write, it is not about you. It is about your readers, and about giving them the same respect and courtesy you believe you deserve.

USING INCLUSIVE LANGUAGE
INCLUDING ALL ETHNICITIES

"ETHNICITY" OR "RACE"?

More and more, scientists argue that *race*—as a genetic basis for categorizing humans—does not exist. We have tended to define someone's race based on the physical appearance of the person, but people may have similar physical appearances (such as skin color) because their ancestors grew up far apart although in similar physical environments; even though two people might look alike, their genetic differences might be so considerable that they share little common heritage.

Because there is controversy over *race*, and because *race* focuses our attention on physical characteristics, we have found it generally better—when we must refer to others through such lenses—to use the term *ethnicity*.

Ethnicity refers to heritage and culture: Ethnic groups tend to come into being because of a people's common ancestry, language, or religion.

TIP: CONSIDERING "RACE"

For centuries, in this country as in many others, the idea of *race* was used to justify the unequal treatment of different peoples. We need to keep this historical fact in mind because, sadly, it is still shaping people's relationships and livelihoods. Therefore, unless you are writing about *race* as a topic, use *ethnicity* to encourage your readers to enact more thoughtful and more accurate relationships.

CHECKING YOUR WRITING

- **Have you referred to a person's ethnicity or national origin only when it is relevant to your argument?**

- **Have you used names that people from an ethnicity prefer for themselves?** As political and social changes affect people of different ethnicities, the names they prefer may change; you will have to ask or do research to find currently preferred names. Members of a group may disagree about their preferred name for different reasons; you can acknowledge this in your writing.

  Learn the names that people find offensive so that you do not inadvertently use them; these are often names that other cultures assigned or used in the past.

- **Have you assumed that your readers share the same ethnicity or experiences as you?** Unless you are writing to people who have precisely the same background as you do, be careful not to assume that your readers hold the same beliefs as you. This can be hard since much of what we believe, think, and feel is implicit; when in doubt, ask someone not of your ethnicity and who has grown up differently from you to read what you have written, to be sure that you are not inadvertently attributing to your readers qualities or beliefs that you hold because of your particular upbringing.

- **Have you been as specific as you can in naming an ethnic group?** The more specific you can be about an ethnicity, the less likely you are to slip into

stereotyping. For example, use *Ojibwa* or *Cherokee* instead of *American Indian*; use *Bahraini* or *Saudi* instead of Arab.

- **Have you used hyphens in multiword names?** In current usage, you should write (for example) *Japanese American* rather than *Japanese-American* because the hyphen implies both dual citizenship (which may not be the case) and that one is not completely American. In the nonhyphenated form, such as *Swedish American*, the first word is an adjective modifying the second word, emphasizing the second word but also holding on to the particular experiences that the first word conveys.

- **Have you avoided phrases that use ethnically tied terms?** You may have grown up with phrases that seem to you just part of language, such as *Latin lover* or *Jewish mother*—but these terms stereotype people. They imply that all people of that ethnicity share some set of broadly defined (and often derogatory) characteristics.

- **Have you capitalized the names of ethnicities?** For example, write *Polish American* or *Filipino American*.

- **Have you checked that any adjectives you put before the name of an ethnic group are appropriate?** To write that someone is (for example) *a quiet American* can imply that Americans are loud.

Because language is social and is therefore continually changing, these usages can change. Keep your ears open to stay current so that your writing is always respectful.

USING INCLUSIVE LANGUAGE
INCLUDING ALL AGES

AGEISM

In other cultures, people who have gray hair and many wrinkles are often respected for the knowledge and understanding that can come with many years of life. In the United States now, however, most people want to stay young as long as possible, with the result that people who are older are often stereotyped as frail, rigid, reactionary, and incompetent—or as soft, kindly, and powerless grandparents. Oddly, however, people who are young are often stereotyped as reckless, loud, selfish and self-absorbed, unambitious, sex-crazed, and lazy.

If you think about all the people you know who are younger than you and all the people you know who are older than you, however, your experiences ought to give you many counter-examples to these stereotypes. Ageism, the stereotyping of people because of how old they are, is therefore—like racism and sexism—a form of prejudice because it shapes our understanding of others in negative, limiting, and rarely true ways.

CHECKING YOUR WRITING TO AVOID AGEISM

- **Have you referred to the age of a person only when your purpose requires it?** To check the necessity of referring to age in your writing, try taking it out; if your readers can still understand your purpose, then remove the reference. If, for example, in an article about poker you have written, *Ms. Jucovy, who is 63, won the final pot,* change the sentence to *Ms. Jucovy won the final pot* and ask others to read the article. If they still understand your article as you intended, then stay with the second version.

- **Have you used ageist terms to describe others?** Terms to avoid for people who are older are the following: *geriatrics, over the hill, ancient, old-timers, matronly, well-preserved.*

  Terms to avoid for young people are the following: *punk, gangbanger, juvie.*

- **Have you used terms that patronize people because of their age?** Treat older—and younger—people with the same respect, using the same titles.

  The standard in Anglo culture in the United States, then, is not to call an old man *Grandpa* (unless he really is your grandfather) or to refer to an older woman as *Honey, Dear*, or *Auntie:* These terms imply a level of familiarity you wouldn't assume with people of other ages.

- **Don't refer to older people as "our seniors" or "our elders."** Again, this is a practice in Anglo culture in the United States. The use of *our* implies that the group of people being discussed is the writer's property or possession instead of individual humans.

- **Have you referred to older people as the vital, interesting, productive people they are?** People who are retired do not share any common characteristic other than that they are retired: Some people retire in their forties, and others retire in their seventies; some retire from one career to take up another while others take on active volunteer work. The more you learn about what a range of older people does, the more you are likely to write respectfully, fairly, and accurately about them.

USING INCLUSIVE LANGUAGE
INCLUDING ALL GENDERS

SEXISM

Language is sexist when it implies that women are not only different from men but also somehow inferior.

CHECKING YOUR WRITING TO AVOID SEXISM

• **Anytime you have described someone's gender—or used descriptive terms that are culturally gender-related—ask yourself if the description is necessary.** One way to check this is to rewrite the sentence, changing the gender. For example, if you have written, *The musician, a pretty redheaded girl, played the Bach concertos effortlessly* but would not write, *The musician, a pretty redheaded boy, played the Bach concertos effortlessly*, then change the original sentence to, simply, *The musician played the Bach concertos effortlessly.*

• **Have you used *man, men, he,* or *him* to refer to a group of people that might include women?** Some argue that these words are always inclusive of both men and women, but look at these sentences:

On this form, everyone should add the name of his husband or wife.

When pregnant, men ought to aim for more sleep.

Pantyhose fit properly if a man feels a slight cling at his waist.

Because these words are not inclusive, revise any such uses so that your words don't exclude the women in your audience.

To revise:

Substitute gender-neutral nouns for *man* or *men* or words that include them. For example, instead of *chairman,* use *chairperson.*

Make a sentence plural so that you can change *he* and *him* to the gender-neutral *they* and *them: Everyone should bring his own umbrella* can become *All visitors should bring their own umbrellas.*

- **Have you used unequal terms to refer to men and women in equal positions?** If, for example, you are writing about the presidents of two countries, it is incorrect to write *Mrs. Halonen and President Bush;* instead, write *Presidents Halonen and Bush.* Similarly, *man and wife* puts the woman in a subordinate position; *husband and wife* treats both with equal respect. If you write *the girls' team,* then refer to the boys' team as *the boys' team;* to call one team *the team* and the other *the girls' team* is to imply that the first team is the standard and the second is a deviation.

- **Have you avoided stereotyped uses of occupations?** The sentences *Each computer programmer has his own style of coding* and *A teacher can have a tremendous impact on her students* imply that these occupations are the domain of one gender only. Make the sentences plural to avoid the stereotypes: Write, *All computer programmers have their particular styles of coding* and *Teachers can have a tremendous impact on their students.*

- **Have you used any words that stereotype behavior according to gender?** If you are describing a group made up only of women or only of men, check that your sentences do not use words that belittle some members.

You can check this by rewriting the sentence for the other gender. For example, if you've written, *The women were gossiping about the senatorial candidate,* see if *The men were gossiping about the senatorial candidate* sounds right. If it does not, then change the original sentence to *The women were discussing the senatorial candidate.*

- **Have you used salutations that include all members of an audience?** Do not start a letter with *Dear Sirs* if you do not know your audience; you can start with *To whom it may concern* or *Dear Colleagues,* or you can leave off the salutation.

USING INCLUSIVE LANGUAGE

INCLUDING ALL SEXUAL ORIENTATIONS

HETEROSEXISM

To write as though all readers have the same sexual orientation is to risk losing their attention and respect just as much as writing as though all readers are male, European American, or of one age risks losing their attention and respect.

CHECK YOUR WRITING TO AVOID HETEROSEXISM

- **When you refer to someone's sexual orientation in your writing, is it necessary to your purpose?** If you would not write, *The heterosexual engineer was fluent with both the aesthetic and the technical aspects of design,* then do not write, *The gay engineer was fluent with both the aesthetic and the technical aspects of design.*

  As we have similarly recommended on the previous pages, if you are unsure about the appropriateness of including references to sexual orientation in your writing, remove the references. If readers still understand your purpose, then you can omit the references from your final draft.

- **Have you used *sexual orientation* rather than *sexual preference*?** To write *sexual preference* is to imply that sexuality is the result of conscious choice, a view that neither scientific research nor the reported experiences of lesbians, gays, or heterosexuals support.

- **Have you used terms that those you are describing themselves prefer?** Currently, *gay* is the preferred term for homosexual men and *lesbian* is the preferred term for homosexual women; people whose sexual orientation includes both men and women prefer *bisexual. Transgendered* is preferred for those whose sex is not congruent with their gender identity.

Homosexual emphasizes sexuality over relationships and in the past has been associated with mental illness and criminality. It has also been used primarily to refer to male sexuality, and thus erases lesbians from the discussion. Many people thus avoid using *homosexual.*

Keep in mind that, in the twenty-first century, *lesbian* and *gay* are primarily about communities of people rather than sexual activity. This is important because some people have sex with others of the same gender but do not consider themselves *lesbian* or *gay.*

If you have any concerns about the terms you are using, ask and do research. As with all your writing, ask a range of people to read what you write, to be sure none feel pushed away by your word choices.

- **Have you avoided assuming heterosexuality?** In a manual for a large corporation, the sentence *All employees are encouraged to bring their wives to these yearly events* is a problem because it assumes that all the employees are married heterosexual males. In contrast, *all employees are encouraged to bring their partners or significant others to these yearly events* includes employees of all genders and sexual orientations as well as those who are not married.

USING INCLUSIVE LANGUAGE
INCLUDING ALL RELIGIONS

EXCLUSIONARY LANGUAGE ABOUT RELIGION

While there is no single term to define language that promotes one religion while discouraging or being derogatory toward others, the matter of religion is just as sensitive in our time as any of the other aspects of people's identities we have been discussing in Part 6.

As with the other aspects of identity, our beliefs about deities—that they exist or not—and religions—whether or not to belong to an organized religion—matter very deeply to each of us. Therefore, as with each of the other aspects of identity we have discussed in this part, the main guideline for writing when you want to build common ground with a wide audience is to respect others' beliefs as you would want yours respected.

CHECK YOUR WRITING TO AVOID DISCRIMINATING BASED ON RELIGION

- **Have you referred to someone's religion only when it is central to your purpose?** Whenever you include a reference to someone's religion in your writing, try taking it out and having others read your writing. If your readers still understand your purpose, then leave the reference out from your final draft. We recommend this not because we believe that religion should be excluded from all writing but rather because, given the weight of religious beliefs in people's lives, particular care is warranted.

- **When you write about religious beliefs and practices in general, have you used terms that reflect a range of religions?** For example, if you are writing about how varying communities construct special buildings for religious observances, you should not write, *All over the world, members of communities build churches for practicing their religions;* instead, write, *All over the world, people build mosques, temples, churches, and other specially named buildings used specifically for religious practices.*

   Similarly, be alert to the names religions use for their members and leaders. *Rabbi, priest, reverend, imam,* and *bishop* are only some of the possibilities. This is another case where doing a little research can help you show your respect for your readers.

- **Have you avoided assuming that your readers hold the same religious beliefs as you?** Many people who believe in a deity do not belong to an established church, and many people do not believe in a deity. Also, the names of deities in different religions are different. If you are trying to reach a broad audience—whether on a national or international level—be careful that any references you include about your own faith and religion do not imply that everyone else does or should believe just as you do.

- **Have you used the terms the people you are describing use for their beliefs?** When you want your writing to be read by a wide audience, be careful about your use of terms like *cult* instead of *religion* or *myth* instead of *religious belief.*

   If you need to describe religious practices and beliefs, do research. Have a range of others read your writing to be sure it is respectful.

- **Have you acknowledged the broad beliefs that people in the same religion might hold?** When you write about a religion, do not assume that its members hold the same beliefs or act the same. Catholics, for example, hold a range of views on abortion, the death penalty, birth control, and the status of women. The same is true of Muslims, Jews, Baptists, and the members of any other religion you can name, on any topic.

USING AN ESL DICTIONARY

There are English-English dictionaries specifically designed to support learning English as a new language. Such dictionaries have special features to help you learn the subtleties of the language; below is a sample excerpt from such a dictionary:

entry word

This dictionary color-codes each entry word. Not only does this help you see the words being defined, but in this dictionary, pink tells you a word is a noun; blue tells you it is a verb.

frequency information

These codes tell you that the word "card" is one of the top 1,000 words used in spoken English and one of the top 2,000 words used in written English; you can look through the dictionary to learn the most commonly used words.

pronunciation

This phonetic transcription tells you how the word is pronounced.

part of speech

n: noun
v: verb
adj: adjective
adv: adverb
prep: preposition

usage categories

The highlighted words tell you that the use of this word shifts in different categories.

definitions

ESL dictionaries provide definitions in easier-to-understand language than other dictionaries do.

sample sentences

Sample sentences can be more useful to you than definitions because they show a word in use and help you remember usage patterns.

frequency use of definition

The numbers before the categories indicate that the definitions are listed by frequency of use.

card¹ S1 W2 / kɑːd $ kɑːrd / n

1 INFORMATION [C] a small piece of plastic or paper containing information about a person or showing, for example, that they belong to a particular organization, club etc: *Employees must show their **identity cards** at the gate.* | *I haven't got my **membership card** yet.*

2 MONEY [C] a small piece of plastic, especially one that you get from a bank or shop, which you use to pay for goods or get money: *Lost or stolen cards must be reported immediately.* | *a £10 phone card* | *Every time you use your store card, you get air miles.* → CHARGE CARD, CHEQUE CARD, CREDIT CARD, DEBIT CARD

3 GREETINGS [C] a piece of folded thick stiff paper with a picture on the front, that you send to people on special occasions: *birthday/Christmas/greetings etc card* *a Mother's Day card*

4 HOLIDAY [C] a card with a photograph or picture on one side, that you send to someone when you are on holiday; ▤ **postcard**: *I sent you a card from Madrid.*

5 STIFF PAPER [U] *BrE* thick stiff paper; → **card-board**: *Cut a piece of white card 12 x 10cm.*

6 FOR WRITING INFORMATION [C] a small piece of thick stiff paper that information can be written or printed on: *a set of recipe cards* | *a score card*

count and noncount nouns

C: count noun
U: noncount noun

→ See pages 511–512 to learn about this important distinction between kinds of nouns.

PART 7
COMPOSING WITH STYLE

CONTENTS

WHERE ARE WE IN THE PROCESS FOR COMPOSING?

Understanding your project

Getting started

Asking questions

Shaping your project for others

Drafting a paper

Getting feedback

Revising   Paying attention to style

Polishing

STYLE AND AUDIENCE

ALL COMMUNICATIONS HAVE STYLE

This paragraph comes from a book about the senses:

One scent can be unexpected, momentary, and fleeting, yet conjure up a childhood summer beside a lake in the Poconos, when wild blueberry bushes teemed with succulent fruit and the opposite sex was as mysterious as space travel; another, hours of passion on a moonlit beach in Florida, while the night-blooming cereus drenched the air with thick curds of perfume and huge sphinx moths visited the cereus in a loud purr of wings; a third, a family dinner of pot roast, noodle pudding, and sweet potatoes, during a myrtle-mad August in a midwestern town, when both of one's parents were alive.

This paragraph comes from a webpage describing the work of two scientists:

In 1991 Axel and Buck discovered a family of roughly 1,000 genes that encode the odorant receptors of the olfactory epithelium, a patch of cells on the wall of the nasal cavity. The olfactory epithelium contains neurons that send messages directly to the olfactory bulb of the brain. When an odor excites a neuron, the signal travels along the nerve cell's axon and is transferred to the neurons in the olfactory bulb.

Both paragraphs describe the sense of smell. The differences between the paragraphs result because the writing is aimed at two different audiences:

- The first paragraph is for an audience of general readers, who have no particular scientific background. The paragraph is the opening of a chapter; it leads into passages that contain somewhat technical information. The style of the paragraph suggests to the readers that even though what the chapter covers is somewhat technical, readers will still enjoy it because the information will be detailed, sensual, and concrete.

- The second paragraph, as you could probably tell, was written by scientists for scientists. Individual words are not defined, because the writer assumes the reader knows them. The sentences are much shorter than in the first example, and they focus on describing processes as directly as possible, with few adjectives.

Although the second paragraph may not seem to have much style, many choices went into it, choices about individual words, the length of sentences, and the grammatical construction of the sentences.

OVERALL STYLE—AND FINELY DETAILED STYLE

The two example paragraphs probably suggest to you what the larger pieces from which each comes are like: The first paragraph comes from a book that is full of fine and luscious descriptions; the second comes from a short, to-the-point, descriptive piece of writing.

Notice, then, that style is about:

- **The overall feel a piece has for a reader.** Does the piece feel lush and detailed, or quick and precise? In what contexts and for what purposes will audiences expect writing like the first example paragraph or like the second?

- **The feel of words, sentences, and paragraphs.** The overall style of a piece is built from the choices you make at the level of words and sentences. We've already pointed out the differences in sentence length and word choice between the two examples; what other differences can you see between the two?

Style is not about being fancy;
it is about the detailed choices you make
to design your ideas for your audience.

STYLE IN WRITING

STYLING FOR CLARITY, CONCISION, COHERENCE, EMPHASIS, AND ENGAGEMENT

If you construct your writing to be clear, concise, coherent, emphatic, and engaging, you will have writing that works for present-day readers in most contexts. Your readers may not be able to name those five values, but in the United States we are in a culture that desires information to come quickly and easily as well as with some pleasure. (Or, to look at it in another way, no one likes having to work hard for boring information.)

If you are to construct writing that has these values, you need to know your purposes in writing. To decide how to style a sentence or paragraph, you need to ask how your choices will help your readers understand your purposes.

CLARITY

Clarity comes from a Latin word that means **clear**, as when the air is clear on a bright day. When you strive for clarity in writing, you shape sentences to help your readers see what is most important, quickly and easily.

CONCISION

Being concise means getting to the point. To be concise in writing, use as few words as possible. Concision supports clarity.

COHERENCE

When writing is coherent, it feels as though all its parts belong together. Readers see connections between the parts of a writing, and can easily grasp the overall purpose of the writing.

EMPHASIS

To persuade others to listen to your concerns, you need to make your purposes clear and you need to offer reasons. Some reasons will be more persuasive to your audience than others, and so the following pages offer strategies for emphasizing the parts of writing that you want your audience most to notice and remember.

Keep in mind, when you want to emphasize specific parts of your writing, that you cannot emphasize every single word or phrase. That would be like yelling continually at your audience—and, as you know, when someone yells at you continually, you stop listening. Instead, emphasis is when someone has been talking in a regular tone for a while and only now and then raises (or lowers) her voice.

ENGAGEMENT

Humans are lively, energetic, social beings. We like to tell jokes. We like to hear about odd events in the lives of others. We need to learn the practical details of living well and healthily. We need to learn how others live with the sorrows of death and pain.

We learn best from each other when our minds are active and engaged.

Writing that helps readers feel and understand someone else's delight or sorrow will be more effective than writing that doesn't. Writing that helps readers understand concretely and comfortably how to put together a stereo system will be more effective than writing that doesn't. Writing that helps readers understand the consequences of a melted polar ice cap is much more likely to bring readers to action than writing that just lists sterile facts.

■ ■ ■

The following pages discuss strategies you can use—with your own choices of individual words and your own constructions of sentences and paragraphs—to shape your writing to include all these values.

Because style is present in all levels of writing, we divide the following pages into the following order:

WORDS

SENTENCES

PARAGRAPHS

STYLING WORDS

All writing takes shape from the particular words you choose. On the next pages we offer you specific strategies for choosing words that will help you achieve your specific purposes in writing.

Compare these two sentences:

What did the first settlers of Easter Island eat when they were not eating the local equivalent of maple syrup?

What did the first settlers of Easter Island eat when they were not glutting themselves on the local equivalent of maple syrup?

Which sentence gives you a clearer and sharper sense of action? Why? When might you use one sentence rather than the other?

Compare these sentences:

The Canadian Rangers protect the Canadian Arctic, an area of Precambrian earth covered with 1,000-year-old Inuit settlements and ice.

The Canadian Rangers protect the Canadian Arctic, an old hunk of Precambrian earth, ice carpeted and spotted with Inuit settlements dating back 1,000 years.

The differences are subtle—but the second sentence (we think) asks you to think about the Canadian Arctic as a familiar, almost living, piece of the earth.

In what writing contexts would the second sentence be appropriate for shaping an audience's relations to the topic?

The dictionary defines cancer as "A malignant growth of cells caused by their abnormal and uncontrolled division." Chances are, however, that you cannot read **cancer** without some fear; it's possible you read the word with memories of someone close to you who has had cancer.

The definition of **cancer** is what we call the **denotation** of the word. The denotation of any word is simply its analytic definition, what we can count on most anyone else knowing.

Connotation, on the other hand, is what individuals bring to a word because of their personal or cultural background. Connotation describes the ideas or mental pictures that come to people's minds—unbidden from their memories and experiences—when they hear a word.

As you choose words, consider what associations—the ideas and mental pictures—your readers are likely to have. Do you want your readers to have positive or negative associations?

Most importantly—and especially if you are writing for an audience you do not know very well—you want to avoid using words that will have associations opposite to those that will help you achieve your purposes.

DICTIONARY DEFINITIONS & ASSOCIATIONS WITH WORDS

What is on this page will help you style your writing for:

- ☑ CLARITY
- ☐ CONCISION
- ☐ COHERENCE
- ☐ EMPHASIS
- ☑ ENGAGEMENT

TIP: FIND A READER

To be sure your word choices do not encourage readers to think of connotations that will undermine your purpose, have people from your audience read drafts of your writing.

STYLING WORDS
THE NAMES WE USE

What is on this page will help you style your writing for:

- ☑ CLARITY
- ☐ CONCISION
- ☐ COHERENCE
- ☐ EMPHASIS
- ☑ ENGAGEMENT

If the problem were called *Atmosphere cancer* or *Pollution death*, the entire conversation would be framed differently.

The writer of the above sentence is discussing **global warming**, and argues that we might, as individuals and as a culture, be less sanguine about global warming if the concept had been named more compellingly.

The words used to name a condition, a syndrome, or a place carry considerable weight through their connotations (→ discussed on page 271). Consider how the following terms ask readers to think about the person or position named:

pro-choice	pro-abortion
right-wing	conservative
heterosexual	straight
gun rights	gun control
affirmative action	racial preferences
illegal alien	undocumented immigrant

Readers respond to the names you use based on how they interpret the names. Someone in favor of affirmative action, for example, will likely be less amenable to writing that uses *racial preferences*.

> **TIP: KNOW YOUR AUDIENCE**
> Ask people from your audience about any terms you are considering so that you can learn how they respond. This will help you decide which terms help you make the arguments you desire.

Jump. Giggle. Estimate. Play. Clarify. Balance. Sing. Compare. Interpret.

These are action verbs: They name actions readers can imagine themselves taking. (This is connotation at work again.) Because action verbs encourage readers to imagine doing what a sentence describes, action verbs help readers connect with writing.

Action verbs describe concrete actions and so clarify what is going on:

He is enjoying performing.

He revels in performing.

The second sentence uses an action verb instead of **is**. **Revels** carries associations of energetic delight, and so will likely convey that emotion to readers.

Here are other examples:

The wasp put her stinger through the roach's exoskeleton and directly into its brain.

The wasp slipped her stinger through the roach's exoskeleton and directly into its brain.

The second sentence helps a reader understand more precisely what the wasp did—and makes the wasp's action scarier and more compelling.

ACTION VERBS

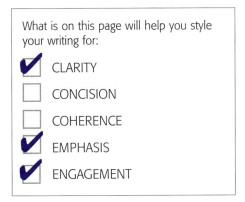

What is on this page will help you style your writing for:

- ✔ CLARITY
- ☐ CONCISION
- ☐ COHERENCE
- ✔ EMPHASIS
- ✔ ENGAGEMENT

TIP: REPLACING "IS"

When you want your writing to connect with readers, underline every use of **is** (including its variations, such as **are** and **was** and **will be**) in your writing, and if you see more than a few, replace those words with action verbs.

STYLING WORDS
JARGON

What is on this page will help you style your writing for:

☑ CLARITY

☑ CONCISION

☐ COHERENCE

☐ EMPHASIS

☑ ENGAGEMENT

Jargon can describe the specialized language of an organization or a profession; it can also describe fancy-sounding words someone else uses that you don't understand. Jargon, then, is useful when you are writing to those inside your profession and need to be precise; it is bad to use outside the profession because readers can't follow your writing.

To a reader immersed in computer culture, this probably makes sense:

In architecting our software, build systems, and engineering processes, we have given considerable thought to how our code will be able to evolve alongside the Mozilla code, without forking it.

Most readers know **architect** and **fork** as nouns, not verbs, and probably do not know what a **build system** or **Mozilla** is. A general audience is more likely to understand:

In developing our software and engineering processes, we have considered how our code will be able to evolve alongside the existing code with which it must work—without messing up that existing code.

TIP: KNOW YOUR AUDIENCE

If you are writing for people who share a vocabulary, use that vocabulary to be precise. If you do not know your audience, err on the side of caution: Use only words almost anyone would understand. Check this by having someone else read your writing.

As far as we can see, it is a fact that there are a whole lot of ways you can end up with way too many words in your sentences and, as a result of the too many words, make your readers bored or make it too hard for them to figure out your purpose.

When we see sentences like the above, it is usually a sign that the writer isn't sure what to say and is fumbling for a way to say it; sometimes people write like that when they aren't confident.

The sentence above is characterized by both empty words (words that add nothing to the purpose of the sentence) and redundant words (words that repeat uselessly what has already been said).

If we modify the sentence, we can end up with this, which is more concise and hence clearer for readers:

There are many ways to have too many words in a sentence, boring your readers, and getting in the way of their understanding.

To compose focused sentences, ask yourself, *What is it exactly that I want readers to take from this sentence?*

TOO MANY WORDS

What is on this page will help you style your writing for:

- ✓ CLARITY
- ✓ CONCISION
- ☐ COHERENCE
- ☐ EMPHASIS
- ✓ ENGAGEMENT

TIP: REREAD

Put your writing aside for a while, and then reread it: Looking at your writing anew will help you see where you have used more words than you need. You can also ask others to read it, to help you find the sentences that need tightening to clarify your points.

STYLING
SENTENCES

Style is all about how you connect with audiences in order to achieve your purposes.

On the next pages, we consider sentence style from two angles:

1 How do you construct sentences with the grammatical structures that readers expect in a formal, academic style of writing?

2 How do you construct sentences that readers want to read and that help you make your points?

Perhaps you think these two angles are really the same. After all, if sentences have the structures audiences expect, doesn't that mean readers will want to read them? Doesn't that mean the sentences will help writers make their points?

Consider this paragraph:

I must be real. Hear what I'm saying. We ain't going nowhere, as the boys in the hood be saying. Nowhere. If you promote all the surviving Afghans to the status of honorary Americans, Mr. President, where exactly on the bus does that leave me. When do I get paid. When can I expect my invitation to the ranch. I hear Mr. Putin's wearing jingle-jangle silver spurs around his dacha. Heard you fixed him up with an eight-figure advance on his memoirs. Is it true he's iced up to be the Marlboro man after he retires from Russia. Anything left under the table for me. And mine.

That paragraph breaks just about every rule one can imagine for formal writing. The writer uses periods instead of question marks. There are sentence fragments. The writer uses what some would call **colloquial phrasing**.

The paragraph's writer is John Edgar Wideman, who has won many prestigious awards for his writing and has taught writing at the university level. The paragraph comes from an essay, "Whose War," that appeared in the highly respected collection *The Best Essays of 2003*.

Given what he understood about his purposes—questioning the U. S. government's use of resources in the opening years of the twenty-first century—Wideman chose to write as he did. He chose to go against expectations of formal writing so that his essay would stand out, so that his essay would convey anger and frustration, so that his essay would read as though it were being spoken, passionately.

■ ■ ■

Wideman chose to break expectations because he was in a position to do so. He was in a position to do so both because he is a practiced writer who knows and can use the expectations and standards of formal writing when he wants, and also because he is a well-known writer. Because he is a well-known writer, others know that he usually does write in more expected formats, and that he must therefore have had his reasons for writing differently.

As you are styling your sentences, then, keep in mind the expectations of your readers, in regard to your words and to you. Will your readers expect a formal piece? Do your readers know you well enough to know that, if you break expectations, it is because you chose to do so? If you break expectations, how do you let readers know that you did so for a reason?

■ ■ ■

On the next pages, we offer angles for learning the expectations readers have for formal, academic writing.

Learn these well so that you can use them but also so that you can modify them as your purposes demand.

ACADEMIC SENTENCES

All academic writing will have the stylistic features listed below:

What is on this page will help you style your writing for:

 CLARITY

 CONCISION

 COHERENCE

 EMPHASIS

 ENGAGEMENT

CHECKLIST FOR FORMAL, ACADEMIC SENTENCES

❑ Your sentences have positive structures.

→ See page 281 to learn about sentences without double negatives.

→ See page 281 to learn about sentences that are positive rather than negative.

❑ Each sentence fits one of the four sentence patterns.

→ See pages 470–471.

❑ You use no sentence fragments—except, rarely, for emphasis.

→ See pages 490–493.

❑ Your sentences do not shift among grammatical forms.

→ See page 537 to learn about shifts in person and number.

→ See pages 522–523 to learn about shifts in verb tense.

→ See pages 538–539 to learn about shifts in voice.

→ See page 536 to learn about shifts in direct and indirect discourse.

→ See page 539 to learn about shifts in levels of formality.

❑ Your sentences are easy to read.

→ See pages 282–283.

SENTENCES DO NOT USE DOUBLE NEGATIVES

In formal writing, convention requires using only one negative in a sentence.

NEGATIVES: *barely hardly neither no not never none nothing scarcely*

Sometimes there will be more than one way to fix a double negative:

INCORRECT Bob did **not** have **no** solution for the problem.
NEGATIVE   NEGATIVE

CORRECT Bob had **no** solution for the problem.
NEGATIVE

CORRECT Bob did **not** have a solution for the problem.
NEGATIVE

Sometimes only one solution will be obvious:

INCORRECT **Nobody** said **nothing** about how to make quotations in a paper.
NEGATIVE   NEGATIVE

CORRECT **Nobody** said anything about how to make quotations in a paper.
NEGATIVE

SENTENCES ARE POSITIVE, NOT NEGATIVE

The following two sentences are both grammatically correct—but the second sentence is easier to read and understand because it presents its information in a straightforward, positive manner.

Classic gangster films were not without a message, showing audiences that if a gangster's life had no order, it was because society had no order.

Classic gangster films had a message, showing audiences that the chaos of a gangster's life mirrored the chaos of society.

TIP: READ!

Formal, academic writing—even in scientific disciplines—leaves considerable room for working with style. Reading widely respected writers in a discipline is the best way to learn the leeway you have.

TIP: WHERE TO FOCUS?

You are probably already in good control of several of these features of academic sentences. Ask someone who is familiar with your writing—a teacher or someone in your Writing Center—which of these features needs your attention, and then focus your attention just on those.

USING COORDINATION AND SUBORDINATION

What is on this page will help you style your writing for:

- ☑ CLARITY
- ☐ CONCISION
- ☑ COHERENCE
- ☑ EMPHASIS
- ☐ ENGAGEMENT

When you have two ideas to express to readers, do you want the ideas to have equal weight in their minds, or is one idea less important than the other?

When the ideas are equal, they are coordinate.

When one idea is less important than another, it is subordinate.

As you build sentences with independent clauses, you relate the clauses through coordination or subordination.

Both coordination and subordination are signs of formal, academic writing.

TO COORDINATE OR TO SUBORDINATE?

It's up to you: What understanding do you want readers to have of a sentence?

For example, if you want readers to consider knitting's traditional role to be equal to its more recent role, use *coordination*:

Knitting has traditionally been a domestic activity for women, but in the last decades it has been turned into a fine art.

Knitting has traditionally been a domestic activity for women; however, in the last decades it has been turned into a fine art.

If, however, you want to emphasize the recently growing importance of knitting over its past role, use *subordination*:

Although knitting has traditionally been a domestic activity for women, in the last decades it has been turned into a fine art.

→ To learn more about independent and dependent clauses, see pages 483–487.

→ To learn more about conjunctions, see pages 532–535.

COORDINATION

There are two patterns for building a sentence that uses coordination:

1 independent clause + **,** + coordinating conjunction + independent clause + **•**

COORDINATING CONJUNCTIONS: *and but for nor or so yet*

Stone is bad insulating material, but it makes a tight wall that radiates stored heat for hours.

2 independent clause + **;** + conjunctive adverb + independent clause + **•**

CONJUNCTIVE ADVERBS: *consequently furthermore however moreover otherwise therefore thus nevertheless*

With normal communication channels cut down during the war in Bosnia, the only news came by word of mouth; consequently posters became a cheap and easy way to spread information.

SUBORDINATION

There is one pattern for building a sentence that uses subordination, but you can reverse its order:

independent clause + **,** + subordinating conjunction + dependent clause + **•**

OR

subordinating conjunction + dependent clause + **,** + independent clause **•**

SUBORDINATING CONJUNCTIONS: *after although as because before if since that though unless until when where whether which while who whom whose*

After she placed a doily on top of a cupcake, my grandmother would sift sugar on top to make a lacy pattern.

My grandmother would sift sugar on top of a cupcake to make a lacy pattern, after she had placed a doily on top of the cupcake.

STYLING SENTENCES
FIGURATIVE LANGUAGE

What is on this page will help you style your writing for:

- [ ] CLARITY
- [ ] CONCISION
- [ ] COHERENCE
- [x] EMPHASIS
- [x] ENGAGEMENT

When you want readers to understand or remember a crucial concept, use figurative language. *Figurative language* refers to a range of strategies that make concepts stand out.

FIGURATIVE COMPARISONS

As we said when we discussed analogy in Part 3 (➜ see page 106), you can help readers understand new or complex ideas by describing the ideas in terms readers already know. Similarly, you can make ideas more vivid—and so more memorable—with unexpected comparisons.

COMPARISONS TO MAKE NEW IDEAS FAMILIAR

This passage uses concepts of building blocks and atoms to explain mathematical concepts:

Prime numbers, such as 17 and 23, are those that can be divided only by themselves and 1. They are the most important objects in mathematics because, as the ancient Greeks discovered, they are the building blocks of all numbers—any of which can be broken down into a product of primes. (For example, 105 = 3 x 5 x 7.) They are the hydrogen and oxygen of the world of mathematics, the atoms of arithmetic.

COMPARISONS TO MAKE IDEAS MEMORABLE

Microsoft is a middle-aged company struggling to figure out how to dance with the teenagers, and its body simply can't keep up with its intentions, no matter how correct they may be.

The passage could instead read, *Microsoft is having trouble attracting young audiences*—but would that have created such a funny picture in your head?

Michael Ondaatje's *The English Patient* is a novel whose nervous system connects books, visual art, and war.

By giving the novel it discusses a **nervous system**, the example above compares the novel to a living being, giving it a vibrancy it wouldn't otherwise have.

"Goya's Last Works," at the Frick, isn't large, but neither are grenades.

The one little word **grenades**—emphasized by its placement as the last word of the sentence—suggests that the exhibit of paintings being described is explosive and even somehow dangerous.

"I think of her as the human embodiment of Wal-Mart," said Kevvy Schlaucher, a 25-year-old engineer from Calgary, Canada, who used to watch the show with his mother. "The Oprah Empire is everywhere. She makes sure you don't get out of the system."

Saying that Oprah Winfrey's empire is a big business is not as memorable as making you hold her and Wal-Mart in your head at the same time.

FIGURATIVE PATTERNS

Experiments with familiar language patterns can make memorable sentences:

On Monday, engineers repaired the ruptured 17th Street Canal levee in New Orleans and floodwaters receded a bit as some suburban residents, carrying suitcases and heavy hearts, briefly returned to their homes and sifted through the sodden debris.

When you read *carrying suitcases and…*, you might expect the next words to be *backpacks* or *boxes*. *Heavy hearts* can slow your reading, making palpable the residents' emotions.

Experiment with any language pattern, such as those of conjunctions:

All day I keep the Shabbos. This means I do not turn on a light or tear paper or write or bathe or cook or sew or do any of the hundred kinds of work involved in building the Holy Temple.

The **or**'s stretch out the list of actions to emphasize the number of items.

Just as you can multiply conjunctions, you can also take them away:

I smiled. We smoked. We looked up at the stars. We shook from cold.

Grammatical disconnection and emotional disconnection between people are shown by a lack of conjunctions.

TIP: HOW MUCH?
Like spice, figurative language works best in small quantities. Because figurative language can heighten readers' attention to important points in your writing, using it a lot would diffuse its effects.

TIP: NEED INSPIRATION?
Listen to country-western music. Figurative language abounds there, sometimes funny, sometimes not, as when Julie Roberts sings, "Men and mascara always run."

STYLING PARAGRAPHS
CONCLUDING PARAGRAPHS

What is on this page will help you style your writing for:

 CLARITY

☐ CONCISION

 COHERENCE

 EMPHASIS

 ENGAGEMENT

Why talk about concluding paragraphs before introductory paragraphs?

Because you cannot have a shining, strong introductory paragraph until you know the exact end toward which that paragraph points readers.

FUNCTIONS OF CONCLUDING PARAGRAPHS FOR READERS

- Concluding paragraphs sum up the arguments of the paper.
- Concluding paragraphs give readers a take-away memory of the writing.

STRATEGIES FOR CONCLUDING

As you write, you cannot separate the two functions of concluding paragraphs. As you read the following examples, look for how they mix functions, but also try to imagine what preceded the conclusion; a strong conclusion should enable that.

RESTATING OR SUMMARIZING YOUR ARGUMENT

Provide a crisp summary, not a rote repetition. You can include a question, quotation, or recommended action:

In sum, the globalization of English does not mean that if we who speak only English just sit back and wait, we'll soon be able to exchange ideas with anyone who has anything to say. We can't count on having much more around the world than a very basic ability to communicate. Outside of certain professional fields, if English-speaking Americans hope to exchange ideas with people in a nuanced way, we may be well advised to do as people elsewhere are doing: become bilingual.

RECOMMENDING ACTION

The following conclusion recommends specific actions its audience can take:

The problem at hand is so huge it requires a response like our national mobilization to fight—and win—World War II. To move our nation off of fossil fuels, we need inspired, Churchillian leadership and sweeping statutes à la the Big War or the Civil Rights Movement. So, frankly, I feel a twinge of nausea each time I see that predictable "10 Things You Can Do" sidebar in a well-meaning magazine or newspaper article. In truth, the only list that actually matters is the one we should all be sending to Congress *post haste*, full of 10 muscular clean-energy statutes that would finally do what we say we want: rescue our life-giving Earth from climate catastrophe.

(Note: In the examples of introductory paragraphs on page 294 is the intro-duction that leads to this conclusion.)

SUGGESTING MORE QUESTIONS FOR RESEARCH

Such suggestions about the conduct of technical writing courses, however, must remain suggestions and not firm recommendations, until we know more about the composing processes of engineers. Additional research on composing might reveal how Nelson, his firm, and his subdiscipline are and are not typical. It might show how his composing habits are more efficient or less efficient than those of his colleagues. It might suggest that some tasks call for very different composing habits and skills than others, or it might imply that technical writers should develop several composing styles that they can call upon in different composing situations. One thing seems certain, however: Only when more research is completed will teachers know how to better prepare students for the kinds of writing they will do at work.

REFLECTING ON HOW YOUR WRITING OR RESEARCH HAS AFFECTED YOU

Using your own voice pulls readers closer, making your observations more compelling.

In the interviews I conducted for this paper, I learned that men and women learn to be men and women through experiencing all the photographs, movies, magazine covers, and popular songs that portray what men and women are supposed to be and do. I've also learned how the simplest of tossed-off sentences in different situations can shape someone's sense of what's proper behavior. I heard how a teacher's comments are remembered for a long time. As an education major, it's that last observation I will carry with me, to help me think about the responsibilities I'll be taking on.

> ### TIP: FUNCTIONS OF CONCLUDING PARAGRAPHS FOR WRITERS
> Once they are drafted, concluding paragraphs provide surprisingly useful suggestions to writers about revising.
> → See page 306.

TRANSITIONS BETWEEN PARAGRAPHS

What is on this page will help you style your writing for:

- ☑ CLARITY
- ☐ CONCISION
- ☑ COHERENCE
- ☑ EMPHASIS
- ☑ ENGAGEMENT

In Part 5, we discussed creating coherence within paragraphs; here we discuss creating coherence *between* paragraphs.

Most writers need to learn how to provide transitions between paragraphs, but learning how to do this will help your writing be confident and effective. When you use the strategies we discuss here, you tell readers why one paragraph follows another; you enable readers to follow and so better understand your arguments.

STRATEGIES FOR BUILDING TRANSITIONS

- Repeat crucial words, phrases, or concepts from one paragraph to the next.
- Repeat crucial concepts by using synonyms.
- Use the linking words listed on page 216 to show relationships between the paragraphs.

LINK THE LAST SENTENCE OF ONE PARAGRAPH TO THE FIRST SENTENCE OF THE NEXT

In constructing transitions from one paragraph to the next, choose the most important words, phrases, or concepts of the last sentence of a paragraph; and then weave those words, phrases, or concepts into the the first sentence of the next paragraph.

The paragraphs to the right use the strategies above to build transitions.

ozone in Mexico City have exceeded the country's air-quality standards 284 days per year, on average. Geography doesn't help: Mexico City lies on a broad basin ringed by tall mountains that can block the movement of air masses that might clear out pollution.

Furthermore, the city's rapid spread in recent decades has aggravated its pollution problems. Mexico City now covers about 1,500 square kilometers—about 10 times as much as it occupied just 50 years ago.

In this example, the writer uses the first paragraph to discuss connections between pollution in Mexico City and the city's geography; in the second paragraph, he turns to discussing how the city's size contributes to its pollution problems. **Furthermore** tells readers that additional information is being added, and **city** and **pollution** carry the topic from one paragraph to the next.

■ ■ ■

still-unawakened self, a collective psyche dangerously out of balance, and this awareness united many of the poets in an effort to support and produce a poetry of protest whose fundamental aim was not to destroy the establishment but to rethink it, heal it, render it more flexible and self-aware.

The work of Allen Ginsberg paved the way for this sensibility by claiming the right of the self to be what it has to be and write the poetry it has to write; but Ginsberg also went a step further "to insist" as James E. Mersmann points out in his

In this example's first paragraph, the writer generally describes poets' desires in the mid-twentieth century; in the second paragraph, he turns to discussing how one poet helped shape those desires. Note how **this sensibility** summarizes and repeats the description of the poets' desires, thus linking the two paragraphs.

■ ■ ■

the same thing he does, you do it using plain words without instruments. Words are like music. Well-reasoned thoughts, conveyed with well-chosen words, can touch us deeply as a moving symphony or a driving drum beat.

But Maggie Simpson doesn't possess language and doesn't speak. In the twentieth century, philosophers concerned with humanity's place in the universe have turned to the relationship between words and thoughts. How do we think if

In this example, the writer argues first that words matter in communication; in the second paragraph, the discussion shifts to focus on a character who doesn't use words. **But** signals this shift to readers. The two paragraphs are still strongly connected by the repetition of concepts concerning words and language.

STYLE IN VISUAL TEXTS

TYPOGRAPHY

SERIF AND SANS SERIF TYPEFACES

Knowing this major distinction between kinds of typefaces will help you choose typefaces to fit your purposes.

serif   sans serif

Serif is a French word meaning **tail**, and it describes typefaces that have little swashes (circled above) added to the ends of letters. *Sans* is French for **without**; thus *sans serif* typefaces have no serifs.

Serifed typefaces generally look more classical or old-fashioned than sans serif typefaces. Audiences in the United States are accustomed to seeing serifed typefaces in long sections of text that are meant to be readable.

DECORATIVE TYPEFACES

Typefaces that look like this are called "DECORATIVE." They are not easy to read in anything but short phrases and so they are most often used for short pieces of text like titles and headers. OCCASIONALLY A PARTICULAR PURPOSE JUSTIFIES USING THEM FOR BLOCKS OF TEXT YOU WANT PEOPLE TO READ, BUT ONLY OCCASIONALLY.

SOME NOTES ON USING TYPEFACES

Since the invention of the printing press in the fifteenth century, conventions for the use of type in different genres have developed.

- Academic and other texts that are meant to be serious or formal almost always use one size of a single, serifed typeface throughout. For example, teachers might expect you to use the typeface Times in 12-point type for papers; at most, then, you would use the plain, italic, and bold versions of the Times typeface.

  Occasionally, writers will use a second typeface in such writings: A plain, sans serifed typeface such as Helvetica or Arial, in its bold version, can provide sufficient contrast for headings, as described to the right.

- Visual unity, a value of many genres, underlies the number of typefaces experienced visual designers use. Even in genres that have considerable wiggle room in choice of type—genres such as posters or brochures—designers most often use only two or three typefaces: one for the title or main head, another for the information or body text, and perhaps a third if there is another text function that needs to be visually differentiated.

HEADINGS

When you chunk a text by inserting headings, you allow readers to better see the sections of your text. This can help readers both comprehend and remember your arguments.

- Headings should be short, taking up only one line, so that readers can see them at a glance.

- Headings should have space before them so that readers see a heading as part of the text that follows it.

- The typeface of a heading should be different (in size, thickness, or style) from the typeface used in the body of the text, again so that readers can see and read the heading easily.

To create a conservative look in a heading
Use a bold version of the typeface you use for the body of text.

To create a more modern look in a heading
Use a sans serif typeface heading with a serifed typeface for the body of the text. Usually, you will have to use a bold version of the sans serif typeface to create an easy-to-see contrast between the heading and the body.

NOTE: Unless a heading is very short, use upper- and lowercase letters. Using only uppercase letters is hard to read for more than just a few words.

STYLE IN ORAL PRESENTATIONS

In oral presentations, the main component of style is you: Your voice and gestures will be your main strategies for creating emphasis and engagement.

CONNECTING WITH AN AUDIENCE

Public speaking might make you anxious. In addition to remembering to breathe deeply before and during a talk, making eye contact with people in your audience and even addressing them directly can help you relax. These actions are also style decisions.

As you prepare, decide how to connect with your audience. Few presentation contexts and purposes require formality. Rather, in almost all circumstances, you can engage your audience—and thus encourage their generosity toward your arguments—by asking them questions, speaking directly to them while looking into their faces, or smiling.

SPEAKING STYLES

Your voice—its volume, speed, and tone—gives you a wonderful range of style choices while you speak. To take advantage of your voice, have your presentation organized in time so you can practice often: Seek a conversational style and avoid reading.

Identify the presentation parts (words or sentences) you wish to emphasize. Then experiment with different ways of saying those parts. Exaggerate volume and tone, playfully, and make yourself laugh. This will help you relax—but will also help you find what works best for the real presentation.

BODY LANGUAGE

For most presentations, you need to use your body language—expressions and gestures—to put your audience at ease and to emphasize the major points of your presentation.

Look over what you have written for your presentation, and decide what facial expressions, and where, support your arguments. In the past, audiences expected almost theatrical gestures and expressions; now, simple smiles, frowns, nods, or occasional head shakes are enough.

Similarly, current audiences do not expect grand hand gestures. You will make audiences uncomfortable if you nervously wring your hands, but you can instead keep your hands clasped in front of or behind you, placed on the lectern, or holding your notes.

Do check over your words, seeing where a gesture will emphasize what needs emphasizing. And then practice.

Practicing your presentation over and over will help you make your body language relaxed and friendly.

USING VISUAL SUPPORTS

Visual supports can be slide presentations (using software like PowerPoint or Keynote), overheads, handouts, or physical objects.

Use visual supports to help your audience see the main points of your presentation.

Use objects that help you demonstrate procedures you are discussing or that illustrate your main points: A stretched-out plastic bag holding the amount of trash an average American throws out in one day will make the point about

American's resource use much more strongly than a spoken statistic.

Whatever your visual aids, practice with them. You need to be able to use them comfortably so that your audience focuses on the points you are making rather than on your trying to use a projector. Also, using visual aids slows down a presentation; if you have a time limit, practicing with your visuals will help you stay within that time limit.

PARALLELISM IN ORAL PRESENTATIONS

Apply to the paragraphs you will speak the same guidelines for building parallelism in sentences that we described on page 286. Paragraphs that use parallelism create rhythmic and emotionally compelling paragraphs, as in this Convocation Address by Nikki Giovanni:

We are Virginia Tech.

The Hokie Nation embraces our own and reaches out with open hearts and hands to those who offer their hearts and minds. We are strong, and brave, and innocent, and unafraid. We are better than we think and not quite what we want to be. We are alive to the imaginations and the possibilities. We will continue to invent the future through our blood and tears and through all our sadness.

We are the Hokies.

We will prevail.

We will prevail.

We will prevail.

We are Virginia Tech.

HINTS & TIPS FOR CONCLUDING PARAGRAPHS

USING CONCLUDING PARAGRAPHS TO HELP YOU REVISE

You are writing your first draft. You type the last period for the last sentence, and breathe deeply: You are done.

But, no, wait, sorry: You are not done, not if you want the strongest possible writing. Definitely take a deep breath and leave your paper for a while—but come back several hours or a day later.

For writers, the first draft of a conclusion provides crucial information:

- Often, a conclusion is when you realize what your argument really is. Experienced writers know that a first draft is only a beginning, and that often they don't know what they really want to argue until that first attempt at a conclusion. Sometimes writers use the concluding paragraph of a first draft—because it is often a succinct and passionate statement of an argument—as the first paragraph of the next draft.

- If you do feel that the concluding paragraph is an accurate and strong statement of your argument, go back through the rest of the paper to ask yourself: Do all the other paragraphs lead up to and support the conclusion?

- Because most writers intuitively know that concluding paragraphs should include a little passion, they include passion—but often there is no passion in the rest of the writing, and so the conclusion will seem unsuitable to readers. When you finish a conclusion, check that its emotional tone is supported by the rest of the writing, just as you check to make sure its logical claims are likewise supported.

- Use the concluding paragraph to help you make your introductory paragraph as strong and engaging as possible. Knowing the end point where you want to take readers, what might be the most effective starting point?

PART 8
DOCUMENTING

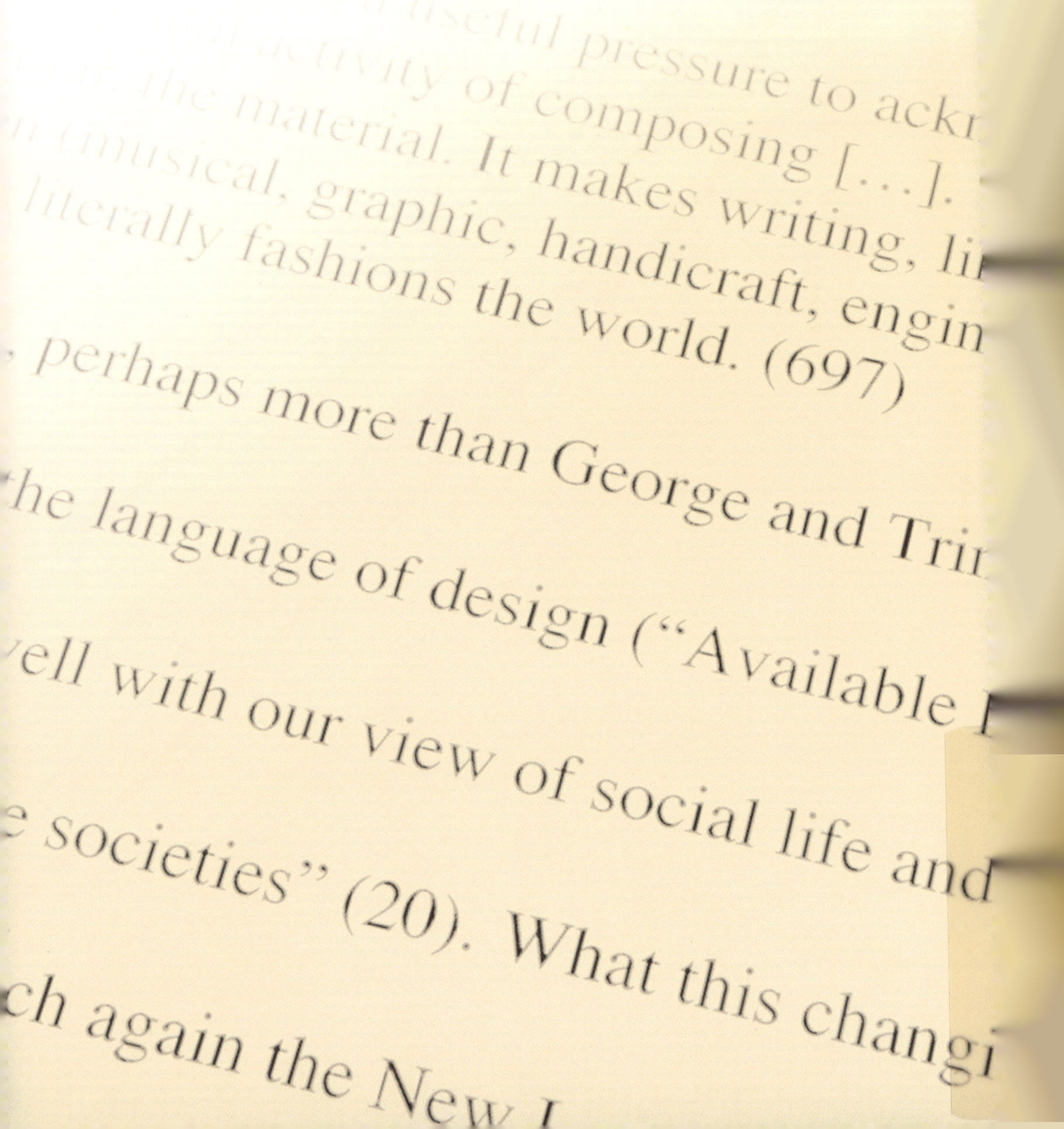

CONTENTS

WHERE ARE WE IN THE PROCESS FOR COMPOSING?

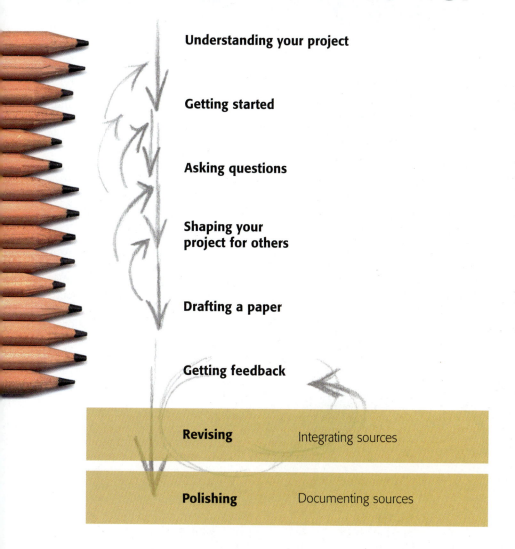

Understanding your project

Getting started

Asking questions

Shaping your project for others

Drafting a paper

Getting feedback

Revising   Integrating sources

Polishing   Documenting sources

WHY CITE AND DOCUMENT SOURCES?
CONSIDERING PLAGIARISM—AND HOW TO AVOID IT

Do you want to live and work in communities—school districts, neighborhoods, cities, countries—where people respect each other and each other's ideas, and where people try to persuade you and each other based on the best possible evidence?

If you do, some of your part in shaping such communities is knowing cultural expectations for showing respect in spoken or written deliberations—even when you disagree. Your part is understanding how to determine and use the best possible evidence and letting others know where that evidence comes from, so that they can judge and check it.

To cite is to name the people from whom you drew your ideas; **to document** is to record where—print or online books, journals, or newspapers—you found the ideas.

Many people think that using, citing, and documenting sources is only for academic writing. There are certainly academic conventions for doing such work—and helping you learn those conventions is a large part of the following pages. But these conventions exist because people who write academic papers, no matter what discipline, want to be sure that they are using the best possible evidence and that they are making that evidence available to others to check.

Citing and documenting sources shows that you want to take part in ongoing deliberations while being respectful of the research and thinking others have done before you. It shows that you want others to understand where your good reasons and thinking come from.

WHAT IS PLAGIARISM?

Plagiarism is using the ideas or words of others without acknowledgment, as though they were your own.

Plagiarism can happen inadvertently: While doing research, you might take notes or copy some text from a webpage and in the rush to finish a paper, lose track of where the words came from and put them straight into your paper. Plagiarism can also happen when you don't have enough confidence in your own ideas or the quality of your research to take your own positions; you let the words of others stand in for your words.

Whether plagiarism is inadvertent, purposeful, or the result of not enough confidence, it is considered wrong in the United States. It can cause you to have to redo an assignment, to fail an assignment or a class, or to be expelled from school. It stops you from learning how to have confidence in presenting your ideas in ways others will respect; it also stops you from developing your own ideas and learning.

PLAGIARISM—OR MISUSE OF SOURCES?

Sometimes students and other novice writers are accused of plagiarism because they did not cite all their sources or did not cite their sources conventionally. This can happen when writers are inexperienced with or simply do not know the conventions.

To avoid this happening to you, here are steps you can take:

- If you receive an assignment that asks you to use sources, be sure you know what citation style your teacher wants you to use. If an assignment does not specify a style, ask.

- Ask your teacher or someone in a Writing or Learning Center to look at a draft of your writing: Are you using citation styles as conventions ask?

- Pay close attention to the conventions as they are presented in this handbook. The conventions are detailed, and can seem tedious to learn, but the conventions are detailed precisely because it is a cultural practice in the United States to be very careful with the words and ideas of others.

CULTURAL ATTITUDES TOWARD THE WORDS AND IDEAS OF OTHERS

In some cultures, using the words of respected authorities and knowing when others are using them, without mentioning the source, are signs of being educated. In some cultures, students use the words of their teachers and other authorities as their own to indicate that they have learned what they were supposed to. In the United States, however, concern for the value of property—and a belief that words and ideas can be individual property—lead to a valuing of and the development of conventions for acknowledging uses of others' words or ideas.

WHAT WORDS AND IDEAS DON'T NEED TO BE CITED

You don't need to cite sources when the ideas you are using are

- *Common and shared knowledge.* Most people will accept without question that there are seven days in a week or that the capital of Maryland is Annapolis. To be sure whether you need to give a source, ask yourself if everyone in your audience will know. If the answer is **yes**, then you can write without citing a source. If you're unsure if what you are writing is common knowledge, find and cite a source for it.

- *Facts that are available in a wide range of sources.* If every encyclopedia or newspaper article you check states that Joan of Arc died in 1431 or that somewhere between 22 and 26 inches of snow fell in upstate New York on Monday, then you can include these facts in your writing without citing any source for the facts.

- *The results of your own field research.*

WHAT WORDS AND IDEAS ALWAYS NEED TO BE CITED

Cite the origins of ideas and words you use in writing or oral presentations if the words and ideas are

- *Someone else's exact words* that you copied from a book, website, or interview.

- *Your paraphrase or summary of someone else's words or ideas.* (→ See pages 322–325 on paraphrasing and summarizing.)

- *Facts not known or accepted by everyone in your audience.* While global climate change is accepted by almost all scientists, many nonscientific audiences are still unsure about the details. If you are writing to a nonscientific audience, you should provide sources for any evidence you offer that the climate is changing.

- *Photographs, charts, graphs, or illustrations.* Give the source—and permissions, if necessary—for any visual object you place into writing or a webpage. Do this even if you made the object, to calm any concerns readers might have.

HOW TEACHERS TRY TO PREVENT OR RECOGNIZE PLAGIARISM

Teachers have developed ways both to avoid and to detect plagiarism. Teachers help you avoid plagiarism by asking you to develop research projects through notes, drafts, and revisions so that they can see and encourage the progress of your ideas. (Teachers who ask you to do this will therefore be curious if you abandon a topic at the last moment and turn in a final paper on a new topic.) Some software programs can check papers online against existing writing to recognize if writers have used words from others; this software is controversial because it is not always accurate and can impinge on students' privacy and intellectual property rights.

TIPS FOR AVOIDING PLAGIARISM

The best way to avoid plagiarism is to have integrity toward your sources and toward yourself as a researcher: Respect the words and ideas of others as you would like your own words and ideas respected.

Your work habits can help you: If you take notes carefully and record your research, you will know when you are using the words and ideas of others.

• Keep a working bibliography of all sources you might use. This will help you have at hand the information you need when you need it so that you can cite sources as others expect.

→ To learn about working bibliographies, see pages 82–83.

• If you record someone else's words because you might use them later, mark that they are someone else's words; this will help keep you from inadvertently using those words as though they were yours.

If you copy words from a webpage into your notes, color-code the notes or put quotation marks around them; always record the information you need for citing the words.

→ See pages 342–347 for the information you need to record to cite webpages.

If you record words from print sources, put quotation marks around them immediately and record the source information.

→ See pages 326–341 for the information to record to cite print texts.

• If you work online, take advantage of websites like furl.com or citeulike.com to track your sources. Similarly, make copies of print sources you might use so that you can check—after you've finished your writing—that you have cited with integrity.

• Understand how to quote, summarize, and paraphrase.

→ See pages 314–325.

• Understand how to cite the words of others in your text.

→ For MLA in-text citations, see pages 350–359; for APA, see pages 421–425; for CSE, see pages 452–457; for CMS, see pages 458–459.

• Understand how to build an appropriate and accurate Works Cited page.

→ For sample sets of MLA Works Cited pages, see pages 404–405 and 416–418; for a sample APA References list, see pages 450–451.

TIP: HOW TO CHECK THAT YOU HAVE CITED ALL YOUR SOURCES

When your writing is very close to finished, give it to a friend (one who is a careful reader) with two different colored highlighters. Ask the friend to mark your paper, highlighting your ideas in one color and the ideas of everyone else in the other color. If your friend highlights the ideas correctly, then your paper should be good to go. If not, you need to add citations and other indications—as we show later in these pages—so that it is clear when the ideas and words in your paper are not your own.

There are four facets to
CITING AND DOCUMENTING

1

USING OTHERS' WORDS IN YOUR WRITING BY QUOTING, SUMMARIZING, OR PARAPHRASING

Quoting is using others' exact words; summarizing is reporting the main idea of someone else's words, without details; paraphrasing is putting others' ideas into your own words.

QUOTING
"We started making videos to send home that showed what our life here was like," says Wright in an e-mail from his Antarctic base.

SUMMARIZING
Pollan's book tells us about the origins of four meals from widely different sources, asking us to question how our eating habits embed us in social, economic, political, and ecological webs.

PARAPHRASING
Sabido describes how he wants his *telenovelas* to reach his audience's limbic brain, which governs emotions.

→ Go to pages 314–325.

2

COLLECTING THE CITATION INFORMATION YOU NEED FOR ANY SOURCE YOU USE

Anytime you quote, summarize, paraphrase, or otherwise use any kind of source (including photographs, drawings, charts, and graphs) in your writing, you need to give readers information about the source.

For different sources you need to collect different information.

→ To learn the information to collect, see pages 326–349.

→ To determine the kinds of sources you have, see pages 44–59.

→ For help figuring out if the kinds of sources you are using are right for your arguments, see pages 42–43.

THE STYLES OF CITATIONS

There are four styles for citing sources: MLA, APA, CMS, and CSE. Each style is used by a different set of disciplines. As we note on the opposite page, we devote separate pages of this book to each of these styles; see the section on a style to learn who uses it.

3

CREATING IN-TEXT CITATIONS FOR YOUR SOURCES

When you use the words or ideas of someone else, provide information to help readers find those words themselves. Each style provides ways for you to give this information.

MLA STYLE

Monroe reminds us that there is no generic access to computers: Access at home is not the same as access at work or school (19–20, 26–27).

APA STYLE

Whalen (1995) analyzed how the talk of operators responding to emergency 911 calls was organized in part by the task of filling in required information on a computer screen with a specific visual organization.

4

CREATING WORKS CITED, REFERENCES LISTS, AND BIBLIOGRAPHIES

Each style has its own name for the list of sources at the end of a piece of writing, but all of them require writers to list all the sources used in their writing.

APA STYLE

Panofsky, E. (1970). *Meaning in the visual arts.* Harmondsworth, England: Penguin.

CSE STYLE

20. Latchman DS. From genetics to gene therapy: the molecular pathology of human disease. London: Bios Scientific Publishers; 1994. 362 p. (UCL molecular pathology series).

Because each style for in-text citations and works cited lists is different, we provide separate sections for each style.

→ The **MLA style** for in-text citations is described on pages 350–359; the style for the list of works cited at the end of a paper is described on pages 360–405.

→ The **APA style** for in-text citations is described on pages 421–425; the style for the list of works cited at the end of a paper is described on pages 426–451.

→ The **CSE style** for in-text citations is described on page 453; the style for the list of works cited at the end of a paper is described on pages 454–457.

→ The **CMS style** for in-text citations is described on pages 458–459; the style for the list of works cited at the end of a paper is described on pages 460–462.

QUOTING THE WORDS OF OTHERS

Here is one way to use the words of the journal excerpt on page 315:

Because of the "addictive qualities" of massively multiplayer online games (MMOGs), a researcher of uses of digital technologies for language learning, Ravi Purushotma, argues that teachers ought to use such games "to capture the attention of adolescent audiences and bring them into a manipulatable world with players from all over the planet" (86).

When you quote the words of others, it is as though you invite the words to speak for you: You bring both the sense of speaking and the authority of the speaker into your writing.

Because of this, use the exact words of others in your writing when those words add something to your argument that you cannot provide with your own words.

- Use words from those whom your readers are likely to recognize either by name, work, or affiliation. This will give readers more reason to accept your points.

- Quote words that will be funny, poignant, striking, or otherwise memorable for your readers. This will help readers better remember your points.

- When in your writing you are considering the positions of people with whom you disagree, it can be useful to quote their words. This shows your audience that you are being fair by letting others speak for themselves.

THE PARTS OF QUOTING WELL

Here is the example of quoting the journal article excerpt on page 315. We repeat the example—with color coding—to show the many conventions that readers of more formal texts have come to expect:

Because of the " addictive qualities " of massively multiplayer online games (MMOGs), a researcher of uses of digital technologies for language learning, Ravi Purushotma, argues that teachers ought to use such games " to capture the attention of adolescent audiences and bring them into a manipulatable world with players from all over the planet " (86).

The points to the right can be a checklist for when you quoting another's words, to be sure you follow the conventions.

It is a convention that all direct quotations are indicated by quotation marks.
→ See page 318 for details on using quotation marks.

The words you are quoting should be the exact words, with no changes.
→ Sometimes, however, you will need to modify the words you are quoting—perhaps to shorten the quotation, to give an explanation readers might need, or to correct spelling—see page 319.

Using a title or affiliation of the person you are quoting, or the source of the quote, can help your audience understand why they should pay attention to this person.
→ See page 319 for ways to do this.

It is a fairly consistent convention to give the name of the person(s) responsible for the words you are quoting.
→ See page 320 for ways to do this.

Signal to your readers that you are quoting the words of others with the verb you choose to introduce the quoted words; use these verbs to weave the quotation into your writing.
→ See pages 320–321 for a list of signal words and for hints on weaving others' words into your own writing.

Each citation style specifies how to reference the page or paragraph of a citation's source. Readers can then find the exact place from which you drew your cite.
→ For MLA style, see pages 350–359.
→ For APA style, see pages 421–425.
→ For CSE style, see page 453.
→ For CMS style, see pages 458–459.

USING THE NAME OF THE PERSON BEING QUOTED

Giving the full name of the person or persons you are citing—and referring to them formally by last name or appropriate pronoun in following sentences—is a convention in formal writing. It is a way of acknowledging that ideas are always connected to thinkers.

The sports historian James Riordan suggests that after the revolutionary stirrings of 1905, factory owners introduced soccer to their workers "as an attempt to encourage a form of civil loyalty and to divert their employees from revolutionary and other disruptive actions."

SIGNALLING THAT YOU ARE QUOTING: CHOOSING AN INTRODUCTORY VERB AND WEAVING IN THE WORDS OF OTHERS

It is a convention to introduce others' words with phrases that

• signal to readers that you are about to quote.

• weave the quoted words into your writing so that they fit the structure of your own words.

CHOOSING SIGNALLING VERBS

You can choose among many verbs to signal to readers that they are about to read the words of others; we list many of them to the right.

Note, however, that the verb you choose not only signals that you are about to quote the words of someone; your verb choice can also signal to readers your position about the words you are quoting. Consider these examples, looking at how they ask you to think about what Paulk says.

In his article about interior design in the computer game *The Sims*, Charles Paulk says that the Sims are "hard-wired social climbers" (n.p.).

In his article about interior design in the computer game *The Sims*, Charles Paulk charges that the Sims are "hard-wired social climbers" (n.p.).

In his article about interior design in the computer game *The Sims*, Charles Paulk complains that the Sims are "hard-wired social climbers" (n.p.).

Signalling verbs

acknowledges	*adds*	*admits*
advises	*agrees*	*analyzes*
answers	*argues*	*asks*
asserts	*believes*	*charges*
claims	*comments*	*complains*
concedes	*concludes*	*concurs*
condemns	*confirms*	*considers*
contends	*criticizes*	*declares*
denies	*describes*	*disagrees*
disputes	*emphasizes*	*explains*
expresses	*finds*	*holds*
illustrates	*implies*	*insists*
interprets	*lists*	*maintains*
notes	*objects*	*observes*
offers	*opposes*	*points out*
predicts	*proposes*	*refutes*
rejects	*remarks*	*replies*
reports	*responds*	*reveals*
says	*shows*	*speculates*
states	*suggests*	*thinks*

WEAVING QUOTED WORDS INTO YOUR WRITING

Anytime you quote, watch that:

- Your own words weave together with the quoted words to make a sentence that is **logical**.

"Poverty is more than a problem of economics," Farah claims, because it is also a public health problem.

The words that follow the quotation do not explain why Farah thinks poverty is a public health problem. Here is a fix:

"Poverty is more than a problem of economics," Farah claims, because it can adversely affect how the brain functions and so effect what people are capable of doing.

- Your own words weave together with the quoted words to make a sentence that is **grammatical**.

If poverty can "literally damage our brains," as Farah asserts, then it "directly affecting the biological substrate of who we are and what we can become."

Because the verb forms used above are inconsistent, the sentence is ungrammatical. Here is a fix:

If poverty can "damage our brains," as Farah asserts, then it damages also "the biological substrate of who we are and what we can become."

TIPS: **FOR QUOTING**

- Papers composed completely or mostly of quotations would be viewed by most readers as potentially interesting experimental writing. For more formal writing, there are no hard-and-fast conventions for how many quotes are acceptable—but even though quotations can memorably and powerfully support your points, do not use so many that they lose their strength. Check your drafts with readers to see if they think you are using too many (or too few) quotations.

- To ensure that you are respecting the words of others, make it a part of your final proofreading of any writing to check your quotations against the originals.

- Anytime you quote the words or ideas of others, ask yourself if you are being honest to the other person's intent and meaning. Build thoughtful and respectful communities by using the words and ideas of others as you would want them to use your words and ideas.

QUOTING, SUMMARIZING, AND PARAPHRASING

PARAPHRASING THE WORDS OF OTHERS

A paraphrase is about as long as the original passage, but it is a restatement of the original in your own words. You paraphrase when you do not want to quote someone else's words, perhaps because you already have used many quotations or because the original words are not memorable or need modification so that your audience will understand them.

Here is a passage from the journal article excerpted on page 315:

Besides merging international editions to form bilingual versions, another almost effortless modification game designers could make to interest language learners would be to create incentives and ways in which players could find and partner with native speakers of their L2 trying to learn their L1. This would not only provide the above-mentioned benefits of playing a bilingual game, but also provide learners with an L2 native from whom to learn about culture and language while performing a series of entertaining tasks requiring communicative exchanges.

Here is a paraphrase of the passage:

Purushotma suggests that if game designers want to make their software more useful to adolescent language learners, they could design games that encourage the language learners to play alongside and talk with native speakers of the language being learned; in the process of solving game tasks together, the language learners would also learn about culture from a native.

Notice that this paraphrase:

- Retells in new words all the points of the passage's sentences.
- Makes the passage more accessible to a nonspecialist audience, often a reason for paraphrasing.
- Is more detailed than a summary would be: Summaries tend to be about whole arguments; paraphrases are usually of parts of arguments.

AVOIDING PLAGIARISM IN PARAPHRASES

This summary—

Purushotma argues that the extreme success of some massively multiplayer online games should interest anyone trying to get the attention of adolescents: In contrast to high school language teachers trying to get their students to do half an hour of homework, computer games have been so successful at attracting teenagers for long periods of time that some governments are trying to control their use.

—is plagiarism because:

- It repeats, overall, the grammatical and sentence structures of the original; it also repeats the order of the sentences.
- It simply removes a few words from the original, rearranges a few others, and replaces some words with synonyms.

TIP: HOW TO PARAPHRASE TO AVOID PLAGIARISM

- Read several times the passage you want to paraphrase.
- On a piece of paper, break the passage up into its parts: What are the main points of the passage?
- Without looking at the passage or your notes, write down what you understand the passage to be communicating.
- Check your writing against the original to be sure you have the main ideas and have not inadvertently used the same words and structures in the original.

TIP: PARAPHRASING WELL

- A paraphrase is usually shorter than the original.
- Weave paraphrases into your writing using the same sorts of introductory phrases and strategies you use with quotations. (→ See pages 320–321.)
- Use the same sorts of strategies for alerting readers to the authority of the authors of the piece you are paraphrasing as you use for quotations. (→ See pages 319–320.)
- The point of a paraphrase is to present the ideas of another as you think that writer wants others to understand them—so don't offer your interpretation or any comments until after you have finished a full and honest paraphrase.

COLLECTING CITATION INFORMATION FROM PRINTED BOOKS

Most often, you find a book's citation information in two places:

• On the Title page, which is usually the second or third page of a book and has the title, the author's name, and the name and location of the publisher.

• On the Copyright page, which usually is the back of the Title page. (In some books, this information is on the very last page.)

No matter what citation style you use, record the five pieces of information described on the next page, some of which you will use for in-text citations and all of which you will use for the works cited section of your paper. All the styles require this same information; they just use it differently.

YOU MIGHT ALSO NEED…

→ See pages 395–397 for the additional information you need for dissertations, translations, multiple-volume series, and second (or later) editions.

→ See pages 332–335 for the additional information you need if the book you are using is a collection of essays or articles written by different authors; a chapter in a reference work; a poem in an anthology.

Girls Make Media

Mary Celeste Kearney

Routledge
Taylor & Francis Group
New York · London

Routledge is an imprint of
Taylor & Francis Group, an informa business

Title page

Published in 2006 by
Routledge
Taylor & Francis Group
270 Madison Avenue
New York, NY 10016

Published in Great Britain by
Routledge
Taylor & Francis Group
2 Park Square
Milton Park, Abingdon
Oxton OX14 4RN

© 2006 by Taylor & Francis Group, LLC
Routledge is an imprint of Taylor & Francis Group

Printed in the United States of America on acid-free paper
10 9 8 7 6 5 4 3 2 1

International Standard Book Number-10: 0-415-97278-7 (Softcover)
International Standard Book Number-13: 978-0-415-97278-9 (Softcover)
Library of Congress Card Number 2005029586

No Part of this book may be reprinted, reproduced, transmitted, or utilized in any form
by electronic, mechanical, or other means, now known or hereafter invented, including
photocopying, microfilming, and recording, or in any information storage or retrieval
system, without written permission from the publishers.

Trademark Notice: Product or corporate names may be trademarks or registered
trademarks, and are used only for identification without intent to infringe.

Library of Congress Cataloging-in-Publication Data

Copyright page (detail)

BOOK'S TITLE

Record the book's title exactly as it appears on the Title page of the book, including punctuation (also record the subtitle if there is one). If the book's title is not in English, copy it exactly, including any punctuation.

AUTHOR'S NAME

Record the author's name exactly as it appears on the Title page of the book.

→ See pages 330–331 for what to record in cases of no or multiple authors, if a company or organization is listed, or if the author is described as an editor.

PUBLISHER'S NAME

Record the publisher's name exactly as it appears on either the Title or the Copyright page. (For the sample to the left, you would record *Routledge*; the other corporate information is not used in citations.)

PLACE OF PUBLICATION

Record the city and state, or the city and country if the book was not published in the United States. If you cannot find a place of publication, make a note of this. If more than one place is listed, use the first.

DATE OF PUBLICATION

Record the year listed on the Copyright page (sometimes it is also on the Title page). If no year is listed, record that there is no date. Record the latest date if more than one is listed.

COLLECTING CITATION INFORMATION WHEN YOU ARE CITING PART OF A PRINTED BOOK

When you are citing a part of a book—

- a poem in an anthology
- one essay or article from an edited collection of essays or articles
- a chapter in a reference work
- the preface, foreword, introduction, or afterword to a book

—collect the same information you would for a book, as shown on pages 328–331, as well as the following:

❑ The name of the person(s) who wrote it

❑ Its title

❑ Its page number(s)

On the following pages we show you where to find this information.

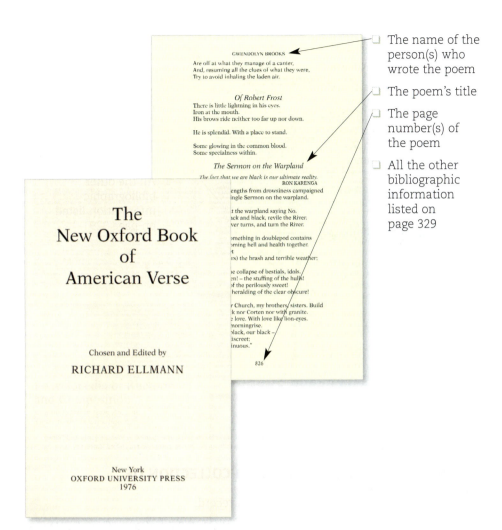

The name of the person(s) who wrote the poem

The poem's title

The page number(s) of the poem

All the other bibliographic information listed on page 329

A POEM IN AN ANTHOLOGY

For the poem on the page above, you would record:

Brooks, Gwendolyn. "The Sermon on the Warpland." <u>The New Oxford Book of American Verse</u>. Ed. Richard Ellmann. New York: Oxford UP, 1976. 826. Print.

(Note that this is not the final format for a works cited page.)

COLLECTING CITATION INFORMATION WHEN YOU ARE CITING PRINTED PERIODICALS

The six pieces of information listed to the right are used by every citation style, with some minor shifts.

IF YOU ARE WORKING WITH THE FOLLOWING…

you will need to record some additional or different information:

❏ if you are citing a letter to the editor, an editorial, a published interview, a review (of a book, movie, CD, performance, or anything else), or a microfilm, **record the kind of publication** (that is, along with all the other information listed to the right, record *letter to the editor* or *review*).

❏ a daily newspaper; see page 338.

❏ a periodical that is published every week or every other week; see page 339.

❏ a periodical that is published every month or once a season; see page 340.

❏ an article whose pages are numbered by volume, not by issue; see page 341.

❏ an article that does not have sequential page numbering; see page 341.

→ See pages 48–49 for descriptions of different kinds of periodicals and how they can be useful for different projects.

→ What do *volume*, *issue*, and *number* mean? See page 341.

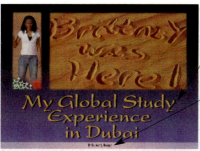

TITLE OF ARTICLE
Record the title exactly as appears. If the title is not in English, copy it exactly, including the punctuation.

AUTHOR'S NAME
Record this exactly as it appears. In some periodicals, the author's name is at the end of the writing.

PERIODICAL NAME
Record the name exactly as it appears on the periodical's Table of Contents or in the header or footer.

PAGE NUMBERS
Record the page numbers for all the pages, even if the article is not on sequential pages. The example to the left is on pages 62–63, but you might have an article that goes from pages 72–75 and from 120–123; record all the pages.

DATE OF PUBLICATION
Record the exact date: It may be a month and year, two months, or a specific day. The date can appear in a page header or footer, but it is always on the Table of Contents. In this example, the date is 2006.

VOLUME AND ISSUE NUMBER
Record the volume and issue number from the Table of Contents. Sometimes this information is at the top of the page, but it might be at the bottom or on a second page. Look carefully—but know that some periodicals do not include this information. Record what you can find.

A PERIODICAL THAT IS PUBLISHED EVERY MONTH
OR ONCE A SEASON

Different citation styles use different citation information for periodicals that are published every month or seasonally, so to be safe, record every item listed for periodical articles (as shown on page 337).

For the book review shown below, here is what you would record:

Kunkel, Benjamin. "Last Things: The Sinister Charm of Frederick Seidel." Rev. of Ooga-Booga, by Frederick Seidel. Harper's 315.1888 (Sept. 2007): 92+. Print.

❑ Date (month and year)

❑ Volume and issue numbers

❑ Page number(s). If the article is on multiple pages, record all of its pages, even if they are not sequential.

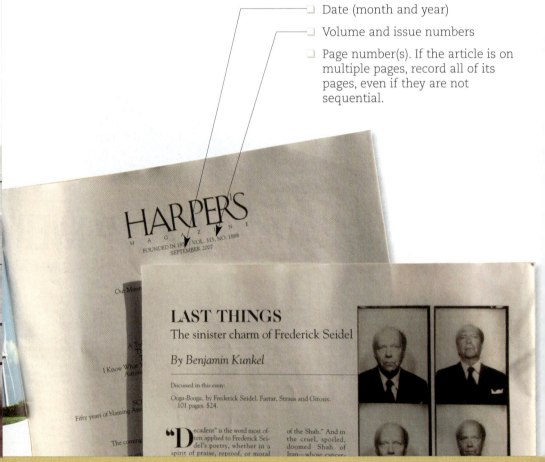

AN ARTICLE WHOSE PAGES ARE NUMBERED BY VOLUME INSTEAD OF ISSUE

Some journals start each new issue with a page numbered **1**. Some start the volume that way and do not change the page numbering throughout the whole volume: For example, if volume 25, issue 1, starts at page 1, and issue 1 has 176 pages, issue 2 will start on page 177.

When you are citing an article whose pages are numbered by volume, you need to record only the volume number, the date, and the page numbers of the article you are citing; you do **not** need to record the issue number. Readers will be able to find the article based simply on the volume number, date, and page numbering.

AN ARTICLE THAT DOES NOT HAVE SEQUENTIAL PAGE NUMBERING

In many magazines and newspapers, articles will start on one page of the periodical and then be interrupted by another article; the original article will start up again after several pages or in the back of the periodical.

Different citation styles record nonsequential page numbering differently. To be well prepared for composing your bibliography, record all the pages on which the article appears.

For example, in a newspaper you might record:

B3, B5

In a magazine, you might record:

32–35, 62–65.

WHAT DO "VOLUME," "ISSUE," AND "NUMBER" MEAN?

An **issue** is probably what comes to your mind when you hear **magazine** or **journal**: It is the paper-bound collection of articles that comes out once a week, once a month, or seasonally.

Often, after a year, an organization that publishes magazines or journals will bind together all the issues published in that year. The bound-together set of issues is the **volume**.

When you look at the Table of Contents page of a magazine or journal and see Volume 25, Issue 8, what that means is that the periodical has been published for 25 years, and that you are looking at the eighth issue published in that year.

Sometimes, instead of **issue**, you'll see **number**: This is just another way of referring to **issue**.

COLLECTING CITATION INFORMATION WHEN YOU ARE CITING WEBPAGES

For the purposes of citation, there are two kinds of websites:

• Databases of journals

• All others

We start with **all others** because it requires collecting less information than when you cite an article you found through an online database.

→ To determine the kind of webpage you are using, see pages 50–59.

ALL WEBPAGES EXCEPT THOSE FROM DATABASES

To the right we list the seven pieces of information you should try to collect for most webpages you cite. Because webpages can be so different, on the two following pages we show some examples of what to do when you can't find all seven pieces of information.

For the website shown to the right, here is a way to record the information you would collect; what we show is not the final format for a citation, but will help you keep track of a website in a running list.

Zinn, Lennard. "Tech Talk: Real Bikes for Real People." *VeloNews*. Inside Communications, 3 Oct. 2006. Web. 5 June 2009.

URL
Record the whole URL.

WEBSITE NAME
If there is a name for the overall webpage or website, record it exactly.

TITLE OF ARTICLE YOU ARE CITING/ TITLE OF WEBPAGE
Record the title exactly as it appears on the webpage, with its punctuation.

AUTHOR'S NAME
Record this exactly.

PUBLICATION DATE
This can be near the author's name, at the end of the text you are citing, or at the bottom of the page. If you find only a year, record that. If you find nothing, note that, too.

SPONSORING ORGANIZATION
If there is a company or organization that sponsors the information on the page, copy the name exactly. If this information is not obvious at the top of the page, look at the bottom of the page.

DATE ACCESSED
Record the date on which you visited the webpage. If readers visit later, they can then see if the information has changed.

TIP: LOOK EVERYWHERE!
The information listed to the right could be anywhere on a webpage. If some of this information is not included on a webpage, leave it out of your final citation.

INDIVIDUAL'S WEBSITE OR BLOG

Sometimes a personal website or blog will have a sponsoring organization, but often it won't, as with the website above. Note that the website does have a name, different from the entry, and that you can find the writer's name (at both top and side) and that the date is given in European format, with the day of the week coming before the month. Here is what you would record:

Rettberg, Jill Walker. "The Swedish Minister for Foreign Affairs Blogs Differently to U.S. Politicians." jill/txt. N.p., 5 May 2007. Web. 27 May 2009.

GOVERNMENT WEBSITE

This website gives no date; in such cases, it is a good idea to note that the date you record for accessing the site is the access date, as shown below.

"How Do I Register as a Candidate for Federal Office?" Federal Election Commission. US Federal Election Commission, n.d. Web. 10 Nov. 2008.

NONPROFIT ORGANIZATION

This webpage does not give an individual writer for the article being cited, and the sponsoring organization is the same as the website name, so record the following:

"Automakers Summer Prescription for American Drivers." <u>Union of Concerned Scientists</u>. Union of Concerned Scientists, 24 May 2007. Web. 26 June 2009.

ONLINE PERIODICAL

Here is what you record for an article like the above, where the website and the sponsoring organization are the same:

Miller, Laura. "Panic in the Pages." Rev. of <u>The Ten-Cent Plague</u>, by David Hajdu. <u>Salon.com</u>. Salon, 25 Mar. 2008. Web. 15 May 2009.

CITATION INFORMATION FOR DATABASES OF JOURNALS

Because it is often easier and more convenient to find relevant and credible journal articles through online databases than through print searches, more and more researchers are having to learn how to cite these sources.

When you cite an article that you found through an online database, you need to collect the same information you would for a print article—but you also need to collect information about the database, as we show on the next page.

→ See pages 64–71 to learn how to use online databases.

First, collect the same information as you would for a print article; this will usually be in one place on the page, as in the example to the right.

❏ **THE NAME(S) OF THE AUTHOR(S)**
❏ **THE TITLE OF THE ARTICLE**
❏ **THE NAME OF THE PERIODICAL**
❏ **THE PUBLICATION DATE**
❏ **THE VOLUME AND ISSUE NUMBERS**
❏ **THE ARTICLE'S PAGE NUMBERS**

—but note that some databases will give you the article as a pdf and some will not. *When the article is a pdf*, the page numbers will be the same anywhere, and so you can copy the page numbers exactly as they are given. *When the article is **not** a pdf*, like the example to the right, copy only the first page number, however it is presented. (The *p50(16)* in the information to the right means that the article starts on page 50 in the journal, and is 16 pages long.)

For the article shown on the right, you would record what is shown below.

Schultz, Ulrike, Asia Maccawi, and Tayseer El-Fatih. "The credit helps me to improve my business: The experiences of two microcredit programs in greater Khartoum." <u>Ahfad Journal</u> 23.1 (June 2006): 50. subscription service: Thomson Gale. database: InfoTrac OneFile. Michigan Technological University. 5 June 2007.

Then, collect information about the database and your use of it:

☐ THE NAME OF THE SUBSCRIPTION SERVICE

This is the name of the service you used to search for the database. The name will usually be on the webpage you click to access the full-text article, but if not, you need to keep track of which service you used. (It is a good idea to record which is the subscription service and which is the database name so that you can keep them straight.)

☐ THE NAME OF THE DATABASE

This is usually at the top left of the webpage.

☐ LIBRARY NAME

This is the name of the library where you accessed the database.

☐ THE URL OF THE DATABASE

Record the URL for the database, not the URL for the article you are citing.

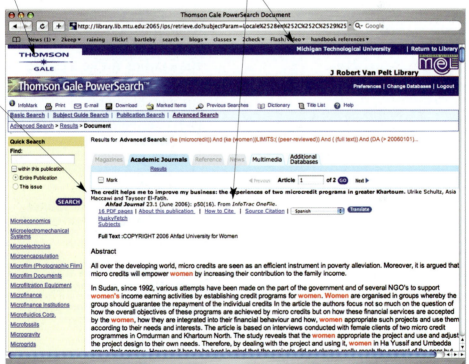

COLLECTING CITATION INFORMATION FOR OTHER KINDS OF SOURCES

Any time you hear or see someone else's ideas and those ideas can support an argument you are making, you can use those ideas as a source—but you have to cite the source.

Because there are so many possible places you can find the ideas of others, it is impossible to list every possible kind of citation. Instead, collect as much information as you can as that listed in the pattern below.

THE PATTERN

Collect as much of the following information as you can:

- ❏ **NAME(S) OF AUTHOR(S) OR COMPOSER(S)**

- ❏ **THE NAME OF THE SOURCE YOU ARE CITING**

- ❏ **THE KIND OF SOURCE**

- ❏ **WHO IS RESPONSIBLE FOR THE PUBLICATION**
  If there is a company or organization that supported the publication, record this.

- ❏ **THE PLACE WHERE THE SOURCE WAS PUBLISHED OR PERFORMED**
  Record the city and state—or the URL.

- ❏ **THE DATE THE SOURCE WAS PUBLISHED OR PERFORMED**

- ❏ **PAGE NUMBERS, IF THEY EXIST**

SPECIFIC INFORMATION YOU NEED FOR PARTICULAR KINDS OF TEXTS

For the following kinds of sources, record what is listed in addition to what is in the pattern shown on the left.

FILM OR VIDEO

Record the title; the names of the director, the main actors, or the narrator; the name of the distributor; and the year of release. If it is an online film or video, record the name of the website on which you see the piece, as well as the URL and the date you see the piece.

INTERVIEW YOU CONDUCT

Record the name of the person you interview and the date.

LECTURE

Record the name(s) of the speaker(s), the title of the lecture, and the organization sponsoring the lecture, as well as the location and date. If you see the lecture online, record the name of the website on which you see it, as well as the URL and date you see it.

LEGAL DOCUMENTS

Record the name of the document, its Public Law number, the date it was enacted, and its Statutes at large number.

LIVE PERFORMANCE

Record the title of the work being performed and the name of the artist, author, or composer. Also get as much information as you can about the director, the choreographer, the conductor, and the major performers. If there is a group or company doing the performance, record this as well. Record the name of the theater.

MUSICAL SOUND RECORDING

Record the name of the recording company and the date.

PERSONAL LETTER

Record the name of the person who wrote the letter and the letter's date.

RADIO OR TELEVISION INTERVIEW

Record the name of the person being interviewed and the name of the person doing the interview, as well as the information listed below for a radio or television program.

RADIO OR TELEVISION PROGRAM

Record the name of the particular episode, if there is one, as well as the series title. If there is a host or a writer, get the name. Record the network name, the local station (if there is one), and the date of the broadcast.

■ ■ ■

→ For MLA citation formats for a range of such texts, see pages 398–403.

→ For APA citation formats, see pages 448–449.

→ For CSE citation formats, see pages 455–457.

→ For CMS citation formats, see page 462.

HINTS & TIPS FOR COLLECTING CITATION INFORMATION

COLLECT IT NOW!

If there is any possibility that you might use a source, record its citation information immediately.

Nothing will vex you more than having to try to find a source at the last minute, as you are putting the finishing touches on a paper.

KEEP ALL YOUR SOURCE INFORMATION IN ONE PLACE

Get in the habit of having a notebook or folder or single online document in which you keep track of all your sources.

You want to be able to put together your final, formal list of works cited all at once, and you want to be able to check your in-text citations all at once.

DO COLLECT INFORMATION ABOUT ONLINE SOURCES

Even though you can bookmark webpages and go back to them later, two problems will confront you if you do not collect citation information immediately:

- You have to wade through all your other bookmarks to find the ones you want.

- The information on the page might have changed from when you first visited it.

If you are publishing your paper online, you might think that you do not need to provide a works cited list because you can provide links directly to the webpages you cite. But many readers will still want to see the full list, in one place, of all your citations—and, because websites can change (or disappear), a citation will reference when you saw the site.

IF YOU KNOW THE STYLE EXPECTED FOR YOUR FINAL PAPER, PUT YOUR SOURCES INTO THAT FORMAT RIGHT AWAY

This will save you time when you are finishing your paper.

→ For MLA style, see pages 360–405.

→ For APA style, see pages 426–451.

→ For CSE style, see pages 454–457.

→ For CMS style, see pages 460–462.

KEEP IN MIND THAT YOU MIGHT NOT USE ALL THE SOURCES YOU COLLECT

Until you have the absolute, final version of a paper, you will not know exactly which sources you will need. Sometimes you can become attached to a source, or to all your sources, because of the time and energy you put into researching—but this doesn't mean you will need the source.

Remember that you cite only the sources that you quote, paraphrase, summarize, or otherwise reference in your writing.

MLA DOCUMENTATION FOR IN-TEXT CITATIONS

understandings between word and

mple dichotomous opposition. For example, i

conoclasm—rejection of images—in Marx an

ell argues that images contain more than the

m by those he labels iconoclasts; instead, he

as having a dialectical nature, containing both

e—as object in the world, as representation, a

as figure—most of all as a Janus-faced emble

istory, and a window beyond it" (*Iconology*, 20

articular dichotomies Mitchell lists are pre

The MLA style comes from the Modern Language Association, which is an organization of scholars and teachers of languages and literature. *The MLA Handbook for Writers of Research Papers* is now in its seventh edition, published in 2009. The MLA style is used primarily in English studies, comparative literature, foreign-language, literary criticism, and humanities fields.

PURPOSES OF IN-TEXT CITATIONS

The overall purpose of an in-text citation is to help readers see your cited sources for themselves. People who value the free exchange of ideas—who want to think for themselves—want to trace the sources of your ideas.

In-text citations also help give your writing authority: When readers see that your sources are respected and well established, they are more likely to take your writing seriously.

Stemming from these overall purposes, in-text citations in the MLA style have two more focused purposes:

1 In-text citations are guides to the Works Cited page: By giving authors' names or the title of a reference, they help readers learn from the Works Cited list where you found the words and ideas that you quote, paraphrase, or summarize.

2 By giving a page number, in-text citations also tell readers exactly where in a source to find the words or ideas being referenced.

natural to today's student cohort, there's nothing innate about knowing how to apply their skills to the processes of democracy.

Although there is nothing innate about such knowledge, David Buckingham argues that this knowledge is necessary for young people because "to become an active participant in public life necessarily involves making use of modern media" (5) and eng...

technologies provides a "bas...

media production in the fut...

amplification of global econ...

the quoted person's name

WORKS CITED

Barry, Lynda. "Common Scents." *One Hundred Demons*. Seattle: Sasquatch, 2002. Print.

Berger, John. *The Success and Failure of Picasso*. London: Penguin, 1965. Print.

Buckingham, David. *Media Education: Literacy, Learning, and Contemporary Culture*. Cambridge, UK: Polity, 2004. Print.

Clark, T. J. *The Painting of Modern Life: Paris in the Art of Manet and His Followers*. Rev. ed. Princeton: Princeton UP, 1999. Print.

page number of the quoted piece

full information of the source's publication

HOW IN-TEXT CITATIONS FUNCTION

In an in-text citation in the MLA style, as shown above, the writer gives—at a minimum—the name of the person being quoted and the page number from which the quotation comes.

- A reader can use the quoted person's name to find full information about the source's publication in the Works Cited list at the end of the paper.

- The reader can then use the page number from the body of the paper to find the exact passage being cited.

THE BACK-AND-FORTH OF CREATING IN-TEXT CITATIONS

In composing a research paper, you move back and forth between creating in-text citations and a Works Cited list. Here is one way to create these essential parts of a research paper:

- Whenever you weave a citation into your paper, put the basic information for the citation into the body of your writing. → See pages 352–359.

- As soon as you weave a citation into your paper, add the source to the Works Cited list. → See pages 360–420 to learn about MLA Works Cited lists.

- Because you may have to make some adjustments to your in-text citations after your Works Cited page is complete, always leave time to double-check your citations against your Works Cited. You will need to make such adjustments if, for example, you use two or more sources from the same author or use sources by authors who have the same last name. → See pages 404–405 to learn what to do about these conditions.

IN-TEXT CITATIONS IN THE MLA STYLE

Whether you are citing books or electronic sources, in-text citations in the MLA style generally contain:

1

The **name of the author** of the words or ideas being quoted, summarized, or paraphrased.

The author's name can appear within the sentence containing the quoted words, or it can appear within parentheses at the end of the sentence.

2

The **page number(s)** of or some other reference to the words or ideas being cited.

The number of the page from which quoted words come goes at the end of the sentence, in parentheses.

In her article on two nineteenth-century women preachers, Patricia Bizzell argues that "a conjunction between the female sex and moral activism is traditional in Methodism" (379).

One writer on nineteenth-century women preachers argues that "a conjunction between the female sex and moral activism is traditional in Methodism" (Bizzell 379).

PUNCTUATION IN MLA IN-TEXT CITATIONS

- The parentheses that contain page numbers go at the end of the sentence, followed by the punctuation that ends the sentence.
- When you put an author's name in the parentheses with the page number, put a single space between the name and the page number.
- If the words you are quoting run across several pages, cite them like this: (23-25).
- If the words you are quoting are from several nonsequential pages, cite them like this: (45, 76).

VARIATIONS ON THE PATTERN

What if you run into one of the following cases?

→ No author is named for the source.
See page 354.

→ There is no page number (for example, you are citing a brochure or a webpage).
See page 354.

→ Your Works Cited contains two or more sources by the same author.
See page 355.

→ Your Works Cited contains sources by two authors with the same last name.
See page 355.

→ The work you are citing has two or three authors.
See page 356.

→ The work you are citing has four or more authors.
See page 356.

→ The work you are citing has a corporate author or is a government document.
See page 357.

   → See page 331 for what *corporate author* means.

→ You are quoting words that another writer quoted.
See page 357.

→ You are citing part of an edited collection or anthology.
See page 357.

→ You are citing an encyclopedia or dictionary.
See page 357.

→ Your sentence references a whole source (such as a whole book or webpage).
See page 358.

→ Your sentence references two or more sources.
See page 358.

→ You are citing a novel.
See page 358.

→ You are citing a short story.
See page 359.

→ You are citing a sacred text, such as the Bible or Koran.
See page 359.

→ You are citing lines from a play.
See page 359.

→ You are citing lines from a poem that is divided into parts or that has line numbers.
See page 359.

Aristotle's *Rhetoric* brings together understandings of situations in which people communicate, the psychology of audiences, the character of communicators, the structures of communication, and politics (A. Rorty).

→ See page 405 for how these two citations appear in the Works Cited listing.

THE WORK YOU ARE CITING HAS TWO OR THREE AUTHORS

List the names in the same order as they are given in the source.

For two names, use **and** between the names, whether you use the names in your sentence or in parentheses at the end of a sentence:

As "much an activist as an analytical method" is how Moeller and Moberly, in an online review, describe McAllister's approach to computer games.

As "much an activist as an analytical method" is how two online reviewers describe McAllister's approach to computer games (Moeller and Moberly).

→ See page 375 for the corresponding Works Cited listing.

With three names, put commas between the names:

DeVoss, Cushman, and Grabill draw our attention to "the institutional and political arrangements" that make new media compositions possible (16).

A recent article draws our attention to "the institutional and political arrangements" that make new media compositions possible (DeVoss, Cushman, and Grabill 16).

→ See page 375 for the corresponding Works Cited listing.

THE WORK YOU ARE CITING HAS FOUR OR MORE AUTHORS

If the work you cite has four or more authors, you can list each author's name (following the same guidelines as for two or three authors). You can also use only the first author's name, followed by the expression **et al. Et al.** is Latin for **and others**. When you use **et al.**, put a period after **al**.

What happens when a ninth-grade World Literatures class is offered at the high honors level for all students, without tracking? Fine, Anand, Jordan, and Sherman offer a two-year study of such a class in "Before the Bleach Gets Us All."

What happens when a ninth-grade World Literatures class is offered at the high honors level for all students, without tracking? Fine et al. offer a two-year study of such a class in "Before the Bleach Gets Us All."

When a ninth-grade World Literatures class is offered at the high honors level for everyone, without tracking, students "who never expected to be seen as smart" come to see themselves as capable and sharp, and "questions of power are engaged" (Fine et al. 174, 175).

→ See page 376 for the corresponding Works Cited listing.

THE WORK YOU ARE CITING HAS A CORPORATE AUTHOR OR IS A GOVERNMENT DOCUMENT

Use the name of the corporation or government office in full, unless there is a common shortened form of it. (If the name is long, including it in the sentence will read less awkwardly than including it within the parentheses.)

In a pamphlet published by the U.S. Dept. of the Interior, the Keweenaw National Historic Park is described as giving a "view of the birth of an industrialized society" in the United States.

Because the writer explains that the quotation comes from a pamphlet, readers will not expect a page number; they will look in the Works Cited for a listing under *United States. Dept. of the Interior*.

→ See page 377 for the corresponding Works Cited listing.

YOU ARE QUOTING WORDS THAT ANOTHER WRITER QUOTED

Use the expression *qtd. in* (for *quoted in*) before the source reference to show where you found the quoted words.

Elizabeth Durack, a blogger, argues that *Star Wars* "and other popular media creations take the place in modern America that culture myths like those of the Greeks or Native Americans did for earlier peoples" (qtd. in Jenkins 153).

Readers will look for the corresponding Works Cited listing under *Jenkins*.

YOU ARE CITING PART OF AN EDITED COLLECTION OR ANTHOLOGY

Use the name of the author who wrote the words you quote, not the name of the collection's editor. For example, if you are citing an article on soap operas by Tania Modleski in a collection on visual culture edited by Amelia Jones, use Modleski in your in-text citations:

Tania Modleski's article "The Search for Tomorrow in Today's Soap Operas" examines the different pleasures women find in soap opera narratives.

One researcher has argued that women find many different pleasures in soap opera narratives (Modleski).

→ See page 375 for the corresponding Works Cited listing.

YOU ARE CITING AN ENCYCLOPEDIA OR DICTIONARY

If you cite a section of a reference work that has a named author, then set up your citation and Works Cited entry just as you would for a part of a book, starting with the author's name.

If you cite a section of a reference work that does not list an author, put the section into your Works Cited list alphabetically, by the title. Because such sections are usually arranged in alphabetical order, you do not need to give a page number; readers can easily find what you are referencing without the page number.

MLA DOCUMENTATION FOR WORKS CITED

The following pages show you how to format the individual entries of the Works Cited listing at the end of any research project.

This is the basic format for all texts you list in the Works Cited section of an MLA-style paper:

Author's Name. *Title of Text*. Where and When the Text Was Published. Medium.

For example, here is a citation for a book:

Treichler, Paula. *How to Have Theory in an Epidemic: Cultural Chronicles of AIDS*. Durham: Duke UP, 1999. Print.

(Note the indenting: This is standard when formatting your list of Works Cited, as we describe on pages 404–405.)

Most often your sources will be books, periodicals, webpages, or online databases, so we focus on those formats. But because there are so many other kinds of texts you can also cite, we include those as well.

In MLA style, you need to include the medium of the source you are citing. For sources on paper, the word **Print** appears at the end of a citation. Webpages and online sources are identified as **Web**. For other types of sources, see pages 398–403.

TO MAKE WORKS CITED LISTS

FIRST, MAKE AN INDIVIDUAL LISTING FOR EACH WORK YOU ARE CITING

You should have determined the kind of source you have and collected the kinds of information listed for the source, as described on pages 328–329.

Then go to the page for the kind of source you have.

BOOK Go to page 362.	**PART OF A BOOK** Go to page 364.	**ARTICLE FROM A PERIODICAL** Go to page 366.	**WEBPAGE** Go to page 368.	**TEXTS FROM ONLINE DATABASES** Go to page 370.	**OTHER KINDS OF TEXTS** Go to page 372.

Each page shows the pattern for the Works Cited listing for that kind of source.

• Follow the pattern to construct your listing part by part, starting with the author, moving on to the title, and so on.

• If your citation varies from the pattern, follow the page references to see the format for the variation.

THEN CONSTRUCT YOUR WORKS CITED PAGE

When you have all your individual citations, put them together into the Works Cited page.

➜ See page 404 for how to format the Works Cited page.

FOR WEBPAGES
OTHER THAN DATABASES

Here is a citation for an article from an online journal in the MLA format:

Carroll, Jon. "Soul Resident." *SFGate*. San Francisco Chronicle, 21 Jan. 2009. Web. 21 Jan. 2009.

THE PATTERN

Here is the MLA citation pattern with its parts labeled and with information about how to modify the citation depending on a webpage's particularities:

Author's Name.   "Webpage Title." *Name of Website.*

The pattern for an author's name is on page 374.

WHAT TO DO WHEN YOU HAVE:

• no author named: page 375

• one author: page 375

• two or three authors: page 375

• four or more authors: page 376

• a corporation or business is listed as the author: page 376

• a government author: page 377

This is the title of the webpage itself, which is often different from that of the website within which the page exists.

The pattern for presenting the titles of webpages is the same as for titling articles; see page 379.

For help determining the title of either a webpage or a website, see pages 342–345 and 384–386.

The pattern for giving the title of a website is on page 384.

WHAT TO DO WHEN YOU HAVE:

• a personal website: page 385

• a blog: page 385

• an online scholarly journal: page 385

• an online newspaper: page 386

• a popular magazine, online: page 386

• an article from a database: page 393

• a webpage with no apparent affiliation (that is, you can find no name of a website): page 386

YOU MAY NEED TO ADD INFORMATION HERE...

If you are citing an advertisement, chart, map, graph, performance, interview, or video that has been posted online, you will need to add here the additional information about the medium of your source. See pages 398–403.

Where do you look on webpages to find all this information?
How do you know you have all the information you need for a webpage?

→ See pages 342–345 for help.

Publisher. Publication Date. Medium. Date accessed.

If there is a company or organization associated with the website, give its name exactly as it appears on the webpage, using the same capitalization and including *The* if it is used in the title.

If you cannot find any sponsoring organization listed in the webpages you are citing, put **N.p.**

If you have already listed the sponsoring organization as the author or as the website name, do not repeat the information; instead, just omit it from this place in the citation.

Follow the same formatting for this date as for the date accessed, shown to the right.

If there is no date listed, put **n.d.**

WHAT TO DO WHEN YOU HAVE:

• a date for the last time the page was revised: page 385

It is part of the MLA style to include the medium of the source you are referencing; for all web-pages, then, you will put **Web.** in your citation before the date accessed.

Put the day, then the month (abbreviated as shown), then the year:

5 Jan. 2006
27 Feb. 2008
19 Mar. 2007
1 Apr. 2006
1 May 2006
11 June 2008
22 July 2009
17 Aug. 2006
22 Sept. 2007
31 Oct. 2006
10 Nov. 2006
3 Dec. 2008

Put the URL for the website here if…

you know that your readers won't be able to find your source without a URL, put it here, after the Date Accessed information. See page 387 for examples and for information on inserting URLs.

FOUR OR MORE AUTHORS

You can write out the names of all the authors, following the pattern described earlier for multiple authors—or you can give only the name of the first author listed. All the other authors are then represented by *et al.*, which is a Latin abbreviation meaning *and others*.

CHAPTER, IN EDITED BOOK

Fine, Michelle, Bernadette Anand, Carlton Jordan, and Dana Sherman. "Before the Bleach Gets Us All." *Construction Sites.* Ed. Lois Weiss and Michelle Fine. New York: Teachers College, 2000. 161-79. Print.

ARTICLE, IN ONLINE ACADEMIC JOURNAL

Imus, Anna, et al. "Technology: A Boom or a Bust? An Understanding of Students' Perceptions of Technology Use in the Classroom." *Inventio* 6.1 (2004): n. pag. Web. 1 Mar. 2009.

BOOK

Shema, Mike, et al. *Anti-Hacker Tool Kit.* 3rd ed. Emeryville: McGraw-Osborne, 2006. Print.

A BOOK REVISED BY A SECOND AUTHOR

The second author is considered to be an editor:

BOOK

Strunk, William. *Elements of Style.* Ed. E. B. White. 4th ed. Boston: Allyn, 2000. Print.

→ On page 331 you can see the Title page of a book revised by a second author.

AN EDITED COLLECTION

Put *ed.* (or *eds.*, for multiple editors) after the names that begin the citation.

ONE EDITOR

BOOK, EDITED

Le Faye, Deirdre, ed. *Jane Austen's Letters.* 3rd ed. Oxford: Oxford UP, 1995. Print.

TWO EDITORS

If the book has more than two editors, follow the pattern for a book with multiple authors.

BOOK, EDITED

Hocks, Mary, and Michelle Kendrick, eds. *Eloquent Images: Word and Image in the Age of New Media.* Cambridge: MIT P, 2003. Print.

> **NOTE!**
> If you are citing only a piece from an edited collection and not the whole collection, create the citation following the pattern shown on pages 364–365.

A CORPORATE AUTHOR

Start the citation with the name of the corporate author exactly as it is listed in the source (but omit *A*, *An*, or *The*):

BOOK

Museum of Modern Art. *The Changing of the Avant-Garde: Visionary Architectural Drawings from the Howard Gilman Collection.* New York: Museum of Modern Art, 2002. Print.

A GOVERNMENT AUTHOR

Start the citation with the country name, then give the name of the government organization responsible for the publication, exactly as it appears in the publication:

United States. Dept. of the Interior. *Keweenaw*. Washington: GPO, 2002. Print.

(*GPO* stands for *Government Printing Office* and is a standard abbreviation you can use.)

United Nations. Development Program. *Beyond Scarcity: Power, Poverty, and the Global Water Crisis*. New York: United Nations, 2006. Print.

(Documents from the United Nations start with **United Nations**.)

A PAMPHLET WITHOUT AN AUTHOR

Renoir Lithographs. New York: Dover, 1994. Print.

A PSEUDONYM IN PLACE OF AN AUTHOR'S NAME

Start the citation with the pseudonym, then put the author's real name in brackets:

LeCarre, John [David Cornwell]. *The Russia House*. New York: Knopf, 1989. Print.

THE PREFACE, INTRODUCTION, FOREWORD, OR AFTERWORD TO A BOOK

Put the name of the person who wrote the preface, introduction, foreword, or afterword in the author name position.

After that person's name, put **Preface**, **Introduction**, **Foreword**, or **Afterword**.

Then put the title of the book, followed by the name of the person responsible for the book (preceded by **By** if the person is the author or **Ed.** if the person is the editor).

At the end of the citation, give the page numbers of the cited part.

Zizek, Slavoj. Afterword. *The Politics of Aesthetics*. By Jacques Rancière. Trans. Gabriel Rockhill. London: Continuum, 2004. 67-79. Print.

NOTE!

In the examples on these pages, we show the citations with what is called **hanging indentation**: The first line of a citation sticks farther into the left margin than the other lines. This is the standard form of indenting for MLA works-cited lists. A hanging indent of one-half inch makes the list easier to read.

The examples on these pages are shown single-spaced, but in a formal paper, your list of works cited should be double-spaced.

A BOOK

BOOK

Lawson, Mary. *Crow Lake*. New York: Delta Trade, 2002. Print.

BOOK

Petherbridge, Deanna, and Ludmilla Jordanova. *The Quick and the Dead: Artists and Anatomy*. Berkeley: U of California P, 1997. Print.

BOOK, ONLINE

Sharp, Lesley A. *The Possessed and the Dispossessed: Spirits, Identity, and Power in a Madagascar Migrant Town*. Berkeley: U of California P, 1993. *eScholarship Editions*. Web. 22 Sept. 2008.

AN ESSAY OR CHAPTER IN A BOOK

ESSAY, IN ONLINE BOOK

Makhan, Jha. "Island Ecology and Cultural Perceptions: A Case Study of Lakshdweep." *Lifestyle and Ecology*. Ed. Baidyanath Saraswati. New Delhi: Indira Gandhi National Centre for the Arts, 1998. N. pag. *Kalasampada*. Web. 30 June 2008.

ESSAY, IN EDITED BOOK

Plato. "Meno." *The Collected Dialogues of Plato*. Ed. Edith Hamilton and Huntington Cairns. Trans. W. K. C. Guthrie. Princeton: Princeton UP, 1961. 353-85. Print.

ESSAY, IN EDITED BOOK

Van Proyen, Mark. "The New Dionysianism." *The Sticky Sublime*. Ed. Bill Beckley. New York: Allworth, 2001. 165-75. Print.

AN ESSAY IN AN ONLINE COLLECTION

ESSAY, IN ONLINE COLLECTION

Badger, Meredith. "Visual Blogs." *Into the Blogosphere: Rhetoric, Community, and Culture of Weblogs*. Ed. Laura J. Gurak, Smiljana Antonijevic, Laurie Johnson, Clancy Ratliff, and Jessica Reyman. U of Minnesota, June 2004. Web. 23 Sept. 2008.

AN ARTICLE FROM A REFERENCE BOOK

Reference works rarely give the name of the person who wrote the article. Put the article's title in quotation marks at the beginning of the entry, leaving off A or *The*.

ARTICLE, IN REFERENCE BOOK

"Islam." *The New York Public Library Desk Reference*. 1989. Print.

ARTICLE, IN ONLINE REFERENCE BOOK

"Bovine Spongiform Encephalopathy." *Encyclopædia Britannica Online*. Encyclopædia Britannica, 2007. Web. 25 Feb. 2007.

A POEM OR SHORT STORY IN A BOOK

POEM, IN BOOK BY ONE AUTHOR

Ras, Barbara. "Where I Go When I'm Out of My Mind." *One Hidden Stuff*. New York: Penguin, 2006. 19-20. Print.

SHORT STORY, IN EDITED BOOK
SHORT STORY, TRANSLATED

Mina, Hanna. "On the Sacks." *Literature from the "Axis of Evil."* Trans. Hanadi Al-Samman. New York: New, 2006. 179-206. Print.

POEM, IN EDITED COLLECTION

Mông-Lan. "Trail." *The Best American Poetry 2002*. Ed. Robert Creeley. New York: Scribner's, 2002. 108-17. Print.

In the following example, note that the date of the book's original publication follows the book's title.

SHORT STORY, IN ONLINE BOOK

Woolf, Virginia. "Monday or Tuesday." *A Haunted House*. 1921. N. pag. *Bartleby.com: Great Books Online*. Web. 17 Feb. 2009.

A TITLE THAT IS IN A LANGUAGE OTHER THAN ENGLISH

BOOK OF POETRY, TITLE IN LANGUAGE OTHER THAN ENGLISH

Baudelaire, Charles. *Les Fleurs du mal*. Paris: Pocket, 2000. Print.

BLOG ENTRY, TITLE IN LANGUAGE OTHER THAN ENGLISH

Doreau, Delphine. "Merci à tous ceux qui ont fait coucou hier." *Non Dairy Diary*. N.p., 10 Aug. 2007. Web. 11 Apr. 2009.

ARTICLE, IN ACADEMIC JOURNAL
ARTICLE, TITLE IN LANGUAGE OTHER THAN ENGLISH

Tapia, Rosa. "'Mia o de Naiden.' La Reescritura de la Violencia en 'Pasion de Historia' de Ana Lydia Vega." *Hispanic Review* 75.1 (2007): 47-60. Print.

Note that the citation follows the capitalization conventions of the original language.

A RELIGIOUS TEXT

If you are not citing a particular edition of a religious text such as the Bible or the Koran, you do not need to include it in the Works Cited listing at the end of your paper.

WEBSITE TITLES

Webpages are almost always part of larger websites. When you cite a webpage, you must also cite the website of which it is a part—just as when you cite an article or essay, you also cite the book in which you find the article or essay.

In their capitalization, website titles function just like the titles of books.

In their placement, website titles are like book titles when you are citing part of the book: You place the website title after the title of the webpage being cited.

■ ■ ■

Because of the similarities we've just listed, we could have included information on website titles on the preceding pages. But because citing websites is still new to many, and because there are so many possible variations in websites, we are focusing on them here.

→ On these pages, we demonstrate how to include titles for individual citations for a range of sources; on pages 404–405 we show you how to bring together individual citations like these to create a full Works Cited section that goes at the end of any MLA-style research paper.

WEBSITE TITLES

Take the title exactly as you find it on the website, and follow these steps to build the pattern:

1 Capitalize all the words of the title except for

   articles *(a, an, the)*

   prepositions in the middle of a title

   conjunctions *(and, but, for, or)*

   the word **to** when it is part of an infinitive (as in **to read** or **to write**)

2 Capitalize the first word and the last word even if the words are one of the exceptions above.

3 Italicize the whole title.

4 Put a period after the title. (If the title ends with a question mark or exclamation point, use that instead.)

The Title of the Website.

Electronic Book Review.

Google.

ScientificAmerican.com.

The Institute for the Future of the Book.

We Make Art, Not Money.

PeaceWomen across the Globe.

A PERSONAL WEBSITE

If you are citing a personal website that has a title, include it in italics and add the publisher of the site (use *N.p.* if no publisher's name is listed).

PERSONAL WEBSITE

El-Sayed, Najib M. Home page. *The El-Sayed Laboratory*. El-Sayed Laboratory, n.d. Web. 23 June 2008.

If a personal website does not have a title, use the generic label "home page" instead. A URL is included in this citation because readers would not be able to find the site without it.

PERSONAL WEBSITE

Mullis, Kary. Home page. 2004. Web. 1 Jan. 2009 <http://www.karymullis.com/>.

A BLOG

The general pattern for a blog entry is

Author's Name. "Title of blog entry." *Name of Weblog*. Sponsoring organization, Date posted. Medium (*Web*). Date accessed.

If you can't find a publisher or sponsor listed (look at the bottom of the page, usually), use *N.p*. Include a URL for the site only if you think a reader would not be able to find the website without one.

BLOG BY ONE PERSON

Mueller, Derek. "Everything Inventive Is Good for You." *Earth Wide Moth*. N.p., 13 Feb. 2009. Web. 16 Feb. 2009.

GROUP BLOG

Ifill, Sherrilyn. "Right and Wrong." *Blackprof.com*. Blackprof.com, 15 Feb. 2009. Web. 16 Feb. 2009.

AN ONLINE SCHOLARLY JOURNAL

Scholarly journals published online are cited much like print journals. Many online journals do not use page numbers; use *n. pag*. instead. Include the medium of publication (*Web*) and the date you accessed the site.

ARTICLE, IN ONLINE ACADEMIC JOURNAL

Sorapure, Madeleine. "Between Modes: Assessing Student New Media Compositions." *Kairos* 10.2 (2006): n. pag. Web. 25 June 2008.

INTERVIEW, IN ONLINE ACADEMIC JOURNAL

Metinides, Enrique. Interview with Daniel Hernandez. *Journal of Aesthetics and Protest* 5 (2007): n. pag. Web. 5 Aug. 2008.

MLA WORKS CITED
PLACE OF PUBLICATION

Note how the pattern for listing the place of publication for a text is consistent across citations for all kinds of texts in all kinds of media.

→ On these pages, we show how the place of publication appears in individual citations for a range of sources; on pages 404–405 we show you how to bring together individual citations like these to create a full Works Cited section that goes at the end of any MLA-style research paper.

Put the place of publication after the title of the book, followed by a colon.

Place of Publication:

Boston:

Santa Monica:

Calumet:

If more than one place of publication is listed, use the first one.

EXAMPLE

Jackson, Leslie. *Twentieth-Century Pattern Design: Textile and Wallpaper Pioneers.* Princeton: Princeton Architectural, 2002. Print.

Merrell, Floyd. *Unthinking Thinking: Jorge Luis Borges, Mathematics, and the New Physics.* West Lafayette: Purdue UP, 1991. Print.

Wardlow, Gayle Dean. *Chasin' That Devil Music: Searching for the Blues.* San Francisco: Miller Freeman, 1998. Print.

WHEN TO MENTION THE STATE

According to the new MLA style guidelines, your citation should include only the city in which a work was published. You do not need to list a state or country name. If more than one city is listed in the book, include only the first city listed in your works cited entry.

BOOK

Eisner, Will. *Graphic Storytelling and Visual Narrative.* Tamarac: Poorhouse, 1996. Print.

BOOK

Hargittai, István, and Magdolna Hargittai. *Symmetry: A Unifying Concept.* Bolinas: Shelter, 1994. Print.

BOOK

Harris, Stephen L. *Agents of Chaos: Earthquakes, Volcanoes, and Other Natural Disasters.* Missoula: Mountain, 1990. Print.

WHEN THE BOOK WAS PUBLISHED IN ANOTHER COUNTRY

If the country ought to be obvious to readers because the city is well known, use the same citation pattern for books published in the United States:

BOOK

Yanagi, Soetsu. *The Unknown Craftsman: A Japanese Insight into Beauty.* Tokyo: Kodansha, 1989. Print.

BOOK

Bourriaud, Nicolas. *Relational Aesthetics.* Dijon-Quetigny: Les Presses du Réel, 2004. Print.

A BOOK WITHOUT PUBLICATION INFORMATION

If you find a book that does not include complete information about the place of publication, use the abbreviation *n.p.* (an abbreviation for *no publication information*).

PERIODICAL VOLUME, ISSUE, NUMBER, AND DATE

When periodicals were first printed, publishers would bind a sequential set of issues into one volume; eventually the pattern developed of binding a full year's set into one volume. This made finding and referring to any particular issue easy: One could find the volume first, and then the article in the volume by its issue number or date.

→ On these pages, we show how periodical volume numbers and dates appear in individual citations for a range of sources; on pages 404–405 we show you how to bring together individual citations like these to create a full Works Cited section that goes at the end of any MLA-style research paper.

THE PATTERN

VOLUME AND ISSUE NUMBER, AND DATE

The volume number goes directly after the name of the periodical; there is a space but no punctuation between the two. If there is an issue number, put a period after the volume number and then the issue number.

The date follows, in parentheses.

Volume Number.Issue Number (Year)

5.2 (2004)

27.11 (1976)

EXAMPLES

French, R. M. "Using Guitars to Teach Vibrations and Acoustics." *Experimental Techniques* 29.2 (2005): 47-48. Print.

Watts, Steven. "Walt Disney: Art and Politics in the American Century." *Journal of American History* 82.1 (1995): 84-110. Print.

WHEN THERE IS NO ISSUE NUMBER

The volume number and date still give readers enough information for finding the source.

REVIEW, OF SOUND RECORDING, IN JOURNAL
REVIEW, IN JOURNAL

Ostrow, Saul. Rev. of *Sharp? Monk? Sharp! Monk! Bomb* 100 (2007): 15. Print.

WHEN THERE IS ONLY A DATE

Many popular magazines do not list volume numbers, just a date.

ARTICLE, IN POPULAR MAGAZINE

Birnbaum, Charles A. "Cultivating Appreciation." *Dwell* Sept. 2007: 196+. Print.

A DAILY NEWSPAPER

Because daily newspapers don't have volumes and issues, they are cited only with the date—which does not have parentheses around it.

EDITORIAL, NO AUTHOR NAMED

"Rethinking Abstinence." Editorial. *Bangor Daily News* 17 Sept. 2007: 8. Print.

NEWSPAPER ARTICLE

Rozek, Dan. "Girls' Squabble over iPod Over: And in the End, Neither Will Get Music Player." *Chicago Sun-Times* 10 Nov. 2006: 3. Print.

A WEEKLY OR BIWEEKLY JOURNAL OR MAGAZINE

Do not give the volume and issue numbers even if they are listed. Do not put parentheses around the date.

ARTICLE, IN WEEKLY JOURNAL, RETREIVED FROM ONLINE DATABASE

Gorman, Christine. "To an Athlete, Aching Young." *Time* 18 Sept. 2006: 60. *Expanded Academic ASAP*. Web. 25 Feb. 2007.

REVIEW, OF BOOK, IN WEEKLY JOURNAL

Schlei, Rebecca. "Faithful Comrade: A Monumental Affair." Rev. of *Loving Frank*, by Nancy Horan. *Shepherd Express* 6 Sept. 2007: 48. Print.

A MONTHLY OR SEASONAL JOURNAL OR MAGAZINE

Do not give the volume and issue numbers even if they are listed. Do not put parentheses around the date.

REVIEW, OF BOOK, IN WEEKLY JOURNAL

Fallows, James. "Macau's Big Gamble." *Atlantic* Sept. 2007: 96-105. Print.

IF THE BOOK OR ARTICLE IS TRANSLATED FROM ANOTHER LANGUAGE

In this case, in addition to all the information listed on pages 362–363, you need also to include

- the name of the translator or translators, preceded by **Trans.** to help readers distinguish between the author and the *translator*.
- the page numbers of the article (if you are citing an article).

The translator's name comes after the title of the book or after the names of any editors:

Author's Name. *Title of Book*. Trans. Translator's Name. Place of Publication: Publisher, Year of Publication. Medium.

BOOK, TRANSLATED

Bauby, Jean-Dominique. *The Diving Bell and the Butterfly*. Trans. Jeremy Leggatt. New York: Knopf, 1997. Print.

BOOK, TRANSLATED

Grossman, David. *See Under: Love*. Trans. Betsy Rosenberg. New York: Washington Square, 1989. Print.

ESSAY, IN EDITED BOOK
ESSAY, TRANSLATED

Plato. "Meno." *The Collected Dialogues of Plato*. Ed. Edith Hamilton and Huntington Cairns. Trans. W. K. C. Guthrie. Princeton: Princeton UP, 1961. 353-85. Print.

IF THE BOOK IS A PUBLISHED OR UNPUBLISHED DISSERTATION

If you are citing a published dissertation, follow the pattern for a book but add the abbreviation **Diss.** to make clear that the source is a *dissertation*. Include the name of the university that granted the degree as well as the date the degree was granted in addition to the publication date.

DISSERTATION, PUBLISHED

Arola, Kristin L. *Invitational Listening: Exploring Design in Online Spaces*. Diss. Michigan Technological U, 2006. Ann Arbor: UMI, 2006. Print.

If the dissertation is unpublished, put its title in quotation marks instead of underlining it.

DISSERTATION, UNPUBLISHED

Babior, S. L. "Women of a Tokyo Shelter: Domestic Violence and Sexual Exploitation in Japan." Diss. UCLA, 1993. Print.

IF THE BOOK IS PART OF A MULTIVOLUME SERIES

In some cases, you will use and cite only one part of a multivolume set. In such cases, list only the volume to which you are referring.

BOOK, PART OF MULTIVOLUME SERIES, A PART

Rothenberg, Jerome, and Pierre Joris, eds. *Poems for the Millennium: The University of California Book of Modern & Postmodern Poetry*. Vol. 1. Berkeley: U of California P, 1995. Print.

▪ ▪ ▪

In cases when you need to refer to two or more parts of a multivolume set, give the total number of volumes in the work (**2 vols.**) following the title of the work.

BOOK, PART OF MULTIVOLUME SERIES, COMPLETE

Rothenberg, Jerome, and Pierre Joris, eds. *Poems for the Millennium: The University of California Book of Modern & Postmodern Poetry*. 2 vols. Berkeley: U of California P, 1995-98. Print.

Since the two volumes in this example were published over a period of years, the complete date range is included in the publication information.

IF THE BOOK IS A SECOND (OR LATER) EDITION

Put the number of the edition, followed by *ed.* after the title of the book.

BOOK, SECOND OR LATER EDITION

Lynch, Patrick J., and Sarah Horton. *Web Style Guide: Basic Principles for Creating Web Sites*. 2nd ed. New Haven: Yale UP, 2001. Print.

FILM OR VIDEO

Begin the citation with the name of the film or video, and then list the director(s), the distributor, and the year of release. If your purpose in citing the film or video suggests it, include the names of any writers, performers, or producers before the distributor.

FILM

The Longest Day. Dir. Ken Annakin, Andrew Marton, Bernhard Wicki, and Darryl F. Zanuck. Twentieth Century-Fox, 1962. Film

VIDEO, ONLINE

Fantoche (two times). Animatorblu. *BLU/blog.* 15 Sept. 2007. Web. 10 Nov. 2007.

You do not need to include whether you saw the film or video in a theater or on television. If you saw it on a DVD, however, include that information:

FILM, ON DVD
FILM, FOREIGN

Pan's Labyrinth [El Laberinto del fauno]. Dir. Guillermo del Toro. New Line, 2006. DVD.

(Notice, too, that you include—after the English title—the original title of a film that was made in another country.)

If, in the writing where you cite the film or video, you are commenting on the part played by a particular person, start the citation with that person's name. (**Perf.** abbreviates **performer**.)

FILM, FOCUS ON ACTOR OR DIRECTOR

Newman, Paul, perf. *The Price of Sugar.* Dir. Bill Haney. Uncommon Productions, 2007. Film.

CARTOON OR COMIC STRIP

If you have only an author's name or a title, start with what you have; otherwise, give both the name and then the title. Follow that with **Cartoon.** or **Comic Strip.** End with the full publication information for the source where you found the cartoon or comic strip. (If the source's date matters to your argument, put it after the title.)

CARTOON, IN NEWSPAPER

Carlson, Stuart. Cartoon. *Milwaukee Journal Sentinel* 23 Sept. 2007: 2J. Print.

CARTOON, ONLINE
CARTOON, NO KNOWN AUTHOR

"The Last Rail Split by 'Honest Old Abe.'" Cartoon. 1816. *Explore History.* HarpWeek, 17 May 2006. Web. 15 Apr. 2009.

COMIC STRIP, IN BOOK
COMIC STRIP, REPRINTED

Chapman, Hank, writer. "The Last Tattoo!" Comic strip. Art by Fred Kida. 1952. *Arf Museum.* Ed. Craig Yoe. Seattle: Fantagraphic, 2007. 60-64. Print.

COMIC STRIP, ONLINE
COMIC STRIP, TWO AUTHORS

Horne, Emily, and Joey Comeau. "A Softer World." Comic strip. *A Softer World.* N.p., 15 Sept. 2007. Web. 11 Apr. 2009.

> ### TIP: FINDING INFORMATION ABOUT FILMS
>
> The *Internet Movie Database* (<http://www.imdb.com>) gives you access to all the information you need in citing films.

MUSICAL COMPOSITION

Begin with the composer's name, followed by the title of the work. (If you cite a composition that is identified by a number, do not italicize it or put quotation marks around it.)

MUSICAL COMPOSITION

Price, Florence. *Mississippi River Suite*. Chicago: KOCH Classics, 1940. Print.

MUSICAL COMPOSITION

Sibelius, Jean. Symphony no. 7 in C major. Copenhagen: Wilhelm Hansen, 1980. Print.

TELEVISION OR RADIO PROGRAM

Start with the name of the particular episode you are citing, then give the name of the title of the program. List the writer (using **By**), the director (**Dir.**), or the Host; also list the performers (**perf.**) if appropriate for your use of the source. Give the name of the network and then the call letters of the station (if the station is local, give the city name) on which you saw or heard the broadcast. End with the show's broadcast date.

TELEVISION PROGRAM

"Homer's Phobia." *The Simpsons*. By Ron Hauge. Dir. Mike B. Anderson. Fox. WITI, Milwaukee, 16 Feb. 1997. Television.

RADIO PROGRAM

"Babysitting." *This American Life*. Host Ira Glass. Public Radio International. WNMU, Marquette, 1 June 2001. Radio.

RADIO PROGRAM, ONLINE

"The Melody of Murder." *The Avenger*. 3 Aug. 1945. *RadioLovers*. Bored.com, 4 June 2007. Web. 11 Apr. 2009.

BROADCAST INTERVIEW

For interviews you see on television or hear on the Internet or on the radio, follow the same pattern as for print interviews (→ see page 383).

INTERVIEW, ONLINE VIDEO

Salzmann, Marc. Interview with Jonathan Mann. "Awaiting *Halo 3*." *CNN.com*. Cable News Network, 24 Sept. 2007. Web. 24 Sept. 2007.

INTERVIEW, ONLINE RECORDING

Harper, Ben. Interview with David Dye. "Transcending Genre." *Natl. Public Radio*. Natl. Public Radio, 7 Sept. 2007. Web. 12 Sept. 2007.

AN INTERVIEW YOU CONDUCT

Give the name of the person interviewed, the kind of interview (*Personal interview.*, *Telephone interview.*, or *E-mail interview.*), and the date.

INTERVIEW, CONDUCTED BY YOU

Bok, Hillary. E-mail interview. 24 Feb. 2009.

A WORKS CITED PAGE IN MLA FORMAT

To format an MLA Works Cited listing:

❑ Put the listing at the very end of the paper.

❑ Use the same margin measurements as the rest of the paper (➜ see page 407).

❑ The Works Cited starts on its own page.

❑ Number each Works Cited page at the top right of the page (as you do each page in the MLA format; ➜ see page 407). The number on the first page follows the number of the last page of the paper. For example, if the last page of the paper is 8, the first page of the Works Cited will be 9.

❑ **Works Cited** is centered at the top of the page.

❑ The listings are arranged alphabetically by the author's last name. (If a listing starts with the title of a source, place it into the whole list alphabetically, using the first letter of the title. If the title begins with **A**, **An**, or **The**, alphabetize by the second word of the title.)

❑ If you list two or more sources by the same author, alphabetize them by the source titles. List the author only once; start all subsequent entries with three hyphens and a period.

❑ If you have two authors with the same last name, alphabetize by the first name.

❑ Double-space the entries.

Works Cited

Bauby, Jean-Dominique. *The Diving Bell and the Butterfly*. Trans. Jeremy Leggatt.
New York: Knopf, 1997. Print.

King Lear. By William Shakespeare. Dir. Trevor Nunn. Perf. Ian McKellen. Guthrie
Theater, Minneapolis. 14 Oct. 2007. Performance.

"The Melody of Murder." *The Avenger*. 3 Aug. 1945. *RadioLovers*. Bored.com, 4 June
2007. Web. 11 Apr. 2009.

Pollan, Michael. *Botany of Desire: A Plant's Eye-View of the World*. New York: Random,
2001. Print.

---. *The Omnivore's Dilemma: A Natural History of Four Meals*. New York: Penguin,
2006. Print.

Rorty, Amélie Oksenberg. "Structuring Rhetoric." *Essays on Aristotle's Rhetoric*. Ed.
Amélie Oksenberg Rorty. Berkeley: U of California P, 1996. 1-33. Print.

Rorty, Richard. *Philosophy and the Mirror of Nature*. Princeton: Princeton UP, 1979.
Print.

Shakespeare, William. *Hamlet*. Ed. A. R. Braunmuller. New York: Penguin Classics,
2001. Print.

World Health Organization. *The World Health Report 2005: Make Every Mother and
Child Count*. Geneva: World Health Organization, 2005. *World Health
Organization*. Web. 13 Mar. 2009.

Use hanging indentation

So that readers can scan the
alphabetic list easily and quickly,
indent by 1/2 inch all lines
underneath the first.

Summarizing

This paragraph was a long quotation in Riley's first draft. By summarizing the quotation, Riley keeps her readers focused on the points important to her argument—and also then has more room to make her arguments.

Transitions between paragraphs

By repeating concepts and words from the end of one paragraph at the beginning of the next, Riley helps readers see how her ideas connect from one paragraph to the next.

→ See pages 296–297 about transitions between paragraphs.

Asking questions

Riley focuses the purpose of her paper further by asking whether the microloan system works for borrowers. Questions also challenge readers to answer them, and so can increase their engagement. (Asking questions can be overdone, however; in a paper of this length, two to three questions will seem reasonable to readers.)

Using the words of others to make your point

Riley wants to show that many people expect microloans to end poverty and change the status of women. Because she makes this point using the words of the Nobel Peace Prize Committee—a group that should have considerable authority with readers—her readers are likely to accept her point about people's expectations about microcredit.

so that their communities really are enriched and the women join the global economy in ways that make sense to them and not just to the people who make the loans.

Microcredit originated in Bangladesh. In the 1970s, Muhammad Yunus, an economics professor at a Bangaldeshi university, started making very small loans to villagers so they could buy supplies for their small businesses; Yunus had learned that traditional banks would not give loans to the villagers. Eventually, out of Yunus's loan-making came the Grameen Bank. The Bank makes loans to groups of five villagers, who are responsible for each other's debts. Because of the groups, villagers have repayment incentive: "the threat of being shamed before neighbors and relatives" (Giridharadas and Bradsher).

The successes of Grameen Bank led to many other organizations following the same pattern: Loans are made to a small group, each member of which is responsible that all repay their loans. In addition, Grameen started another pattern, of loan recipients meeting regularly to learn community-building habits. For the loanmakers, this system seems to work: The repayment rate on microloans through microenterprise organizations is at least 95% ("Microenterprise Quick Facts"). But does the system work for borrowers?

The "microloan" Google search described at the beginning of this paper brings up, in addition to microloan organization websites, many newspaper and magazine articles. Almost all the writing celebrates the microloan movement's successes, describing—as in my opening quotations—how women in poor communities turn small loans into small businesses, have enough money to send their children to school, and sometimes even start providing jobs for others. These writings also often show the same expectations about microloans as the Nobel Peace Prize committee did when they gave the 2006 prize to Yunus and the Grameen Bank: The Committee wrote that "Lasting peace can not be achieved unless large population groups find ways in which to break out of poverty" and that "Microcredit has proved to be an important liberating force in societies where women in particular have to struggle against repressive social and economic

A transition paragraph

Riley uses words she quoted earlier to return to her main questions and keep her readers aware of how and why she is moving from one paragraph to the next.

Focused paragraphs

In her first draft, this paragraph and the next were all one (→ see page 173). By turning back to her thesis statement (→ see page 163), Riley was able to break the original paragraph into two. Each of the paragraphs now focuses on one specific point about how microloans work.

When you quote words that you found in a quotation

Riley found the words about Bangladesh and Bolivia quoted in a journal article. She decided to use the exact words, so she has to show that she found them in that article. Putting *qtd. in* before the in-text citation to the source indicates that she is doing this.

Opportunity International, provides evidence that, in one program in the Philippines, "77 percent of incoming clients were classified as 'very poor'; after two years in the program, only 13 percent of mature clients were still 'very poor'" (23). Another writer, in a paper written for the United Nations Research Institute for Social Development, describes how women in India use loans to start work in local markets and keep their families and small businesses going in hard times (Mayoux 39). So no one is wrong to think that microloans can have positive effects in the lives of women.

But can those effects really "liberate women" and help "large population groups.... break out of poverty" as the Nobel Prize committee suggested? Many do not think so, given the evidence.

For example, in terms of poverty, the writer of the paper for the United Nations Research Institute for Social Development, quoted above, says, immediately after the passage I summarized, that most studies of microcredit programs "find very small increases in income for quite large numbers of borrowers; in only a very small number of cases are there significant income increases" (Mayoux 39). In addition, studies also find that microcredit benefits women who are not at the lowest levels of poverty; the poorest of the poor may, in fact, get poorer trying to repay (MacIsaac 11-12; Mayoux 40-44). The benefits from microcredit also don't last long because borrowers often can't use loans for anything but immediate need (MacIsaac 15; Mayoux 41) or the borrowers take up work where they make only a little bit of money and where they gain no economic clout (Feiner and Barker; Roy). Under such conditions, women's positions within the overall economy do not change, meaning that their communities are unlikely to "break out of poverty." Even though microcredit has been in existence for over twenty years, Robert Pollin, co-director of the Political Economy Research Institute at the University of Massachusetts, pointed out in 2006 that "Bangladesh and Bolivia are two countries widely recognized for having the most successful microcredit programs in the world. They also remain two of the poorest countries in the world" (qtd. in Cockburn 9).

Works Cited

Bajaj, Vikas. "Out to Maximize Social Gains, Not Profit." *New York Times*. New York Times, 9 Dec. 2006. Web. 22 Nov. 2007.

Burjorjee, Deena M., Rani Deshpande, and C. Jean Weidemann. *Supporting Women's Livelihoods: Microfinance That Works for the Majority. A Guide to Best Practices*. New York: United Nations Capital Development Fund/Special Unit for Microfinance, 2002. Print.

"Change for the Better in Afghanistan." *FINCA*. FINCA International, July 2007. Web. 20 Nov. 2007.

Cheston, Suzy. "Women and Microfinance: Opening Markets and Minds." *Economic Perspectives: An Electronic Journal of the U.S. Department of State* 9.1 (2004): n. pag. Web. 19 Nov. 2007.

Cockburn, Alexander. "The Myth of Microloans." *Nation* 6 Nov. 2006: 9. Print.

Cowen, Tyler. "Microloans May Work, but There Is Dispute in India over Who Will Make Them." *New York Times*. New York Times, 10 Aug. 2006. Web. 19 Nov. 2007.

Feiner, Susan F., and Drucilla K. Barker. "Microcredit and Women's Poverty." *Dollars and Sense* Nov.-Dec. 2006: 10-11. Print.

Freid, Joseph P. "From a Small Loan, a Jewelry Business Grows." *New York Times*. New York Times, 12 Nov. 2006. Web. 19 Nov. 2007.

"Frequently Asked Questions." *FINCA*. FINCA International, n.d. Web. 20 Nov. 2007.

Giridharadas, Anand, and Keith Bradsher. "Microloan Pioneer and His Bank Win Nobel Peace Prize." *New York Times*. New York Times, 13 Oct. 2006. Web. 19 Nov. 2007.

"Improving Lives: Miriam Carolina Mejía, Juticalpa, Honduras." *Global Partnerships*. Global Partnerships, 2007. Web. 21 Nov. 2007.

Kelly, Sean. "Banking on Women: Microcredit in Northern Ghana." *Natural Life* May-June 2007: 34-35. Print.

Kristof, Nicholas D. "You, Too, Can Be a Banker to the Poor." *New York Times*. New York Times, 27 Mar. 2007. Web. 21 Nov. 2007.

MacIsaac, Norman. "The Role of Microcredit in Poverty Reduction and Promoting Gender Equity: A Discussion Paper." *Canadian International Development Agency*. Strategic Policy and Planning Division, Asia Branch Canadian International Development Agency, 12 June 1997. Web. 18 Nov. 2007.

Mayoux, Linda. "From Vicious to Virtuous Circles? Gender and Micro-Enterprise Development." *United Nations Research Institute for Social Development.* United Nations Research Institute for Social Development, 1995. Web. 18 Nov. 2007.

"Microenterpise Quick Facts." *Economic Perspectives: An Electronic Journal of the U.S. Department of State* 9.1 (2004): n. pag. Web. 16 Nov. 2007.

"Microloans and Literacy Are Contributing to Food Security in Poor Upper Guinea." *USAID Africa Success Stories.* USAID, 2005. Web. 24 Nov. 2007.

"Nobel Peace Prize for 2006." Press release. *The Norwegian Nobel Committee*. Oslo. 13 Oct. 2006. Web. 22 Nov. 2007.

Rahman, Aminur. "Microfinance and Gender-Based Violence: Experience from the Grameen Bank Lending." Slide program. *Canadian International Development Agency*. Canadian International Development Agency, 9 Nov. 2004. Web. 24 Nov. 2007.

Roy, Ananya. "Against the Feminization of Policy." *Woodrow Wilson International Center for Scholars*. Woodrow Wilson International Center for Scholars, Nov. 2002. Web. 23 Nov. 2007.

Smith, Christopher H. "Microcredit Loans Are Critical Tools for Helping the World's
Poor." *Economic Perspectives: An Electronic Journal of the U.S. Department of State*
9.1 (2004): n. pag. Web. 17 Nov. 2007.

Temes, Peter. "Bridgeport v. Bangladesh." *New York Times*. New York Times, 1 July 2007.
Web. 20 Nov. 2007.

GUIDE TO MLA DOCUMENTATION MODELS

WORKS CITED SAMPLES

APA DOCUMEN-TATION FOR IN-TEXT CITATIONS

The American Psychological Association (APA) publishes the *Publication Manual of the American Psychological Association*, which is now in its fifth edition, published in 2001.

This style's title might suggest that only psychologists use this style, but APA style is also used in other disciplines such as business, education, sociology, nursing, social work, and criminology. APA style was developed for researchers to report research results, and—in line with twentieth-century beliefs about how scientific research is supposed to be objective—this style encourages writing in the third person or passive voice; it also encourages the straightforward presentation of data, tables, charts, and graphs.

THE PURPOSES OF IN-TEXT CITATIONS IN APA STYLE

Although (as you will see) APA style uses a slightly different format for in-text citations than the MLA style uses, the reasons for using in-text citations are the same.

→ See page 351 to learn the purposes of in-text citations.

IN-TEXT CITATIONS IN APA STYLE

Whether you are citing books, periodicals, or electronic sources, in-text citations in the APA style generally contain these three elements:

1

The **name of the author** of the words or ideas being quoted, summarized, or paraphrased. The name can appear within a sentence containing quoted words, or it can appear in parentheses at the sentence's end.

2

The **date** when the source being cited was published.

3

The **page number(s)** of or some other reference to the cited words or ideas. The number of the page from which quoted words come goes at the end of the sentence, in parentheses. Note that **p.** goes before the page number.

These three elements can be arranged in one of two different ways to create an in-text citation in the APA style:

In her article on two nineteenth-century women preachers, Bizzell (2006) argues that "a conjunction between the female sex and moral activism is traditional in Methodism" (p. 379).

One writer on nineteenth-century women preachers argues that "a conjunction between the female sex and moral activism is traditional in Methodism" (Bizzell, 2006, p. 379).

→ Pages 422–425 list variations on this pattern for APA in-text citations.

PUNCTUATION IN APA IN-TEXT CITATIONS

- The parentheses that contain page numbers go at the end of the sentence, followed by the punctuation that ends the sentence.
- When you include an author's name in the parentheses with the year and page number, put a comma between each element.
- If the words you are quoting run across several pages, cite them like this: **(pp. 23–25)** (**pp.** stands for **pages**).
- If the words you are quoting are from several nonconsecutive pages, cite them like this: **(pp. 45, 76)**.

VARIATIONS IN THE APA PATTERN OF IN-TEXT CITATIONS

→ No author is named for the source.
See page 422.

→ There is no page number (for example, you are citing a brochure or a webpage).
See page 422.

→ Your Reference list contains two or more sources by the same author.
See page 423.

→ Your Reference list contains sources by two authors with the same last name.
See page 423.

→ The work has two authors.
See page 423.

→ The work has three, four, or five authors.
See page 424.

→ The work has six or more authors.
See page 424.

→ The work has a group or corporate author or is a government document.
See page 424.

   → See page 331 for what "corporate author" means.

→ You are citing two or more sources in one sentence.
See page 424.

→ You are citing a classical work, sacred text, or other work with no date listed.
See page 425.

→ You are citing an electronic source such as a webpage or e-mail.
See page 425.

APA PATTERN FOR IN-TEXT CITATIONS

VARIATIONS ON THE PATTERN

NO AUTHOR IS NAMED

If you cannot find a named author, use the title of the work instead:

To "watch the rejects crash and burn" is why we watch *American Idol*, according to *Rolling Stone* magazine ("Idol Worship," 2007).

→ See page 433 for the corresponding References list entry.

→ If you find that a government or corporate organization is the author, see page 424.

THERE IS NO PAGE NUMBER

If you cite a source that has no page number, give a paragraph or part number if there is one; otherwise, give only the name of the author.

The World Health Organization identifies obstetric fistulas as a global problem, estimating that over two million women suffer from them, with 50 to 100 thousand new cases occurring each year (2006, para. 64).

For the example above, readers will look in the References for a listing under *World Health Organization*.

→ See page 451 for the corresponding References list entry.

YOUR REFERENCES LIST CONTAINS TWO OR MORE SOURCES BY THE SAME AUTHOR

When you use two or more works by the same author, indicate which work you are referencing at any one time, to help your readers. You can do this by giving the date of the work in your sentence or in the in-text citation.

Here is a citation for the first work cited from one author:

That meat from cows fed on grass is more nutritious than that from corn-fed cows is just one of the many arguments Pollan makes (2006, p. 211).

Here is how a second work by the same author is cited:

Because his research shows just what chemicals go into a commercial potato, Pollan cannot bring himself to eat one given to him as a gift (2001, p. 98).

→ See page 451 for how these two citations appear in the References list.

YOUR REFERENCES LIST CONTAINS SOURCES BY TWO AUTHORS WITH THE SAME LAST NAME

In such a case, include the authors' initials in your citations so that readers know which citation to check in the References list. Here are examples from the same paper, using the authors' initials:

R. M. Rorty (1979) argues that we ought no longer to think of our minds as "mirrors" that directly and only reflect what is already in the world.

A. O. Rorty (1996) shows how Aristotle's *Rhetoric* brings together understandings of situations in which
people communicate, the psychology of audiences, the character of communicators, the structures of communication, and politics.

Here are examples that avoid ambiguity in their parenthetical citations:

Some philosophers argue that our understanding of what knowledge is has changed over the last two hundred years: We ought no longer to think of our minds as "mirrors" that directly and only reflect what is already in the world (R. M. Rorty, 1979).

Aristotle's *Rhetoric* brings together understandings of situations in which people communicate, the psychology of audiences, the character of communicators, the structures of communication, and politics (A. O. Rorty, 1996).

→ See page 451 for how these two citations appear in the References list.

THE WORK HAS TWO AUTHORS

List the names in the same order as they are given in the source. Use *and* between the names in the body of your paper, but use an ampersand (&) in parenthetical references:

As "much an activist as an analytical method" is how Moeller and Moberly (2006) describe McAllister's approach to computer games.

As "much an activist as an analytical method" is how two online reviewers describe McAllister's approach to computer games (Moeller & Moberly, 2006).

→ See page 433 for the corresponding References list entry.

THE WORK HAS THREE, FOUR, OR FIVE AUTHORS

The first time you cite the work, list each author's name. After that, list only the first author's name followed by the expression **et al.** (**Et al.** is Latin for **and others.**) When you use **et al.**, put a period after **al**.

What happens when a ninth-grade World Literatures class is offered at the high honors level for all students, without tracking? Fine, Anand, Jordan, and Sherman (2000) offer a two-year study of such a class.

Later in the same paper:

As a result of their study, Fine et al. (2000) argue that students "who never expected to be seen as smart" come to see themselves as capable and sharp, and "questions of power are engaged" (pp. 174, 175).

→ See page 433 for the corresponding References list entry.

THE WORK HAS SIX OR MORE AUTHORS

Include only the first author's name, followed by the expression **et al**. **Et al.** is Latin for **and others**. When you use **et al.**, put a period after **al**.

Statistical data can be useful but is "easily misinterpreted" (Walpole et al., 2006, p. 217).

Walpole et al. (2006, p. 217) argue that statistical data is useful but "easily misinterpreted."

→ See page 434 for a Reference list entry for a source with six or more authors.

THE WORK HAS A GROUP OR CORPORATE AUTHOR OR IS A GOVERNMENT DOCUMENT

If you need to cite a work by a group author (an association, government agency, or corporation), write out the name of the group author in your citation.

When organizing catalogs, librarians typically follow a set of guidelines established by the American Library Association (2004).

When organizing catalogs, librarians typically follow established guidelines (American Library Association, 2004).

→ See page 435 for the corresponding References list entry.

YOUR ARE CITING TWO OR MORE SOURCES IN ONE SENTENCE

If you need to cite two or more sources in a single reference, list the sources in alphabetical order by each author's last name and separate the entries by a semicolon.

The language used to describe issues of race and ethnicity often shapes the way people respond to calls for diversity or social justice (Adams, 2000; Fletcher, 2007).

Adams (2000) and Fletcher (2007) argue that language plays a vital role in shaping the way people respond to calls for diversity and social justice.

→ See pages 433 and 434 for the corresponding References list entries.

YOU ARE CITING A CLASSICAL WORK, SACRED TEXT, OR OTHER WORK WITH NO DATE LISTED

Use the author's name followed by a comma and **n.d.** for **no date**.

Early in its history, rhetoric was defined as the use of the available means of persuasion (Aristotle, n.d.).

You can also use the date of translation, if known, preceded by **trans.**

Early in its history, rhetoric was defined as the use of the available means of persuasion (Aristotle, trans. 1954).

If you are citing passages from a sacred text like the Bible or the Koran, you do not need to provide a References list entry. The first time you cite the work, identify the version you are using.

John 11:7 (Revised Standard Version)

YOU ARE CITING AN ELECTRONIC SOURCE SUCH AS A WEBPAGE OR E-MAIL

Many electronic sources do not have page numbers. If your source includes paragraph numbers, use that number, preceded by **para**.

Some researchers have suggested the concept of "virtual wives" to describe the new role of technology in personal life (Clark-Flory, 2007, para. 12).

If your source does not number paragraphs, you can cite the nearest main heading and number the paragraph following it to refer to a specific passage.

Some researchers have suggested the concept of "virtual wives" to describe the new role of technology in personal life (Clark-Flory, 2007, Introduction section, para. 1).

→ See page 446 for the corresponding References list entries.

Because personal e-mails cannot be retrieved by your readers, do not include them in your References list. You should cite them in your text only.

Austin's famous Congress Avenue bats first appeared in 1980 (E. C. Lupfer, personal communication, March 17, 2003).

APA DOCUMENTA-TION FOR REFERENCES LIST ENTRIES

The following pages show you how to format entries in the References list that goes at the end of any APA-style paper.

This is the basic format for all texts in the References list of an APA-style paper:

Author's Last Name, Initials. (Year the work was published). *Title of work.* **Location: Publisher.**

For example, here is a book citation:

Treichler, P. A. (1999). *How to have theory in an epidemic: Cultural chronicles of AIDS.* **Durham, NC: Duke University Press.**

(Note the indenting: This is standard when formatting your References list, as we describe on pages 450–451.)

In distinguishing among the kinds of sources to be cited, the APA distinguishes between periodicals and nonperiodicals. (Nonperiodicals are books and any other kind of source not printed on a regular schedule.) We follow the same distinction in the pages that follow.

Note that when you cite a book, periodical, or webpage, the format of the citation—the capitalization of the title of a book, the inclusion of a periodical's issue number, or the listing of a URL—tells a reader what kind of text you are citing. When you cite a text that isn't a book, periodical, or webpage, you may also need to indicate what kind of text it is.

TO MAKE APA REFERENCES LISTS

FIRST, MAKE AN INDIVIDUAL LISTING FOR EACH WORK YOU ARE CITING

You should have determined the kind of source you have and collected the kinds of information needed to cite the source, as described on pages 326–350.

Then go to the page for the kind of source you have.

PERIODICALS
Go to
page 428.

NON-PERIODICALS
Go to
page 430.

Each page gives a pattern for the References list entry for that kind of source.

- Follow the pattern to construct your listing part by part, starting with the author, moving on to the year of publication, and so on.
- If your citation varies from the pattern, follow the page references to see the format for the variation.

THEN CONSTRUCT YOUR REFERENCES LIST

When you have all your individual citations, put them together into the References list.

→ See page 450 for how to format the References list.

FOR PERIODICAL SOURCES

Here is a citation for a periodical in the APA format:

Atkinson, M. (2006). Straightedge bodies and civilizing processes. *Body and Society,* 12(1), 69–95.

THE PATTERN

Here is the APA citation pattern with its parts labeled and with information about how to modify the citation depending on a periodical's particularities.

Author's Name. (Date). Title of article.

The pattern for an author's name is on page 432.

WHAT TO DO WHEN YOU HAVE:

- no author named: page 433
- one author: page 433
- two to six authors: page 433
- more than six authors: page 434
- two or more works published by the same author in the same year: page 434
- a government author: page 434
- a corporate author: page 435
- a work signed *Anonymous* author: page 435

The pattern for the article title is on page 439.

WHAT TO DO WHEN YOU HAVE:

- a letter to the editor: page 441
- a review: page 441

The pattern for year of publication is on page 436.

WHAT TO DO WHEN YOU HAVE:

- a monthly magazine article: page 437
- a daily newspaper article: page 437

Where do you look in a periodical to find all this information?
How do you know you have all the information you need to cite a periodical?

→ See pages 337–341 for help.

WHAT COUNTS AS A PERIODICAL?

A periodical is a publication that is published at regular intervals: every week, every month, every season. Journal, magazine, or newspaper articles, *including when they are published online,* are periodicals.

Periodical Name, Volume(Issue), Pages.

If the periodical name begins with **A** or ***The***, you can leave off those words.

Italicize the journal name.

The pattern for the volume and issue numbers is on page 444.

WHAT TO DO WHEN YOU HAVE:

- no issue number: page 445
- only a date: page 445
- a daily newspaper: page 445
- a weekly or biweekly journal or magazine: page 445

IF YOUR SOURCE IS ONLINE:

The pattern for online sources is on pages 446–447.

Give the inclusive page numbers: **37–52** or **121-145**.

If you cite a newspaper article, put **p.** (for single page articles) or **pp.** (for multipage articles) before the page numbers: **p. J3** or **pp. C2-C5**. If the pages are discontinuous, put a comma between the numbers: **pp. B1, B4**.

APA PATTERN FOR REFERENCES
AUTHOR'S NAME

Note how the patterns for author names are consistent across citations for all kinds of texts in all kinds of media.

→ On these pages, we show you how authors' names appear in individual citations for a range of sources; on pages 450–451 we show you how to bring together individual citations like these to create a full References list that goes at the end of any APA-style research paper.

on pages 450–451

THE PATTERN

The first author listed is always written with the last name first, then a comma, and then the initials.

Last Name, Initials.

Singh, A. R.

If an author's first name includes a hyphen, include that hyphen with the initials.

Chen, K.-H.

If a work you are citing has more than one author, the additional names should be listed in the order in which they are given in the source. All authors are cited last name first. Use an ampersand (&) before the last author's name.

Phelps, L. W., & Emig, J.

Fine, M. T., Weis, L., Pruitt, L. P., & Burns, A.

Note that, in a References list entry, there is a period after the author's name or the list of authors' names.

NO AUTHOR NAMED

If you cannot find an author's name, start the entry with the title of the book or article.

MAGAZINE ARTICLE

Idol worship. (2007, February 8). *Rolling Stone, 1016,* 7.

REFERENCE WORK

Ultimate visual dictionary (Rev. ed.). (2002). New York: Dorling Kindersley.

ONE AUTHOR

BOOK

Pollan, M. (2006). *The omnivore's dilemma: A natural history of four meals.* New York: Penguin.

BLOG POSTING

Xavier, J. (2007, June 11). Timo Veikkola (Nokia): A vision for the future. Message posted to http://julianax.blogspot.com/2007/06/timo-veikkola-nokia-vision-of-future.html

ESSAY, IN EDITED BOOK

Fletcher, M. A. (2007). At the corner of progress and peril. In K. Merida (Ed.), *Being a black man: At the corner of progress and peril.* New York: Public Affairs.

TWO TO SIX AUTHORS

In References list entries, include the names of up to six authors. Separate names and initials with commas and use an ampersand (&) before the last author.

BOOK

Levitt, S. D., & Dubner, S. J. (2006). *Freakonomics: A rogue economist explores the hidden side of everything.* New York: HarperCollins.

REVIEW, ONLINE
REVIEW, OF BOOK

Moeller, R. M., & Moberly, K. (2006). [Review of the book *Game work: Language, power, and computer game culture*]. *Kairos, 10,* 2. Retrieved from http://english.ttu.edu/kairos/10.2/binder.html?reviews/moeller_moberley/index.html

ARTICLE, IN ACADEMIC JOURNAL

DeVoss, D. N., Cushman, E., & Grabill, J. T. (2005). Infrastructure and composing: The when of new-media writing. *CCC, 57,* 14–44.

CHAPTER, IN EDITED BOOK

Fine, M., Anand, B., Jordan, C., & Sherman, D. (2000). Before the bleach gets us all. In L. Weiss & M. Fine (Eds.), *Construction Sites* (pp. 161–79). New York: Teachers College Press.

DATE OF PUBLICATION

Note how the pattern for listing the year of publication for a text is consistent across citations for many kinds of texts in many kinds of media.

→ On these pages, we show you how the publication dates appear in individual citations for a range of sources; on pages 450–451 we show you how to bring together individual citations like these to create a references list that goes at the end of any APA-style research paper.

THE PATTERN

Place the copyright date or year of publication in parentheses, followed by a period.

(Year of Publication).

(2007).

If you find more than one copyright date for a book, use the most recent one.

For monthly magazines, newspapers, and newsletters, give the year followed by the month.

(2006, July).

Include the day for periodicals published daily, like newspapers.

(2007, August 23).

WHAT TO DO WITH A BOOK THAT HAS BEEN REPUBLISHED

A republished book is one that has been previously published by a different publisher or published in a different form (for example, a hardback book being republished as a mass-market paperback edition).

For such books, use the standard pattern for book entries, and insert the original publication date at the end.

BOOK, REPUBLISHED

Johnson, S. (2002). *Emergence: The connected lives of ants, brains, cities, and software*. New York: Touchstone-Simon. (Original work published 2001)

WHAT TO DO WITH A BOOK THAT HAS NO PUBLICATION DATE

If a book does not list a date of publication on its copyright page, put the abbreviation **n.d.** (for **no date**) where the year of publication usually goes in a citation.

BOOK, NO PUBLICATION DATE

Baudrillard, J. (n.d.). *Simulations*. New York: Semiotext(e).

MAGAZINE ARTICLE

For magazines and other monthly periodicals, include the month of publication following the year.

ARTICLE, MAGAZINE

Ehrenreich, B. (2000, April). Maid to order: The politics of other women's work. *Harper's*, 59–70.

NEWSPAPER ARTICLE

For newspapers and other daily periodicals, include the month and day of publication following the year.

ARTICLE, NEWSPAPER

Lipton, E. (2007, September 2). Product safety commission bears heavy scrutiny. *Austin American Statesman*, p. A11.

APA PATTERN FOR REFERENCES
TITLES

Note how the patterns for titles are consistent across citations for all kinds of texts in all kinds of media.

→ Sample References list entries follow, on page 440.

→ On these pages, we demonstrate how to include titles for individual citations for a range of sources; on pages 450–451 we show you how to bring together individual citations like these to create a References list that goes at the end of any APA-style research paper.

THE PATTERN

BOOK TITLES
Follow these steps to build the pattern:

1 Capitalize only the first word of the title and the first word of the subtitle.

2 Capitalize any proper nouns within a title.

3 Italicize the whole title. If you are not using a computer, underline the title.

4 Put a period after the title. (If the title ends with a question mark or exclamation point, use that instead.)

The title of the book.

Crow Lake.

The diving bell and the butterfly.

If the book has a subtitle, put the subtitle after a colon and capitalize its first word.

Scribbling the cat: Travels with an African soldier.

The quick and the dead: Artists and anatomy.

A country doctor's casebook: Tales from the north woods.

TITLES OF PARTS OF BOOKS, PERIODICAL ARTICLES, AND WEBPAGES

Follow these steps to build the pattern:

1 Capitalize only the first word of the title and the subtitle.

2 Do not italicize or put quotation marks around the title.

3 Put a period after the last word of the title. (If the title ends with a question mark or exclamation point, use that instead.)

4 Follow the pattern below for finishing the title depending on the source.

PARTS OF BOOKS

For a chapter in an edited book, list the title of the chapter first, followed by the word **In** and the editor's name, followed by the title of the book.

The title of the chapter. In Editor's name (Ed.), *The title of the book.*

At the corner of progress and peril. In K. Merida (Ed.), *Being a black man: At the corner of progress and peril.*

JOURNAL ARTICLES

Put the name of the journal—in italics—after the article name. (If you are not using a computer, underline the journal's title.)

The article. *Journal Name*

Will the next election be hacked? *Rolling Stone*

Animal magnetism and curriculum history. *Inquiry*

WEBPAGES

Put the name of the website—in italics—after the name of the webpage. (If you are not using a computer, underline the webpage's title.)

The article. *Website name.*

Project description. *The Nora Project.*

Pictures without bias: How to avoid discrimination in visual media. *Center for Media Literacy.*

A BOOK

BOOK

Lawson, M. (2002). *Crow Lake*. New York: Delta Trade.

BOOK

Petherbridge, D., & Jordanova, L. (1997). *The quick and the dead: Artists and anatomy*. Berkeley: University of California Press.

A WEBSITE

WEBSITE, ENTIRE SITE

Austin City Connection: The Official Web Site of the City of Austin. (n.d). *Childhood Lead Poisoning Prevention Program*. Retrieved from http://www.ci.austin.tx.us /health/education.htm

AN ESSAY OR CHAPTER IN A BOOK

ESSAY, IN ONLINE BOOK

Makhan, J. (1998). Island ecology and cultural perceptions: A case study of Lakshdweep. In B. Saraswatie (Ed.), *Lifestyle and ecology*. New Delhi: Indira Gandhi National Centre for the Arts. Retrieved from http://www.ignca.nic.in /cd_08012.htm

ESSAY, IN EDITED BOOK
ESSAY, TRANSLATED

Plato. (1961). Meno (W. K. C. Guthrie, Trans.). In E. Hamilton & H. Cairns (Eds.), *The collected dialogues of Plato* (pp. 353–385). Princeton: Princeton University Press.

ESSAY, IN EDITED BOOK

Van Proyen, M. (2001). The new Dionysianism. In B. Beckley (Ed.), *The sticky sublime* (pp. 165–175). New York: Allworth.

AN ESSAY IN AN ONLINE COLLECTION

ESSAY, IN ONLINE COLLECTION

Badger, M. (2004, June). Visual blogs. In L. J. Gurak, S. Antonijevic, L. Johnson, & J. Reyman (Eds.), *Into the blogosphere: Rhetoric, community, and culture of weblogs*. Retrieved from http://blog.lib.umn.edu /blogosphere/visual_blogs.html

AN ARTICLE FROM A REFERENCE BOOK

Reference works rarely give the names of the people who wrote the articles. Put the title in place of the author in these cases.

ARTICLE, IN REFERENCE BOOK

Islam. (1989). In *The New York public library desk reference*.

ARTICLE, IN ONLINE REFERENCE BOOK

Bovine spongiform encephalopathy. (2007). In *Encyclopedia Britannica*. Retrieved from Encyclopedia Britannica Online: http:// www.search.eb.com/eb /article-9002739

APA PATTERN FOR REFERENCES
ADDITIONAL INFORMATION

Sources are published—and cited—under varying circumstances. On these pages, we show you patterns for how to handle citations for several circumstances that occur frequently.

→ On these pages, we show you how to create individual citations for a range of sources; on pages 450–451 we show you how to bring together individual citations like these to create a References list that goes at the end of any APA-style research paper.

REPORT FROM THE EDUCATIONAL RESOURCES INFORMATION CENTER (ERIC)

If you are doing research in the field of education, you are likely to find and use reports available through ERIC. These sources are usually numbered; provide this ERIC number in parentheses at the end of the reference entry.

REPORT, FROM ERIC

Polette, N. (2007). *Teaching thinking skills with picture books, K-3.* Portsmouth, NH: Teacher Ideas Press. (ERIC Document Reproduction Service No. ED497152)

A WORK WITH A TRANSLATOR

BOOK, TRANSLATED

Burgat, F. (2008). *Islamism in the age of al-Qaeda* (P. Hutchinson, Trans.). Austin: University of Texas Press.

A BOOK IN A SECOND OR LATER EDITION

BOOK, IN A SECOND OR LATER EDITION

Rubenstein, J. M. (2004). *The cultural landscape: An introduction to human geography* (8th ed.). Upper Saddle River, NJ: Prentice Hall.

WORK IN MORE THAN ONE VOLUME

BOOK, MULTIVOLUME

Goldman, B. A., & Mitchell, D. F. (2007). *Directory of unpublished experimental mental measures* (Vol. 9). Washington, DC: American Psychological Association.

A BOOK REVIEW

REVIEW, OF BOOK

Julius, A. (2007, September 2). A people and a nation [Review of the book *Jews and power*]. *New York Times Book Review*, p. 27.

AN ABSTRACT

ABSTRACT, JOURNAL ARTICLE

Lacy, E., & Leslie, S. (2007). Library outreach near and far: Programs to staff and patients of the piedmont healthcare system. *Medical Reference Services Quarterly*. Abstract obtained from Library, Information Science & Technology Abstracts database.

LETTER TO THE EDITOR

LETTER TO THE EDITOR

Delaney, J. (2007, August 28). Helping the world's sexually abused children [Letter to the editor]. *Washington Post*, p. A12.

APA PATTERN FOR REFERENCES

PERIODICAL VOLUME AND ISSUE

When periodicals were first printed, publishers would bind a sequential set of issues into one volume; eventually the pattern developed of binding a full year's set into one volume. This makes finding and referring to any particular issue easy: One can find the volume first, and then the article in the volume by its issue number or date.

→ On these pages, we show you how periodical volume and issue numbers appear in individual citations for a range of sources; on pages 450–451 we show you how to bring together individual citations like these to create a full References list that goes at the end of any APA-style research paper.

THE PATTERN

VOLUME AND ISSUE NUMBER

The volume number, italicized, follows the name of the periodical; there is a comma between the two. If there is an issue number, put it in parentheses immediately after the volume number. Issue numbers are not italicized.

Volume(Issue)

5(2)

27(11)

EXAMPLES

French, R. M. (2005, March/April). Using guitars to teach vibrations and acoustics. *Experimental Techniques, 29*(2), 47–48

Watts, S. (1995, June). Walt Disney: Art and politics in the American century. *The Journal of American History, 82*(1), 84–110.

WHEN THERE IS A VOLUME AND AN ISSUE NUMBER

If a journal you are citing paginates each issue separately, include the issue number in your References list entry.

ARTICLE IN A JOURNAL PAGINATED BY ISSUE

Baker, B. (2007). Animal magnetism and curriculum history. *Inquiry, 37*(2), 123–158.

WHEN THERE IS NO ISSUE NUMBER

The volume number and date still give readers enough information for finding the source.

ARTICLE IN A JOURNAL PAGINATED BY VOLUME

Lawrence, R. (2000). Equivalent mass of a coil spring. *Physics Teacher, 38*, 140–141.

WHEN THERE IS ONLY A DATE

Many popular magazines do not list volume numbers, just a date.

ARTICLE, IN POPULAR MAGAZINE

Birnbaum, C. A. (2007, September). Cultivating appreciation. *Dwell,* 196+.

A DAILY NEWSPAPER

Because daily newspapers don't have volumes and issues, they are cited only by the date.

EDITORIAL, NO AUTHOR
NEWSPAPER ARTICLE, NO AUTHOR

Rethinking abstinence. (2007, September 17). [Editorial]. *Bangor Daily News*, p. 8.

NEWSPAPER ARTICLE

Rozek, D. (2006, November 10). Girls' squabble over iPod over: And in the end, neither will get music player. *Chicago Sun-Times*, p. 3.

A WEEKLY OR BIWEEKLY JOURNAL OR MAGAZINE

ARTICLE, IN WEEKLY JOURNAL, RETRIEVED FROM ONLINE DATABASE

Gorman, C. (2006, September 18). To an athlete, aching young. *Time, 168*(12), 60. Retrieved from Expanded Academic ASAP database.

If a weekly or biweekly journal or magazine doesn't have volume and issue numbers, cite only the date.

REVIEW, OF BOOK, IN WEEKLY JOURNAL

Schlei, R. (2007, September 6). Faithful comrade: A monumental affair [Review of the book *Loving Frank*]. *Shepherd Express*, 48.

APA PATTERN FOR REFERENCES
FOR ONLINE TEXTS

APA references to Internet sources and other online works need to include a title or description of the document, a date, and a Web address (URL). If you can identify the authors, include their names as well.

In 2007, APA published the *APA Style Guide to Electronic References,* which updates APA style for online sources. Sample references shown here conform to the updated APA guidelines. Some scholarly publications are now being identified using a Digital Object Identifier (DOI), a unique number intended to be more permanent than a URL. If you are citing a source with a DOI, include the DOI in place of the URL.

Berke, J. H., & Schneider, S. (2007). Nothingness and narcissism. *Mental Health, Religion, and Culture,* 10(4), 335-351. doi:10.1080 /13694670600722452

You do not need to list a database name or URL in a reference if you provide the DOI for your source.

→ On these pages, we show you how to create individual citations for a range of sources; on pages 450–451 we show you how to bring together individual citations like these to create a References list that goes at the end of any APA-style research paper.

CITING AN ENTIRE WEBSITE
WEBSITE

Austin City Connection: The Official Web Site of the City of Austin. (n.d). *Childhood Lead Poisoning Prevention Program.* Retrieved from http://www.ci.austin.tx.us /health/education.htm

CITING ONLINE ARTICLES
ARTICLE, ONLINE VERSION OF PRINT SOURCE

Lieberman, J. E. (2005, November /December). Coming clean [Electronic version]. *Psychology Today, 38*(6), 8.

ARTICLE, ONLINE ONLY

Clark-Flory, T. (2007, August 10). Roundup: Virtual wives, non-ironic feminism and more. Salon.com. 1-1. Retrieved from http:// www.salon.com/mwt/broadsheet /2007/08/10/roundup

ARTICLE, FROM DATABASE

Smith, S. K. (2007). Bioarchaeology: The contextual study of human remains. *Anthropology, 133,* 1171. Retrieved August 31, 2007, from Academic Search Complete database.

NEWSPAPER ARTICLE, ONLINE

Rockwell, L. (2004, January 21). UT task force releases report on race relations. *The Daily Texan.* Retrieved from http://www.dailytexanonline.com

CITING PART OF AN ONLINE DOCUMENT

ONLINE DOCUMENT, PART

Sales, L. (2005). Part II. In *Hurricane Katrina: Reporter's diary*. Retrieved from http://www.abc.net.au/news /newsitems/200509/s1460732

CITING E-MAIL

Because personal e-mail cannot be retrieved or viewed by your readers, the APA says that you should not include it in your references list (➡ see page 425 on in-text citations for e-mail).

For retrievable online postings, like discussion groups or mailing lists, use the following format:

DISCUSSION GROUP OR MAILING LIST POST

McLaughlin, B. (2007, September 4). Webinar for enviromental bench-marking survey. Message posted to AAUP-L mailing list, archived at http://ucp.uchicago.edu/mailman /listinfo/aaup-l

CITING BLOGS AND WIKIS

BLOG POSTING

Xavier, J. (2007, June 11). Timo Veikkola (Nokia): A vision for the future. Message posted to http:// julianax.blogspot.com/2007/06 /timo-veikkola-nokia-vision-of-future.html

WIKI POSTING

Wiki. (2007, 25 October). Retrieved October 28, 2007, from Wikipedia: http://en.wikipedia.org/wiki/Wiki

APA PATTERN FOR REFERENCES

FOR OTHER KINDS OF SOURCES

You may need to create references for other types of sources, including visual and multimedia sources. In APA style, a note or identifying description usually helps clarify the type of source you are citing.

→ On these pages, we show you how to create individual citations for a range of sources; on pages 450–451 we show you how to bring together individual citations like these to create a References list that goes at the end of any APA-style research paper.

SOFTWARE

Cite software as you would a book without a named author (→ see page 433)—but include *Computer software* in brackets after the title. If there is a publisher, include the name and date of publication; for software you have downloaded, give the date of the download and the URL.

SOFTWARE

PsychMate (Version 2.0) [Computer software]. (2007). Philadelphia: Psychology Software Tools.

VISUAL SOURCES

CHART, ONLINE

Fruitrich, C., & Ward, S. (2007). Groups' Goodwill helps [Chart]. USATODAY.com. Retrieved from http://www.usatoday.com/news /snapshots/25anniversary /goodwill.htm

PHOTOGRAPH, ONLINE

Cubitt, C. (2006). *Church*. Katrina: A gallery of images. Retrieved from http://www.claytoncubitt.com /publish/katrina

PHOTOGRAPH

Adams, A. (ca. 1930). *Factory Building, San Francisco*. Santa Fe, NM: Museum of Fine Arts.

FILM AND TELEVISION

FILM, VIDEOTAPE, OR DVD

Gibney, A. (Director). (2005). *Enron: The smartest guys in the room* [Motion picture]. United States: Magnolia.

TELEVISION SHOW OR SERIES

Hanson, H. (Writer), & Yaltanes, G. (Director). (2005, September 13). Pilot [Television series episode]. In B. Josephson & H. Hanson (Producers), *Bones*. New York: Fox Broadcasting.

AN INTERVIEW YOU CONDUCT

Because it does not consider an unpublished interview to be data that someone can check, the APA says not to include such an interview in the References list. You may, however, give an in-text citation for the interview:

> Some music composers believe digital technologies slow down their composing processes because they offer so many options (M. Boracz, personal communication, October 18, 2007).

CONFERENCE PAPER PRESENTATION

Use this format if you need to cite a conference presentation or similar lecture or speech that has not been published.

PRESENTATION OR LECTURE

Kleinberg, S. L. (2005, June). *The changing face of Texas in the twenty-first century: Perspectives on the new immigration.* Paper presented at Gateway on the Gulf, a Humanities Texas Institute for Texas Teachers.

SOUND RECORDING

MUSIC OR AUDIO RECORDING

Arcade Fire. (2004). Neighborhood (Tunnels). On *Funeral* [CD]. Durham, NC: Merge Records.

TIP: FINDING INFORMATION ABOUT FILMS

The *Internet Movie Database* (http://www.imdb.com) gives you access to all the information you need for citing films.

A REFERENCES PAGE IN APA FORMAT

FORMATTING PAGES FOR THE APA STYLE

For a paper in APA style:

❏ Use one inch margins at the top, left, right, and bottom of each page.

❏ Double-space each page.

❏ Use one of the two typefaces recommended by the APA *Publication Manual*: 12 pt. Times Roman or 12 pt. Courier.

❏ Number each page at top right. (The numbers should appear one inch in from the right margin, and approximately 1/2 inch from the top of the page.)

❏ Start the paper with a title page, with the paper's title, and your name centered on it.

❏ If you are asked to include an abstract, include that immediately after the title page, in its own page.

To format an APA References listing:

❏ Put the listing at the very end of the paper.

❏ The References list starts on its own page.

❏ Number each References page at the top right of the page. The number on the first page follows the number of the last page of the paper. For example, if the last page of the paper is 8, the first page of the References will be 9.

❏ "References" is centered at the top of the page.

❏ The listings are arranged alphabetically by the author's last name. (If a listing starts with the title of a source, place it alphabetically in the list by the first letter of the title. If the title begins with **A**, **An**, or **The**, alphabetize by the second word of the title.)

❏ If you list two or more sources by the same author, arrange them by the year of publication, earliest first. If the sources are published in the same year, arrange them alphabetically by title.

❏ If you have two authors with the same last name, alphabetize by the first name.

❏ Double-space the entries.

References

Anonymous. (2007). How to be an anarchist. Retrieved January 29, 2008, from
WikiHow: http://www.wikihow.com/Be-an-Anarchist

Idol worship. (2007, February 8). *RollingStone, 1016*, 7.

Moeller, R. M., & Moberly, K. (2006). [Review of the book *Game work: Language,
power, and computer game culture*]. *Kairos, 10*(2). Retrieved from
http://english.ttu.edu/kairos/10.2/binder.html?reviews
/moeller_moberley/index.html

Pollan, M. (2001). *The botany of desire: A plant's-eye view of the world*. New York:
Random House.

Pollan, M. (2006). *The omnivore's dilemma: A natural history of four meals*. New York:
Penguin.

Rorty, A. O. (1996). Structuring Rhetoric. In A. O. Rorty (Ed.), *Essays on Aristotle's
rhetoric* (pp. 1–33). Berkeley: University of California Press.

Rorty, R. M. (1979). *Philosophy and the mirror of nature*. Princeton: Princeton
University Press.

United States Department of Health and Human Services. (2002). *Mental health
aspects of terrorism*. Retrieved from http://mentalhealth.samhsa.gov
/publications/allpubs/KEN-01-0095/default.asp

World Health Organization. (2005). *The world health report 2005: Make every mother
and child count*. Retreived from http://www.who.int/whr/2005
/whr2005_en.pdf

1/2"

Use hanging indentation
So that readers can scan the alphabetical list easily and
quickly, indent by 1/2 inch all lines underneath the first.

GUIDE TO APA DOCUMENTATION MODELS

REFERENCE LIST SAMPLES

CSE DOCUMEN-TATION

[2] J. Allan: Automatic hypertext
...
04)

... M. Me...
... Informati...

[4] R. Hammwöhner / R. Kuhlen: Se...
Information Science, 20(3), 175-184. ...

[5] R. Hammwöhner / M. Rittber...
Management, 33(2), 243-254. 1997

[6] Z. Zhang: Experiemnteller Aufbau ...
Hypertext-System (KHS). Master Thesis...
Feb.,1995.

[7] M. Agosti / J. Allan: Introduction t...
construction of hypertext. Information Proce...

[8] R. Aßfalg: Integration eines offenen H...
Web. Hartung-Gorre Verlag: Konstanz. 1996...

[9] R. Furuta / C. Plaistant / B. Scheinerman: ...
1(2), 179-195, 1989.

[10] M.H. Chignell et al.: The HEFTI model o...
991.

] P. Thistlewaite: Automatic construction and ...
...anagement, 33(2), 161-174. 1997

This style used to be called CBE, after the Council of Biology Editors, which developed it. But because this style has become so widespread in the sciences, the CBE changed its name in 2000 to the Council of Science Editors (CSE).

In 2006, the CSE published a new seventh edition of their style guide, *Scientific Style and Format*. CSE documentation style is used by authors in the life sciences, physical sciences, and mathematics.

The citation system advocated by the seventh edition of the CSE manual is known as **the citation-name system**. In this system, writers must create their list of references before they can insert their in-text citations—and so to the right we discuss the reference list before we discuss the in-text citation format.

CSE REFERENCES

In the citation-name system, writers complete the list of references and then create the in-text citations. The reference list (called *References*, *Cited References*, *Literature Cited*, or *Bibliography*) is arranged alphabetically by author and then numbered:

References

1. Amann RI, Ludwig W, and Schleifer KH. Phylogenetic identification and in situ detection of individual microbial cells without cultivation. Microhi01 Rev. 1995;59:143-169.

2. Barns SM, Fundyga RE, Jeffries MW, and Pace NR. Remarkable arched diversity detected in a Yellowstone National Park hot spring environment. Proc Natl Acad Sci USA. 1994;91:1609-1613.

3. Dojka, MA, Harris JK, and Pace NR. Expanding the known diversity and environmental distribution of an uncultured phylogenetic division of bacteria. Appi Environ Microbiol. 2000;66:1617-1621.

→ See pages 454–457 for information on how to format CSE style references.

CSE IN-TEXT CITATIONS

The numbers alphabetically assigned to these end references are then used for in-text references, regardless of the sequence in which the works appear in the text:

> Early studies [2] used molecular methods to reveal remarkable microbial diversity in the sediment of Yellowstone hot springs.

or:

> Early studies (2) used molecular methods to reveal remarkable microbial diversity in the sediment of Yellowstone hot springs.

In order to avoid ambiguity, citation numbers appear immediately after the relevant word, title, or phrase rather than at the end of a sentence. Usually, the citation number appears as super-script, but it can also be set in parentheses. Set the citation number with one space both before and after, except when followed by a punctuation mark. This spacing makes the citation number easier to see.

When there are several in-text citations occurring at the same point in the text, put them in numerical order so that a reader can find them easily in the list of references. Separate the numbers by commas; if the numbers are consecutive, they can be joined by a hyphen.

> Researchers have studied brucellosis for the better part of a century [3,5,16-18,43], finding that ...

CSE SAMPLE REFERENCES

NO AUTHOR NAMED

Start the citation with the work's title.

8. Handbook of geriatric drug therapy. Springhouse (PA): Springhouse; c2000.

MORE THAN ONE AUTHOR

17. Sebastini AM, Fishbeck DW. Mammalian anatomy: the cat. 2nd ed. Burlington (NC): Carolina Biological; 2005.

A CORPORATION OR ORGANIZATION AS AUTHOR

Start with the abbreviated name of the corporate author as it appears in the source.

3. [CCPS] Center for Chemical Process Safety. Guidelines for safe and reliable instrumented protective systems. Indianapolis (IN): Wiley Publishing, Inc.; 2007.

AN EDITED BOOK

Put *editor* or *editors* after the name(s) that begin(s) the citation.

2. Brockman J, editor. What we believe but cannot prove: today's leading thinkers on science in the age of certainty. New York (NY): HarperCollins; 2006.

A GOVERNMENT AUTHOR

6. [GPO] US Government Printing Office. Style manual. Washington (DC): The Office; 2000.

GPO stands for *Government Printing Office*.

AN ESSAY OR CHAPTER IN A BOOK

8. Feynman RP. The making of a scientist. In: Leighton R, editor. Classic Feynman: All the adventures of a curious character. New York (NY): Norton; 2006. p. 13-19.

A REVISED OR LATER EDITION OF A BOOK

Add the edition after the title.

22. Tufte ER. The visual display of quantitative information. 2nd ed. Cheshire (CT): Graphics Press; 2001.

AN ONLINE BOOK

7. Ebert D. Ecology, epidemiology, and evolution of Parasitism in Daphnia [Internet]. Bethesda (MD): National Library of Medicine (US), National Center for Biotechnology Information; 2005 [cited 2007 Sep 4]. Available from: http://www.ncbi.nlm.nih.gov/entrez/query.fcgi?db=Books

A VOLUME IN A SERIES

Place the series information in parentheses after the date of publication.

9. Honjo T, Melchers F, editors. Gut-associated lymphoid tissues. Berlin (Germany): Springer-Verlag; 2006. (Current Topics in Microbiology and Immunology; vol. 308).

A TECHNICAL REPORT

Include the performing and/or sponsoring organization. (The following example shows the performing organization [the group that performed the research], the University of Washington Department of Statistics; the sponsoring group funded the research.) Often, the very end of the citation acknowledges the funding; for example: *(Sponsored by the Nuclear Regulatory Commission)*. The report number goes at the end of the citation (before the URL if there is one). If there is a contract number, include it.

14. Krivitsky P, Handcock M, Raftery AE, Hoff P. Representing degree distributions, clustering, and homophily in social networks with latent cluster random effects models. Seattle (WA): University of Washington Department of Statistics; 2007. No. 517. Available from: http://www.stat.washington.edu/www/research/reports/

A CONFERENCE PRESENTATION
Include the location and dates.

2. Braun F, Noterdaeme JM, Colas L. Simulations of different Faraday screen configurations for the ITER ICRH Antenna. In: Ryan PM, Rassmussen D, editors. Radio frequency power in plasmas: 17th topical conference on radio frequency power in plasmas; 2007 May 7-9; Clearwater (FL). Melville (NY): [AIP] American Institute of Physics; 2007. p. 175-178.

A JOURNAL PAGINATED BY VOLUME

8. Gradstein FM, Og JG. Geologic time scale 2004—why, how, and where near! Lethaia. 2004;(37):175-181.

AN ARTICLE IN A DAILY NEWSPAPER
24. Revkin AC. Cooking up a fable of life on melting ice. New York Times. 2007 Jul 22;Sect. 2:11.

AN ONLINE ARTICLE
24. Spiesel S. Can a rollercoaster really scare you to death? And more. Slate [Internet]. Aug 28 [cited 2007 Sep 3]. Available from: http://www.slate.com/id/2172960/fr/flyout

A WEBPAGE
5. DNA Interactive [Internet]. Cold Spring Harbor (NY): Cold Spring Harbor Lab; c2003 [cited 2007 Aug 12]. Available from: http://www.dnai.org/

AN ONLINE DATABASE
3. Catalysts and catalysed reactions [Internet]. London (UK): RSC Publishing. 2002 [updated 2007 Aug; cited 2007 Sep 5]. Available from: http://pubs.rsc.org/Publishing/CurrentAwareness/CCR/CCRSearchPage.cfm

A BLOG POSTING
4. Diganta [screen name]. Pushing the limits of speciesism. In: Desicritics.org [Web log]. [posted 2007 Jun 18; cited 2007 Sep 2].

A WIKI ENTRY
20. Quantum gates. In: Quantiki [Internet]. Available from: http://www.quantiki.org/wiki/index.php/Quantum_gates. [accessed 4:00 pm CST, Sep 5, 2007].

A CD-ROM
11. Hagen EH, Walker PL. Human evolution: a multimedia guide to the fossil record [CD-ROM]. 4th ed. New York (NY): Norton; 2003. 1 CD-ROM: color, 4 3/4 in.

AN AUDIO OR VIDEO RECORDING
1. Arledge B, director. NOVA-Cracking the code of life [DVD]. Boston (MA): WGBH Boston; 2001. 1 DVD: sound, color, 4 3/4 in.

CHICAGO MANUAL OF STYLE DOCUMEN-TATION AND IN-TEXT CITATIONS

The **Chicago Manual of Style** (CMS) is now in its fifteenth edition (published in 2003). It is used by writers in the arts and humanities, especially history.

Rather than using the author and date in-text citation format of MLA and APA, most CMS advocates prefer the footnote or endnote style of citation. In this style, a superscript number is placed after any quotation, paraphrase, or summary. These numbers are consecutive throughout the text, and correspond either to a footnote set at the bottom of the page or to endnotes that come at the end of the text.

Because CMS notes provide full bibliographic information for the sources cited, writers do not need to provide a **Works Cited** or **References** listing—although they can.

[12] Wang, 84. On the increasin the Qing, see the articles by Elvi to ban *Western Chamber*, see I Change and Dissemination," *Act*

[13] Jin's claim is echoed by T kenkyu," 107. Wang Ji-si, howeve a convenient discussion of the au Hargett in the *Indiana Compani* H. Nienhauser (Bloomington: In

CMS IN-TEXT CITATIONS AND FOOTNOTES

Here is a sample sentence containing a quotation as it would appear in the body of a paper with a superscript number at its end, and the footnote to that sentence, linked by the number. (This sample is numbered 12 because there are eleven source references before it.)

> In *Marriage, a History*, Stephanie Coontz states that, "whether it is valued or not, love is rarely seen as the main ingredient for marital success."[12]
>
> 12. Stephanie Coontz, *Marriage, a History: From Obedience to Intimacy or How Love Conquered Marriage* (New York: Viking, 2005), 18.

SUBSEQUENT NOTE ENTRIES

After the first reference to a book or other source, CMS conventions say that writers should put into a footnote the following:

- the author's last name
- the title of the work (or a shortened version if the title is long)
- a page number.

Some writers, however, use only the author's name and the page number if there will be no ambiguity as to which source is being cited. The footnote could thus read

10. Coontz, *Marriage*, 99.

Or

10. Coontz, 99.

If a reference is to the same work as in the preceding note, you can use the abbreviation **Ibid.** (**Ibid.** is a shortened form of the Latin word **ibidem**, which means **in the same place**.)

11. Ibid., 103.

BIBLIOGRAPHY

If the writer of these sample citations were to include a bibliography listing at the paper's end, the citation would be:

Coontz, Stephanie. *Marriage, a History: From Obedience to Intimacy or How Love Conquered Marriage*. New York: Viking, 2005.

(Notice, in this case, that the listing has the same formatting as MLA style.)

→ See pages 460–462 for more sample CMS footnotes.

CMS SAMPLE REFERENCES

BOOKS

For a footnote:

16. J. H. Plumb, *The Italian Renaissance* (New York: Mariner Books, 2001), 86.

In the bibliography:

Plumb, J. H. *The Italian Renaissance*. New York: Mariner Books, 2001.

AN ESSAY OR CHAPTER IN A BOOK

For a footnote:

8. F. J. Byrne, "Early Irish Society (1st–9th Century)," in *The Course of Irish History*, eds. T. W. Moody and F. X. Martin (Lanham, MD: Roberts Rinehart, 2002), 55.

In the bibliography:

Byrne, F. J. "Early Irish Society (1st–9th Century)." In *The Course of Irish History*, eds. T. W. Moody and F. X. Martin, 43–60. Lanham, MD: Roberts Rinehart, 2002.

ARTICLES FROM PERIODICALS (JOURNALS, MAGAZINES, OR NEWSPAPERS)

For a footnote:

13. Valerie A. Kivelson, "On Words, Sources, and Historical Method: Which Truth About Muscovy?" *Kritika: Explorations in Russian and Eurasian History* 3, no. 3 (2002): 490.

In the bibliography:

Kivelson, Valerie A. "On Words, Sources, and Historical Method: Which Truth About Muscovy?" *Kritika: Explorations in Russian and Eurasian History* 3, no. 3 (2002): 487–99.

A JOURNAL ARTICLE RETRIEVED FROM ELECTRONIC DATABASE

The citation should follow the same form for a journal, but the URL for the article is included.

For a footnote:

23. Bryon MacWilliams, "Yale U. Press Strikes Deal with Russian Archive to Open Stalin's Papers to Scholars," *Chronicle of Higher Education* 53, no. 44 (July 2007), http://web.ebscohost.com.ezproxy.lib.utexas.edu/ehost.

In the bibliography:

MacWilliams, Bryon. "Yale U. Press Strikes Deal with Russian Archive to Open Stalin's Papers to Scholars." *Chronicle of Higher Education* 53, no. 44 (July 2007), http://web.ebscohost.com.ezproxy.lib.utexas.edu/ehost.

ONLINE SOURCES (OTHER THAN DATABASES)

For a footnote:

4. Chris Johnson, "Statement from Human Rights Campaign President Joe Solmonese on Recent ENDA Developments," Human Rights Campaign, September 28, 2007, http://www.hrcbackstory.org/2007/09/statement-from-.html.

In the bibliography:

Johnson, Chris. "Statement from Human Rights Campaign President Joe Solmonese on Recent ENDA Developments." Human Rights Campaign, September 28, 2007, http://www.hrcbackstory.org/2007/09/statement-from-.html.

NO AUTHOR NAMED

Start the citation with the work's title.

For a footnote:

4. *Broad Stripes and Bright Stars* (Kansas City, MO: Andrews McMeel, 2002), 15.

In the bibliography:

Broad Stripes and Bright Stars. Kansas City, MO: Andrews McMeel, 2002.

TWO OR THREE AUTHORS

In a footnote, put all of the authors' full names. For subsequent references, give the authors' last names only. In the bibliography, give full names.

For a footnote:

2. Larry J. Reynolds and Gordon Hutner, eds., *National Imaginaries, American Identities: The Cultural Work of American Iconography* (Princeton, NJ: Princeton University Press, 2000), 56.

In the bibliography:

Reynolds, Larry J., and Gordon Hutner, eds. *National Imaginaries, American Identities: The Cultural Work of American Iconography.* Princeton, NJ: Princeton University Press, 2000.

FOUR OR MORE AUTHORS

In a footnote, give the name of the first author listed, followed by **and others**. List all the authors in the bibliography.

For a footnote:

3. James Drake and others, *James Drake* (Austin, TX: UT Press, 2008), 40.

In the bibliography:

Drake, James, Bruce Ferguson, Steven Henry Madoff, and Jimmy Santiago Baca. *James Drake.* Austin, TX: UT Press, 2008.

A CORPORATE AUTHOR

Start with the name of the corporate author as it appears in the source.

For a footnote:

5. Texas State Historical Association, *The Portable Handbook of Texas* (Austin, TX: Texas State Historical Association, 2000).

In the bibliography:

Texas State Historical Association. *The Portable Handbook of Texas.* Austin, TX: Texas State Historical Association, 2000.

A GOVERNMENT AUTHOR

List the full agency or department name as author.

For a footnote:

11. Central Intelligence Agency, *The World Fact Book 2007* (Washington, DC: Potomac Books, Inc., 2007), 136.

In the bibliography:

Central Intelligence Agency. *The World Fact Book 2007.* Washington, DC: Potomac Books, Inc., 2007.

AN EDITED BOOK

Put **ed.** (or **eds.** for multiple editors) after the names that begin the citation.

For a footnote:

14. J. Peter Burkholder and Claude V. Palisca, eds., *Norton Anthology of Western Music,* Vol. 1, *Ancient to Baroque* (New York: Norton, 2005), 550.

In the bibliography:

Burkholder, J. Peter, and Claude V. Palisca, eds. *Norton Anthology of Western Music.* Vol. 1, *Ancient to Baroque.* New York: Norton, 2005.

continued on the next page

CMS SAMPLE REFERENCES, continued

AN ARTICLE FROM A REFERENCE BOOK

Well-known reference materials are not usually listed in a CMS bibliography, so you need to know only the footnote format. Start with the name of the reference work, and then list its edition. Put **s.v.** (*sub verba*, Latin for *under the word*) and then put the title of the entry you are citing in quotation marks:

9. *Riverside Dictionary of Biography*, 2004 ed., s.v. "Aaron, Hank (Henry Lewis)."

AN ARTICLE FROM AN ONLINE REFERENCE

The access date should be included in the citation only for sources that are frequently updated, such as Wikis. (And, as with reference works in print, there should be no listing in the bibliography.)

26. Wikipedia, s.v. "Deadwood, South Dakota," http://en.wikipedia.org/wiki/Deadwood%2C_South_Dakota (accessed September 4, 2007).

A RELIGIOUS TEXT

Citations for religious texts appear in the notes, but not in the bibliography.

12. Qur'an 18:16–20.

A WEBPAGE

For a footnote:

19. New York Historical Society, "Galleries," New York Divided: Slavery and the Civil War, http://www.slaveryinnewyork.org/tour_galleries.htm (accessed September 2, 2007).

In the bibliography:

New York Historical Society. "Galleries." New York Divided: Slavery and the Civil War. http://www.slaveryinnewyork.org/tour_galleries.htm (accessed September 2, 2007).

AN E-MAIL

If you reference e-mails in the text of your paper, you do not need to provide a note. E-mails are not listed in a CMS bibliography.

In an e-mail message to the author on November 6, 2006, Jason Craft noted....

If you do need to include a footnote:

24. Jason Craft, e-mail message to author, November 6, 2006.

A BLOG POSTING

When you give the URL for a blog entry, give the **permalink** to the entry rather than the URL of that blog so a reader can go directly to the entry without having to scroll through the entire blog.

For a footnote:

8. Pink Lady [Screen name], "Howard's End," In the Pink Texas Blog, comment posted June 29, 2007, http://www.inthepinktexas.com/2007/06/29/howards-end-3/ (accessed August 3, 2007).

In the bibliography:

In the Pink Texas Blog. "Howard's End." http:// www.inthepinktexas.com/2007/06/29/howards-end-3/.

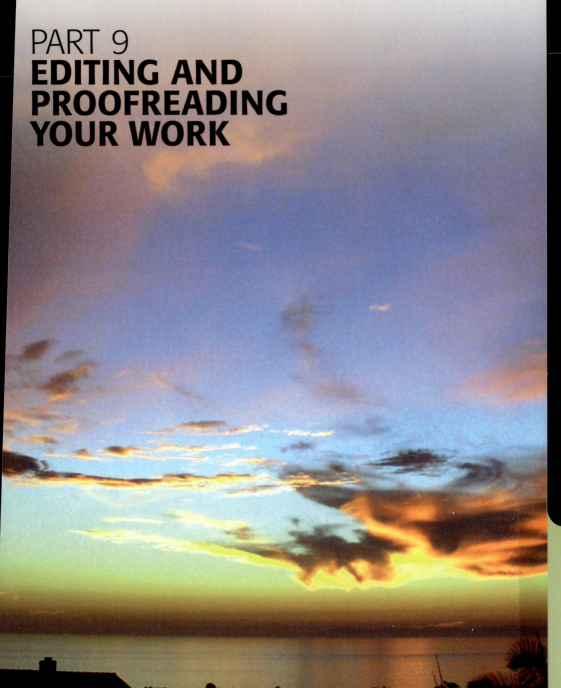

PART 9
EDITING AND PROOFREADING YOUR WORK

CONTENTS

WHERE ARE WE IN THE PROCESS FOR COMPOSING?

Understanding your project

Getting started

Asking questions

Shaping your project for others

Drafting a paper

Getting feedback

Revising

Polishing   Editing and proofreading

EDITING AND PROOFREADING

EDITING

To edit your own writing, try reading it aloud to yourself (which will help you really hear how your words are working) or to someone else (which will really make you aware of how others respond to your words).

Whether you read aloud or work with hardcopy, keep an ear and eye out for the following:

- Are your verbs active? Are your nouns concrete?

  → See pages 273–274.

- Have you avoided jargon?

  → See page 276.

- Will your readers know easily why one sentence or paragraph follows another?

  → See pages 296–297 on transitions.

- Do your sentences have all the qualities that make them easy to read?

  → See pages 282–283.

- Are your introductory and concluding paragraphs engaging and strong?

  → See pages 292–295.

- Have you used inclusive language?

  → See pages 248–263.

PROOFREADING

For both editing and proofreading, keep the following in mind:

- If you have been writing exclusively on a computer screen, **print a hard copy** for editing and proofreading: Seeing the text differently will help you see changes you can and ought to make to help your audience read the text easily.

- Almost all word processing software comes with *grammar checkers*. Use them, but use them carefully: They simply are not as sophisticated as humans. They often miss or misidentify sentence fragments, recommend that you shorten sentences that are just fine, and suggest grammatical changes that are just plain wrong. At this time, there is no better grammar checker than another human.

- Like grammar checkers, *spell checkers* are imperfect. They cannot tell whether you are using **they're**, **there**, or **their** correctly, and they will sometimes recommend replacement words for words they do not have in their reference lists; for example, one spell checker has recommended *salmon's* to replace *someone's*. Spell checkers do not recognize many names. So use spell checkers, but use them carefully: If you are unsure whether a change they recommend is correct, check a dictionary or ask someone whose knowledge you trust.

→ To learn more about using spell checkers, see page 609.

IF ENGLISH IS NOT YOUR HOME LANGUAGE

- Proofread and edit little by little. Don't wait until the paper is finished to edit and proofread. Instead, once you have a thesis, a statement of purpose, and a completed draft, spend a little time editing. If you leave all the language work until the end of the process, you may not have enough time or you may find it too overwhelming and discouraging.

- Determine the aspects of style, punctuation, or grammar that give you trouble. Focus on those aspects when you proofread.

- Proofread your text more than once. Look for a different style, punctuation, or grammar point each time.

- Be an active proofreader. Use strategies that allow you to focus on the mechanics and language of what you have written. In addition to the strategies we have described to the left, try:

  - Underlining or highlighting the aspects of style, punctuation, or grammar on which you are focusing.

  - Moving a pencil along each sentence as you proofread to focus your attention on your words and punctuation.

  - Reading sentence by sentence, covering the rest of the text with a blank sheet of paper.

  - Putting slash marks (//) between each sentence. This will help you focus on the grammar, punctuation, and vocabulary choices you have made in each sentence.

GRAMMAR

WHAT IS GRAMMAR?

The grammars that appear in handbooks and textbooks attempt to capture language patterns that develop as humans talk and write. Not only do grammars change as times change but they shift from group to group.

The grammar we present in the next pages is **the grammar of academic American English writing**. You may have grown up into this pattern if you grew up where people write and read a lot. You may have grown up where other patterns—other grammars—of English are used. You may have grown up in another language.

No matter what your language background, studying the current patterns in academic American English writing can help you move between different grammar communities and help you decide how you want to shape the words you use to reach others.

■ ■ ■

The illustration to the right shows the basic parts—and how they build—of English sentences.

Like any illustration, it is not perfect, but it is accurate enough for you to see how sentences are broken down into clauses, subjects and predicates, noun and verb phrases, and then the parts of speech.

You can also move from the bottom up, to see how words—the parts of speech—come together to form phrases and then subjects and predicates and then clauses and finally sentences.

The nineteenth-century Society for the Diffusion of Really Useful Knowledge published and widely distributed *The Penny Magazine* and *The Penny Cyclopedia*, because its members were worried about the reading practices of its working-class audience.

SENTENCES
are made of…

The nineteenth-century Society for the Diffusion of Really Useful Knowledge published and widely distributed *The Penny Magazine* and *The Penny Cyclopedia*

because its members were worried about the reading practices of its working-class audience.

CLAUSES, of which there are two kinds, both of which are made of…

The nineteenth-century Society for the Diffusion of Really Useful Knowledge

its members

SUBJECTS,
which are made of…

published and widely distributed *The Penny Magazine* and *The Penny Cyclopedia*

were worried about the reading practices of its working-class audience.

PREDICATES,
which are made of…

The nineteenth-century Society for the Diffusion of Really Useful Knowledge

The Penny Magazine and *The Penny Cyclopedia*

its members

the reading practices of its working-class audience

NOUN PHRASES,
which can be made of…

published and widely distributed

were worried

VERB PHRASES,
which can be made of…

VERBS: published, distributed, worried
HELPING VERBS: were
ADVERBS: widely
CONJUNCTIONS: and

NOUNS: Society, Diffusion, Knowledge, members, *Magazine, Cyclopedia,* practices, audience
PRONOUNS: its
ARTICLES: the
ADJECTIVES: nineteenth-century, Useful, working-class
ADVERBS: Really
CONJUNCTIONS: and
PREPOSITIONS: of

Nouns, pronouns, articles, adjectives, adverbs, conjunctions, prepositions, and verbs, taken all together, are referred to as

THE PARTS OF SPEECH.

THERE ARE 4 SENTENCE FUNCTIONS.

With sentences, we can…

1

MAKE STATEMENTS

These kind of sentences are called **DECLARATIVE SENTENCES**, and they are the main kind of sentence you will see in all writing, including academic.

Lyle sits hunched over on the tailgate.

In the fifth and sixth centuries, Ireland was the center of high culture in Europe.

In the last years of his life, Ray began to manifest a strange relationship with snow.

Between the end of the Civil War and the turn of the century, the controversy in American life about who women were and ought to be played itself out in popular self-improvement manuals that offered condensed versions of academic and practical subjects including the principles of elocution, oratory, and composition.

2

ASK QUESTIONS

These are **INTERROGATIVE SENTENCES**, and they matter in all writing. In academic writing, authors often use questions to set up the problems they want to address.

What should we do now?

How can an experiment be "wrong"?

How lethal was the flu of 1918?

Will all broadband infrastructures be privately owned?

What is it like to live in a cell in one of the most notorious prisons in the country?

Why is it that people have such strange attitudes toward images, objects, and media? Why do they behave as though pictures were alive, as if works of art had minds of their own, as if images had a power to influence human beings, demanding things from us, persuading, seducing, and leading us astray?

3

COMMAND

These are **IMPERATIVE SENTENCES.** They tell someone to do something. You also find them in instruction sets and manuals.

Go home.

Put down the weapon and raise your hands.

Watch out that the temperature of the beaker's contents does not rise about 275°.

In a large saucepan over low heat, warm the oil until hot but not smoking. Add the curry paste. It should just sizzle; if it spits and pops wildly, remove the pan from the heat for a moment.

(Note that imperative sentences have an implied subject: It is as though every imperative sentence begins with the implied word **You**.)

4

BE EMOTIONAL

These are **EXCLAMATORY SENTENCES.** Exclamations are expressions of strong feeling. Writers often use exclamatory sentences when they are describing the speech of others. These sentences end with exclamation points.

Anthrax!

When we were little, how we loved to be scared silly!

If the electrons are not seen, we have interference!

THERE ARE 4 SENTENCE PATTERNS.

It is out of these four patterns that all American English sentences are built.

1

SIMPLE SENTENCES

are used in all writing:

Dogs bark.

Jumping dogs bark loudly.

She and I were going to the park.

An autumn wind gusts up to thirty miles an hour.

He pointed to a pile of smooth bricks.

They giggle and laugh.

Simple sentences are the building blocks of the other kinds of sentences, so it is important that you have a good understanding of them because the other kinds of sentences are much used in academic and formal writing. (Notice, too, that simple sentences are neither necessarily short nor uninformative even though they are called **simple**.)

→ **GO TO PAGE 472.**

2

COMPOUND SENTENCES

join two simple sentences:

Dogs bark and cats meow.

She and I were going to the park while everyone else was swimming.

An autumn wind gusts up to thirty miles an hour; a winter wind can gust up to fifty miles an hour.

I am not worried about getting lost in the woods; besides, the point of wilderness is to lose yourself in it.

Compound sentences are important in academic and other kinds of formal writing because they help you express a range of relationships among the elements of your sentences.

→ **GO TO PAGE 480.**

→ The parts out of which sentences are built are words, which we discuss in the Parts of Speech pages beginning on page 496.

3
COMPLEX SENTENCES

allow you to express complicated relations among the elements you are describing. These sentences are also very important in academic and other kinds of formal writing.

Those who want to learn more should come to the Friday-evening classes.

In this chapter I examine the development of Piaget's thought, which has three main features.

Although his mother remarried after his father died, she was soon abandoned by her second husband.

I argue that James's use of metaphor is not so straightforward when one considers it in light of his family background.

→ GO TO PAGE 483.

4
COMPOUND-COMPLEX SENTENCES

As their name suggests, compound-complex sentences result when you combine a compound sentence with a complex sentence. These sentences tend to be long, and are used almost exclusively in academic writing.

Georgette de Montenay, who came from a noble family in southwest France, lived at the court of the Queen of Navarre and she wrote the first religious emblem book.

Chinese mathematical thought was always profoundly algebraic instead of geometrical, and in the Sung and Yuan dynasties of the twelfth to fourteenth centuries A.D., the Chinese school led the world in the solution of equations; thus the triangle we now call Pascal's was already old in China in 1300 A.D.

→ GO TO PAGE 488.

SIMPLE SENTENCES 1

The simplest sentences are most often composed of two words. The first word names a person, place, thing, or idea; the second word describes what that person, place, thing, or idea is, was, or will be doing.

THE PATTERN

person, place, thing, or idea + **action** = **simplest sentence**

NOUN	VERB
Sylvia	walks.
Men	swam.
Chairs	rock.
Lakes	glisten.
Air	moves.
Dogs	barked.
You	smile.
I	sleep.
Happiness	is.
SUBJECT	**PREDICATE**

INDEPENDENT CLAUSE

→ When we wish to speak of persons, places, objects, and ideas as a grammatical category, we call them nouns (pages 498–501).

→ As a grammatical category, actions are called verbs (pages 514–527).

→ The part of a sentence that names who or what acts is the subject (pages 475–478); the part that names the action is the predicate (pages 474–478).

→ A subject and predicate together are a clause (page 483); when they can stand alone as a sentence, they are independent clauses (pages 484–487).

SIMPLE SENTENCES 2

To the simplest sentences you can add descriptions to help readers understand more about the nouns and verbs in them.

THE PATTERN

noun and description + verb and description = sentence

NOUN PHRASE	VERB PHRASE
The woman	walks quickly.
A man	swam slowly.
Rocking chairs	swayed jauntily.
Blue lakes	glisten lightly.
Cool air	moves quietly.
A dog	barked loudly.
You	smile widely.
I, tired,	sleep contentedly.
Our happiness	stays still.
SUBJECT	**PREDICATE**
INDEPENDENT CLAUSE	

→ The words that help us say descriptive things about nouns are called adjectives (pages 508–509). Articles are the words *a, an,* and *the,* and are a special kind of adjective (pages 510–513).

→ The words that help us say descriptive things about verbs are called adverbs (pages 528–529).

→ When nouns and verbs have descriptive words added to them, as above, they are called (respectively) noun phrases (page 474) and verb phrases (page 474).

GRAMMAR: SIMPLE SENTENCES
MORE ON PREDICATES

As we described on the preceding page, a predicate always contains a verb (see pages 514–527 to learn more about verbs). The verb in a predicate can be one of three kinds:

- a verb that takes objects
- a verb that does not take objects
- a linking verb

VERBS THAT TAKE OBJECTS

Objects can be parts of predicates. Objects are the nouns or nouns phrases that describe the person, place, thing, or idea affected by the verb's action. Verbs that take objects are called **transitive verbs**.

She smelled the roses.

Jamieson interviewed a variety of experts.

Neanderthals were cooking shellfish in Italy about 110,000 years ago.

There are two kinds of objects: **direct object** and **indirect objects**. The examples above all show direct objects.

Indirect objects only appear in sentences that have direct objects. Indirect objects answer the questions *For whom was this action carried out?* or *To whom was the object given?*

	indirect objects	direct objects
He gave	me	water.
Mark read	his son	a story.
The carpenter will build	us	new bookshelves.

An indirect object usually comes between the verb and the direct object.

Indirect objects do not follow prepositions (→ see pages 530–531). Sentences with indirect objects can be rewritten with prepositions—

He gave water to me.

Mark read a story to his son.

The carpenter will build new bookshelves for us.

—but then the indirect object becomes the object of the preposition before it and is no longer an indirect object.

VERBS THAT DON'T TAKE OBJECTS

Verbs that don't take objects or subject complements (see below) are called *intransitive verbs.*

Meredith left. • Margarete complained. • The train arrived.

Intransitive sentences can have adverbs (see pages 528–529) or adverbial phrases (see page 486) following the verb, but these modify the verb; they are not objects:

Meredith left sadly. • Margarete complained about her haircut.

The train arrived two hours late.

LINKING VERBS

Linking verbs "link" a noun to a fuller description.

Luisa is happy.

Communication overload may be sapping your productivity.

The words following a linking verb are a *subject complement*: the subject complement fills out (or *complements*) what readers know about the noun. The subject complement in a sentence can be a noun, noun phrase, or pronoun—

"Why Did I Get Married" is the big screen adaptation of Tyler Perry's stage play.

—or it can be an adjective—

The process was difficult for everyone involved.

Linking verbs are usually a form of the verb *be* (see page 519) but can also be verbs such as *appear, become, feel, look, make, seem, smell, sound,* or *taste*:

The cheese smelled stinky but delicious.

TIP: DOES A VERB TAKE A DIRECT OBJECT, NO OBJECT, OR A SUBJECT COMPLEMENT?
A dictionary entry will tell you.

TIP: SOME VERBS CAN BE BOTH TRANSITIVE AND INTRANSITIVE
She moved the furniture to her new house.
Molecules and ions moved through the cell membrane.

In the first sentence above, *moved* functions as a transitive verb, with *the furniture* as its direct object. In the second sentence, *moved* functions as an intransitive verb; *through the cell membrane* is an adverbial phrase. A dictionary entry can help you learn about such verbs and how to use them.

GRAMMAR
COMPOUND SENTENCES

Compound sentences are made up of two or more simple sentences joined by punctuation or conjunctions—or both punctuation and conjunctions.

THE FUNCTION OF COMPOUND SENTENCES

When you write with compound sentences, your sentences can show readers more complex relations among events than simple sentences allow. Compound sentences show up frequently in academic writing.

Because compound sentences are made up of two independent clauses joined together, they show that the writer wants to give equal emphasis to both clauses.

THE PATTERN

MAKING COMPOUND SENTENCES USING PUNCTUATION

INDEPENDENT CLAUSE **;** INDEPENDENT CLAUSE **=** COMPOUND SENTENCE

Cecelia walks; Martha bikes.

I was sleeping; you were reading.

Dogs bark; coyotes howl.

The cell was large; it could attach to the molecule.

You jump; he leaps; we all dance.

This pattern implies that the events described in the joined independent clauses happened at the same time and are of equal importance.

→ To learn more about using semicolons as punctuation to join two independent clauses, see pages 565–567.

MAKING COMPOUND SENTENCES USING CONJUNCTIONS

INDEPENDENT CLAUSE + CONJUNCTION + INDEPENDENT CLAUSE =
COMPOUND SENTENCE

Cecelia walks and Martha bikes.

I was sleeping for you were reading.

Dogs bark but coyotes howl.

The cell was large but it could attach to the molecule.

This pattern—which uses ***coordinating conjunctions***—allows you to show various kinds of relations between the events of the independent clauses.

→ To learn more about coordinating conjunctions and the relations they can help you build between independent clauses, see page 532.

A COMPLEX SENTENCE COMBINES AN INDEPENDENT CLAUSE WITH ONE OR MORE DEPENDENT CLAUSES

There are two kinds of dependent clauses: *adjective clauses* and *adverb clauses*. In formal written English, dependent clauses cannot stand alone as sentences.

THE PATTERN

COMPLEX SENTENCES WITH ADJECTIVE CLAUSES

RELATIVE PRONOUN + PREDICATE = ADJECTIVE CLAUSE

who was biking

which was in the street

that hid under the bushes

whose shape kept changing

Adjective clauses allow you to give additional information about subjects, and so they help you write expressive sentences. Adjective clauses are inserted into independent clauses to make **THE FIRST KIND OF COMPLEX SENTENCE**:

The woman who was biking is my sister.

The bicycle, which was in the street, is missing.

The cell whose shape kept changing has been identified.

→ To learn more about relative pronouns, see page 504.

→ *Whom* is also a relative pronoun, and it can cause writers lots of trouble; see page 507 to learn about the standard ways of using *whom*.

→ To learn more about the punctuation of adjective clauses when you weave them into independent clauses, see pages 558–562. Pay close attention to this; punctuating adjective phrases can cause writers trouble.

WATCH OUT FOR THIS!

Adjective clauses can look like independent clauses because they have a similar structure to sentences: There is a word and then there is a predicate. But, in formal English, relative pronouns cannot take the place of nouns—and so adjective clauses cannot stand alone as sentences.

NOT SENTENCES

who was biking

which was in the street

that hid under the bushes

whose shape kept changing

→ The phrases above are fragments of sentences that can be turned into sentences. To learn more about sentence fragments, see pages 490–493.

SENTENCES

If, in the adjective clauses above, you were to replace the relative pronouns with subjects, you would have sentences:

Mary was biking.

The bicycle was in the street.

The woodchuck hid under the bushes.

The cell's shape kept changing.

SENTENCES

Sometimes, if you put a question mark on the end of an adjective clause—and you capitalize the first letter of the relative pronoun—you can make interrogatory sentences out of adjective clauses:

Who was biking?

Whose shape kept changing?

When you do this, you are changing the function of the pronoun, and so you are changing the type of the pronoun, from a relative pronoun to an interrogative pronoun.

→ To learn more about interrogative pronouns, see page 503.

COMPOUND-COMPLEX SENTENCES

Compound-complex sentences are a sure sign of academic writing. Writers who know how to compose and mix compound and complex sentences into compound-complex sentences are writers who can build sentences for the widest range of contexts and purposes.

THE PATTERN

Compound-complex sentences have at least two independent clauses and one dependent clause, in any order.

**INDEPENDENT CLAUSE + INDEPENDENT CLAUSE + DEPENDENT CLAUSE =
COMPOUND-COMPLEX SENTENCE**

The clauses can be joined together in any of the ways we have described for compound and complex sentences. Look back over the preceding pages for compound and complex patterns to see how they add up in the examples below.

Because compound-complex sentences are made up of many parts, they tend to be long. Because they characterize academic writing, we have taken our examples from essays in various academic disciplines.

> In his essay, Tolman proposed that rats who were able to find food in a maze weren't simply reacting to a conditioned behavioral stimulus but the rats had generated a cognitive map of the overall environment.

The compound-complex sentence above consists of:

- A compound sentence that has a dependent clause (an adjective clause).
- The conjunction **but**.
- A simple sentence.

Below is a compound-complex sentence made of:
- A simple sentence.
- The conjunction *and*.
- A compound sentence that has a dependent clause (an adverb clause).

The American colonies were initially as jealous of their autonomy as the Cherokee chiefdoms, and their first attempt at amalgamation under the Articles of Confederation in 1781 proved unworkable because it reserved too much autonomy for the ex-colonies.

Can you see the parts making up this compound-complex sentence?

We readily recognize people's distinctive handwriting when they put addresses on envelopes, and our signatures remain a key way in which we can identify ourselves during a variety of transactions.

FIXING FRAGMENTS THAT LACK SUBJECTS

Fix fragments that lack subjects by one of the following two approaches:

1 Add a subject

2 Join the fragment to a sentence

ADDING A SUBJECT TO A FRAGMENT

These phrases are fragments because they lack subjects:

Danced in the street.

Sensing their delight in winning.

To add a subject, ask, *Who is doing the action described in the sentence?*—and then give that information:

Mary and Elaine danced in the street.

Christa was sensing their delight in winning. [OR] Christa sensed their delight in winning.

As with the second example, note that you may have to modify the verb when you add a subject.

JOINING A FRAGMENT TO A SENTENCE

Often people inadvertently write fragments in longer descriptions:

Mary and Elaine won the guitar contest last June. They were so happy they threw a party. Danced in the street.

The *danced in the street* fragment can be joined to the sentence before it with a coordinating conjunction:

Mary and Elaine won the guitar contest last June. They were so happy they threw a party and danced in the street.

→ We discuss coordinating conjunctions on page 532 and pages 556–557.

FIXING FRAGMENTS THAT LACK PREDICATES

Fix fragments that lack predicates by one of the following two approaches:

1 Add a predicate

2 Join the fragment to a sentence

ADDING A PREDICATE TO A FRAGMENT

These phrases are fragments because they lack predicates:

The computer on the desk.

Only the lonely.

To add a predicate, ask *What is happening to the objects named the fragment?*—and then give that information:

The computer on the desk was broken.

Only the lonely know how I feel tonight.

JOINING A FRAGMENT TO A SENTENCE

Just as with fragments that lack subjects, fragments without predicates often occur when people write descriptions:

Nobody was out walking after midnight. Only the lonely.

The *only the lonely* fragment can be joined to the sentence before it by making it into the subject:

Only the lonely were out walking after midnight.

Or you can use a conjunction to join the fragment to the end of the sentence:

Nobody was out walking after midnight, except for the lonely.

→ We discuss conjunctions on pages 532–535.

FIXING FRAGMENTS THAT ARE SUBORDINATE CLAUSES WITHOUT ATTACHED INDEPENDENT CLAUSES

This fragment type is a common problem for those learning to write formal prose.

THE PATTERN

To recognize these fragments, you need to be able to recognize dependent clauses. Dependent clauses begin in two ways:

- with one of the **subordinating conjunctions**, which we list on page 534.

  Rather than build a road.

  Although we lived under the Nazi regime for only one year.

  When the people of this part of Peru were building their cities.

- with one of the **relative pronouns**, which we describe on page 504.

  Who regularly sat in hot tubs.   *Whom* he had met in high school.

Anytime you see a phrase that begins with a subordinating conjunction or a relative pronoun, it cannot stand on its own; each gray text above is a fragment.

■ ■ ■

To fix these fragments:

JOIN SUBORDINATE CLAUSE FRAGMENTS TO INDEPENDENT CLAUSES

Rather than build a road, they installed a tram over the trees.

Although my family lived under the Nazi regime for only one year, I will never forget the fear and humiliation I experienced that year in Vienna.

When the people of this part of Peru were building their cities, there was only one other urban complex on earth.

REMOVE THE SUBORDINATING CONJUNCTION TO MAKE A SENTENCE

Note that this gives you two sentences, separated by a period:

We lived under the Nazi regime for only one year. I will never forget the fear and humiliation I experienced that year in Vienna.

INSERT A CLAUSE BEGINNING WITH A RELATIVE PRONOUN INTO AN INDEPENDENT CLAUSE

All the men who regularly sit in hot tubs showed signs of infertility.

Talib Kweli began recording with Mos Def, whom he had met in high school.

PARTS OF SPEECH

The parts of speech are the most basic units of sentences: The parts of speech are the individual words of sentences, named according to the functions they serve in sentences.

The illustration to the right gives a quick introduction to the parts of speech; on the following pages, we go into the parts of speech in more detail.

■ ■ ■

Keep in mind that identifying a word as a particular part of speech depends on how the word is used in a sentence. In the following sentences—

I fish for my dinner.

There aren't many fish in this lake.

I do not like to bait fish hooks.

—the word *fish* serves first as a verb, then as a noun, and then as an adjective.

■ ■ ■

There is one part of speech that we do not mention in the illustration because it does not show up much in academic writing. This kind of word usually stands alone as a sentence:

interjections

Words that describe the person, place, thing, or idea being discussed are **NOUNS.**

Words that describe what the person, place, thing, or idea is doing are **VERBS.**

Alice walks.

She walks.

A certain kind of noun that refers back to an earlier mentioned noun is a **PRONOUN.**

Words that give more details about nouns are **ARTICLES** and **ADJECTIVES.**

Words that give more detail about how an action is done (where, when, or in what manner) are **ADVERBS.**

The smiling woman walked happily yesterday.

Words that allow us to talk about more than one noun or action at a time are **CONJUNCTIONS.**

Alice and Shereen walk and talk.

Words that allow us to describe how the actors and actions in a sentence are placed in space or time are **PREPOSITIONS.**

After saying good-bye, Alice walked into the store.

Prepositions are always the first words of phrases; those phrases can tell us more about nouns (in what shape was Alice?), in which case they are **ADJECTIVAL PREPOSITIONAL PHRASES**...

Out of breath, Alice leaned against the wall.

... or those phrases can tell us more about verbs (where did Alice lean?), in which case they are **ADVERBIAL PREPOSITIONAL PHRASES.**

MAKING NOUNS PLURAL

In English, a noun's ending usually indicates whether it is singular or plural.

THE PATTERNS

PLURAL ENDINGS

> If you have any questions about a noun's plural form, a dictionary will show you the plural form.

SINGULAR	PLURAL	
-s		
a boy	the boys	If a noun ends in an *-o* preceded by a *vowel*, it usually takes an *-s* to make it plural.
the site	many sites	
freedom	seven freedoms	
my radio	their radios	With compound hyphenated words, add *-s* to the main noun, even if that noun is not at the end of the word.
father-in-law	fathers-in-law	
-es		
a box	six boxes	Nouns that end in *-s, -sh, -ch,* and *-x* add *-es* to become plural.
my church	our churches	
one potato	two potatoes	If a noun ends in an *-o* preceded by a *consonant*, it usually takes an *-es* to make a plural.
-ies		
the summary	several summaries	Nouns that end in *-y* lose the *-y* and add *-ies* to become plural.
a boundary	the boundaries	
-ves		
my life	our lives	Nouns that end in *-f* or *-fe* replace the *-f* or *-fe* with *-ves* to become plural.
a calf	six calves	
other endings		
one medium	the media	Sometimes the plurals of words that derive from other languages take their plural form from the original language.
the analysis	the analyses	
one criterion	three criteria	
his child	his children	
changed form		
one man	many men	Words that have been in use since the beginning of language often change their forms to make plurals.
a mouse	three mice	
no change		
one moose	two moose	Many names for large animals keep the same form in both singular and plural.
one deer	many deer	

MAKING NOUNS POSSESSIVE

A possessive noun comes before another noun, and its possessive form indicates possession of or other close association with the noun it precedes.

POSSESSIVES USING SINGULAR NOUNS

Add **-'s** to the end of the noun even if the noun ends in **-s:**

a cell's wall	Magnolia's cupcakes	my life's story
Luis's award	the grass's height	a potato's texture

With nouns ending in **-s**, you can leave off the **-'s** and simply use an apostrophe if pronouncing the words would be awkward:

Jesus's sayings   **Jesus' sayings**

Aesops's stories   **Aesops' stories**

POSSESSIVES USING PLURAL NOUNS

If the plural noun does not end in **-s**, add **-'s**.

the children's choir	the media's analysis	the deer's diseases

If the plural noun *does* end in **-s**, add only an apostrophe.

a bakers' dozen	the Kennedys' compound	the grasses' heights
the boxes' interiors	many potatoes' textures	our lives' stories

POSSESSIVES USING COMPOUND NOUNS

The last word in a compound noun becomes possessive, following the above guidelines:

a NASCAR driver's car	the school nurse's office
the fathers-in-law's meeting	some swimming pools' depths

POSSESSIVES USING TWO OR MORE NOUNS

If the object in question is owned jointly by the nouns, make the last noun possessive:

Abbott and Costello's "Who's on first?" routine was developed in the 1930s.

If each of the two nouns has possession, make both possesive:

Abbott's and Costello's lives had very different endings.

TIP: **LEARN THE DIFFERENCE BETWEEN PLURALS AND POSSESSIVES**

Both plurals and possessives usually add an **-s** at the end of a noun. The difference is that possessives always have an apostrophe; plurals do not.

| RELATIVE PRONOUNS | who, whoever, whom, which, that, what, whatever |

Relative pronouns allow us to combine sentences that are about the same person, place, thing, or idea. By using them, we can help readers see the connections that exist between two sentences:

The man was tired. The man climbed all the stairs.

The man who climbed all the stairs was tired.

(The single sentence implies more strongly than the two separate sentences that the man was probably tired because he climbed the stairs. Note that *who* replaces *The man*.)

The dogs like the beach. The beach has many sticks.

The dogs like the beach that has many sticks.

(The single sentence implies more strongly than the two separate sentences that the dogs like the beach because of the sticks. Note that *that* replaces *The beach*.)

The buildings burned. The buildings were old.

The buildings that burned were old.

(The single sentence implies more strongly than the two separate sentences that the buildings burned because they were old. Note that *that* replaces *The buildings*.)

■ ■ ■

Relative pronouns function as the first words of clauses (page 483) that give additional information about a noun. Clauses made with relative pronouns are called dependent clauses (pages 484–487) because they are not sentences by themselves; to make a sentence with such a dependent clause, join it to an independent clause (page 483):

DEPENDENT CLAUSE: who climbed all the stairs

INDEPENDENT CLAUSE: The man was tired.

SENTENCE: The man who climbed all the stairs was tired.

→ For more on using relative pronouns, see pages 484–485, 493, and 507.

DEMONSTRATIVE PRONOUNS this, that   these, those

These pronouns help us be specific about a person or object we want to discuss.

This woman is my friend. • **That** dog belongs to Mavis.

These people went to the museum. • **Those** buildings are on Washington Street.

In the examples above, the demonstrative pronouns function like adjectives, telling readers or listeners exactly what person or thing is meant. In the examples below, the pronouns function like nouns:

This is the most important issue of our time: Are we running out of oil?

That is my best pen. • **Those** who care for others will themselves be cared for.

REFLEXIVE PRONOUNS   myself, oneself, himself,   ourselves, themselves
                        herself, itself

Reflexive pronouns refer back to the person or thing performing an action, to emphasize who did the action.

Mark cut **himself**. • Luisa made **herself** dinner. • The dog licked **itself**.

The men took **themselves** out of the race.

The buildings were **themselves** victims of time.

RECIPROCAL PRONOUNS   each other, one another

Use reciprocal pronouns when you want to show people or objects acting on each other.

The survivors helped **one another**. • The dogs chased **each other**.

IF YOU GREW UP SPEAKING A LANGUAGE OTHER THAN ENGLISH…

→ See page 506 to make sure you have chosen the correct pronoun for the noun to which you are referring.

→ See page 507 for help with using *who* and *whom*.

ADJECTIVES

Adjectives help us make writing precise by allowing us to describe the particular qualities of people, places, objects, and ideas.

WHICH ONE? WHAT KIND?

Adjectives allow us to specify exactly which people, places, objects, or ideas we are discussing.

He wore his green shoes. • Could you bring me the red shoes, please?

HOW MANY?

Adjectives help us say how many people, places, objects, or ideas are at stake.

Four potatoes make enough mashed potatoes for three people.

HOW DO THEY COMPARE?

Adjectives help us specify which people, places, objects, or ideas we mean by allowing us to make comparisons.

He asked for the smallest book. I would like the largest book. She asked for a book that was smaller than mine.

PLACEMENT OF ADJECTIVES

1 Adjectives usually come before the nouns they modify:

Use only the sharpest tools to prune your bushes.

A brilliant green aurora shimmers in the dark night.

There is no biological reason for this condition.

The jubilant procession advanced through the narrow streets.

2 Adjectives come after the verbs *appear*, *be*, *feel*, *look*, *seem*, *smell*, *sound*, and *taste*:

She was not at her sharpest.

The frog looked a brilliant green in the sun.

The reason is purely biological.

The team sounded jubilant after their win.

The bay appeared narrow after we had been out on the lake.

IF YOU GREW UP SPEAKING A LANGUAGE OTHER THAN ENGLISH...

→ Pages 552–553 give you more help with placing adjectives correctly and ordering multiple adjectives.

THE TENSES OF ENGLISH VERBS

The examples below show the tense forms for the first person singular forms of the regular verb **talk** and the irregular verbs **begin** and **be**.

THE PATTERNS

SIMPLE TENSES

In the present, the simple tense describes actions taking place at the time a sentence is written or spoken, or for actions that occur regularly. The simple past describes actions that were completed in the past. The simple future describes actions that have not yet begun.

PRESENT	I talk.	I begin.	I am.
PAST	I talked.	I began.	I was.
FUTURE	I will talk.	I will begin.	I will be.

PROGRESSIVE TENSES

The progressive tenses describe actions that continue—or will continue—over time.

PRESENT	I am talking.	I am beginning.	I am being.
PAST	I was talking.	I was beginning.	I was being.
FUTURE	I will be talking.	I will be beginning.	I will be being.

PERFECT TENSES

The perfect tenses describe actions that have been (or will have been) completed.

PRESENT	I have talked.	I have begun.	I have been.
PAST	I had talked.	I had begun.	I had been.
FUTURE	I will have talked.	I will have begun.	I will have been.

PERFECT PROGRESSIVE TENSES

The present perfect progressive tense describes an action that began in the past, continues in the present, and may continue into the future. The past perfect progressive tense describes a stretched-out action that was completed before some other past action; this tense usually appears in sentences that describe the other past action (→ see pages 520–521). The future perfect progressive tense describes a stretched-out action that will occur before some specified future time.

PRESENT	I have been talking.	I have been beginning.	I have been being.
PAST	I had been talking.	I had been beginning.	I had been being.
FUTURE	I will have been talking.	I will have been beginning.	I will have been being.

→ To learn more about these tenses and how they are used in academic English writing, see pages 520–521.

FORMING THE TENSES OF ENGLISH VERBS, PART 1

Except for the verb *be*, all English verbs have five forms.

	BASE FORM	-S FORM	PRESENT PARTICIPLE	PAST FORM	PAST PARTICIPLE
REGULAR VERB	walk	walks	walking	walked	walked
IRREGULAR VERB	sing	sings	singing	sang	sung
IRREGULAR VERB	ride	rides	riding	rode	ridden

THE BASE FORM

The base form is how you find a verb in a dictionary, and it is the form from which all the verb's tenses are built. If you place **to** in front of the base form, you make what is called **the infinitive**.

THE -s FORM

This form is the third person singular present tense of any verb.

THE PRESENT PARTICIPLE

The present participle, made by adding **-ing** to the base form, is used with a helping verb to construct the progressive tenses of any verb. (Note that if a verb's base form ends in **-e**, the **-e** is dropped before the **-ing** is added.)

The present participle can also be used as an adjective: **Let sleeping dogs lie**.

THE PAST FORM

The past form is used for the simple past tense. Because English has been formed from so many other languages, many frequently used verbs have irregular past forms. A dictionary will show you the past form of any verb.

THE PAST PARTICIPLE

With a helping verb, the past particple is used to construct the perfect tenses of any verb. For regular verbs, the past participle is the same as the past form; for irregular verbs, you will need to check a dictionary to learn the past participle.

MAIN VERBS AND HELPING VERBS

In the patterns to the left, note that—except for the simple present and simple past—verb tenses are constructed from a main verb and a helping verb, as shown on page 518.

The main verb is one of the five forms of a verb described above; a helping verb is one of the forms of the irregular verbs *be*, *have*, and *do*.

→ In addition to the helping verbs *be*, *have*, and *do*, there is another kind of helping verb. To learn about these modal auxiliary verbs, see page 519.

USING THE TENSES OF ENGLISH VERBS IN ACADEMIC WRITING

Because verb tenses convey so much information, writers use them to show relationships among the events about which they write. In turn, readers understand verb tenses as signals that help them understand the relationships and order of events.

The descriptions below focus on verb tenses in academic writing. Look at different types of writing—lab reports, summaries and responses to literature, research proposals—to learn what verb tenses tend to be used in each type of writing.

THE SIMPLE PRESENT
is used to...

- describe the present situation
  Conservationists at the Masai Mara work hard to protect the wildebeest from poachers.

- generalize
  Studies show that chronic stress contributes to heart attacks and other diseases.

- describe the contents of a book, movie, or other text
  In his thesis, "Intimate Relationships with Artificial Partners," Levy conjectures that robots will become so human-like that people will fall in love with them.

THE PRESENT PROGRESSIVE
is used to...

- describe actions in progress at the moment of speaking
  Women are dying from complicated pregnancies and childbirth at almost the same rate they were in 1990.

- compare two present actions. One action is described in simple present, the other in present progressive.
  Children with strict parents follow rules when under supervision, but often engage in reckless actions when their parents are not watching.

THE PRESENT PERFECT
is used to...

- describe actions begun in the past but not completed
  The once vanished gray wolf has made a comeback in the Northern Rockies.

- describe actions begun at an unspecified past time
  Over half of adolescents have tried alcohol and drugs at least once.

- introduce a topic
  Once a disease of the Western world, breast cancer has become a global concern.

THE SIMPLE PAST
is used to...

- describe completed events or states
  Charles M. Schulz drew "Peanuts" for nearly half a century.

- report past research or events, summarize lab or research results, and to give narrative examples
  Steven C. Amstrup of the United States Geological Survey led a recent exhaustive study of polar bears.

THE PAST PERFECT
is used to...

- compare two past events. The past perfect signals the event that happened first.
  The protesters were demanding the freedom and democracy for which their parents had fought.

THE SIMPLE FUTURE
is used to describe...

- intentions and promises
  In this paper I will explore the relations between media portrayals of men and men's body images.

- predictions
  American employers will hire 270,000 fewer IT workers this year than they did in 2003.

TIP: EDITING WRITING FOR VERB TENSES

1 Underline or highlight each sentence's main verb. The main verb has a subject.

2 Each sentence should contain a complete verb phrase: **Main verb** or **Helping verb + Main verb**.

3 For each sentence, ask if your verb tenses signal your desired meaning.

CONJUNCTIONS

Conjunctions connect words or groups of words. There are four kinds of conjunctions, each of which helps you express different kinds of relations between the words you are connecting.

COORDINATING CONJUNCTIONS

Coordinating conjunctions can connect nouns (including pronouns), adjectives, adverbs, prepositions, clauses, and sentences.

Use a coordinating conjunction when you want a reader to see that the words you are connecting have equal—coordinate—emphasis. The coordinating conjunctions, together with the relations they show, are

and	addition	Jacob and Ali went to the store. Loretta cooked and ate dinner.
for	cause	The dog is wet, for she swam. I am hungry, for I forgot to eat.
but, yet	contrast	Jacob went to the store, but Ali stayed home. Loretta cooked dinner, yet she did not eat right away.
or	choice	Jacob or Ali can go. • Loretta can cook dinner or eat out.
so	effect	I am hungry, so I will eat. The dog is wet from the rain, so I will dry her.
nor	exclusion	José doesn't swim, nor do I.

To connect individual words—such as nouns (including pronouns), adjectives, adverbs, and prepositions—**or phrases** use this pattern:

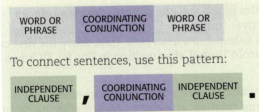

| WORD OR PHRASE | COORDINATING CONJUNCTION | WORD OR PHRASE |

To connect sentences, use this pattern:

| INDEPENDENT CLAUSE | **,** | COORDINATING CONJUNCTION | INDEPENDENT CLAUSE | ■ |

CORRELATIVE CONJUNCTIONS

Correlative conjunctions are like coordinating conjunctions in that they help you give equal emphasis to the words you are connecting—but correlative conjunctions come in two parts, and readers always expect to see both parts:

both…and, not only…but also	Both Miguel and Rav are on vacation.
addition	She did both her English and her math work.
either…or, whether…or	I could hire either Paul or Shawna.
choice	I want either to go out for dinner or to sleep.
	Either you will eat at home, or you will go out.
just as…so	Just as the smell of the air brought back
equality	memories, so too did the taste of the bread
	bring back memories.
neither…nor	Neither this car nor that is running.
exclusion	Neither will Omi go out, nor will she stay in!

To connect individual words—such as nouns (including pronouns), adjectives, adverbs, and prepositions—**or phrases**, use this pattern:

CORRELATIVE CONJUNCTION, PART 1	WORD OR PHRASE	CORRELATIVE CONJUNCTION, PART 2	WORD OR PHRASE

To connect sentences, use this pattern:

CORRELATIVE CONJUNCTION, PART 1	INDEPENDENT CLAUSE	CORRELATIVE CONJUNCTION, PART 2	INDEPENDENT CLAUSE

, ■

GRAMMAR
AVOIDING SHIFTS IN GRAMMATICAL FORMS

Shifts occur when a sentence begins with one grammatical form but ends with another. The conventions of formal, academic writing call for none of the five kinds of shifts we describe on these four pages.

SHIFTS BETWEEN DIRECT AND INDIRECT DISCOURSE

When you quote someone's words directly, you are using *direct discourse*:

"Are you going to the store without me?" Harriet's sister wanted to know.

In *indirect discourse*, you report what someone else said:

Harriet's sister wanted to know if we were going to the store without her.

A convention of formal written English is not to shift from one of these forms to another in a sentence:

Harriet's sister wanted to know are we going to the store without her.

SHIFTS IN PERSON AND NUMBER

To understand what it means to make a shift in person and number in a sentence or across sentences, keep in mind the chart to the right.

Whenever you mention the same noun twice, or use a noun and a pronoun, check that both have the same person and number. The pattern below shows you what to look for:

NUMBER PERSON	singular	plural
first person	I, me	we, us
second person	you	you
third person	it, one, she, he, her, him	they, them

THE PATTERN

USING PERSON CONSISTENTLY

correct **You can write. All you have to do is pick up a pen.**
second person, singular / second person, singular

incorrect **Anyone can write. All you have to do is pick up a pen.**
third person, singular / second person, singular

USING NUMBER CONSISTENTLY

correct **We all have to be careful about our effects on the environment. To help, each of us should drive less, recycle more, and talk to our political representatives.**
first person, plural / first person, plural / first person, plural

incorrect **We all have to be careful about our effects on the environment. To help, I should drive less, recycle more, and talk to my political representatives.**
first person, plural / first person, singular / first person, singular

→ For more information about using pronouns, see pages 502–507.

GRAMMAR
AVOIDING MISPLACED AND DANGLING MODIFIERS

Modifier is the collective name for adjectives, adjectival phrases, adverbs, and adverbial phrases.

Modifiers make writing concrete and engaging—if readers can tell what words are being modified. Unfortunately, writers can easily put modifiers in odd places, which is why we offer the following suggestions.

PUT MODIFIERS CLOSE TO THE WORDS THEY MODIFY

In this sentence—

Covered in chocolate icing, my friends will love this cake.

—the friends sound like people we should approach with spoons in hand. When the adjectival phrase *covered in chocolate icing* is moved closer to the noun it is meant to modify, the result—

My friends will love this cake covered in chocolate icing.

—is clearer about the icing's location.

You are most likely to produce such slips when you write sentences with several modifiers. The following sentence has two modifiers (*all over Europe* and *passing close to earth*) placed to make it sound as though Europe passed close to earth in 1577:

The Great Comet of 1577 was viewed by people all over Europe passing close to earth.

When *passing close to earth* is moved closer to the noun phrase it should modify, the sentence is clearer:

Passing close to earth, the Great Comet of 1577 was viewed by people all over Europe.

TIP: CHECKING YOUR MODIFIERS

Modification slips are easy to produce as you write—and easy to fix. Fixing them requires finding them, however, and finding them takes time and careful reading.
To check your modifiers:

1 Underline every modifier in your writing and then draw a line from each to the word it modifies.

2 Move modifiers that are far from the words they modify closer to those words.

3 If the underlined word is a limiting modifier (→ see page 541), is it placed so that the sentence means what you desire it to?

4 If you cannot find a noun to which the modifier refers, you have a dangling modifier. Choose one of the options on page 541 to fix the dangling modifier.

PAY PARTICULAR ATTENTION TO LIMITING MODIFIERS

Limiting modifiers are words such as *almost*, *even*, *hardly*, *just*, *nearly*, *not*, *only*, and *simply*. They can be placed almost anywhere in a sentence, which makes them dangerous: Their placement can change a sentence's meaning.

For example, this sentence says that Luther thought about donating his collection, but didn't:

Luther almost donated his entire collection of LPs to the auction.

This sentence says that Luther *did* donate a large part of his collection:

Luther donated almost his entire collection of LPs to the auction.

Check each instance of limiting modifiers in your writing to be sure your sentences say what you want.

MOVE DISRUPTIVE MODIFIERS

Modifiers are disruptive when they disrupt a sentence's grammatical elements. In the first sentence below, a long phrase creates a distracting pause for readers between the sentence's subject and predicate:

Palenquero, although its grammar is so different that Spanish speakers cannot understand it, is thought to be the only Spanish-based Creole language in Latin America.

Moving the phrase makes the sentence easier to read:

Although its grammar is so different that Spanish speakers cannot understand it, Palenquero is thought to be the only Spanish-based Creole language in Latin America.

FIX DANGLING MODIFIERS

A modifier *dangles* when it cannot logically modify anything in its sentence. For example, unless the writer of this sentence has an unusual dog—

Reading a book, my dog rested her head on my knee.

—the sentence describes an impossible situation because the position of the modifier *reading a book* implies that the dog can read.

In addition, the person we assume is reading is not made explicit as a noun in this sentence. Because there is no such noun, the sentence cannot be fixed by moving the modifier closer to the nonexistent noun.

Because dangling modifers cannot be fixed by being moved, there are two other options for fixing them:

1 Revise the dangling modifier to make explicit the noun that is to be modified:

As I was reading a book, my dog rested her head on my knee.

2 Revise the rest of the sentence so that the noun appears elsewhere:

Reading a book, I was warmed when my dog rested her head on my knee.

PUNCTUATION

Before writing, there was no punctuation: People simply spoke, not thinking of what they said as being words, much less as being divided up by punctuation. People simply put sounds together in different orders, and they understood each other.

After the invention of writing, it was still many centuries before punctuation (or even spaces between words) was invented. What seems to have given rise to punctuation was the need for speakers to read printed words aloud to listeners, as in churches. Imagine reading this passage aloud if you hadn't had time to figure out the passage beforehand:

most punctuation marks are composed to be seen but not heard these subtle often understated devices are quite important however for they are the meter that determines the measure within the silent voice of typography punctuation directs tempo pitch volume and the separation of words periods signify full stops commas slow the reader down question marks change pitch quotation marks indicate references

Punctuation is thus an important part of writing to communicate: It shows readers how you are shaping your ideas, where you are putting emphasis, and when you are using others' words.

There is considerable room for you to choose how to punctuate in order to reach the audiences for whom you write—but the information in the following pages will help you make informed decisions.

THERE ARE TWO MAIN DIVISIONS OF PUNCTUATION MARKS:

PUNCTUATION THAT GOES WITHIN SENTENCES

- commas
- semicolons
- colons
- parentheses
- dashes
- brackets
- hyphens
- slashes
- quotation marks
- apostrophes

PUNCTUATION THAT GOES AT THE END OF SENTENCES

- periods
- exclamation points
- question marks

AND…

There is another form of punctuation that is not really a mark and that you might not think of as punctuation, but—like all punctuation—it is very important for helping readers understand where sentences begin and end:

CAPITALIZATION

Punctuation, then, is a matter of care. Care for words, yes, but also, and more important, for what the words imply. Only a lover notices the small things: the way the afternoon light catches the nape of a neck, or how a strand of hair slips out from behind an ear, or the way a finger curls around a cup. And no one scans a letter so closely as a lover, searching for its small print, straining to hear its nuances, its gasps, its sighs and hesitations, poring over the secret messages that lie in every cadence. The difference between "Jane (whom I adore)" and "Jane, whom I adore," and the difference between them both and "Jane—whom I adore—" marks all the distance between ecstasy and heartache.

PICO IYER,
"In Praise of the Humble Comma"

COMMAS
have four main uses.

1

USING COMMAS TO MAKE NUMBERS, PLACE-NAMES, AND DATES CLEAR

To learn how and when to use commas in sentences like the following—

Virginia's population was 1,000,000 in 1830. It took eighty more years for it to reach its second million (2,061,612 in 1910).

If you visit Emily Dickinson's house in Amherst, Massachusetts, you won't see anything that truly belonged to Emily Dickinson.

Abraham Lincoln was shot the night of April 14, 1865, and died the following morning.

→ **GO TO PAGE 546.**

2

USING COMMAS TO HELP INDICATE WHEN YOU ARE QUOTING (EXACTLY) THE WORDS OF SOMEONE ELSE

To learn how and when to use commas in sentences like the following—

"Hello," she said, "can I help you with that?"

"The real problem with having a robot to dinner," argues Ellen Ullman, "is pleasure."

—or to learn about the following kinds of sentences (in which you aren't quoting someone else's words directly)—

She asked if she could help me.

Ellen Ullman has argued that pleasure (or the lack of it) is why people don't have robots to dinner.

→ **GO TO PAGE 548.**

3

USING COMMAS TO SEPARATE WORDS THAT ARE PARTS OF LISTS IN SENTENCES

To learn how and when to use commas in sentences like the following—

At lunch I ate potato chips, a peanut butter and jelly sandwich, a banana, two cupcakes, and some barbecued eel.

The stinking, reeking water roiled down the street.

She caught a cab, her breath, and then the flu.

He was livid, he was angry, and he was mad.

→ GO TO PAGE 550.

4

USING COMMAS TO BUILD SENTENCES THAT CONTAIN MULTIPLE PARTS

To learn how and when to use commas in sentences like the following—

To hear him tell it, the bananas were not exactly conducive to a happy stomach.

Her father, who was born in Saudi Arabia, always longed for the hottest days in August.

Can you bring me the ladder, which is in the backyard?

You'd think it would be enough that she earned A's in all her classes, but my roommate, a biomechanical engineering major, also wanted to have the highest GPA on campus.

He looked up at me, and he burst into tears.

→ GO TO PAGE 554.

WHEN SHOULDN'T YOU USE COMMAS? → GO TO PAGE 563.

COMMA USE 2
USING COMMAS TO HELP INDICATE WHEN YOU ARE QUOTING (EXACTLY) THE WORDS OF SOMEONE ELSE

When you embed someone else's spoken or written words into your own, use commas to separate the words you are quoting from the phrases that signal you are quoting:

"I've got to sing," he said, hoarsely.

WHEN YOU **DON'T** BREAK UP THE SENTENCES YOU ARE QUOTING

You can put quoted words at the beginning or at the end of a sentence.

"Keep the hard hat on," she said to me when we parked.

As the poet W. H. Auden put it, "The chances are that, in the course of his lifetime, the major poet will write more bad poems than the minor."

In the first case, notice that the comma goes *inside* the quotation mark and *before* the *she said* phrase. In the second case, the comma goes *after* the (equivalent of the) *she said* phrase, *before* and *outside* the quotation mark.

WHEN YOU **DO** BREAK UP THE SENTENCES YOU ARE QUOTING

You can break up the words of others for effect:

"Why," asks Jonathan Burt, "should the rat be such an apt figure for horror and the target of so much hatred and loathing?"

Note that the first comma goes *inside* the quotation marks and *before* the (equivalent of the) *he said* phrase; the second comma goes *after* the (equivalent of the) *he said* phrase, *before* and *outside* the quotation mark.

WHEN YOU DON'T QUOTE A WHOLE SENTENCE

These examples use no comma before the quoted words because the quoted words are not sentences.

In describing his cityscapes of Paris, Fox Talbot says that photography "chronicles whatever it sees," noting the complex and jumbled array of chimney pots and lightning rods.

She finally cobbled together some mumbo jumbo about a "man from the West" who would "walk on water" to the "East."

WHEN YOU QUOTE SEVERAL SENTENCES

The following example starts in the usual way, with a comma following *observed*—but notice that there are two complete sentences being quoted, separated by a period.

The cop observed, "In the older generations we didn't even drink a beer. If your mom and dad smelled a beer on you, oh my God, you might have to stay in for a year."

In the next example, because the *he said* words break up the sentences being quoted, the *he said* has a comma before it:

"It was the sociological nadir of the American spirit," a Pepsi executive recalled. "Protests. Woodstock. Drugs. A surly and sullen generation occupying the dean's office, burning it down—whatever it was. It was all that sixties stuff."

WHEN YOU DON'T QUOTE WORDS EXACTLY

When you refer to something that someone else said but don't use the person's exact words, you are using indirect quotation. In indirect quotation, you do not use quotation marks or commas. Very often, *that* introduces the words that are being indirectly quoted.

INDIRECT QUOTATION:

Mr. Quiring has told me that essays and stories generally come, organically, to a preordained ending that is quite out of a writer's control.

DIRECT QUOTATION:

In class, Mr. Quiring said, "Essays and stories come to a preordained ending organically—completely out of a writer's control!"

→ See pages 314–325 for help in thinking about how and why to incorporate the words of others in your academic writing.

→ See pages 597–599 for more information on using quotation marks to punctuate quotations.

COMMA USE 3 continued

USING COMMAS IN LISTS OF PHRASES AND CLAUSES

As with nouns and verbs, when you list **three or more** phrases or clauses, use a comma between each.

Furious, Buffmeier walked through the front door, exited to the back, crossed the parking lot, and went into his shack.

Gilligan's work emphasizes relationships over rules, connection over isolation, caring over violence, and a web of relationships over hierarchy.

The Egyptians mummified their dead in a complex process that involved pulling the brain through the nostrils with an iron hook, washing the body with incense, and, in later dynasties, covering it with bitumen and linen.

BUT!

Use semicolons—and not commas—between a series of phrases that themselves contain commas:

The four common principles that ran through much of this thought through the end of the Cold War were a concern with democracy, human rights, and, more generally, the internal politics of states; a belief that American power can be used for moral purposes; a skepticism about the ability of international law and institutions to solve serious security problems; and, finally, a view that ambitious social engineering often leads to unexpected consequences and thereby undermines its own ends.

USING COMMAS IN LISTS OF INDIVIDUAL ADJECTIVES

When you put together **two or more adjectives**, you have to decide two things:

1

whether or not to use a comma between them

AND

2

whether to use **and** between them.

WHEN TO USE A COMMA OR "AND" IN LISTS OF ADJECTIVES

*Use a comma or **and*** to separate two adjectives if you can change their order without changing the meaning of the sentence. For example, the meaning of

He was a thin, dapper fellow who preferred a suit and vest to ordinary clothes.

isn't changed when it is written as

He was a dapper, thin fellow who preferred a suit and vest to ordinary clothes.

or as

He was a thin and dapper fellow who preferred a suit and vest to ordinary clothes.

In these examples, *thin* and *dapper* are called **coordinate adjectives**, the name for adjectives whose order can be changed without the meaning of the sentence changing.

WHEN TO USE NEITHER A COMMA NOR "AND" IN LISTS OF ADJECTIVES

If you cannot rearrange the adjectives in a sentence without changing the meaning of the sentence, do not put a comma between them, *no matter how many adjectives you are using*:

The prize for my banana costume was a radio designed to look like a box of frozen niblets corn.

This sentence doesn't have a comma between *frozen* and *niblets* because, in the United States, we would not say *niblets frozen corn* or *niblets and frozen corn*.

Here is another example:

Three huge gray whales swam by.

Because *three* is describing how many *huge gray whales* this writer saw, *three* goes before the other adjectives.

Adjectives that cannot be rearranged are called **noncoordinate adjectives**, and they do not have commas between them.

WHEN TO USE A COMMA AND "AND" IN LISTS OF ADJECTIVES

When you have three adjectives whose order can be changed without changing the meaning of the sentence, use the same pattern as with lists of nouns, verbs, phrases, and clauses. Put a comma after each of the adjectives except the last:

Reappropriate.com is a political, current-events, and personal blog written from the perspective of a loud and proud Asian-American woman.

We have come to know zero intimately in its mathematical, physical, and psychological embodiments.

WHEN SHOULDN'T YOU USE COMMAS IN A LIST OF WORDS?

Sometimes writers want to emphasize the length of time that goes into a series of actions, so they link the words or phrases of a series with *and* or *or*:

Instead, we arrange the platters of food and remove bread from the oven and fill cups with grape juice and wine.

The example at the left is correct, as is the example below (which creates a quicker sense of the time involved in all the actions):

Instead, we arrange the platters of food, remove bread from the oven, and fill cups with grape juice and wine.

PATTERN 1

USING COMMAS TO ADD ONE SENTENCE ONTO THE END OF ANOTHER

When you combine two sentences, the convention of written English is to put a comma and then a coordinating conjunction between the two:

| independent clause | **,** | coordinating conjunction | independent clause | **.** |

and
but
or
nor
for
so
yet

For example,

We passed them buckets of water **,** and they threw the water onto the fire .

or

He swung his arms wildly **,** but the mosquitoes still swarmed around him .

or

The molecules attach to this material **,** for they have proper affinity with it .

When you combine sentences in this way, be sure to put a comma before the coordinating conjunction.

Here are more examples. Note how each follows this pattern:

independent clause + **,** + coordinating conjunction + independent clause •

I tried to draw him out, but it saddens Hugh to discuss his childhood monkey.

The sweaters I've made aren't impressive specimens, but they've taught me a lot.

Part of Goldstein's work was concerned with the effects of brain damage, and he found that, whenever there was extensive damage, there tended to be an impairment of abstract-categorical capacity.

Twenty years later there were 3,000 factory hands at Baldwin, and by 1900 there were more than 8,000.

Several selective pressures may act similarly and simultaneously on trees, so it is difficult to tease apart the contributions those pressures make to tree evolution.

It sounds like something you'd read on a movie poster, but sometimes the sins you haven't committed are all you have to hold on to.

Like most Kenyans, I was not taught about my culture or about the things my parents learned from their parents in school, yet I was taught about the American Revolution, Niagara Falls, and the Second World War.

BE CAREFUL...

If you were to take these sentences—

In this section I focus on fluorescent biological samples.

The techniques may be applied to material science.

—and combine them without using a coordinating conjunction—

In this section I focus on fluorescent biological samples, the techniques may be applied to material science.

—you would have *a comma splice*. Writing teachers notice comma splices—so if you have been making this error without knowing it, now is the time to learn how to keep your writing teacher smiling at you.

Here is the version that will make a writing teacher put away the red pen:

In this section I focus on fluorescent biological samples, but the techniques may be applied to material science.

You can avoid comma splices by following the pattern shown on these two pages, joining two sentences with a comma and a coordinating conjunction.

→ There are other strategies for mending comma splices; see pages 494–495.
→ For more on coordinating conjunctions, see page 532.

NONESSENTIAL INFORMATION IN THE MIDDLE OF A SENTENCE

Short interjections of words can add a conversational tone to writing; these interjections remind readers that a person wrote the words, so interjections can help writers build relations with their readers. Put a comma before and after such interjections:

Dirt, it seems, is an important ingredient in particle physics experiments.

Some sequels, as we all know, are better than the originals.

Let me clarify two points that will, I hope, make clear our disagreement.

■ ■ ■

When you use explanatory words and phrases such as *though* and *for example*, they should be set off by commas:

Once I'm awake, though, I tend to lie there wondering if I've made a terrible mistake.

Among Plains tribes, for example, certain forms of design knowledge, such as quill embroidery and beadwork, are sacred.

BUT!

Do not put a comma after *though* if the word introduces a phrase:

Though she had already been executed, Joan of Arc was acquitted on July 7, 1456.

■ ■ ■

The following sentences have phrases that come after nouns (very often names) and that explain what the noun is; put a comma before and after all such phrases:

Aunty Lau, an accomplished weaver, teaches Hawaiian culture in the schools.

My son, who is eleven, has a memory like wet cement.

Lascelles Brown, an athletic Jamaican butcher who had briefly dabbled in boxing, first got interested in bobsledding after seeing the 1993 Disney film *Cool Running*, based on Jamaica's 1988 Olympic team.

Scissors, a mundane object to which we are introduced in kindergarten, are a sophisticated tool requiring opposable thumbs and some dexterity.

The Space Shuttle, on track and on schedule, came into view just after 5:53 Pacific time.

Nature, when abused, may react eventually like a tiger whose tail has been pulled.

We know from research that dogs, even kennel-raised puppies, do much better than generally more brilliant wolves or human-like chimpanzees in responding to human cues in a food-finding test.

STEPS FOR DECIDING IF INFORMATION IS ESSENTIAL OR NOT

1

For a sentence about which you are unsure, describe to yourself exactly what is most important to you in the sentence: *What exactly is it that you want your readers to take away from your sentence?*

Example 1
Your sentence emphasizes some events that took place in New York City.

Example 2
Your sentence focuses your readers' attention on society's responses to the women who died in Vietnam.

2

Identify in the sentence the information that may or may not be essential.

All of this took place in New York City, <u>which is cruelly, insanely expensive</u>.

This website is dedicated to women <u>who died in the Vietnam War</u>.

3

Remove the information you identified in step 2.

All of this took place in New York City.

This website is dedicated to women.

4

Ask yourself this question about the shortened sentence: Does it give your readers exactly what you want them to take from the sentence?

If you are writing this sentence to emphasize that the events you are describing took place in New York City and not to emphasize the cost of being in New York City, the answer is **yes**.

If you are writing this sentence to focus your readers' attention on society's responses to the women who died in Vietnam and not on all women, the answer is **no**.

5

If the answer is **yes**, then the information you identified in step 2 is nonessential, and should be separated from the rest of the sentence with commas.

If the answer is **no**, then the information you identified in step 2 is essential and should not be separated with commas.

All of this took place in New York City, which is cruelly, insanely expensive.

This website is dedicated to women who died in the Vietnam War.

BETWEEN A SENTENCE'S VERB AND ITS SUBJECT OR OBJECT

delete

Everything good, is bad for you.

Everything good is bad for you.

delete

One of the dominant themes in American science policy this past year was, how we can maintain a competitive edge in a global economy.

One of the dominant themes in American science policy this past year was how we can maintain a competitive edge in a global economy.

If you include more than one word in a subject, it can be tempting to put a comma after it because you might read the sentence out loud with a pause after the subject—which can suggest that a comma should go there. The same temptation can happen with long objects: If you were reading it out loud, you would probably pause before the object. But in writing, the convention is not to put commas in these places.

BEFORE OR AFTER PARENTHESES

delete

A political career, (or a legal one) is the surest ticket to a historical legacy.

A political career (or a legal one) is the surest ticket to a historical legacy.

or

A political career, or a legal one, is the surest ticket to a historical legacy.

The convention is to use parentheses or commas around parenthetical comments, but not both.

AFTER A SUBORDINATING CONJUNCTION

delete

Although, scientists no longer consider Pluto to be a planet, many still seek that little celestial body in their telescopes.

Although scientists no longer consider Pluto to be a planet, many still seek that little celestial body in their telescopes.

→ Page 534 lists and explains subordinating conjunctions.

BEFORE THE FIRST ITEM IN A LIST, OR AFTER THE LAST ITEM

delete

E-mail spammers endure, legal harassment, exclusion from polite society, and the disgust of nearly every computer user.

E-mail spammers endure legal harassment, exclusion from polite society, and the disgust of nearly every computer user.

delete

Many accidents of geography, history, and biology, created our lopsided world.

Many accidents of geography, history, and biology created our lopsided world.

→ See pages 550–553 for the conventional uses of commas with lists.

SEMICOLONS
have two main uses.

1

USING SEMICOLONS TO SEPARATE THE ITEMS IN A LIST WHEN THE ITEMS ARE COMPLEX.

To learn how and when to use semicolons in a sentence like the following—

Arbus's subjects included a child in the park, holding a toy grenade; a woman, cozily ensconced in her kitchen, holding a chimpanzee; and the fire-eater of a Maryland circus.

→ GO TO PAGE 566.

2

USING SEMICOLONS TO JOIN TWO SENTENCES

To learn how and when to use commas in sentences like the following—

Some writers write many drafts of a piece; some write one draft, at the pace of snail after a night on the town.

I'm not arguing that the postmodern shift erases traditional texts or narratives; instead, I'm trying to make clear that our traditional texts are changing.

→ GO TO PAGE 567.

SEMICOLON USE 1

USING SEMICOLONS TO SEPARATE
THE ITEMS IN A LIST WHEN THE
ITEMS ARE COMPLEX

USING SEMICOLONS TO JOIN ELEMENTS THAT CONTAIN THEIR OWN PUNCTUATION

Usually, we use commas to build lists of items—

A hat, gloves, and boots are necessary for winter.

—but in a complex sentence, commas might not be of help to readers:

Istanbul's steep hills and harbor views remind you of San Francisco, its overcrowded streets recall Bombay, its transportation facilities evoke Venice, for you can go many places by boats, which are continually making stops.

Instead, with semicolons separating the items, it is easier to see the separate items:

Istanbul's steep hills and harbor views remind you of San Francisco; its overcrowded streets recall Bombay; its transportation facilities evoke Venice, for you can go many places by boats, which are continually making stops.

If you are building a list using items that contain their own punctuation, use semicolons to separate the items:

As the leech began to suck, it released several other substances into his ear: a powerful anticoagulant, which prevented his blood from clotting; a vasodilator, which opened his vessels, helping to increase blood flow; and a spreading factor, which moved these chemicals quickly into tissue farthest from the bite, liquefying any hardening blood.

SEMICOLON USE 2

USING SEMICOLONS TO JOIN TWO SENTENCES

JOINING SENTENCES

Be sure you have two complete sentences (that is, independent clauses), and then join them with a semicolon. The first letter of the word following the semicolon is not capitalized, unless it is a proper noun.

The father didn't move out; he just moved to a different bedroom.

The ceiling, freshly painted, was luminous as the sky; I almost thought I could smell the paint.

My fears were powerful and troubling and annoyingly vague; I couldn't establish exactly what it was that frightened me.

The highway went for miles between high mud walls and canebrakes; the black tracery of date palms rose above them, against the brilliant night sky.

You can use semicolons to join multiple sentences:

Work made people useful in a world of economic scarcity; it staved off the doubts and temptations that preyed on idleness; it opened the way to deserved wealth and status; it allowed one to put the impress of mind and skill on the material world.

→ To be sure you are joining complete sentences, read about independent and dependent clauses, pages 483–487.

COLONS
have three main uses.

1

USING COLONS IN CERTAIN CONVENTIONAL PATTERNS.

To learn how and when to use colons in writing situations like the following—

Dear Senator Gonzaga:

The experiment took place at 3:22 P.M.

Her article is titled "Concrete: A Hard History."

New York: Longman, 2008.

→ GO TO PAGE 570.

2

USING COLONS TO PREPARE READERS FOR INFORMATION AT THE END OF A SENTENCE.

To learn how and when to use colons in sentences like the following—

He brought along his equipment: some collecting jars, a microscope, and his lunch.

The shops gave the street a strange air: They all looked alike from the outside.

→ GO TO PAGE 572.

3

USING COLONS TO LINK TWO SENTENCES.

To learn how and when to use colons in sentences like the following—

In April, Stefano and his team completed preliminary research on the medicinal leech: They found morphine in its head region, which contains the leech's salivary glands.

→ GO TO PAGE 573.

TIP: CHOOSING HOW MUCH EMPHASIS YOU WANT TO GIVE

The next three punctuation marks— colons, parentheses, and dashes— have some overlaps in their uses: Each of these punctuation marks can be used to emphasize parts of a sentence.

For you to decide which punctuation mark to use in your writing, you have to decide how much emphasis you want to give. Look at the examples here and on the following pages, where words are set off by colons, parentheses, or dashes, in order to determine the level of emphasis you want your words to have.

COLON USE 1
USING COLONS IN CERTAIN CONVENTIONAL PATTERNS

SALUTATIONS

In formal or business letters, colons are used after the greeting at the beginning of the letter:

Dear Sir or Madam:

Dear Dr. Lucchesi:

Dear Ms. Poole:

BUT!

In the past, it was acceptable to start any business letter with *Dear Sirs:*—but now, with more women than ever before in workplaces, you cannot know the gender of the person opening a letter you send. It is better to write, "Dear Sir or Madam:"

MEMO HEADINGS

In workplaces, memos (less formal than letters) are often used to inform others of the progress of a project, or of meetings or other events. The top of a memo will usually look like this:

To: The members of the Research Committee

From: Ralph Bunker

Re: Next Steps

(**Re:** means *regarding*; think of it as being like the subject heading of an e-mail.)

TIME

When you are writing the time of day, use a colon between the hour, the minutes, and the seconds (if you include them):

12:32 P.M.   4:50:32 P.M.

I awoke just before the alarm went off, at 5:59:59 A.M.

Similarly, when you are recording the duration of an event, such as a race or experiment, use colons between the hour, minutes, and seconds:

She ran her first mile in 4:35 and her second in 4:50.

Sometimes, however, you need to spell out the time:

The cells separated after 2 hours and 35 seconds.

Otherwise, it might be unclear to readers whether you are describing the time of day or the duration you are recording:

The cells separated after 2:35.

BETWEEN TITLE AND SUBTITLE

When you are writing the title of any communication—book, article, movie, television show—that has a subtitle, put the title, then a colon, then the subtitle:

Katherine Dunham: Dancing Queen

Wind: How the Flow of Air Has Shaped Life, Myth, and the Land

Fibroids: Women Seek Answers, Treatment

MLA WORKS CITED LISTINGS

When you are putting together a listing of the works you have cited in a paper, put a colon after the name of the city where the book was published, and then put the name of the publisher:

Le Faye, Deirdre, ed. *Jane Austen's Letters*. 3rd ed. Oxford: Oxford UP, 1995.

Mông-Lan. "Trail." *The Best American Poetry 2002*. Ed. Robert Creeley. New York: Scribner, 2002. 108–17.

Monroe, Barbara. *Crossing the Digital Divide; Race, Writing, and Technology in the Classroom*. New York: Teachers College Press, 2004.

→ For fuller explanation of how to punctuate MLA citations, see pages 360–403.

BIBLE VERSES

If you cite verses from the Bible, put a colon between the chapter and the verse:

Matthew 6:5

Deuteronomy 5:17

Psalm 46:9

PARENTHESES
have four main uses.

1

USING PARENTHESES TO EXPLAIN ABBREVIATIONS

To learn how to use parentheses in a sentence like the following—

Technobabe Times (TBT) produces our campus's feminist newspaper.

Burning Man participants who wish to bring motorized art cars or mutant vehicles must submit their designs in advance to the event's own "Department of Mutant Vehicles" (DMV) for approval.

Nevertheless, the NRA (National Restaurant Association) has vehemently opposed any rise in the minimum wage.

→ GO TO PAGE 576.

2

USING PARENTHESES FOR NUMBERS IN LISTS

To learn how to use parentheses in a sentence like the following—

The steps are (1) punctuate, (2) capitalize, (3) proofread.

Writer John Hodgman's steps for winning a fight are (1) always make eye contact, (2) go ahead and use henchmen, (3) run lots of attack ads.

If you want to get over your fear of clowns, (1) make a list of why you are afraid of clowns, (2) sort items on the list into rational and irrational fears, (3) work your way down the list until all your fears are in the irrational category, (4) stop being afraid.

→ GO TO PAGE 577.

Words go here.

3

USING PARENTHESES FOR IN-TEXT CITATIONS

To learn how to use parentheses to refer to a source in your writing—

Bronson (1950) notes that since their muscles are so flexible, cats seem to bounce when they fall rather than break any bones (p. 32).

"Whatever is profound loves masks; what is most profound even hates image and parable" (Nietzsche 50).

→ GO TO PAGE 578.

4

USING PARENTHESES TO ADD INFORMATION

To learn how to use parentheses in a sentence like the following—

According to Clara Pinto-Correia, some tombs were even outfitted with toilet facilities for the *ka* (soul).

Anything that you include in your paper that is not from you (or from the piece of literature with which you are working) is considered *a secondary source*.

Fundamentally, a *ragú* is an equation involving a solid (meat) and a liquid (broth or wine), plus a slow heat, until you reach a result that is neither solid nor liquid.

→ GO TO PAGE 579.

PARENTHESES USE 3

USING PARENTHESES FOR IN-TEXT CITATIONS

Readers of academic research writing expect—whenever a writer quotes another's words—that the writer will give readers the information they need to find those words in the original source. One part of providing this information is to give the name of the author being quoted as well as the number of the page from which the quoted words come (readers can then look to the list of works cited at the end of the essay to find the bibliographic information that will help them find the cited work):

In Carruther's argument, a sacred book is given a bejeweled cover to signify to readers that one's memory, growing out of the book, was "a storehouse, a treasure-chest, a vessel, into which the jewels, coins, fruits, and flowers of text are placed" (246). But, by the twelfth century, for those who could not afford treasure chests, the same books could also appear in "cheap and decorative binding" (Foot 118).

Notice that, if the author's name is included as part of a sentence, it is not noted in the parentheses; if the author's name is not included, then it is put in the parentheses along with the page number.

To be an academic writer yourself, you need to learn these conventions.

→ The example above is for the MLA citation style, about which there is more on pages 360–403. For the APA style, see pages 426–452.

Words go here.

PARENTHESES USE 4

USING PARENTHESES TO ADD INFORMATION

You can use parentheses to insert comments or additional information into a sentence. When you do this, you are adding *parenthetical remarks* to the sentence. Many writers use this strategy to add humor to a sentence:

Sometimes in the morning Mrs. Murrow asks me if I heard the cobras singing during the night. I have never been able to answer in the affirmative, because in spite of her description ("like a silver coin falling against a rock"), I have no clear idea of what to listen for.

This afternoon, Johnny Depp is wearing a white undershirt tucked into gray tweed slacks hiked a tad too high (in the style of certain retirement-aged Italian gentlemen).

You can also use parenthetical information to add dates, definitions, a URL, or anything else you think will help readers understand:

Katherine Dunham's dance piece "Southland" (1951), which was a protest against lynching and depicted a lynching on stage, created a lot of controversy in America.

Traditionally, a hysterectomy (removal of the uterus) was the primary way to treat fibroids, and it remains the only permanent cure.

"I'm not an ice cream guy," says Jim Baxter, the technologist behind the design of the MooBella vending machine (www.moobella.com), which churns out a 4.5-ounce cup of ice cream in 45 seconds.

Words go here.

BRACKETS
have two main uses.

1

USING BRACKETS INSIDE PARENTHETICAL COMMENTS

Sometimes writers need to put parenthetical information inside other parenthetical information. When this is the case, the convention is to put the embedded information inside brackets instead of inside another set of parentheses:

(For further discussion, see Abdo [2000] and Burgat [2003].)

Khubz marquq (also called *lavash tannour* [mountain bread]) is a flat bread with a slightly tangy taste.

2

USING BRACKETS TO INSERT INFORMATION INTO A QUOTATION

Anytime writers use the words of someone else, the words are removed from their full context; sometimes, then, writers have to fill in some information or change a few words so that readers can understand the quotation.

If writers need to do this in the middle of a quotation, the convention is to put the changed or added information inside brackets so that readers can see where the original has been changed. For example, here are words as they were originally spoken by Anthony B. Pinn, a professor of Humanities and Religion at Rice University in Houston:

What you get with mega-churches is a kind of caricature of the social gospel thrust. In terms of the hard issue of social justice, such churches tend to be theology-lite.

Here is how a magazine article quoted those words, in order to fit them to its needs:

What you get with mega-churches is a...caricature of the social gospel thrust. In terms of...social justice, [they] tend to be theology-lite.

→ If you need to leave words out of quotations, use ellipses, a punctuation mark explained on pages 588–589, to show the omissions.

■ ■ ■

To figure out whether you need to add or modify the information in a quotation, ask yourself if your readers will understand a quotation exactly as it is written. If not, modify the quotation in the smallest way you can while still helping your readers.

For example, imagine that the words in brackets below contained someone's name (which was in the original quotation); would the quotation make sense?

In Field's most recent novel, *The Lawyer's Tale*, Harry Cain asks his private eye to dig up dirt on an opponent. Harry "didn't want to commit extortion if he could avoid it," Fields writes. "But he had to get a message to [the opponent] that would change his mind."

Here is a quotation in which the bracketed words are used to explain a term that comes from the British educational system:

Miss Lee reports that "the other day a child in the reception class [kindergarten] in Myatt Gardens told me a story about September 11."

Without the bracketed information, would you have known what a *reception class* is?

With quotations, then, notice how you can use brackets to replace a term that readers might not know with familiar information or to add explanatory information.

HY ▬
PHENS have three main uses.

1

USING HYPHENS TO BREAK WORDS AT THE END OF LINES

If you are using a typewriter, you need to know about hyphens in order to fit part of a word at the end of a line when you run out of space for the whole word. Watch the lines as you type them, and—if you need to break a word—break if after a syllable and put a hyphen at the end of the line. (If you are unsure, check a dictionary to learn where the syllables break in a word.)

Clarkston High School now has students from more than 50 countries.

Poets use hyphens to create wordplay:

when sunsnap
sheet-
back-
boys-
slip
pinned
to shade

If you are writing with a word processing program on a computer, the computer will automatically break words at syllables and insert hyphens at the end of lines.

2

USING HYPHENS FOR CLARITY

A precise reader sees considerable difference between these two sentences:

He was a big city man.

He was a big-city man.

The first is about a man from the city who is big; the second is about a man from a big city. When using two words as an adjective, put a hyphen between them if you wonder whether others will read your words as you intend.

■ ■ ■

When you use the prefixes *re-*, *anti-*, and *pre-* with verbs, use a hyphen between the prefix and the verb if, without the hyphen, a different meaning is made.

I resent her letter.

I re-sent her letter.

■ ■ ■

Use hyphens if the first word of a compound word you are making begins with the same letter as the second:

doll-like   **non-native**

3

USING HYPHENS IN COMPOUND WORDS

Compound words are made when writers put together any two (or more) other words to make one new word:

Operating on an off-the-shelf Linux-based computer, MooBella's fresh-on-the-spot system changes the blueprint of traditional ice-cream vending machines, which spit out months-old bars.

In the above sentence, the compound words are *off-the-shelf*, *Linux-based*, *fresh-on-the-spot*, *blueprint*, *ice-cream*, and *months-old*.

The longer a compound word has been in use, the more likely it won't have a hyphen in it (think of **bathtub**, **earthquake**, **bookshelf**, or **website**); conversely, the newest compound words will most likely have hyphens in them. (Some writers who want to sound cool make up compound words; you'll find new compound words in blogs and science fiction writing.)

■ ■ ■

Some compound words, however, do conventionally keep their hyphens:

In Rochester, Dr. Bonnez's solution was to approach veterinarians treating dairy cows, which grow grapefruit-sized warts loaded with virus. He still has a block of 20-year-old cow warts in his freezer.

When compound words are used as adjectives before nouns—such as **20-year-old** and **grapefruit-sized** above or in the term **nineteenth-century art**—they tend to be hyphenated.

To be safest, check a dictionary: Because our uses of compound words are time-sensitive, it is wise to check whether a compound word is in the dictionary. If you cannot find the word in a dictionary, put hyphens in it.

■ ■ ■

When you write out numbers between 21 and 99, a hyphen is conventional:

twenty-three

one hundred twenty-three

one thousand two hundred and ninety-four

TIP: U.S. HYPHENS

In the United States, it is customary **not** to put spaces around hyphens or dashes: write **nineteenth-century**, *not* **nineteenth - century**.

ELLIPSES...
have two main uses.

1

USING ELLIPSES TO SHOW A PAUSE OR AN INTERRUPTION IN SPEECH THAT YOU ARE QUOTING

Because readers cannot hear words that you quote but can only see your transcription of them on a page, use ellipses to signal, visually, where someone you are quoting paused:

In an interview with Powells.com's Dave Weich, chef and writer Anthony Bourdain said: "I knew already that the best meal in the world, the perfect meal, is very rarely the most sophisticated or expensive one.... Context and memory play powerful roles in all the truly great meals in one's life."

In contexts less formal than the academic one, writers sometimes use ellipses to show hesitation or surprise; the following sentence, for example, comes from a science magazine for general audiences:

In the grand tradition of linking raunchy music with irresponsible sexual activity comes a new study touting a link between sexual risk taking and listening to...gospel music.

→ You can also use dashes to show hesitation in speech that you are quoting; see page 581.

2

USING ELLIPSES TO SHOW THAT YOU HAVE OMITTED WORDS FROM A QUOTATION

IN A PROSE QUOTATION

If you need to drop words from a sentence you are quoting, use ellipses.

Here are George Lucas's original words from an interview:

> **When I was younger, I had a collection of history books that I was addicted to, a whole series about famous people in history from Ancient Greece and Alexander the Great, up to the Civil War—the Monitor and the Merrimac. I think they were called "Landmark" books, and I collected a whole library of them. I used to love to read those books. It started me on a lifelong love of history.**

Here is one way to quote those words:

> **When I was younger, I had a collection of history books that I was addicted to, a whole series about famous people in history from Ancient Greece and Alexander the Great, up to the Civil War [...]. I collected a whole library of them. I used to love to read those books. It started me on a lifelong love of history.**

By putting the ellipsis inside brackets, you show that you have removed words; an ellipsis alone would indicate that the speaker or writer had paused in the original. (You do not need to use an ellipsis if you are taking words from the beginning or end of someone's words.)

IN A QUOTATION OF POETRY

Sometimes when you are quoting poetry, you need to emphasize several lines while omitting others. If you ever need to quote a passage from which you must drop one or more lines, use a whole line of ellipses to show where you have dropped the lines.

> **In "Elegy for Thelonius," Yusef Komunyakaa brings Thelonius Monk back to life:**

> damn the alley cat
> wailing a muted dirge
> off Lenox Ave.
> Thelonious is dead.
>
> ....
>
> Let's go to Minton's
> & play "modern malice"
> till daybreak. Lord,
> there's Thelonious
> wearing that old funky hat
> pulled down over his eyes.

QUOTATION MARKS USE 1

USING QUOTATION MARKS FOR TITLES OF SHORT WORKS

Use quotation marks to indicate the name of a show or exhibition—

"Goya's Last Works," at the Frick, isn't large, but neither are grenades.

—the titles of poems and musical pieces—

I had to study why Van Halen moved (certain) people as much as the Beatles, but, folks, they did, in the same way Whitman did. "Hot For Teacher" is "Song of Myself" with crappier words but much better lead guitar.

—and the titles of essays—

"The Making of Americans" was a work that Stein evidently had to get out of her system—almost like a person having to vomit—before she could become Gertrude Stein as we know her.

—or the titles of almost any work that is not book length.

→ Information on how to indicate the titles of book-length works is on page 607.

Words go here.

QUOTATION MARKS USE 2

USING QUOTATION MARKS TO INDICATE YOU ARE USING A WORD AS A WORD

Sometimes, writers need to refer to a word as a word. If ever you need to do this, put quotation marks around the word:

"Doctor" comes from the Latin word *docere*, "to teach."

The term "preservation" usually comes up in reference to buildings, not to the graffiti that covers them.

His student asked him how to use "until" according to English conventions.

Franziska often spews repetitive insults using the word "fool."

→ The use of quotation marks for this function goes back to the days of typewriters. With computers, italics can replace quotation marks; see page 607 on using italics.

→ Because quotation marks are almost always woven with other punctuation, it is tricky to use them as academic readers and readers of published work expect. On pages 598–599 we go over the little but important details of using quotation marks in expected ways.

Words go here.

QUOTATION MARKS USE 5

USING QUOTATION MARKS TO INDICATE DIRECT QUOTATION

Over the centuries, conventions have developed in different languages for indicating to readers that writers are quoting the words of others. In English, quotation marks—placed on either side of the words being quoted—have become the expected way of doing this, even if a writer is quoting only one word from someone else:

Fukasawa's approach to designing electronic gadgets, based on over 25 years' experience, has been called "anti-technical" because it dispenses with unnecessary buttons, displays, and other high-tech signifiers.

A comparison to make a point is Sarah Vowell's claim that "Going to Ford's Theatre to watch the play is like going to Hooter's for the food."

At the time the Wright brothers invented the airplane, American law held that a property owner owned not just the surface of his land, but all the land below, down to the center of the earth, and all the space above, to "an indefinite extent, upwards."

→ Because quotation marks are almost always woven with other punctuation, it is tricky to use them as academic readers expect. On pages 598–599 we go over the details of using quotation marks in expected ways.

Words go here.

QUOTATION MARKS USE 6

USING QUOTATION MARKS TO
INDICATE SPEECH

When you wish to suggest to your readers that the words you are writing were spoken out loud by someone else, quotation marks are the customary strategy in English:

"He was going to write the definitive book on leeches," she says. "It was his primary ambition in life."

"Reading ability is a proxy for intelligence in American culture," said Dr. Sally E. Shaywitz of Yale University School of Medicine, a pediatrician who is an expert on dyslexia.

"You have to listen to music before you go out on a mission and get real hyped," says Sgt. Junelle Daniels, a twenty-five-year-old generator mechanic from Miami who is gearing up for a second deployment to Iraq. "If not, you start thinking, 'What if? What if this happens? What if that happens?' You start to get the fear."

Note that indicating speech is sometimes the same as indicating a direct quotation.

→ Because quotation marks are almost always woven with other punctuation, it is tricky to use them as academic readers and readers of published work expect. On pages 598–599 we go over the little but important details of using quotation marks in expected ways.

→ In academic writing, any time you quote someone else, the expectation is that you will give a source of the quotation; see pages 308–350 for how to do this.

Words go here.

APOSTROPHES
have three main uses.

1

USING APOSTROPHES TO MAKE PLURALS OF CERTAIN KINDS OF WORDS

Use an apostrophe to make plurals of lowercase letters; if you do not use an apostrophe, readers might confuse the plural with a word or think you have made a mistake:

Is it "cross your is and dot your ts," or is it the other way around?

Is it "cross your i's and dot your t's," or is it the other way around?

Use an apostrophe to make plurals of uppercase letters if the addition of an **-s** without an apostrophe would make a word:

She earned As throughout school but could never rise above an entry-level position.

She earned A's throughout school but could never rise above an entry-level position.

Otherwise:

He never earned higher than Cs or Ds in school, yet he's a well-known newscaster.

2

USING APOSTROPHES TO MAKE CONTRACTIONS

Use apostrophes to show where letters have been taken out of a contraction:

I am	=	I'm
I would	=	I'd
you are	=	you're
she is	=	she's
he is	=	he's
it is	=	it's
we are	=	we're
we have	=	we've
they are	=	they're
do not	=	don't
did not	=	didn't
cannot	=	can't

One odd pattern to learn:

will not	=	won't

I'm sure that we didn't leave the window open, but shouldn't we go back and check?

We've got time; he won't expect us to arrive until late.

3

USING APOSTROPHES TO MAKE POSSESSIVES

When readers see a word ending with an apostrophe and the letter **s**, they will usually assume that the word is in the possessive case.

This blog's underlying message is "Stop Buying Crap."

Discovery Channel's new reality television show is *Last One Standing*.

The New Mexico Spaceport Authority's design for Spaceport America—the world's first public launching and landing site for space vehicles—includes a passenger terminal and a hangar big enough for seven craft.

→ To learn more about the possessive case, see page 501.

TIP: LEARN THE DIFFERENCE BETWEEN *it's* AND *its*

it's = it is

its = the possessive form of the pronoun it

It's going to rain. (It is going to rain.)

Democracy can be said to be its own biggest threat. (*its* is a stand-in for *democracy's*)

QUESTION MARKS ?
have two main uses.

1

USING QUESTION MARKS TO END SENTENCES THAT ARE QUESTIONS

Of the four functions that sentences can have (➔ pages 468–469), asking questions is one; sentences that ask questions are called interrogatory sentences:

What is education?

Have you ever browsed a sperm bank catalog?

You bought the CD or DVD, and that means you own it, right?

If prisons are meant to make troubled men and women into citizens, he wondered, might there be a social cost to bad prison design?

BUT!

The examples above are *direct questions*; there are also *indirect questions*, in which a writer describes someone else asking a question, without direct quotation. *These end with a period, not a question mark:*

I heard her ask whether the mail had arrived.

He asked how the test had gone.

2

USING QUESTION MARKS TO SHOW DOUBT ABOUT DATES AND NUMBERS

Ir you have doubts about a date or quantity, or if your sources describe doubt about a date or quantity, put **(?)** after the date or quantity.

In this photograph, Reynolds is seen with his mother in 1928 (?).

Witness reports put the number of people trapped in the building at 180 (?).

➔ Using question marks with quotation marks requires careful attention. See pages 598–599.

EXCLAMATION POINTS !
have one main use.

1

USING EXCLAMATION POINTS TO INDICATE TO READERS THAT A SENTENCE CARRIES EMOTIONAL WEIGHT

It is customary in written American English to put a single exclamation point after a sentence when the sentence is an exclamation—

Yikes! Oh no!

—a strong command—

Help!

Don't touch that burner!

Don't go beyond the perimeter!

—or is meant by its writer to encourage a strong emotional response in a reader—

Each treehouse is built in two main pieces: the playhouse and the log. The log is a real, old, fallen tree that we hollow out using a chainsaw!

Age is absolutely no barrier in today's world. In fact, some 30 percent of students today are "non-traditional," meaning us, of course! Your age is not an issue unless you choose to make it one; don't!

In academic writing, exclamation points are almost nonexistent because academic writing is meant to appeal primarily to reason. In most other kinds of writing, the exclamation point is also rare, because people who grow up into American English tend to think that exclamation points are a sign of youth or silliness—especially when several sentences in a row have them or when a single sentence ends in many of them.

There are exceptions: In blogs, for example, writers sometimes use them excessively, as a self-conscious indication that they know exclamation points are dangerous but still potent:

It's not that we know we aren't writing well—and so tack on some exclamations!!!—it's that we know what we're saying doesn't deserve to be written at all.

→ Using exclamation points with quotation marks requires careful attention. See pages 598–599.

→ Many interjections use exclamation points. See page 496.

MECHANICS
SPELLING

In Shakespeare's time, spelling was not standardized: *Been* was spelled *beene*, *bene*, or **bin**—and *Shakespeare* was spelled **Shakspere**, **Shaksper**, **Shakespere**, and **Shackspeare**. As governments grew and required standardized documents— and as printing presses replaced scribes for reproducing documents—people came to expect that a word would be spelled the same way every time it appeared on a page.

In our time, then, it is an expected sign of formal documents that the words are all spelled according to conventions that have developed over time and that are recorded in dictionaries.

SPELLING RULES? CHECK A DICTIONARY!

Spelling is the attempt to put spoken language into consistent patterns on the page, using just the twenty-six characters of the English alphabet. Because English developed out of many different languages, the spelling of a word often results from an attempt in the past to use the English alphabet to translate sounds made in other languages.

English spelling can therefore be vexing, even if your home language is English. There are some spelling rules for English, but all have considerable exceptions and variations, and many people find them confusing.

The best advice we can give you when you are trying to spell a word is to use a dictionary.

USING SPELL CHECKERS

Spell checkers only check spelling; they cannot tell if you are using the wrong word or have made other mistakes.

To use spell checkers well, follow these steps:

1 Use a spell checker after you have a complete draft to catch obvious spelling errors.

2 Use the items listed below under *What spell checkers miss* to find specific kinds of mistakes.

3 Proofread the whole text at least one more time, using any of the strategies we describe on page 465.

WHAT SPELL CHECKERS MISS

- **Incorrect words that are spelled correctly.** In the sentence "He might loose his job," all the words are spelled correctly, but **loose** should be **lose**. The Glossary shows many words that are commonly confused.

- **Homonyms.** *Peace* and *piece* are homonyms: They are words that are spelled differently but sound the same. When writing quickly, it is easy to use a homonym in place of the word you want. The Glossary on pages 616–623 contains some common homonyms.

- **Possessives used as plurals—and vice versa.** If you are writing about more than one dress, it is easy to write **dress's** instead of **dresses**.

→ See page 501 to learn about possessives.

→ See page 500 to learn about plurals.

- **Pronouns that don't match their antecedents.** For example, *If a person wants to write well, you have to write a lot* should be *If you want to write well, you have to write a lot.*

    → See pages 502 and 506 to learn about pronouns and antecedents.

- **Words that are missing.** A spell checker will not catch when you have left a word out of a sentence. Reading your work out loud, slowly, will help you hear if you have left out any words.

- **Misspelling someone's name.** Spell checkers rarely check for proper nouns because there are so many of them. Misspelling the name of an author or major figure about whom you are writing is not only embarrassing, but readers can also interpret this as a sign you were not paying close and careful attention while you were writing. Anytime you use a proper noun, check its spelling by looking up the name in a newspaper, magazine, or biographical dictionary.

ABBREVIATIONS

TITLES

Dr. and *St.* (*Saint*) are abbreviated before a name but not after.

…said Dr. Robert Cantu.

…said Robert Cantu, a doctor specializing in neurosurgery.

Prof., Sen., Gen., Capt., and other titles can be abbreviated when placed before a full name (i.e., first and last names, or initials and last name) but not before the last name when it is given alone:

Sen. Hattie Wyatt Caraway
Sen. H. W. Caraway
Senator Caraway

Put academic and professional titles—*Sr., Jr., J.D., Ph.D., M.F.A., R.N., C.P.A.*—after names. (The periods are often left out of abbreviated titles.)

Ralph Simmons, Ph.D., will speak.

PLACE-NAMES

Spell out the names of continents, rivers, countries, states, cities, streets, and so on, except in these three cases:

1 Use **D.C.** when referring to Washington, D.C.
   Citizens of Washington, D.C., have no voting representation in Congress.

2 Use U.S. as an adjective, not as a noun:
   U.S. soldiers
   soldiers from the United States

3 To put a full address in a sentence, write it as you would on an envelope, using the state's postal abbreviation.
   Please send your applications to Habitat for Humanity International, 121 Habitat St., Americus, GA 31709.

> **TIP: MAKING ABBREVIATIONS PLURAL AND POSSESSIVE**
> To make an abbreviation plural, put **-s** after it.
>
> **Analysts estimate that more than 6,000 PCs become obsolete in California every day.**
>
> To make an abbreviation possessive, put **'s** after it.
>
> **IBM's earning forecast was grim.**

> **TIP: ABBREVIATIONS IN DIFFERENT DISCIPLINES**
> Different disciplines—mathematics, social sciences—use abbreviations differently. The advice we offer on these pages is general, so if you are writing for a specific discipline, ask someone familiar with the field (or a reference librarian) for help in learning the field's conventions.

Otherwise, spell out the state name:
Habitat for Humanity International's head office is in Americus, Georgia.

COMPANY NAMES

If a company name contains an abbreviation, write the name as the company does:

Charlie and the Chocolate Factory, **distributed by Warner Bros. Studios, is based on a novel by Roald Dahl.**

MEASUREMENTS

In the body of a paper, spell out units of measurement—such as *foot, percent, meter*—but abbreviate them in charts, tables, and graphs.

HMS Titanic was 883.75 feet long and 92.5 feet wide.

DATES

Spell out months and days of the week.

"Statistically, you are more likely to have an accident on Monday, November 27, than any other day of the year," the insurance official said.

For dates, the following abbreviations are customary:

399 B.C.	**399 B.C.E.**
1215 C.E.	**A.D. 1215**

B.C. (*Before Christ*), B.C.E. (*Before the Common Era*), and C.E. (*Common Era*) are placed after the year. A.D. (*Anno Domini*, *Year of Our Lord*) goes before the year. B.C.E. and C.E. are currently the most favored abbreviations.

TIMES

The conventional abbreviations for time of day are A.M. or a.m. for before noon and P.M. or p.m. for afternoon.

ACRONYMS

An acronym is a word formed by the initial letters of a phrase or title.

PC	*personal computer*
NPM	*National Poetry Month*
BBC	*British Broadcasting Corporation*

If you use an acronym that readers might not know, spell it out first, put the acronym in parentheses, and then use the acronym for all later references.

Folding At Home (FAH) is Stanford University's distributed computing project to study and understand protein folding, protein aggregation, and related diseases. So far, almost 500,000 users have donated processing time to FAH's projects.

LATIN EXPRESSIONS

Some Latin expressions, commonly used in academic writing, appear only as abbreviations:

cf.	*compare*	**e.g.**	*for example*
et al.	*and others*	**etc.**	*and so forth*
i.e.	*that is*	**n.b.**	*note well*

IN DOCUMENTING SOURCES

Different documentation styles use different abbreviations for words like *anonymous, editor,* or *no date.* Check the style manual you are using for any abbreviations you need to use.

→ See page 602 for how to use periods with abbreviations.

NUMBERS

WRITING NUMBERS

Spell out numbers that can be expressed in one or two words (and note the hyphen). Give the numerals for longer numbers.

seven	**178**
sixty-one	**1,347**
forty-one dollars	**$77.17**
twenty-two years	**250 years**
ninety people	**2,200 people**
ten miles	**352 miles**

Spell out any number that precedes another number expressed in numerals; otherwise readers might have trouble understanding the numbers. (For example, in the first sentence below, it is possible to see the two numbers as 10,250.)

The game is run from 10 250 gigabyte servers.

The game is run from ten 250 gigabyte servers.

WRITE OUT NUMBERS THAT BEGIN SENTENCES

19% of survey respondents knew when the U.S. Constitution was written.

Nineteen percent of survey respondents knew when the U.S. Constitution was written.

Except: Sentences can begin with a year:

1787 is the year the U.S. Constitution was written.

TIP: NUMBERS IN DIFFERENT DISCIPLINES

Different disciplines—mathematics, social sciences—use numbers differently. The advice we offer on these pages is general, so if you are writing for a specific discipline, ask someone familiar with the field (or a reference librarian) for help in learning the field's conventions.

USE NUMBERS CONSISTENTLY IN WRITING
If you spell numbers out or use numerals in a series, do so consistently.

Walsh notes that on average there are between 10,000 and fifteen thousand avatars in Second Life at any given time.

Walsh notes that on average there are between 10,000 and 15,000 avatars in Second Life at any given time.

DATES AND TIMES
Use numerals for dates and times.

On July 22, 1929, Alvin Macauley, president of Packard Motor Company, was on the cover of *Time* magazine.

President John F. Kennedy was shot and killed on November 22, 1963, at 12:30 P.M.

ADDRESSES AND PHONE NUMBERS
Use numerals for addresses and phone numbers.

Grauman's Chinese Theatre is located at 6801 Hollywood Boulevard in Hollywood. For showtimes, call (323) 464-8111.

DECIMALS AND PERCENTAGES
Use numerals for percentages and use the percentage sign (%).

By one estimate, 26% of all electric-cable breaks and 18% of all phone-cable disruptions are caused by rats.

(If the percentages come at the beginning of a sentence, however, spell out both the number and the percentage sign, as shown in the U.S. Constitution example on the preceding page.)

SCORES AND STATISTICS
Use numerals for scores and statistics.

The average age of the most frequent game buyer is 38 years old. In 2007, 92% of computer game buyers and 80% of console game buyers were over the age of 18.

The home run hit by New York Giants outfielder Bobby Thomson to win the National League pennant at 3:58 P.M. on October 3, 1951, is called the "Shot Heard 'Round the World." The Giants won the game 5 to 4, defeating the Dodgers in their pennant playoff series, two games to one.

PAGES AND OTHER PARTS OF BOOKS
Use numerals for pages, chapters, and other book divisions.

In his book *The Uses of Disorder*, Richard Sennett defines adulthood as the time when people "learn to tolerate painful ambiguity and uncertainty" (108).

Chapter 3 of John Stuart Mill's *On Liberty* is titled, "On Individuality, as one of the elements of well-being."

but/however/yet   **But, however,** and **yet** can all be used to indicate a contrast. Using them together in the same sentence will make it wordy.

can/may   In academic writing, **can** indicates the ability to do something, while **may** indicates permission to do something. Informally, these words are often used interchangeably.

capital/capitol   A **capital** is the main governmental city of a state or country. *Annapolis is the capital of Maryland.* A **capitol** is the building in which government bodies meet. *The senator gave a press conference on the steps of the capitol.*

case   Case is the form of a noun or pronoun that indicates its function. Nouns change case only to show possession. (See p. 501.) *I wrote a letter outlining my concerns* (subject). *He wrote a letter to me outlining his concerns* (object of preposition). *The letter's purpose was clear* (possessive noun).

censor/censure   To **censor** is to ban or silence. To **censure** is to reprimand publicly.

cite/sight/site   **Cite** is a verb meaning to "reference specifically." **Sight** is used as a verb meaning "to view" and as a noun meaning "vision." **Site** is usually used as a noun to mean "location," but it can also be used as a verb to mean "to locate."

clause   A clause is a group of words containing a subject and a verb. A **main** or **independent clause** can stand alone as a sentence (see p. 483), but a **subordinate** or **dependent clause** acts as a part of speech and cannot stand alone (see pp. 484–487).

comma splice   A comma splice occurs when two independent clauses are joined incorrectly by a comma. (See pp. 494–495.) *Jose did not approve of our choice, he wanted to hire the other candidate* (incorrect). *Jose did not approve of our choice; he wanted to hire the other candidate* (correct).

common noun   A common noun names a general person, place, or thing. Common nouns are not capitalized unless they are the first word of a sentence. (See pp. 498–499.) *Did Johnny Depp portray a pirate in that movie?*

complement/compliment   To **complement** something is to complete it. To **compliment** is to flatter. Because they are spelled so similarly, they are often confused.

complex sentence   A complex sentence is a sentence that contains at least one subordinate clause attached to an independent clause. (See pp. 483–487.) *Despite the heat, we had a really good time at the festival.*

compound sentence   A compound sentence contains at least two main clauses. (See pp. 480–482.) *We ate dinner and then we went for a walk.*

compound-complex sentence   A compound-complex sentence contains at least two independent clauses and a subordinate clause. (See pp. 488–489.) *Even though my parents are both Italian, I have not visited Italy and I do not speak the language.*

conjunction   A conjunction is a word that links and relates parts of a sentence. (See pp. 532–535.) *Eric arrived late, but the movie had not started yet.* See **coordinating conjunction**, **correlative conjunction**, and **subordinating conjunction**.

conjunctive adverb   A conjunctive adverb is an adverb (such as *however, besides, consequently,* or *therefore*) that relates two main or independent clauses. (See p. 535.) *Our car is broken; consequently, we had to carpool with the neighbors.*

conscience/conscious   **Conscience** is a noun meaning "a sense of right or wrong." **Conscious** is an adjective meaning "awake."

continual/continuous   **Continual** is an adjective meaning "recurring." **Continuous** is an adjective meaning "constant." *That continual noise is a continuous bother.*

coordinating conjunction   A coordinating conjunction is a word (such as *and, but, or, for, nor, yet,* and *so*) that links two grammatically equal parts of a sentence. (See p. 532 and pp. 556–557.) *I brushed my teeth and went to bed.*

correlative conjunction   Correlative conjunctions are two or more words (*neither…nor, either…or, not only…but also*) that work together to link parts of a sentence. (See p. 533.) *Not only were we excited, but we were also a little bit afraid.*

could of   **Could of** is often used in informal writing, but *could have* is more appropriate.

count noun   A count noun names things that can be counted. (See pp. 511–513.) *goats, shoes, computers*

criteria/criterion   A **criterion** is a singular noun that means "a measure" or "a condition." **Criteria** is the plural form of **criterion**.

dangling modifier   A dangling modifier does not have a clear connection to the word it modifies. (See pp. 540–541.) *Spicier than expected, she spat out the soup.*

data/datum   Datum is a singular noun that refers to a piece of information or a fact. **Data** is the plural of **datum**, and although it is often used as a singular noun, it should be treated as a plural noun and take a plural verb.

declarative   A declarative sentence is a statement. (See p. 468.) *The measurements were incorrect.*

dependent clause   See **subordinate clause**.

differ from/differ with   To **differ from** means "to be unlike." To **differ with** means "to disagree with."

different from/different than   Different from is preferred in academic writing to **different than** except in situations where **different from** would be wordy.

direct object   A direct object is the noun, pronoun, or noun clause naming the person or thing that takes the action of a transitive verb. (See pp. 476–472.) *The chef threw the meatloaf in the trash.*

discreet/discrete   Discreet is an adjective meaning "careful" or "prudent." **Discrete** is an adjective meaning "separate."

disinterested/uninterested   Disinterested is an adjective that means "impartial." It is often used incorrectly in place of **uninterested**.

double negative   A double negative is the use of two negatives to convey one negative idea. It should be avoided in academic writing. (See p. 281.) *I don't have no time to go with you.*

due to the fact that   Due to the fact that is a wordy substitute for **because**.

each other/one another   Each other should be used for two things; **one another** should be used for more than two things.

effect   See **affect/effect**.

elicit/illicit   Elicit is a verb that means "to bring out." **Illicit** is an adjective that means "unlawful." These words are often incorrectly used in place of each other.

emigrate from/immigrate to   Emigrate is a verb meaning "to leave one's country." **Immigrate** is a verb that means "to settle in another country."

ensure   See **assure/ensure/insure**.

etc.   Etc. is an abbreviation for the Latin *et cetera* and is used to shorten a list of items. **Etc.** is mostly used in informal writing.

every body/everybody/every one/everyone   Everybody and **everyone** are both collective nouns referring to all parties under discussion. **Every body** and **every one** are both adjective-noun combinations that refer to individuals within the larger group.

except   See **accept/except/expect**.

except for the fact that   Except for the fact that is a wordy substitute for *except that*.

expect   See **accept/except/expect**.

expletive   *There* and *it* are expletives, or "dummy subjects" that are used to fill a grammatical slot in a sentence. (See p. 282.) *It is very clear.*

farther/further   Farther refers to distance, while **further** refers to time or another abstract concept.

fewer/less   Fewer is used for things that can be counted, while **less** is used for things that cannot be counted.

fragment   A fragment is a group of words that is capitalized and punctuated like a sentence but lacks a subject and predicate. Fragments are used in some forms of writing, such as fiction and advertising copy, but they are usually not acceptable in academic writing. (See pp. 490–493.) *A representative who cares.*

further   See **farther/further**.

gender   Gender is the classification of nouns or pronouns as masculine and feminine. (See p. 507.)

good/well   Good can be used only as an adjective, while **well** can be used as both an adjective and an adverb. *His last album was good. He sings well. Is your mother well?*

hanged/hung   Hanged is a verb that specifically refers to an execution. **Hung** is used in all other instances. *In the past, criminals were often hanged. The noose hung from the gallows.*

have/of   Have, rather than **of**, should be used after auxiliary or helping verbs such as *could, should, would, might,* and so on.

he/she; s/he   Academic audiences prefer writing that is gender inclusive (unless a distinction of gender is necessary). (See pp. 256–257.)

predicate   The predicate is the part of a clause that expresses the action or tells something about the subject. The predicate includes the verb and its complements, objects, and modifiers. (See pp. 474–478.)

prejudice/prejudiced   **Prejudice** is a noun meaning "bias." **Prejudiced** is an adjective meaning "biased" or "intolerant."

preposition   A preposition is a part of speech that shows relationships or qualities. (See pp. 530–531.)

prepositional phrase   A prepositional phrase is a phrase formed by a preposition and its object. A prepositional phrase includes the modifiers of the object. (See p. 479.)

pretty   **Pretty** is often used as a colloquial substitute for *very*. Avoid using **pretty** to mean *very* in academic writing.

principal/principle   **Principal** can be a noun, meaning "the head of a school" or it can be an adjective, meaning "the most important element." **Principle** is a noun meaning "a rule or standard."

pronoun   A pronoun is a part of speech that stands for other nouns or pronouns. Classes of pronouns include: **possessive pronouns**, **personal pronouns**, **demonstrative pronouns**, **indefinite pronouns**, **relative pronouns**, **interrogative pronouns**, **reflexive pronouns**, and **reciprocal pronouns**. (See pp. 502–507.)

pronoun case   Pronouns that act as the subject of a sentence are in the **subjective case** (*I, you, he, she, it, we, they*). Pronouns that act as direct or indirect objects are in the **objective case** (*me, you, him, her, it, us, them*). Pronouns that indicate ownership are in the **possessive case** (*my, your, his, her, its, our, their*). (See pp. 502–507.)

proper noun   A proper noun is a noun that names a particular person, place, thing, or group. Proper nouns are capitalized. (See pp. 498–499.) *Anthony Bourdain, Dublin, Yom Kippur*

question as to whether/question of whether   These phrases are both wordy substitutes for *whether*.

raise/rise   The verb **raise** means "lift up" and takes a direct object. The verb **rise** means "get up." It does not take a direct object.

real/really   **Real** is an adjective, while **really** is an adverb. These words are often used incorrectly in place of each other.

reason is because   **Reason is because** is often used to explain causality. *Reason is* and *is because* are less wordy.

reason why   **Reason why** is a redundant construction that should be avoided in academic writing. Instead of *The reason why he went to Malaysia is for work,* you can write, *He went to Malaysia for work.*

relative pronoun   A <u>relative pronoun</u> initiates <u>clauses</u>. *That, which, what, who, whom,* and *whose* are relative pronouns. (See p. 504.) *The woman <u>who makes those funny, furry purses</u> will have a booth at the fair.*

restrictive modifier   A restrictive modifier is essential to the meaning of the word, phrase, or clause it modifies. Unlike a nonrestrictive modifier, it is not set off by punctuation. (See pp. 559–562.) *My uncle <u>who lives in Canada</u> is visiting next week.*

rise/raise   See **raise/rise.**

run-on sentence   A run-on sentence occurs when two main clauses are fused together without punctuation or a conjunction. (See pp. 494–495.) *I don't like Wednesdays they are too far away from the weekend.*

sentence   A sentence is a grammatically independent group of words that contains at least one independent clause. (See pp. 468–495.)

set/sit   The verb **set** means "to put" and it takes a direct object. **Sit** means "to be seated" and does not take a direct object.

shall/will   **Shall** is very formal, and is most often used in first person questions, while **will** can be used in the future tense with all persons.

should of   See **have/of.**

simple/simplistic   Although it is often used as such, **simplistic** is not a synonym of *simple*. **Simplistic** means "crude" or "unsophisticated," while **simple** means "easy."

since   **Since** most commonly refers to time, but it can also be used as a synonym of *because*. Keep in mind, though, that some readers prefer that **since** not be used as a synonym of *because*.

sit/set   See **set/sit.**

some time/sometime/sometimes   **Some time** refers to a period of time, while **sometime** refers to an unspecified time. **Sometimes** means "occasionally."

somebody/some body; someone/some one
Somebody and **someone** are indefinite pronouns that mean the same thing. **Some body** and **some one** are adjective-noun combinations.

sort of   See **kind of/sort of/type of.**

subject   A subject is a noun, pronoun, or noun phrase that identifies what the clause is about and is connected to the predicate. (See p. 475.)

subject-verb agreement   See **agreement.**

subjunctive mood   The subjunctive mood expresses a wish, a condition contrary to fact, a recommendation, or a request. (See p. 527.)

subordinate   A subordinate relationship is a relationship of unequal importance, in either grammar or meaning. (See pp. 284–285.)

subordinate clause   A subordinate clause, also called a dependent clause, is a clause that cannot stand alone but must be attached to a main clause. (See pp. 483–487 and p. 493.)

subordinating conjunction   A subordinating conjunction is a word that introduces a subordinate clause. Some subordinating conjunctions are *after, although, as, because, before, if, since, that, unless, until, when, where,* and *while.* (See p. 534.)

such   **Such** means "of the previous kind" (*such behavior, such praise*), but it is often used informally as a synonym for *very.*

sure   **Sure** is often used as an adverb to mean *certainly,* but it is more properly used as an adjective.

sure and/sure to; try and/try to   **Sure to** and **try to** are correct; do not add *and* after *sure* or *try.*

take   See **bring/take.**

than/then   **Than** is a conjunction expressing difference. *I would rather watch a movie than go out tonight.* **Then** is an adverb expressing time. *First we went to church, then we went shopping.*

that/which   **That** introduces a restrictive or essential clause, while **which** is usually used to introduce nonrestrictive or nonessential clauses.

their/there/they're   **Their** is a possessive pronoun (see p. 503); **there** is most commonly used as an

expletive (see p. 282); and **they're** is a contraction of *they are* (see p. 503).

to/too/two   **To** is a preposition, while **too** is an adverb. **Two** is a number.

transition   A transition is a word or phrase that notes movement from one unit of writing to another. (See pp. 296–297.)

transitive verb   A transitive verb is a verb that takes a direct object. (See pp. 476–477.)

try and/try to   See **sure and/sure to.**

unique   If something is **unique,** it is one of a kind and can't be compared to anything else. Consequently, it is not necessary to use words such as *most* to modify **unique.**

usage/use/utilize   **Utilize** and **usage** are often used in informal writing as synonyms for **use.**

verb   A verb is a word that shows action or characterizes a subject in some way. (See pp. 514–527.)

well/good   See **good/well.**

weather/whether   **Weather** is a noun, describing whether it is sunny, raining, hot, or cold outside. **Whether** is a conjunction that can mean "if" or can introduce a set of opinions.

which/that   See t**hat/which.**

who/whom   **Who** is the subject pronoun, while **whom** is the object pronoun. *Who is that in the yard? With whom did you dance?*

who's/whose   **Who's** is a contraction of *who is,* while **whose** is a possessive. *Who's there? Whose shoes are those?*

will/shall   See **shall/will.**

-wise/-ize   See **-ize/-wise.**

would of   See **have/of.**

you   **You** is primarily used to directly address the reader, but it is often used informally to refer to people in general.

your/you're   **Your** and **you're** are not interchangeable. **Your** is the possessive form of *you. Your conscience will rest easier after you vote.* **You're** is the contraction of *you are. You're a citizen, and so you are expected to vote.* (See p. 503 on possessives; see p. 601 on contractions.)

INDEX

A

to indicate technical terms/ words from other languages, 591, 594
to indicate word is used as a word, 590, 593
MLA style for, 598
quoting parts of a sentence, 599
for referring to words used as words, 607
in sentence ending with question mark or exclamation point, 599
to show irony, 591, 595
single quotation marks, 318
straight and "curly," 596
for titles of short works, 590, 592
when not to use, 318
when quote contains its own quotation marks, 318
when quoting someone, 318
Quotes/quotations, 314–315
adding explanatory comment to, 319
affiliation or title of person quoted, 317, 319
block quotation, 318
brackets used to insert information in, 583
capitalizing first word in direct quotation, 612
direct and indirect quotations, 549
ellipses to signal pause or interruption, 588
example, 317
honoring intent and meaning of, 321
in-text citations, use of parentheses, 578
in introductory paragraph, 295
introductory verb and weaving in words of others, 317, 320
modifying words in, 317, 319
naming persons quoted, 317, 320
obsolete or misspelled words in, 319

omitted words signaled by ellipses, 589
pull-quote, 199
quotation marks and, 317, 318, 596
slashes to indicate line breaks in poems, 587
tips, 321
use of colon when introducing, 573
use of commas in, 544, 548–549
weaving quoted words into writing, 321
words of others, 316–321

R

race vs. ethnicity, 252
Radio interview, collecting citing information for, 349
Radio program, MLA style for works cited, 401
Re:, 570
Reason, 121, 125
Reason (component of thesis statement), 103, 202
recommend, 527
Redesigned, 1
Reference article, CSE style documentation, 462
Reference lists. *See also* MLA documentation style, works cited lists
APA style, 205, 426–435
CSE style, 204, 454
optional in CMS style, 458
Reference sources. *See also* Research sources
books, 46
collecting citation information for chapter used, 335
indexes of, 62
online, 58, 74
reference librarian, 41, 62
Relative pronouns, 283, 493, 504
Religion, avoiding exclusionary language, 262–263
re (prefix), 584

request, 527
Research
ethical, 144–145
questions for, 85
sufficiency of, 165, 174, 176
Research paper or project
audience, defining, 14
composing process, 12–16
context, defining, 15
organizational "wiggle room," 191
purpose, defining, 14–15
schedule, 25
understanding project or assignment, 14–16
Research process, 20–23
from broad to deep research, 22
example, 24
online research, 40
pattern, 21
questions to guide research, 21, 34–37
sample, 23
schedule, 25
search terms, developing, 42
shaping, with narrowed topic, 28
topic, finding, 26–27
Research report
abstract, 204
conclusion, 204
discussion, 204
introduction, 204
methods, 204
references list, 204
results, 204
title, 204
Research sources, 22. *See also* Sources
archives and special library collections, 41
characteristics that distinguish, 45
choosing, 42–45, 46–47
comparing and making judgments on, 44
considerations, 45
determining, 42–43
field research, 41, 78–79
finding, 60–79

REVISION SYMBOLS

Boldface numbers refer to pages in the handbook

ab	abbreviation	**612**
agr	agreement	**524**
awk	awkward diction or construction	**274, 282**
cap	capitalization	**610**
coh	coherence	**214**
coord	coordination	**284**
cs	comma splice	**557**
d	diction, word choice	**270**
dev	development needed	**36, 218**
dm	dangling modifier	**540**
doc	check documentation	**308**
frag	sentence fragment	**490**
fs	fused sentence	**494**
hyph	hyphen	**584**
ital	italics	**607**
lc	lowercase letter	**610**
log	logic	**96, 100**
mm	misplaced modifier	**540**
no ¶	no paragraph needed	**290**
num	number	**614**
¶	paragraph	**290**
¶ dev	paragraph development needed	**218**
ref	unclear pronoun reference	**506**
search	check research or citation	**38, 60, 308**

sp	spelling error	**608**
shift	shift in voice or number	**536**
sub	sentence subordination	**284**
t	verb tense error	**516**
trans	transition needed	**296**
var	sentence variety	**278**
vb	verb form error	**515**
w	wordy	**277**
ww/wc	wrong word; word choice	**270**
//	faulty parallelism	**286**
. ? !	end punctuation	**602, 604, 605**
:	colon	**568**
؛	appostrophe	**600**
—	dash	**580**
( )	parentheses	**574**
[ ]	brackets	**582**
...	ellipses	**588**
/	slash	**586**
;	semicolon	**565**
" "	quotation marks	**590**
؟	comma	**544**
⌒	close up	
^	insert a missing element	
ℓ	delete	
∿	transpose order	

DETAILED CONTENTS

A PROCESS FOR COMPOSING

Understanding your project	**PART 1**	
Getting started	**PART 2**	Finding a topic Narrowing the topic Developing research questions Finding sources Keeping track of sources
Asking questions	**PART 3**	Critical thinking and questioning Evaluating sources Developing a thesis statement
Shaping your project for others	**PART 4**	Thinking in depth about audience Developing a statement of purpose
	PART 5	Choosing a genre Choosing an overall arrangement Arranging paragraphs
Drafting a paper	**PART 4**	Writing a rough darft
	PART 6	Varieties of English Writing for global audiences Inclusive language uses
Getting feedback	**PART 4**	Receiving feedback to drafts Developing a revision plan
Revising	**PART 7**	Paying attention to style
	PART 8	Integrating sources
Polishing	**PART 8**	Documenting sources
	PART 9	Editing and proofreading

Introducing a revolutionary new handbook . . .

Just open to any page and look!

An unprecedented marriage of design and text, *The DK Handbook*, by Anne Frances Wysocki and Dennis A. Lynch, makes finding the information you need—and understanding it—so much easier. Whether you're wondering how to start a paper, how to use the Web for research, or when to use a comma, *The DK Handbook* gives you quick and reliable answers that will help you write better papers and do better research—and get better grades.

Uniquely suited to the questions you face and the way you learn, *The DK Handbook* will help you succeed in any course that involves writing and research.

Another amazing resource for writing and research . . .

Explore it today!
www.mycomplab.com

Longman
is an imprint of

www.pearsonhighered.com

ISBN-13: 978-0-205-74332-2
ISBN-10:   0-205-74332-3

EAN

9 780205 743322

T4-ASC-043